FAITH
THAT
WORKS

FAITH
THAT
WORKS

MORRIS L. VENDEN

REVIEW AND HERALD® PUBLISHING ASSOCIATION
HAGERSTOWN, MD 21740

Texts credited to NEB are from *The New English Bible.* The Delegates of the Oxford University Press and the Syndics of the Cambridge University Press 1961, 1970. Reprinted by permission.

Bible texts credited to RSV are from the Revised Standard Version of the Bible, copyright 1946, 1952, 1971, by the Division of Christian Education of the National Council of the Churches of Christ in the U.S.A. Used by permission.

Bible texts credited to TEV are from the *Good News Bible*—Old Testament: Copyright American Bible Society 1976; New Testament: Copyright American Bible Society 1966, 1971, 1976.

This book was
Edited by Raymond H. Woolsey
Cover design by GenesisDesign/Bryan Gray
Electronic makeup by Shirley M. Bolivar
Typeset: 11/12.5 Minion

PRINTED IN U.S.A.

03 02 01 00 99   5 4 3 2 1

R&H Cataloging Service
Venden, Morris L
    Faith that works.

    1. Devotional calendar—Seventh-day Adventists.
I. Woolsey, Raymond H.   II. Title.
BV4811.V46   242'.2   80-13863

Printed in U.S.A. (Reprinted 1999)

ISBN 0-8280-1453-3

CONTENTS

WHAT GOD IS LIKE

Jesus saith unto him, Have I been so long time with you, and yet hast thou not known me, Philip? he that hath seen me hath seen the Father. John 14:9.

An inscription on an early-American grave reads: "Here lies Lem S. Frame, who killed 89 Indians in his lifetime. He was hoping to have killed 100 by the end of the year, when he fell asleep in Jesus in his house at Hawk's Ferry." Do you think this gives a true picture of God or does it show that someone has misunderstood His character?

The proper blend of God's love and justice has often been debated. The cheap brand of Christianity pictures Him as being a God who never harms anyone, and eventually lets everyone into heaven. The other extreme views God as looking for every chance He can get to destroy His creatures.

This misunderstanding of God's character has caused some people to stay away from religion. If many had accepted what they have been mistakenly taught to believe about God, perhaps God Himself would have been unhappy.

Philip said, "Show us the Father." Jesus replied, "Have I been with you all this time, and yet you haven't known Me? If you've seen Me, you've seen the Father." Jesus came to a world that was in complete misapprehension of God, in order to demonstrate what the Father is really like— what He always has been like and always will be like.

You see a man coming to the edge of a large crowd down by a lake. He has leprosy. As he comes, the people fall back. But Jesus invites him into His presence and touches him. And He says, "They consider you under the curse of God? I will make you clean." Who was this talking? This was God talking!

You see a woman being dragged through the dust into the presence of Jesus. Her accusers stand ready to heave huge rocks at her to crush her skull. Jesus says, "I don't condemn you. Go, and sin no more." Who was that? It was God—His love and justice perfectly blended.

You see a man hanging on a cross. He turns his head and manages to speak a few words, "Lord, remember me." And Jesus says, "I will. You'll be with Me in heaven." Who is that? That's God. That's God—the same yesterday, today, and forever.

GOD'S LOVE FOR SINNERS

For God so loved the world, that he gave his only begotten Son, that whosoever believeth in him should not perish, but have everlasting life. John 3:16.

The apostle Paul tells us that God's character has been misunderstood and misinterpreted since the beginning of the world. People knew something about Him once, but they didn't glorify Him as God. As a result they "became vain in their imaginations, and their foolish heart was darkened. Professing themselves to be wise, they became fools, and changed the glory of the uncorruptible God into an image made like to corruptible man, and to birds, and fourfooted beasts, and creeping things" (Rom. 1:21-23).

It is possible for us, in our minds, to change God into something other than He really is, even if we don't bow down to idols of wood and stone. If we don't have the proper understanding of His character, then we're worshiping a false God! We understand that the last rays of merciful light, the last message of mercy to be given to the world, is a revelation of His character of love. Unless we know what God is really like, we won't be able to reveal Him to the rest of the world! Jesus came to demonstrate to the world what the Father is really like.

One day Jesus and His disciples passed by a blind man (John 9:1). The disciples asked, "Master, who sinned? this man, or his parents, that he was born blind?"

Their question was based on the common concept of God and evil. The people of Christ's day believed that disease and death were God's arbitrary punishment for wrongdoing, either by the sufferer himself or by his parents. Because of this, the suffering person had the additional burden of being considered a great sinner.

Jesus corrected their error by explaining that sickness and pain are caused by Satan. But one of the devil's clever traps is to project his own attributes onto God, and as a result millions of people through the centuries have blamed God for suffering, sickness, and death.

John 3:16 and 17 tell us that God loved the world enough to send His own Son to redeem us. He "sent not his Son into the world to condemn the world; but that the world through him might be saved." That's the gospel! That's redemption!

THE JUSTICE OF GOD

Shall not the Judge of all the earth do right? Gen. 18:25.

There had been popular uprisings against Pilate, governor of Judea, and to restore order to the province, he had allowed his soldiers to invade the Temple and kill Galilean pilgrims who were offering sacrifices to God.

The Jews told Jesus about this calamity, not from a sense of pity and sympathy, but with a deep-down sense of satisfaction that "this hasn't happened to me—therefore I must be better and more favored than those people to whom it happened." Jesus knew that, and said, "I suppose you think this happened because they were great sinners above the rest of you." He continued: "Not so. Unless you repent, you are all going to perish."

Jesus does not ignore the justice of God. In fact, it is an important thing to recognize the justice and judgment of God.

We know that a time will come when mercy will no longer plead and justice will be dealt. The Bible describes times in the past when God "spared not," because His justice could no longer permit conditions to continue as they were. One of the times when God "spared not" is recorded in Genesis 18. Abraham, "the friend of God," was bargaining with Him about Sodom's fate. He must have had a deep relationship with a friendly God to bargain in this way.

He questioned, "Are You going to destroy the righteous along with the wicked? Suppose there are 50 righteous people within the city. Will You spare it for the righteous that are within?" He appealed to God's fairness.

God was patient with this man who was trying to tell his Creator the proper thing to do, for He answered, "If I find in Sodom 50 righteous within the city, then I will spare all the place for their sakes."

Then Abraham became nervous. What if there *weren't* 50? So he continued to bargain for a lower number—45, 30, 20, and finally 10. And the Lord replied, "I will not destroy it for 10's sake." You know the rest of the story. God saw a point past which iniquity and rebellion could no longer be allowed to continue, because He is a God of justice. There weren't even 10 righteous people, and Sodom was destroyed. But the pitiful handful of righteous were spared.

WHEN GOD SPARED NOT

He that spared not his own Son, but delivered him up for us all, how shall he not with him also freely give us all things? Rom. 8:32.

God could not spare the cities of Sodom and Gomorrah when rebellion reached a certain point. Another time that God "spared not" is found in Romans 11:21. Paul was writing to the Christians at Rome, imploring them to change their ways. He reminded them that even though they were wild branches that had been grafted into the olive tree, God had broken off the natural branches because there came a point where He could no longer spare the entire Jewish nation.

A third instance when God "spared not" because of His justice is described in 2 Peter 2:5: God "spared not the old world, but saved [only] Noah the eighth person, a preacher of righteousness, bringing in the flood upon the world."

The fourth time that God "spared not" involves the very universe—2 Peter 2:4: "God spared not the angels that sinned." Sin went on in the very presence of God—rebellion broke out in His courts, led by a mighty angel. Although God was extremely patient, He eventually had to call a halt to the rebellion. You know the results of that war in heaven. Those angels who were cast out are still present in our world today.

Well, the justice of God looks rather grim, doesn't it? He didn't spare a city, a nation, a world, or even a universe because of sin! How can this same God ever find enough mercy to pardon one individual sinner?

There is hope for each of us because God "spared not" one more time. Romans 8:32 tells us that He "spared not his own Son, but delivered him up for us all."

If you will study the sacrifice of Jesus on the cross you will discover that this is the greatest time when God "spared not." Here is demonstrated the realization that God gave Himself. None of this idea of God pleading for His Son to go, or Jesus pleading with His irate Father to spare these people! Away with such concepts!

Instead, you can see the Father and the Son involved together in this great sacrifice. Jesus was the greatest gift that God could have given us. He spared not His own Son so that His justice could remain true and His love could equal it.

THE PATIENCE OF GOD

Then said Jesus, Father, forgive them; for they know not what they do. Luke 23:34.

One day, centuries ago, Jesus was in close conversation with the Father. The angels looked on. The air was heavy with suspense. Everyone was wondering how God's original plan had gone wrong after sin entered, and they were wondering what God would do to complete the plan.

After a long time, Jesus came from that close communion with His Father, and it was revealed that He had offered Himself to die in man's place. God gave all heaven, His own Son. He couldn't have given anything more.

Here you see God and Jesus together, one in purpose. They're together in this great plan of redemption. God's character is best revealed by Jesus and how Jesus related to sinners when He was on this earth.

He gave the Jews mercy time and time again. They had turned God down earlier, killing the prophets and stoning those who had been sent to help them. Finally, God sent His Son Jesus in person, as the greatest manifestation of Himself. "Give them another opportunity." What a demonstration of His mercy!

If we had been on the cross, with evil men mocking us, we would have said, "Bring on the twelve legions of angels. Bring them on. We'll deal with these people." But instead, Jesus uttered the pardoning words, "Father, forgive them; for they know not what they do."

Even after the cross, God's patience wasn't over. After the nation was rejected, He continued to plead with individuals.

The Shekinah glory was removed from the Temple, but God sent the disciples first of all to Jerusalem, to the place where Jesus had issued the words of doom, "Your house is left unto you desolate." During all the missionary journeys of the apostles, the Jewish people were included year after year.

As Stephen was stoned to death by an angry mob, the Holy Spirit came upon him, and he prayed, "Forgive them. Don't give up on them yet."

Don't let this story rest simply with the people in Christ's day. Apply it to your life, to your family, to those you've been praying for. His call of mercy and love continues today—to every person, to every heart.

11

MERCY AND JUSTICE FOR ALL

The Lord is not slack concerning his promise, as some men count slackness; but is longsuffering to us-ward, not willing that any should perish, but that all should come to repentance. 2 Peter 3:9.

He spake also this parable; A certain man had a fig tree planted in his vineyard; and he came and sought fruit thereon, and found none. Then said he unto the dresser of his vineyard, Behold, these three years I come seeking fruit on this fig tree, and find none: cut it down; why cumbereth it the ground? And he answering said unto him, Lord, let it alone this year also, till I shall dig about it, and dung it [fertilize it, as we would say today]: and if it bear fruit, well: and if not, then after that thou shalt cut it down" (Luke 13: 6-9). Let it alone this year also. Don't cut it down yet.

And did He cut it down after one more year? What does the "Let it alone this year" really mean? It suggests today that the mercy and patience of God is almost limitless. "Almost" because we know that there comes a time when mercy no longer pleads and justice must be dealt. But Jesus in His life here on earth gave considerable evidence that God is exceedingly merciful.

The combination of the proper blend of mercy and judgment is one of the things that Christians have struggled with for a long time. We try to figure through all the whys and wherefores of all the possible differences between the God of the Old Testament and the God of the New Testament. This at times brings question upon the Old Testament and its validity. However, there are equal evidences of judgment in the New Testament. It's rather hard to surpass the story of Ananias and Sapphira for judgment. There are points that we cannot understand fully in both the Old and New Testaments.

But it is for sure that a father of love will not let his boy hurt his girl without doing something to stop his boy. He doesn't love his girl *or* his boy if he doesn't do something in that kind of situation. We've heard a lot of angles in regard to God's justice and judgment, but there is one great beautiful truth that lasts to your day and to this moment. God's patience continues. Spare them this year also. Don't cut them down yet. Give them a little more time. Somehow the mercy and the patience of God blends with His justice and judgment, and we have redemption.

TWO KINDS OF TREES

And he shall be like a tree planted by the rivers of water, that bringeth forth his fruit in his season; his leaf also shall not wither; and whatsoever he doeth shall prosper. Ps. 1:3.

In the Bible, Israel and God's people have often been likened to trees. Isaiah 61:3: "They might be called trees of righteousness, the planting of the Lord, that he might be glorified." Beautiful trees, to bring forth fruit and foliage, shelter and hope.

The people of Christ's day made a great show of piety. They had a lot of leaves, much foliage. You remember the story of the fig tree, cursed because of all the foliage but no fruit. In Jesus' day the Jews made a great show of piety, more than did those of earlier ages. But they were "more destitute of the sweet graces of the Spirit."—*Christ's Object Lessons*, p. 215.

Sometimes we confuse what the fruit is all about on these trees. The statistician says that the fruit is *x* number of souls saved, that the fruit of the Christian is how many people he can count on his list that he has converted, or how many stars he will have in his crown. That's *not* the fruit. The fruit that Jesus is really talking about here is the fruit of the Spirit.

The sweet graces of the Spirit—what are they? We are told in Galatians 5:22 and 23. "Love, joy." You see a person who goes around gloomy—that means that he probably doesn't have a fruit of the Spirit. One of them is missing. "Peace, longsuffering, gentleness, goodness, faith, meekness, temperance." The people of Christ's day had many leaves, but few of the sweet graces.

As we approach the very end of time, we discover that God's patience goes on and on and on until the time of Revelation 11:18. There we find what it is that finally ends things in this world, that finally results in the unfruitful trees' being cut down. Evidently God's patience is going to continue until man has come to the place of *destroying himself.* It will go to that point. You know, if your eyes are open, that we have almost reached that place. Therefore the rest of it must be fulfilled very soon.

In the meantime, Jesus "is not come to destroy men's lives" (Luke 9:56). And when the disciples said, "Let's call down fire," Jesus said, "You don't know your spirit. I came not to destroy, but to save."

STILL MORE TIME

For I am persuaded, that neither death, nor life, nor angels, nor principalities, nor powers, nor things present, nor things to come, nor height, nor depth, nor any other creature, shall be able to separate us from the love of God, which is in Christ Jesus our Lord. Rom. 8:38, 39.

A certain man had a fig tree planted in his vineyard; and he came and sought fruit thereon, and found none. Then said he unto the dresser of his vineyard, Behold, these three years I come seeking fruit on this fig tree, and find none: cut it down; why cumbereth it the ground?" (Luke 13:6, 7).

The owner of the vineyard says, "This tree is filling the place that a useful tree might occupy." When a tree has lots of foliage but no fruit, the first tendency could be, "Let it alone—it's not doing any damage." But, according to this parable, it is doing damage, because it's robbing the world of the blessing of another tree that might bring forth fruit. It misrepresents God in the world, and is not merely useless but a hindrance.

In the climax to this story, when the drama seems particularly tense and you wonder whether the tree is going to be cut down or not, there is this argument from the dresser. He does not argue that the master's statement isn't true. It *is* true, and he admits it, but he says, "Let it alone this year. Give it a little more time till I shall dig about it and dress it."

God and Jesus are together here, the Father and Son, in unity of purpose, and this is a dialogue between them. "Shall we cut it down? Shall *we?*" And they say, "No, we will not cut it down. Instead, we'll let it alone this year. We'll try something else. We'll give it more advantage."

Listen, friend. Do you feel that you've about gone the limit and that all you deserve is to be cut down? Here you have the evidence of God's judgment concerning you in His day of mercy and grace. "Let it alone. Give that young person, give that older person who has bartered away God's grace for years—give him another year. And then another one after that, and then another."

Man cuts off quicker than God does. What a God we serve! He doesn't treat us as human beings treat one another, but continues to offer His mercy and His love.

MERCY STILL PLEADS

And he answering said unto him, Lord, let it alone this year also, till I shall dig about it, and dung it: and if it bear fruit, well: and if not, then after that thou shalt cut it down. Luke 13:8, 9.

Are you, O careless heart, a fruitless tree in the Lord's vineyard? Shall the words of doom erelong be spoken of you? How long have you received His gifts? . . . How often has the tender gospel message thrilled your heart! You have taken the name of Christ, you are outwardly a member of the church which is His body, and yet you are conscious of no living connection with the great heart of love."—*Christ's Object Lessons*, p. 216. The issue is not how much foliage. It is whether you are conscious of a living connection, a personal, vibrant, living connection with Jesus.

Wouldn't you like to be in the group who bear fruit and are never cut down? This is possible. We can respond to God's mercy by accepting and receiving His gift of Christ each day. There's no other way, because in order to realize the goodness and mercy of our patient God of justice, we need to study and contemplate Him continually. We may hear about His love from the pulpit, but this happens only once a week, or perhaps even less often. In order to repent daily, we need to contemplate and understand the goodness of God for our lives each day.

Listen, friend, even if you've run away from God because you've misunderstood His character: if you're now tired of running, but afraid He won't accept you back, hear His friendly words of invitation, "Come unto me, all ye that labour and are heavy laden, and I will give you rest" (Matt. 11:28). Find out what it means to fall low before the cross and to communicate with your Saviour, Lord, and Friend. "In His great mercy God has not cut you down. He does not look coldly upon you. He does not turn away with indifference, or leave you to destruction. Looking upon you He cries, as He cried so many centuries ago concerning Israel, 'How shall I give thee up?'"—*Ibid.*, pp. 217, 218.

As we recognize His acceptance of us just as we are, and as we daily behold His love and mercy, fruit springs forth spontaneously. The secret lies in the living connection with the great heart of love.

THE FRIEND OF GOD

By faith Abraham, when he was called to go out into a place which he should after receive for an inheritance, obeyed; and he went out, not knowing whither he went. Heb. 11:8.

Many people question the God of the Old Testament versus the God of the New Testament. One person says, "The God of the Old Testament was a God of judgment, a God who put to death men, women, and children." This is what man has done to God in the Old Testament. Let's look again at one Old Testament example of what God is like.

You see a man who has left his country, his kindred, and his father's house. He has gone out, not knowing where he was going, believing God's promise to make of him a great nation. He is called the friend of God.

Even after he reaches the Promised Land, the story has just begun. A famine comes, and Abraham is forced temporarily to seek refuge in the land of Egypt. There his faith fails. He fears that God isn't big enough to protect Sarah, his wife, who is fair to look upon. So he decides to help God out. He tells a half-truth, which is really a falsehood, that Sarah is his sister. When the king of Egypt hears of her great beauty, he has her brought to his palace, intending to have her for his wife.

How did God handle this? Did He rain fire down from heaven to destroy Abraham? Did He withdraw His protection from him, from Sarah? Did He say to Abraham, "Some friend you turned out to be—forget you"?

"And the Lord plagued Pharaoh and his house with great plagues, because of Sarai Abram's wife" (Gen. 12:17). "Pharaoh saw in this stranger a man whom the God of heaven honored, and he feared to have in his kingdom one who was so evidently under divine favor."—*Patriarchs and Prophets*, p. 131.

A man who lied is under divine favor? How can that be? Abraham had sinned, he had failed, but he was still God's child, still His friend. This did not mean that God approved of Abraham's deception. But it must mean that God approved of Abraham.

Apparently Abraham's friendship with God was based on something other than the occasional good deed or misdeed. What a picture of the God of the Old Testament—His mercy, His justice, and His love.

CAN'T RUN FROM GOD'S LOVE

Like as a father pitieth his children, so the Lord pitieth them that fear him. Ps. 103:13.

One day you see a large crowd gathered on a mountaintop. They have been there since early morning, called together by a man the king has hunted futilely for more than three years. It's rumored that he is responsible for the three-year drought in the land, and the people wait, whisper, and wonder near the two altars that have been erected at Elijah's direction.

With a blaze of fire from heaven, Elijah's sacrifice, the water, and even the altar are consumed, and all present are brought to acknowledge the God of heaven.

That very night, aroused from sleep by a palace messenger, Elijah flees for his life before an angry woman. He fears that even the God who answers by fire is not big enough to protect him from the wicked Jezebel.

He flees in terror through the darkness of the night, with the greater darkness of his own fears and discouragement accompanying him. Finally he comes to the end of his own resources, sits down under a juniper tree, and prays that he might die.

"Did God forsake Elijah in his hour of trial? Oh, no! He loved His servant no less when Elijah felt himself forsaken of God and man than when, in answer to his prayer, fire flashed from heaven and illuminated the mountaintop."—*Prophets and Kings*, p. 166.

Instead of answering Elijah's prayer to take his life, a God of infinite love and pity, who knew his frame and sympathized with his humanity, sent a heavenly messenger with food and water to sustain his life. A second time the angel came saying, "Arise and eat; because the journey is too great for thee."

When our faith fails, when discouragement comes to our lives, do we flee in terror, expecting an angry God to consume us for our lack of trust? Are we any less inclined to misunderstand His love and compassion? Do we constantly expect a God of fire and lightning to execute judgment, and fail to recognize the gentle touch, the still small voice, of our best Friend, who says, "I love you just as much when the journey becomes too great for you"?

That's God speaking. That's God. The Old Testament God—the God of the New Testament, the God of today.

TODAY I MUST ABIDE AT THY HOUSE

For the Son of man is come to seek and to save that which was lost. Luke 19:10.

And Jesus entered and passed through Jericho. And, behold, there was a man named Zacchaeus, which was the chief among the publicans, and he was rich" (Luke 19:1, 2).

Jericho was known for its publicans and its tax collectors. It was the place where a Jewish man could turn traitor to his own people, give up to the Romans, and thereby make a good living. It was a place where a man could become rich, because he was given a portion of his collections. And if his collections were greater, so was his portion, and if his dividing of the portion was fraudulent, so was his increase in riches. So it was with Zacchaeus, chief among the publicans.

Zacchaeus had heard that Jesus was coming to town. Already Jesus had sent His Spirit before Him. And the heart of Zacchaeus had been touched. He was desperately concerned with the possibility of seeing this Man from Nazareth, and the Bible says he wanted to see who He was. Who He was. It doesn't say he wanted to see what He did, or what He said; he wanted to see who He was. He was interested in getting to the heart of the matter. It's one thing to know something about what Jesus said; it's another thing to know who He is.

"And he sought to see Jesus who he was; and could not for the press, because he was little of stature" (verse 3). Imagine seeing this man Zacchaeus, who ordinarily would walk with all of his five-foot dignity down the streets of Jericho with as much composure as possible, running for a tree with the street urchins. Obviously, in seeking Jesus he had forgotten himself.

"When Jesus came to the place, he looked up, and saw him, and said unto him, Zacchaeus, make haste, and come down; for to day I must abide at thy house. And he made haste, and came down, and received him joyfully" (verses 5, 6).

In inviting Himself to Zacchaeus' house, Jesus was simply accepting the invitation that had already gone out from the heart of this publican. He was meeting him where he was; He was making it easy for him to come down out of his tree not only physically but spiritually, and to find the solution to his great problem.

FAITH EQUALS TRUST

He that cometh to God must believe that he is, and that he is a rewarder of them that diligently seek him. Heb. 11:6.

Jesus went thence, and departed into the coasts of Tyre and Sidon. And, behold, a woman of Canaan came out of the same coasts, and cried unto him, saying, Have mercy on me, O Lord, thou son of David; my daughter is grievously vexed with a devil. But he answered her not a word."

Have you ever been ignored? How did you like it? It's surprising that she stayed around. "And his disciples came and besought him, saying, Send her away; for she crieth after us." She's bothering us. Why don't you get rid of her? Jesus' first words, apparently going along with the disciples, were, "I am not sent but unto the lost sheep of the house of Israel." "Then came she and worshipped him." Worshiped Him? Do you worship the people who ignore you and say they didn't come to help you? And she said, "Lord, help me. But he answered and said, It is not meet [right] to take the children's bread and cast it to dogs." But this was the opening she had been looking for. "She said, Truth, Lord: yet the dogs eat of the crumbs which fall from their masters' table." If I am a dog, I am entitled to some dog food.

Jesus must have had a twinkle in His eye during this whole conversation. She must have seen it. "Then Jesus answered and said unto her, O woman, great is thy *faith*: be it unto thee even as thou wilt. And her daughter was made whole from that very hour" (Matt. 15:21-28).

How do you define "faith" in this story? Taking God at His word? If she had taken God at His word, she would have been gone long before He got to the "dogs" part. Do you define faith in terms of believing? Believing what Jesus said? You can't. It doesn't fit. Faith, in her case, was *dis*believing what Jesus said. Faith was *not* taking Him at His word.

So you come to the definition of faith as Jesus used it. It is the real definition of faith. One word: trust. The book *Education*, page 253, says, "Faith is trusting God."

The premise is that Jesus is completely trustworthy. If you don't believe that, you don't know Him yet. The person who is not quite sure that he can trust Jesus is the one who doesn't know Him. Faith comes, not to those who seek it, but to those who seek it not, who seek only to know Jesus.

BUT, GOD, I'M A GOOD MAN!

Behold, one came and said unto him, Good Master, what good thing shall I do, that I may have eternal life? Matt. 19:16.

Here is a behaviorist. And he had a lot of company. In John 6, a whole group came and said, "What shall we do, that we might work the works of God?" Jesus said, "This is the work of God, that ye believe on him whom he hath sent"—immediately transferring them from behavior to relationship.

This man said, "What good thing shall I do?" And He saith unto him, "Why callest thou me good? there is none good but one, that is, God: but if thou wilt enter into life, keep the commandments." Oh-oh. Is Jesus is shifting into a behaviorism pattern Himself?

Jesus knew that no one could keep the commandments in his own strength. He knew that we don't get to heaven by keeping the commandments. But that's what He said. "If thou wilt enter into life, keep the commandments." The rich young ruler asked, "Which?" "Thou shalt do no murder, Thou shalt not commit adultery, Thou shalt not steal," and so on. And the young man said, "All these things have I kept from my youth up: what lack I yet?" Here is the strong man, the behaviorist. He is a good liver. Wouldn't think of doing anything wrong. And then Jesus reveals what He was really after with this man. "Jesus said unto him, If you wilt be perfect, go and sell that thou hast, and give to the poor, . . . and come and follow me."

Jesus didn't always come right to the point with people who were searching for truth. In fact, He was pretty clever in His approach, not for the sake of cleverness, but because He had wisdom that came from His Father and His connection with His Father.

"What shall I do to enter into life?" "Keep the commandments." "I *have*." "Oh, yes? Let Me give you one more." He gave him one more, and the man hung his head and began kicking his toe in the dust. He was a strong, successful, external moral behaviorist, and he had nothing within. He was helpless.

Now, that is the point to which each of us must come when we genuinely come to Christ. We have to admit that we're helpless to do anything in our own strength, except give up trying to do something apart from Christ, and come to Him, just as we are.

SORROW FOR THE BROKEN HEART

Despisest thou the riches of his goodness and forbearance and longsuffering; not knowing that the goodness of God leadeth thee to repentance? Rom. 2:4.

Jesus came to demonstrate to His disciples, and to all of us, the love and forgiveness of our heavenly Father. He wanted to show us that God does not condemn us—that's the work of the enemy. He wanted to show that God is constantly working in every possible way to get as many people to accept His love as He possibly can. His lovingkindness leads us to repentance, as it did in the experience of Peter.

Peter stood by the fire and they pointed the finger at him. He said, "Oh, no. No, I'm not. I'm not, either." And they said, "Yes, you are." Finally, he began to curse and swear and to deny that he ever knew Jesus.

Right in the middle of his cursing and swearing, he looked across the way and saw Jesus looking at him. In that look was no anger or resentment or hurt feelings. There was a look of pity, of sorrow. As Peter looked upon the face of Jesus, a flood of memories began to come back. He saw himself by the sea when Jesus called him to follow Him. Again he saw himself in the hassle over the Temple authorities and tax coins, and Jesus went to his aid and got him out of the jam. Once more he saw himself out in the sea. Jesus is reaching down and pulling him up out of the angry waters. And again, just a few hours earlier—he could still see it—walking in the Garden with Jesus, and He had said, "Peter, Satan is determined to have you, but I've prayed for you. I've prayed for you."

And all these memories came flooding in. Peter was transfixed on the spot. Suddenly, as he stood there, he saw another hand raised to slap Jesus, and he realized that that was the same as his hand, and that he had dealt the hardest blow to the heart of Jesus that night. Blindly he turned from the fire and rushed out of the courtyard gate, out of the city, across the brook, into the Garden.

There he groped around in the darkness until he found the place where Jesus had been praying. He fell on his face and wished he could die. He was really sorry. He had broken the heart of his best Friend. Peter's was real repentance.

21

HOPE FOR THE HOPELESS SINNER

Lord, if thou wilt, thou canst make me clean. Matt. 8:2.

There was a man who was a lonely figure in the country of Palestine in the days of Christ. He had been driven from the city, from home, from friends, from all loved ones. He had no more friends; he was a wretch of humanity, dirty, disheveled. His clothes were in rags, his skin was eaten away, and parts of his body were gone. He was a victim of one of the most loathed diseases of all the East. He had leprosy! He sat by the roadside publishing his mournful condition by crying, "Unclean, unclean!" But he heard of Jesus, of how He'd raised the dead, opened blind eyes, forgiven people's sins. Ah, sin was what plagued *his* heart. Could Jesus somehow do anything for him?

This man thought and pondered and planned and hoped, until one day he began creeping along the road toward a lakeshore. He was looking for that large crowd around Jesus. As he came to the crowd, some of those on the outer fringe saw him. They fell back in horror and began to rebuke him, to get him to leave. This happens many times among human beings today. Remember this: it is human nature that a person who desperately needs attention, and seeks it, repulses other people. But never does he repulse Jesus Christ—never!

As this man came to the edge of the crowd, he was rebuked, but he could not be stopped. The crowd fell back in fear, but as they did, a way was made for him to get to Jesus. This poor man came into the presence of Jesus. As he came, he fell on his face in front of Him, right there on the ground. He said, "Lord, if You will You can make me clean."

He had tried everything! He had tried doctors, he had tried will-power, he had tried "trying." He tried friends who had finally deserted him. He had tried everything he knew of, until there was only one choice left for him. "Lord, if You will You can make me clean." Immediately the words came from Jesus' lips, "I will; be thou clean." And he was made whole from that very hour!

A heart still incapable of goodness but capable of love is accepted. God accepts the person, not for what he *is*, but for what God sees he can *become*, through the indwelling of Jesus Christ.

HOPE FOR THE HELPLESS SINNER

There is none that seeketh after God. Rom. 3:11.

The tax-gatherers and other bad characters were all crowding in to listen to him [Jesus]; and the Pharisees and the doctors of the law began grumbling among themselves: 'This fellow,' they said, 'welcomes sinners and eats with them.'" Now that was a great truth. This man, Jesus, welcomes sinners. They didn't know what they were saying, but they were saying something of great worth. And Jesus "answered them with this parable: 'If one of you has a hundred sheep and loses one of them, does he not leave the ninety-nine in the open pasture and go after the missing one until he has found it? How delighted he is then! He lifts it on to his shoulders, and home he goes to call his friends and neighbors together. "Rejoice with me!" he cries. "I have found my lost sheep." In the same way, I tell you, there will be greater joy in heaven over one sinner who repents than over ninety-nine righteous people who do not need to repent'" (Luke 15:2-8, NEB).

Sheep. A sheep knows that it's lost when it's lost, but it does not know the way back. One sheep is the smallest number of sheep that can be lost, and it will wander helplessly and perish unless it is brought back. In the story of the sheep, Jesus makes it clear that salvation does not come from our seeking after God, but from God seeking after us. We may not always know the way back. We may not even know that we are lost. Yet God goes out looking.

We are not after an evasive God. We are not trying to find, somewhere, a God who is trying to elude us. That is not the kind of God we serve. We serve, and we believe in, a God who followed Adam when he was running away. A God who followed Jacob when he was running away. A God who followed Jonah when he was deliberately running away. A God who followed Saul of Tarsus as he ran from those scenes in Jerusalem that had almost broken his heart. Instead of us seeking and trying to find God or to find Christ, as a rule, we are in the process of running away from Him. To begin with, and sometimes even after we have accepted Him at first, we do some running, too. And He keeps running after us. God is always the One who takes the initiative. And He is seeking each one of us today.

HOPE FOR THE IGNORANT SINNER

And ye shall seek me, and find me, when ye shall search for me with all your heart.
Jer. 29:13.

In Romans 3, Paul says there are people who are inescapably lost in their inability to seek God. In fact, he said, "There is none that seeketh after God" (verse 11). If we will seek Him, we'll find Him when we have searched for Him with all our hearts, but none seeketh after God. Then where does the seeking begin? We are supposed to seek, but none seek.

"'If a woman has ten silver pieces and loses one of them, does she not light the lamp, sweep out the house, look in every corner till she has found it? And when she has, she calls her friends and neighbours together, and says, "Rejoice with me! I have found the piece that I lost." In the same way, I tell you, there is joy among the angels of God over one sinner who repents'" (Luke 15:8-10, NEB).

In this story Jesus is telling us, through the symbol of the coin, that it is possible to be lost and not to know that we are lost, and not to know the way back. And the One goes out and looks for this lost coin. In the lost-coin symbol, it was lost in the house instead of out in the mountains somewhere, and perhaps we could go so far as to say it was lost within the church. Or lost in the family. And it's lost among the rubbish and the rubble of an ancient Middle East dwelling, but the search continues because it is still a piece of silver. It's still of value, and the value of one soul can never be overestimated in the eyes of Heaven.

"And ye shall seek me, and find me, when ye shall search for me . . ." How? "With all your heart." "With all your heart."

It is the sense of need that makes the difference. It is the great finding point. It is the point when we find Christ and the point when Christ finds us. "The Lord can do nothing toward the recovery of man until, convinced of his own weakness, and stripped of all self-sufficiency, he yields himself to the control of God. Then he can receive the gift that God is waiting to bestow."—*The Desire of Ages,* p. 300.

HOPE FOR THE DELIBERATE SINNER

I will arise and go to my father. Luke 15:18.

In the parable of the lost son we have the story of someone who was in the fold, decided—*planned*—to go out and be lost and knew the way back. And the father followed him all the time—with his binoculars, shall we say—and was out looking for him on the day of his return.

And so through this parable, Jesus is demonstrating the goodness and kindness of the Father, and He is saying, "For any type of person, we are out looking. We're out looking for you." The truth is that that is God's business and the great plan of salvation. The God who allowed you to be born, about which you had no choice, is not a God who is going to leave you wandering and lost, whether we know we are lost or whether we don't know it, whether we know the way back or whether we don't. He is going to stay with us until that moment of truth in our lives when by our own conscious intelligence and our reasoning we can accept Him or reject Him.

Like the prodigal son, we are running away from self-surrender. We are running away from the moment of truth in which we face ourselves with the realization that we are incapable for life and for handling the things of eternity.

One way we run away is by just plain busy-ness. We feel we have to keep busy, whether it is with books or studies, work or pleasure—just keep busy, occupied. It's possible for this to become a convenient route for running away. And all the time God is following, staying close, helping when we don't know it.

Then there is the pseudoreligionist who wants to forget God but does not want to give the impression that he wants to forget God, and so he spends a great deal of time discussing and dissecting and analyzing God and Christ and religion. There are probably as many ways of running from God as there are people who are running.

But when we realize that He is out looking for us, we can arise and go to our Father. He will meet us a great way off. "If you take even one step toward Him in repentance, He will hasten to enfold you in His arms of infinite love."—*Christ's Object Lessons,* p. 206.

GOSPEL ACCORDING TO MARY

Come unto me, all ye that labour and are heavy laden, and I will give you rest. Matt. 11:28.

In the village of Bethany lived two women, Mary and Martha, with their brother Lazarus, who evidently was the breadwinner for the family. Father and mother must have been gone. Both women were well known, but Mary was more outgoing than Martha. She felt at home with the crowd. Everybody liked Mary. And whenever there was a banquet or church potluck Mary was always there to make people feel at home.

One day, one of the church leaders, named Simon, began to notice Mary in a special way. He decided deep down inside that he was going to get better acquainted with her. And he did. Mary suspected nothing, at first. She was friendly to everybody. With the help of the archenemy, Simon was able, little by little, to lead Mary into sin.

She wasn't able to hide it forever, and gradually it became known around town that Mary was a "loose" woman. Things got so unbearable in Bethany that Mary packed her few belongings and left town. She traveled down Mount Moriah to a town called Magdala. She later became known as Mary of Magdala.

There Mary began to make some "easy" money. It turned out not to be so easy in the end. She found some people who were willing to pay her price, and oddly enough, she even found a degree of acceptance among these—people who became her friends and came back again and again. But the load got heavier and heavier on her shoulders. She found the easy money turning to bitterness.

One day a traveling preacher came to town. He stood in the streets of Magdala and began to tell people things they had never heard before. In those days, no one accepted publicans and harlots and thieves. But Jesus said, "Come unto me, all ye that labour and are heavy laden, and I will give you rest." *Rest?* For Mary, who had been lying awake at night? She heard words such as, "Him that cometh to me I will in no wise cast out" (John 6:37).

For the first time in her life, Mary saw a glimpse of the true character of God—of His love, which was revealed through Jesus—and she realized that God would accept her. She no longer had to run away from a God she feared.

26

LOVING ACCEPTANCE

Him that cometh to me I will in no wise cast out. John 6:37.

W e've often heard the idea that conversion is an immediate, complete, absolute, final change of life—that we'll have no more problems from then on, no more weaknesses, no more failures. And when problems do arise, then we think we haven't really been converted. But remember this: conversion is a supernatural work of the Holy Spirit on the human heart, producing *a change of attitude toward God;* instead of being against Him, now you're for Him. Conversion creates in the person *a new capacity for knowing and loving God*—it's the turning-around point, the beginning, but that's all it is. And we're told we need to be converted every day, not just once and for all.

The first time Mary of Magdala heard Jesus speaking, she couldn't believe the words of comfort. Religious leaders accepted only the good, moral churchgoers—not sinners, harlots, and thieves! It was almost more than she could stand. With her broken heart, she pressed through the crowd after the outdoor service, and right there in the open, she poured out her heart to Jesus and told Him of her burden. Jesus accepted her. He prayed for her with strong prayers, seeking His Father's presence in her behalf. And Mary was converted right there on the spot. Her load of sin and guilt left her. Conversion, as usually happens, came when she was desperate enough to give up on herself entirely.

We'd like to say that the story ends there. But the truth is that Mary failed, evidently shortly after Jesus left town. She stayed where she was, the same crowd was around, the same voices whispered to her in the marketplace. When Jesus was not in town, she found it difficult to hold on to the peace she had found from hearing His words and from being with Him. But she still had that change of attitude toward God, and her capacity for knowing Him was still down inside. And the next time Jesus came through town, she poured out her troubles to Him, and again He worked in her behalf. He accepted her again. The Bible records that Jesus cast out seven devils from her. But He always accepted her, as He always accepts anyone who comes to Him. It was in this attitude of loving acceptance that Mary's heart was broken anew.

SITTING AT JESUS' FEET

Acquaint now thyself with him, and be at peace. Job 22:21.

Jesus cast seven devils out of Mary of Magdala. Seven times He worked in her behalf, but finally, one day, she learned the secret of righteousness by faith. It was the experience that being with Him produces, and He must have helped her to find it out. What is the secret? It is in sitting at the feet of Jesus, *even when Jesus isn't in town.* Is that possible? Yes, it is. And when Mary learned that, she began to go to her own knees with strong prayers, seeking communion with the Father each day, growing in a relationship with Him. And things began to get better. Why? Because as Jesus comes in, sin is crowded out. There's no point in trying to stamp it out ourselves; it will never work that way. It happens only by Jesus coming in, for our weaknesses are then surmounted by His power. That's why Jesus accepts people just as they are. Only *He* can make the changes. If we look at our sins, we'll become more like them, but if we behold Christ, we'll become like Him. Mary learned that rather than dwelling on her sins and her failures, she should concentrate on God's love.

Things got so much better for Mary, there in Magdala, where she was living, that she began to get up new hopes about going home to Bethany again. Maybe they would accept her now. It would be nice to see Martha and Lazarus again. She packed up her things, and headed back up to the top of the mountain to Bethany.

There was a beautiful reunion between Mary and Martha and Lazarus. But the people in the town were the same kind of people. Some said, "Good, Mary's back!" But more of them said, "Watch out for Mary!" How did Mary succeed in not letting the gossip get her down? How did she manage to retain her peace of mind?

Jesus had taught her the secret—that communication with God each day would bring her power over her problems and worries. How could she communicate with God even when Jesus wasn't in town? Through the same way we can today, by a meaningful devotional time of Bible study and prayer, talking with God and listening to Him, and then sharing with others.

ONLY ONE THING NEEDFUL

But one thing is needful: and Mary hath chosen that good part, which shall not be taken away from her. Luke 10:42.

One day Jesus and His disciples came on the long trip up from Jericho to Bethany. Martha thought it would be a good idea to invite them over for dinner, because they'd all get a chance to know one another better. When Martha asked Jesus to get Mary to help in the kitchen, Martha was troubled. She was worried about making a good impression on Jesus. But Jesus replied, *"There is only one thing needful . . ."* This was His statement on the sum and substance, the beginning, the middle, and the end—everything concerning the Christian life. There's only one thing that is necessary in the Christian life, but it's also the one thing that many of us haven't tried yet.

"I can't sit at Jesus' feet now. He's not in town!" Oh, yes; yes, you can! Please remember that all the intangible phrases we use in describing the Christian life—"coming to Christ," "sitting at Jesus' feet," "giving Him your heart or your will"—are made tangible by three things that we can do. How do we know one another better? By communicating and by doing things together. The same is true in getting to know God—communication with Him at the beginning of every day through Bible study and prayer. You study about the life of Jesus as given in the Bible, especially in the Gospels, and apply it to your own life, your own experiences, your own wants and needs, and then you talk with God about what you've learned. Then share with your friends what you've received from your personal encounter with God. Telling them what Jesus has done for you will make them desire to seek Him for themselves.

Someone asks, "Won't we do anything else besides read the Bible and pray?" Of course we will! There are plenty of other things that are necessary—good works, obedience, high standards, doctrines of the church. But all these will grow out of this one needful thing, sitting at the feet of Jesus. It is the basis of the entire Christian experience. And many of us don't realize it yet; we don't think the Christian life can be that simple. But Mary had realized her need for that "good part," as Jesus said, and it wouldn't be taken away from her.

SPIRITUAL PRESCRIPTION

But to him that worketh not, but believeth on him that justifieth the ungodly, his faith is counted for righteousness. Rom. 4:5.

If you want to produce apples, the best thing for you to do is to find an apple tree somewhere. And if you want to produce the right kind of fruit in the Christian life, the best thing for you to do is to be a Christian. Because an apple tree, remember, bears apples because it *is* an apple tree, never in order *to be* an apple tree. And a Christian does what is right because he *is* a Christian, never in order *to be* a Christian. The problem of so many young people today is that they're trying to do what is right in order to be Christians.

So what is the real faith that works? Faith is best defined as trust. The question is, How do we learn to trust? We learn to trust someone else by learning to know him. And we don't usually really trust anyone until we know him. God is one who is completely trustworthy, but you'll never believe that until you know Him. If you know God, you will trust Him, and you will trust Him spontaneously. If you don't know God, you will distrust Him. Whenever you see a person giving evidence of distrust of God, he is advertising the fact that he doesn't know God.

When you really catch a glimpse of what Christianity is all about, you realize that it is involved in knowing Jesus. There are many professed Christians who will scrap it at that point, and will say, No, thanks; I want a religion, I want a Christianity, in which I can do something for myself. It is ego-deflating to come to Jesus and say, "Lord, I guess You're right. I guess I can't do it. I would like to turn it all over to You."

Now, how is this done? Here is where we get elementary. Here is the prescription: Take time, alone, at the beginning of every day, *to seek Jesus* through His Word and through prayer. That is all you can do, with the surrender of your will, to be a Christian. There is nothing else you can do to be a Christian. If you don't do that, you're not a Christian. All you are is a good liver. And there are a lot of good livers in the church who don't know God, who don't care a whole lot about the Lord Jesus Christ. God invites you to be more than simply a good liver. He invites you to know His presence and power in your life today, every day—that is Christianity.

FLOWERS BEFORE THE FUNERAL

Verily I say unto you, Wheresoever this gospel shall be preached in the whole world, there shall also this, that this woman hath done, be told for a memorial of her. Matt. 26:13.

There is a feast at Simon's house. Jesus is there, and Mary is at Jesus' feet. Her heart is breaking because she's heard Jesus talk about going to Jerusalem, where evil men will put Him to death. Mary heard—when even His disciples refused to listen. And she can't stand the thought, for Jesus is her best Friend.

She doesn't like the synthetic custom of sending flowers after loved ones have gone. So you see her slipping quietly across the room to where Jesus is sitting. She carries the precious box of ointment, and thinks that if she's careful, no one will ever know.

And that's where her plan goes wrong. Whenever you open a box of spikenard, it *screams.* Suddenly all eyes are upon her, including Simon's at the head of the table. The guests begin to murmur as she pours the ointment over Jesus' head and feet.

That's when she discovers she'd forgotten something else, too—she has no towel, or anything else like it with her. In those days, only a woman of the streets would let her long, flowing hair down, but Mary never gives it a thought. She lets down her hair and wipes up the ointment. Imagine her there in her embarrassment. Everyone is staring at her and whispering, and down there at the other end of the table Simon is thinking, If this man Jesus knows what kind of woman she is and yet still allows her to touch Him, He must not be a prophet! It seems strange that anyone with Simon's record could have thought that way, but he did.

"Mary knew not the full significance of her deed of love. She could not answer her accusers. She could not explain why she had chosen that occasion for anointing Jesus. The Holy Spirit had planned for her, and she had obeyed His promptings."—*The Desire of Ages*, p. 560. Christ explained to Mary, and to those present, the meaning of her act. "And as He went down into the darkness of His great trial, He carried with Him the memory of that deed, an earnest of the love that would be His from His redeemed ones forever."—*Ibid.*

The Love of God

TROUBLED ABOUT MANY THINGS

Casting all your care upon him; for he careth for you. 1 Peter 5:7.

Now it came to pass, as they went, that he entered into a certain village: and a certain woman named Martha received him into her house. And she had a sister called Mary, which also sat at Jesus' feet, and heard his word. But Martha was cumbered about much serving, and came to him, and said, Lord, dost thou not care that my sister hath left me to serve alone? bid her therefore that she help me. And Jesus answered and said unto her, Martha, Martha, thou art careful and troubled about many things: but one thing is needful: and Mary hath chosen that good part, which shall not be taken away from her" (Luke 10:38-42).

What would you do if you heard that Jesus was in town? Where would you be? Would you be sleeping on the sidewalk in front of wherever He was going to appear, or would you be on your way out of town?

Martha made certain that Jesus received an invitation to her house. And then she left Him sitting in the living room and went out to the kitchen, to do what Martha types do out in the kitchen. But you see here that Martha's concern was not just about the kitchen, and Mary helping, for she was troubled about *many* things. She was troubled about everything. When Jesus gently rebuked her, He wasn't simply talking about the kitchen and the pots and the pans. He was talking about a way of life for Martha. Martha was a good girl. She wouldn't think of doing anything wrong. Probably the worst thing she ever did was chew her fingernails when the mixer didn't work.

Often good people feel that they don't need Jesus. They can get along fine being religious. But that thoughtful hour alone with Jesus every day is not something we do in addition to being Christians. It is the entire basis of the Christian life. Those who don't know what that is are invariably going to be careful and troubled about many things. There is only one way to victory and peace in the Christian life. Do you know what it is to sit at Jesus' feet, today, tomorrow, and every day until Jesus comes?

JESUS LOVES PHARISEES, TOO!

Who is like unto the Lord our God, who dwelleth on high! Ps. 113:5.

Jesus came one day to the town of Bethany. There He met the man who had led Mary of Magdala into sin. Simon—wretched Simon—now a victim of leprosy. We would have let him suffer by the side of the road. *Simon* didn't deserve healing! Yet the same power that cast the devils out of Mary and raised Lazarus from the dead cleansed Simon from leprosy. And Jesus healed Simon before he had even accepted Him as Messiah, as his Lord and Saviour, or as anything!

This miracle created a real problem for Simon, because a Pharisee, a legalist, who has been used to earning what he gets all his life, is going to be driven up the wall when someone gives him something *free.* You see Simon lying awake at night, you see him making a path across his plush carpets during the day, trying to figure out what to do. He can't stand it— he's been *given* something.

Finally, he has a bright idea. He'll pay Jesus back! He didn't have a chance to earn it, but he'll pay Him back. So he plans a huge banquet in honor of Jesus. There, the reaction of Jesus to Mary's anointing His feet gave Simon reason to justify his rejection of the Christ.

At that moment Jesus turned to Simon and said, "Simon, I have something to say." And Simon got tight stomach muscles. He'd heard about this Man—this Man who could read people's thoughts. Simon stiffened. He expected to be humiliated in his own house, at his own feast, in front of everybody. He was already beginning to feel the pain and embarrassment when Jesus, in a kind, tender manner, simply told him a little story—a story that only Simon could understand, but did he ever understand it! It went deep down into his heart, and for the first time, Simon saw himself as he really was. And he saw himself in the presence of Someone who knew what he was really like but who still loved him, who showed kindness and tenderness in not publicly tearing the mask from his face. His heart was broken, and he was converted right there at his own banquet. Jesus got Simon, too!

WE SHALL NEVER DIE

And whosoever liveth and believeth in me shall never die. Believest thou this? John 11:26.

A certain man was sick, a man named Lazarus, of Bethany, the town of Mary and her sister, Martha. It was that Mary who anointed the Lord with ointment and wiped His feet with her hair whose brother Lazarus was sick.

The Desire of Ages tells us that from their very first meeting, Lazarus' faith in Christ was strong; he became one of the most steadfast of Christ's disciples (page 524). All of them—Mary, Martha, and Lazarus—became close friends of Jesus, and whenever He came to Bethany, He went to see them. They were united in a close bond of fellowship and love.

Jesus did a lot of traveling, and He was far away from Judea, where Bethany is, when Lazarus became ill. Mary and Martha sent a message to Jesus, "He whom You love is sick." Surely because Jesus loved them so much, He would come back immediately to heal Lazarus. But Jesus sent back the words, "This sickness is not unto death." They rushed to Lazarus' bedroom. "Lazarus, can you hear us?" "Yes." "Don't worry, Lazarus, you're not going to die. Jesus said so."

And then he died. That must have been hard to take. The person who doesn't sit at Jesus' feet invariably ends up getting mad at God, blaming God for allowing all his troubles. But for the one who sits at Jesus' feet, it's different. And despite the shock and grief they must have been feeling, Mary and Martha did not waver in their faith; they did not blame Jesus for Lazarus' death.

After an unhurried wait of two days, Jesus said to His disciples, "We're going back to Bethany now. Lazarus is asleep." His disciples thought Jesus was talking about sleep in terms of resting, and couldn't understand why Jesus wanted to go to wake him up. Finally Jesus said reluctantly, in language they were familiar with, "Lazarus is dead. But I'm going to wake him up."

Jesus went back to Bethany and was met by Mary and Martha. Their faith had remained despite their loss. You know the rest of the story. The stone was rolled away, and Lazarus was awakened to life. What we call death is only a temporary separation. It's not eternal. And each of us can look forward to the great reunion when Jesus comes again.

WHY JESUS WEPT

Jesus wept. John 11:35.

When Jesus went with Mary and Martha to the tomb of Lazarus, Jesus knew what plans He had for turning the scene of sorrow into one of rejoicing. Yet we see in the Bible record that "Jesus wept." How could this be?

Jesus wasn't afraid that Lazarus was stuck there, behind that stone. What we call death is no problem to God. Death has never been any problem to God. Raising Lazarus to life was probably one of the easiest things on earth that Jesus ever did. And when the Lord Himself descends from heaven with a shout, with the voice of the archangel, and the dead in Christ come forth from their sleeping beds, wherever they are, that will be one of the easiest things that God has ever done.

The only problem for God that still goes on is unbelief. That's the problem. It's a far greater miracle to see a person go from skepticism and atheism to Jesus, far greater than the raising of Lazarus. Jesus wept at the grave of Lazarus because of the unbelief.

They said, "Oh, He's weeping because He loved him." No, that wasn't why He was weeping. He was weeping because of the people in the crowd that didn't believe. They did not accept what He had to offer. As He had said, "Ye will not come to me, that ye might have life."

There was another reason why Jesus wept at the tomb of Lazarus. He wept in sympathy with those who were hurting. Not only with Mary and Martha but with all the sorrowing of all ages, as His glance swept over the centuries, seeing the pain of the human family for ages to come.

His love was so great that He sympathized with the sorrow of His friends, even though He knew it would last but a little while. He longs to relieve the distress of each of His children. He weeps, today, with those of us who weep. And because of the sacrifice He made in our behalf, we have the promise of a time and a place where all our tears will be wiped away.

WHEN JESUS WEPT FOR SATAN

He is despised and rejected of men; a man of sorrows, and acquainted with grief.
Isa. 53:3.

After sin and rebellion entered our universe, after there had been war in heaven, and after Satan and his angels had been cast out, Satan was not satisfied with what he had accomplished. He experienced no genuine sorrow that he had sinned and hurt Someone who loved him, but he became terrified as he saw the results, even from that point, of his rebellion.

"Satan trembled as he viewed his work. He was alone in meditation upon the past, the present, and his future plans. His mighty frame shook as with a tempest. An angel from heaven was passing. He called him and entreated an interview with Christ. This was granted him. He then related to the Son of God that he repented of his rebellion and wished again the favor of God." Now notice: "Christ wept at Satan's woe but told him, as the mind of God, that he could never be received into heaven. Heaven must not be placed in jeopardy."—*The Story of Redemption*, p. 26.

Jesus wept—at the beginning of the separation and sorrow caused by sin; as He looked ahead and saw Adam and Eve forced to leave the beautiful Garden He had created with them in mind; as He saw Cain, unable to tolerate the righteous Abel, violently ending his brother's life, and then refusing to repent.

He saw the growing wickedness of the world, the wars, the crimes, the hatred, until all but eight souls were destroyed from the earth.

He saw those in misery, in slavery, the masses who looked with longing eyes for a Deliverer, and yet rejected Him when He appeared among them.

He saw Gethsemane, Calvary. He saw how few would accept His sacrifice, and how feeble was the faith of even the few. He wept because of the unbelief, the sorrow, the fear, the pain. He saw martyrs suffering for His sake. He saw those who denied Him to escape suffering.

He sorrowed because Satan, whom He still loved, could not be saved. His heart was broken with the pain of separation from a loved one, from an unnumbered multitude of loved ones, with whom He could never be reunited. What a tremendous commentary on the love of God is the statement "Jesus wept."

THE MAN OF SORROWS

Surely he hath borne our griefs, and carried our sorrows. Isa. 53:4.

It is evening. The sun is setting and the sky is ablaze with color. The hearts of Jesus' disciples are also ablaze. Never have their hopes been so high, their plans and dreams seemed so sure of speedy fulfillment.

They've put up with quite a bit these past three years, and at times it has hardly seemed worth it. But now they are on their way to Jerusalem. Jesus is traveling as a *king*, on a donkey, and multitudes have joined the twelve and are shouting their support. Surely now the new government will be set up.

The procession pauses at the crest of the hill. The sounds of praise are quieted momentarily as the people see the sunset, and the sunset reflected from the white marble of the Temple. For a moment they look in pride and admiration; then they turn to see their own sentiments reflected in the face of Jesus.

Jesus is weeping. Not the glistening eye with the smiling face that speaks tears of joy. But agony. Sobs. Sorrow so deep that it could find expression only in open grief. The people are stunned. Jesus had wept at the tomb of Lazarus, and they had understood that time—or thought they understood. But this is different. They look quickly at the disciples, searching for a clue. What has happened that perhaps they missed? But the faces of the disciples wear the same expression of puzzlement.

From our vantage point in time, knowing what was about to take place, we might associate His sorrow with the sheepgate, beside the Temple. But *The Desire of Ages*, page 576, says, "The tears of Jesus were not in anticipation of His own suffering." As we continue the inspired commentary, we discover that Jesus is weeping in an anguish of separation as He looks upon His children, whom He cannot save because they will not let Him. His glance takes in the sorrow of a world separated from God, from that moment to this. And to the Jews who would cry, "Crucify Him," to the people of all ages who have turned every one to his own way, yes, to you and to me, who are simply too busy to find time for God, Jesus uttered the cry of a God with a breaking heart, "How can I give thee up? How often would I have gathered thee, even as a hen gathereth her chicks, but you would not."

DESIRE FOR SOMETHING BETTER |

That was the true Light, which lighteth every man that cometh into the world. John 1:9.

"The first step toward salvation is to respond to the drawing of the love of Christ."—*Selected Messages*, book 1, p. 323. Everyone, everywhere, is being drawn, except possibly those who have already been brought to a confrontation with God and have turned Him down. Jesus said that the Holy Spirit would "convince the world of sin" (John 16:8, RSV). He didn't say only church members. Not just a few, but the whole world. He told us about His Father: "No man can come to me, except the Father which hath sent me draw him" (John 6:44). And Jesus Himself is involved. "I, if I be lifted up from the earth, will draw all men unto me" (John 12:32). The three mighty persons of the Godhead are drawing every person to face the real issues of time and eternity and make their decision.

Do you have a desire for something better than you presently know? If you do, it is God who gives you that desire. Whether you are ready to admit it or not, whether you'd identify it as that or not, it is God. He is drawing you. He is drawing your heart, your life, your mind, to Him.

The desire will not be satisfied by just being religious. There's a big difference between being religious and being spiritual. There's a difference between knowing the rules and knowing the Lord. There can be a big gap between going through the forms, playing the game called church, and really knowing God.

My telephone rang at 2:00 one morning. I stumbled down the hall to the phone and heard a woman's voice on the other end of the line. She said, "Sir, can you help me?"

I asked, "What kind of help do you need at this time of day?"

"I need to find God. Do you know God?"

Would you think for a moment of all the answers I could have given? "I'm a preacher." No, do you know God? "I studied Greek." No, do you know God? "I keep the Sabbath and pay tithe." Sir, *do you know God?*

That's the question for each one today. Do you know God? Do you know Him personally? That's your biggest need.

THE LONG SEARCH

Wherefore do ye spend money for that which is not bread? and your labour for that which satisfieth not? Isa. 55:2.

My brother and I went with Dr. Siegfried Horn on a tour of Europe and the Middle East in 1959. By the end of the tour we had bought too many souvenirs, and we ran out of money in Frankfurt, Germany. We had our tickets home, but only about 70 cents apiece. So we decided we'd walk up and down the streets of Frankfurt and pick out the best meal we could for 70 cents before we starved! We finally found a cafeteria that offered a pretty good meal for 70 cents—German black bread, potatoes and gravy, and lots of other good food.

We had thought that this would be our choice, but walked for a few more blocks, just to be sure. Suddenly we came to a German pastry shop. We went to the window and looked in. There was the most beautiful pastry we had ever seen. The frosting was as thick as the cake. We went in, and spent the last of our money on German pastry. Then we hurried to the nearest park, sat down by a little pond, and began to eat. We got through about half a bag apiece, and then everything began to look sort of black. We didn't want to throw any of it away, so we finally ate the whole thing! And then we took turns, one keeping watch, while the other groaned in a horizontal position on the park bench. Half the night we sat there. Eating that pastry was really *fun,* while it lasted. But it didn't last. The fun the world offers never lasts.

Satan has a counterfeit for everything real that God has to offer. The counterfeit may seem to satisfy for a time, but it leaves only emptiness in the end. The one who is out trying to get rich or become famous is searching for God and doesn't know it. The poor man who is lying in the gutter in his own vomit is searching for God. The amusement parks and resort cities are filled with people searching for God. The young person who has made oatmeal out of his brain is searching for God but doesn't know it and wouldn't admit it. Everybody, in the mad search for something to take the place of that vacuum within, is searching for God. The only lasting answer to our desire for something better must center upon Jesus. The desire is for Him. Nothing can take His place.

A RIGHT KNOWLEDGE OF GOD

Study to shew thyself approved unto God, a workman that needeth not to be ashamed, rightly dividing the word of truth. 2 Tim. 2:15.

Once we respond to the God-given desire for something better, we must then gain a knowledge of what that "something" is. Knowledge, a correct knowledge, of God and His love is our second step in coming to Him.

If a person simply receives his information about salvation from other people, there's a good chance his information concerning Christianity is going to be based on behavior, because most people define it in terms of behavior. If you rely upon other people for your information, you're likely to end up with a misunderstanding of God.

"Study to show *yourself* approved unto God." If you don't, you're going to be ashamed sometime. Study for *yourself*. Get the right knowledge for yourself. Don't depend upon what others tell you concerning God. Don't depend on the preacher. We have churches full of people today who are depending on the preachers for their information. God help them. The preacher may be just as wrong as the next person. You'd better go and find out for yourself what is right and what isn't.

This involves more than searching the Scriptures for information. The Jewish people did plenty of searching of the Scriptures, but they didn't find the One the Scriptures were intended to help them find. Don't read the Bible just for the sake of reading the Bible. Study for more than information. Study for communication. Don't pray just to get answers to your problems. Pray for communication.

"Seek, and ye *shall* find" (Matt. 7:7). Paul says to seek God, and find Him, "though he be not far from every one of us" (Acts 17:27). It is planned that we find Him.

But remember that we are not after an evasive God. We are not trying to find a God that is lost or trying to elude us. That is not the God of the Bible. We have a God who followed Adam when he hid in the Garden. A God who followed Jonah when he was deliberately running from his duty. A God who followed Saul of Tarsus as he fled from the stoning in Jerusalem that had brought conviction to his heart. It is only as we see the love of God for us that we will be willing for Him to catch up with us.

A WRONG KNOWLEDGE OF GOD

"You study the Scriptures, because you think that in them you will find eternal life. And these very Scriptures speak about me! Yet you are not willing to come to me in order to have life." John 5:39, 40, TEV.

When the devil sees us trying to gain a correct knowledge of God through the study of His Word, he gets nervous. As with every step toward Christ, he has sidetracks designed to hinder us from our goal.

Sometimes the devil is able to sidetrack a person by getting him to start at the wrong place in the Bible. Is there a right and a wrong place to start? For a beginner? Is there? Have you ever made a vow to read your Bible through every year, and become an authority on the book of Genesis? Or have you ever gotten as far as Chronicles and been finished off there? One time I saw a *Reader's Digest* title, "We're Up to Chronicles." *That* was worth putting in the *Reader's Digest!* The devil will do anything he can do to keep us from a knowledge of the love of God. It is possible to have a knowledge of everything *but* the love of God. It is possible to understand about history and prophecy and beasts and symbols and all that, and still to have missed the love of God.

Then there are the pseudointellectuals, who like to talk about religion but spend very little time with the Word, for communication with God. They spend a great deal of time discussing and dissecting and analyzing God and religion. They want a way of forgetting God that will pass as a way of remembering Him. They spend time considering what happens to a flower in heaven when you pick it, whether angels' wings have feathers, or more sophisticated side trips. The name of Jesus is never mentioned, and the devil sits back and laughs.

Some substitute behavioral changes for a personal relationship with God. If they succeed in changing their behavior, they think they have found Him. Some depend on other people, and their spiritual life is high or low according to what kind of people they are around. Some become preoccupied with the psychological approach, without God as the center, analyzing themselves and forgetting Christ. Some people escape by being just too busy to take time for God. But all the time, God is following, staying close, helping when we don't know it, guiding when we don't intend it, ever trying to bring us to a true knowledge of Himself, whom to know is life eternal.

A SENSE OF NEED

They that be whole need not a physician, but they that are sick. But go ye and learn what that meaneth, I will have mercy, and not sacrifice: for I am not come to call the righteous, but sinners to repentance. Matt. 9:12, 13.

One morning one of the fellows who worked at a college farm returned to the dormitory with a gunnysack full of dry cereal. It had been stored at the farm to feed the cows. "The cows can eat grass," he said. "*We'll* eat the cereal." And he put it in his closet. Everyone at his end of the hall came every morning with a bowl and dipped in for a bowlful of dry cereal. Who needs a cafeteria, anyway? They didn't know that the reason the cows had been given the cereal was because it had been swept up off the floor at the cereal factory—until the morning they discovered some "pets" in the bag. Then the fellows made a beeline for the cafeteria. Suddenly they decided they needed the cafeteria after all.

You never feel the need for fire insurance as much as when your house is on fire. You never feel your need for a service station as you do when your car sputters and stops on the side of the road and you are out of gas. It's when you feel sick that you realize your need for a doctor. "It is absurd, therefore, to offer a physician to them that are whole, or that at least imagine themselves so to be. You are first to convince them that they are sick; otherwise they will not thank you for your labor. It is equally absurd to offer Christ to them whose heart is whole, having never yet been broken."—*The Great Controversy*, p. 264.

It is the sense of need that makes the difference. This sense of need comes from the contemplation of the love of God. You don't have to wait for some other person to introduce you into His presence. You can sit down and, even though you find it hard at first, deliberately study and contemplate the revelation in God's Word of the love of God through the life of Jesus Christ. This is the short route that can bring you to a sense of need that perhaps a lifetime would not accomplish otherwise. Come to Him where He is revealed, realizing at the same time that He has been out looking for each one of us. "If you take even one step toward Him in repentance, He will hasten to enfold you in His arms of infinite love."—*Christ's Object Lessons*, p. 206.

THE LONG ROUTE TO GOD

As I live, saith the Lord God, I have no pleasure in the death of the wicked; but that the wicked turn from his way and live. Eze. 33:11.

There are many who refuse the short route of coming to God, the deliberate search and study into the life and character of Christ where God's love is revealed. Probably most of us take the long route. It's too bad, because it's not God's plan. But it's there. It's the route of trouble, ulcers, teetering on the edge of the Golden Gate Bridge. It's a long life of heartache and trouble, of pain and frustration.

It took the thief on the cross the marathon run all the way to the gallows before he was willing to listen. Then he heard the friendly words, "Father, forgive them; for they know not what they do." And there it was, in the presence of the love of God, at the moment of his extremity, that he finally came to the moment of truth.

Saul had resisted. He had tried to erase the memory of a dying man at whom they were throwing rocks, who had said, "Lord, lay not this sin to their charge." Yet finally on the road to Damascus his heart was broken, and he faced the love he had been running away from.

Nicodemus waited for three years. It wasn't until the Friend he must have *intended* to get better acquainted with—someday—was crucified that he finally understood the love that had been offered to him, and he accepted the offer as he and Joseph removed the bruised body of Jesus from the cross.

"Oh," you may say, "if we have all these ways of escape, and the human heart is running from God, what are we going to do?" Just remember that God is running after us. His appeal to you today is to let Him find you, by faith, as the Bible says, not of yourselves. Even faith is the gift of God (Eph. 2:8). "His ear is open to the cry of the contrite soul. The very first reaching out of the heart after God is known to Him. Never a prayer is offered, however faltering, never a tear is shed, however secret, never a sincere desire after God is cherished, however feeble, but the Spirit of God goes forth to meet it. Even before the prayer is uttered or the yearning of the heart is made known, grace from Christ goes forth to meet the grace that is working upon the human soul."—*Christ's Object Lessons*, p. 206.

43

CONVICTION OF SIN

When he is come, he will reprove the world of sin, and of righteousness, and of judgment: of sin, because they believe not on me. John 16:8, 9.

The knowledge of the love of God as revealed in the plan of salvation will lead to the third step in coming to Christ, *conviction of sin*. The behaviorist defines sin in terms of transgression of the law, and it's true—that is the only legal, forensic definition for sin in the Bible. But there are some experiential definitions for sin in the Bible that go deeper than that. One of the best is in Romans 14:23: "Whatsoever is not of faith is sin." Whatever I do, if it isn't done through faith in Christ, it is sin.

There are two definitions for sin. One of them we will call the definition of sin, *singular*, and the other the definition for sin*s, plural. Sin is living a life without Christ. Sins are transgressions of the law.* Living a life apart from Christ (sin) is the cause of doing wrong things (sins). It is interesting the way the King James Version reads on 1 John 3:4: "Whosoever committeth sin [who, as we say, lives a life apart from Christ] transgresses *also* the law."

When did Eve sin? When she ate the fruit? She sinned when she distrusted what God had told her and wandered away. Eating the fruit was simply the natural result of that. If I am having a problem with doing wrong things, my real problem is that I am living a life apart from Christ. Either that, or I haven't known Him long enough yet to grow to victory, and Jesus Himself allowed for growth.

So when we talk about conviction, we are talking about the realization that we are sinners, *regardless of what we have done. Regardless of how good or bad we have been.* We were born sinners, born sinful by nature. 1 John 5:17: "All unrighteousness is sin." Roman 3:10: "There is none righteous." So there is nobody righteous, we are all unrighteous, and all unrighteousness is sin. But don't ever feel that we are held responsible for being born in a world of sin. Jesus knows the way we were born, and the only thing we are responsible for is what we do with His plan of salvation.

When we face ourselves in the presence of Jesus, suddenly we are convicted that we are sinners. *Not because of what we have done, but because of what we are.* Through this conviction we realize our need of Him.

COUNTERFEIT CONVICTION

But what things were gain to me, those I counted loss for Christ. Yea doubtless, and I count all things but loss for the excellency of the knowledge of Christ Jesus my Lord. Phil. 3:7, 8.

If the knowledge about the love of God as revealed in Jesus has been inadequate, it may send a person off the track and hinder his coming to the conviction of sin in the right sense. If the knowledge I have received has to do only with the Ten Commandments, I'll be convinced merely that I have done sinful deeds, and right there is where the sidetrack begins.

People may be divided into two classes, the strong and the weak. By virtue of heredity and environment, we are either among the strong or the weak, or somewhere between. The strong person who is convinced that he has done sinful deeds, and that's as far as his knowledge of the plan of salvation and the problem of sin goes, will change his ways, stop doing the sinful deeds, and become a "good" moral person. This may be his downfall, because morality is not Christianity. Morality has never been Christianity and never will be Christianity. *You don't do what is right by not doing what is wrong. Trying to be good by trying not to be bad is not being good.* Badness held in check is not goodness and never has been goodness. So the peculiar pit for the strong-willed and the backboned and the self-disciplined person is morality without Christ. Thus he deceives himself into thinking that he is a good person, and therefore a Christian—and he may be further from being a Christian than the drunk in the gutter, because he may become blind to his need of Christ. The Pharisees were good moral people. They were such good Sabbathkeepers that they hurried back from the cross to be in time for sundown worship. But that did not make them righteous before God.

If you see from a distance someone who is 10 feet tall, he may not look tall to you. In fact, he may look about your size, maybe a little shorter. But when you get close to him and look up at him, suddenly you feel like a dwarf at his feet. And if you are walking along, no matter how good or bad you are, at some distance from Jesus, He may not look tall—maybe about your size. It's when you come into His immediate presence that you suddenly see yourself as you really are and are convicted of your need.

CONVICTION OF NEED

God be merciful to me a sinner. Luke 18:13.

One time I went to see a man who was drunk. His wife was a member of the church. He looked at me through his bloodshot eyes and said with his thick tongue, "I really admire the Adventists. It takes a strong person, it takes a good man, to be an Adventist." Does it take a strong person to be an Adventist? Is it possible for a *weak* person to be a good Adventist? Yes or no? If your Christian belief is based upon behaviorism only, then it takes a strong person to be a Seventh-day Adventist Christian, or any other kind of Christian. But where religion is based upon relationship with Jesus Christ, the strong and the weak are equal.

Have you ever considered who hated Jesus more when He was here—the strong or the weak? It was the strong. Why? Because for the first time in their spotless lives they saw Someone who went deeper than the externals, and they got nervous. In His presence, suddenly all of their morality and good living added up to nothing, and they knew it.

There is a type of person in this world who says, "Smoking causes lung cancer? I quit!" He quits and he never touches cigarettes again. Another person says, "Smoking causes lung cancer? I quit, too." And that afternoon he goes out and buys another carton. The strong succeed and the weak fail.

It is possible to keep the Sabbath (and we should change that to keep Saturday), to become Saturday keepers, and in the very process of keeping Saturday to be sinning. It is possible to stay out of jail because of a good moral life, and in the very process of staying out of jail, still be living in sin, because you are doing it on your own, apart from Christ. It is possible to abide by all the rules and regulations and to be a good person, and be considered so by everyone else, and still be living in sin. There is going to be a great revival one of these days in the church, but it is not going to be based upon the confession of heinous sins. It's going to be based upon the sudden realization on the part of people who have been living good moral lives that they have been living *apart from Jesus,* and are just as much sinners as the harlots and thieves. This conviction is the step that will lead all, strong and weak, to realize their need of a Saviour.

MORALITY IS NOT ENOUGH

But we all, with open face beholding as in a glass the glory of the Lord, are changed into the same image from glory to glory even as by the Spirit of the Lord. 2 Cor. 3:18.

The enemy of God knows that if a person seeks Jesus, the first by-product of that experience will be genuine faith. He knows that the second by-product of that experience will be righteousness—a natural, spontaneous righteousness that comes from Christ instead of from our own backbone. So one of his favorite gimmicks is to get us to focus on anything but the relationship with Jesus.

He has succeeded by getting people to focus on righteousness. He says, "Now, listen. In order to be a Christian you've got to do what's right. Now work at it." So a person begins trying all the gimmicks. He tries to develop more backbone. Have you ever tried that? I've tried it. Tried to force myself to do things I didn't want to do. I listed out my "seven sins," and I began working on sin No. 1. But before I got to sin No. 7, sin No. 1 was back again! And when I was working the hardest on it, someone from southern California sent me a pamphlet, "One Hundred Sins Laodicea Must Repent Of!"

Then someone came along and said, "No, that's not it. What you need to do is to control your thoughts, because as a man 'thinketh in his heart, so is he.'" So I began to try to control my thoughts. "Now, let's see. Today I'm not going to think about . . . Whoops! I just thought about it." Have you ever been over that road? It is possible to look at yourself in the mirror so long that you become more like yourself.

Someone said, "Suppose you hate Jones, and slap him every time you see him. Your part in overcoming is to try hard to keep from slapping Jones. If you will keep from slapping Jones, then God will do the rest, by taking the hate and temper out of your heart." But when I tried it, I discovered that I couldn't keep from slapping Jones.

We are not against morality. Morality is worthwhile. It will keep you out of jail. It will keep you from getting traffic tickets. It will keep you from lying in the gutter. But *morality is not Christianity, and it will not get you to heaven.* The only way for a person to have any kind of righteousness whatever is to have Jesus, through a relationship with Him.

EVERYBODY'S HELPLESS

I am the vine, ye are the branches: He that abideth in me, and I in him, the same bringeth forth much fruit: for without me ye can do nothing. John 15:5.

Once we have been convicted that we are sinners, whether or not we have ever done anything "wrong," the next step in coming to Christ is to admit that we are helpless to change our lives. We do not change our lives in order to come to Christ. We come to Christ, and *He* changes our lives. There are many who are saying, "Well, when I can fix up my life so that it is good enough, then I will come to Him." Stop wasting your time and energy. It is a hopeless task. We are helpless.

If you would like to have the whole message of salvation through faith in Christ alone, you can sum it up with two verses: John 15:5, which says, "Without me ye can do"—how much?—"nothing." Now, how much is nothing? Nothing is *nothing!* That's how much it is! The other text is Philippians 4:13, "I can do all things through Christ." How many things? *All.* It's just that simple. The smallest boy and girl can understand it. Without Him, I can do nothing. With Him, I can do everything. So the only possible thing I can do is get with Christ. That's all I can do to be saved.

If getting with Christ is still nebulous in your mind, I'd like to remind you that every intangible thing in the area of spiritual life is made tangible by the three tangibles for relationship. How do I get with Christ? Through Bible study—listening to God; prayer—talking with God; and sharing—working with God. Through these avenues the Holy Spirit will work on us and bring us to the right relationship.

"But," you say, "some people are helpless and some aren't." What about the strong person who's doing pretty good? Is he helpless? Yes, he is! The strong person can control the externals. The weak can't. But the problem is deeper than the externals. "Education, culture, the exercise of the will, human effort, all have their proper sphere, but *here* they are powerless."—*Steps to Christ*, p. 18. (Italics supplied.) "Our *hearts* are evil, and we cannot change them."—*Ibid.* (Italics supplied.) Both the strong and the weak are incapable of changing their inward life. Both must admit their helplessness and come to Christ just as they are.

WHEN YOU CAN'T HELP YOURSELF

Ye shall not need to fight in this battle: set yourselves, stand ye still, and see the salvation of the Lord with you. 2 Chron. 20:17.

A man came to a new country with his wife, his cattle, his herds, and his relatives. The people of the land came out to meet them, and they said to him, "What's your name, anyway?" And he said, "My name is Father of a Great Multitude." "Oh, is that right? How many children do you have?" "Well, er . . . ah . . . I don't have any." "You don't?" And they smiled. Then they said to his wife, "What's your name?" "My name is Mother of Nations." "Oh, must be a second marriage. How many children do you have?" "Er, it's a nice day in the land of Canaan, isn't it?" "How many children do you have?" "I don't have any children, either." "How old are you?" "Ninety."

This man and wife put their heads together, and they said, "God has promised something bigger than He can do. We'd better help Him. God helps those who help themselves!" So they worked out a clever plan. And in the Middle East today we still have the problem that resulted from their plan.

We see another man in the palace with its marble statues and ivory throne. His name is Moses. God comes to him and says, "Moses, you're the one to lead Israel out of Egypt." And Moses says, "You've got the right man. I've just graduated from military school. I'll start tomorrow morning." He did, and he got one Egyptian. Then he took off on a flight through the wilderness to the borders of Mount Sinai, and there at its base he herded sheep for 40 years. Then God came to him again, and He said, "Moses, now it's time for you to lead Israel out of Egypt." "Oh, no, not me! I'm a born sheepherder." God smiled and said, "Now you're ready." It didn't take Moses long, when he realized his helplessness, to lead the people out to a great victory. Yet the people had to learn the same lesson for themselves. God said, "You won't have to fight. The Lord will fight for you." And the first thing they did was to begin scrapping with their enemies. They too had to learn that God has the power to do what He's promised, and *He doesn't need our help to do what He has promised to do for us.* Admitting our helplessness to do it ourselves is the final step before coming to Him.

49

THE END THAT IS THE BEGINNING

For Christ is the end of the law for righteousness to every one that believeth. Rom. 10:4.

Today we are talking about surrender, the final step in the sequence of how we come to Christ. Notice Romans 9, the last few verses, and chapter 10, the first few verses. "What shall we say then? That the Gentiles, which followed not after righteousness, have attained to righteousness, even the righteousness which is of faith. But Israel, which followed after the law of righteousness, hath not attained to the law of righteousness. Wherefore?" Or why? "Because they sought it not by faith, but as it were by the works of the law." They were behaviorists. "For they stumbled at that stumblingstone; as it is written, Behold, I lay in Sion a stumblingstone and rock of offence: and whosoever believeth on him shall not be ashamed. . . . For I bear them record that they have a zeal of God, but not according to knowledge. For they being ignorant of God's righteousness, and going about to establish their own righteousness, have not submitted themselves unto the righteousness of God."

Remember this premise: An apple tree bears apples because it *is* an apple tree, never in order *to be* one. If you would like to have some apples, the best thing for you to do is get an apple tree. And an apple tree doesn't have to try hard to produce apples; it's natural for an apple tree to produce apples. Let's go over the scripture again and paraphrase it: "What shall we say then? That the Gentiles who were not trying to produce apples have produced apples, even the apples that come from the apple tree. But Israel, which was trying to produce apples, have not produced apples. Why? Because they didn't try to become apple trees but instead tried to produce apples by their own efforts. For they, being ignorant of God's way of producing fruit, and going about to produce their own apples, have not submitted themselves unto becoming apple trees. For Christ is the end of trying to produce apples apart from the apple tree to everyone who will become an apple tree." That's Venden's Revised Standard Version!

A Christian does right because he *is* a Christian, never in order *to be* a Christian. Giving up on our own ability to produce the fruits of righteousness is the beginning of the Christian life.

STRENGTH IN ADMITTING WEAKNESS

When I am weak, then am I strong. 2 Cor. 12:10.

The term *surrender* is grossly misunderstood by thousands of Christians. If a person's idea of Christianity is based upon behavior, then his primary focus will be on the Ten Commandments and trying hard to obey them. If he is strong, he will "succeed"; if he is weak, he will fail. The behaviorist philosophy never gets the person to the point of helplessness to take him on to surrender. The behaviorist who is strong and apparently succeeds doesn't realize he is helpless. The behaviorist who is weak says, "I can't do it; I give up," quits trying, and goes away from God at the very point, if he only knew it, at which he is the closest to God that he may ever be.

The behaviorist thinks that surrender is giving up certain *things* in his life—giving up his sins, giving up his problems and his weaknesses. So the behaviorist says, "I stand before God and this audience, and I promise that from now on I won't smoke, drink, or dance anymore." If he is strong, he never does them again, and he becomes a so-called "good" church member. If surrender has primarily to do with giving up *things*, the strong succeed and the weak fail.

I've heard a lot of different gimmicks for giving up sins, giving up things. I've even heard of people writing their sins on a piece of paper and passing them to the aisle, where they are all collected and brought down to the front of the church. There is a little altar there, and someone lights a match and burns the "sins" all up. Wonderful! The sins are gone now. The sins are all burned up. Psychological and mass-psychology gimmicks. The problem is that the weak person who wrote his sins down on a piece of paper in order to burn them up gets home and discovers he still has them. There are people who have tried every gimmick in the book until finally they say, "I guess some people were born to be fuel for the fires of hell, and I must be one of them." And they begin to believe in predestination.

I'd like to point out what surrender really is. Surrender is not giving up *things*. Surrender is giving up the idea that I can do anything at all about things, except one: to come to Christ just as I am. We must surrender *ourselves* to Him.

WHERE THE EFFORT COUNTS

Fight the good fight of faith, lay hold on eternal life, whereunto thou art also called, and hast professed a good profession before many witnesses. 1 Tim. 6:12.

There are two ways to fight God. One way is to say, "I don't believe in God. I have no use for Him, no time for Him." So I don't go to Him. There is a more subtle way that is just as effective. That is to go to God with the thought that God helps those who help themselves. I take my problems to Him, but I don't leave them with Him. Instead I get myself mixed up in the whole situation.

I can have trouble with my car, and I can keep the auto mechanic from fixing my car by not going to him. But there's a much more subtle way of fighting the mechanic. I can take my car to him, and after he gets it in the garage and lifts up the hood, I can put my head in from the other side and I can say, "Now just a minute. Don't touch the spark plugs. I just put those in two years ago. And don't touch the carburetor. The carburetor is very delicate and you might knock it out of kilter. And keep your hands away from the fan belt and the fuel pump. And whatever you do, don't touch the power steering." Finally, he throws down his tools and says, "Here, take your car and fix it yourself." I come to God and I say, "Now, God, I'd like to have You do this and this for me." But then I get myself all mixed up in the operation. I'm trying to do part of it and trying to let God do part of it, and in this confusion, the mixing of my own efforts with God's power, comes defeat.

The reason that so many people are frustrated in the Christian life is that they are working on the *results* instead of the *cause.* Even boys and girls know the answer to the question "If you had to choose between working on eating and working on growing, which would you choose?" It doesn't take them long to say, "Well, if you choose to work on eating, you'll do both, but if you choose to work on growing, you'll do neither." The cause of our Christian growth has to do with knowing Jesus as our personal Friend. The result comes in His living His life within us.

WHAT IS NEW IN THE NEW BIRTH?

Except a man be born again, he cannot see the kingdom of God. John 3:3.

A great many people who in the past have come to Christ think they must not have really come, because the surrender didn't last. That's one of the big dilemmas in the Christian world today. There are hundreds of people who have sincerely come to Jesus with a great sense of need and have later become disenchanted when the "conversion" seemed to fade away. It is possible to have genuinely accepted Christ and given up on self during a Week of Prayer last year or on the sawdust trail 40 years ago, but to have the commitment die from doing nothing about it ever since. In order to grow in the Christian life we must learn how to renew our conversion every day.

Conversion is more than saying Yes to God one time. When someone wakes up the week after the week before and discovers that he still has some of the same problems, weaknesses, and fears, he is tempted to think it must not have really "happened" after all. And he waits for the next revival or camp meeting or altar call to run it by again. He does not realize that often the devil works harder when he sees someone come to Christ than he ever did before. Things may go worse for a period of time after conversion than they did before. There may be more trials, more temptations, and more defeats than before the decision was made. Have you seen it happen? The devil tries everything he knows to get us to give up and forget about God.

If conversion is not immediate victory, peace, and freedom from temptation and trial, what is it? Here is a definition of conversion, based on two chapters in *The Desire of Ages*, "Nicodemus" and "At Jacob's Well": Conversion is a supernatural work of the Holy Spirit upon the human heart, producing a change of attitude toward God and creating a new capacity for knowing God that we didn't even have before.

Conversion is God's work, never ours. When we are born again, instead of being against God, we're now on His side. And we then have a relish for spiritual things that were foolishness to us while we were at enmity with God. It is not the end, any more than physical birth is the end of physical life. It is only the equipment to get started. It is only the beginning.

53

ZACCHAEUS COMES TO JESUS

Zacchaeus, make haste, and come down; for to day I must abide at thy house. Luke 19:5.

Jericho is a familiar name to many Christians, who have memories of stories connected with that place way back to childhood. There was the battle of Jericho, and the curse upon the city at the time of Joshua, in the Old Testament, which resulted in the old city of Jericho never being rebuilt. Then there is the newer city, which is still there today. It was the city toward which the good Samaritan was headed, as was the man he helped. It was the city outside of which blind Bartimaeus sat begging. And it was the city of Zacchaeus, who was a wee little man, "A wee little man was he!"

The story of Zacchaeus is an intriguing one. It has all the drama of real life. It has a comical side and it has deeply spiritual implications as an account of a true seeker after God.

Zacchaeus was the chief among the publicans, and he was rich. If you analyze the regard that we have for the income-tax people today, perhaps you can understand somewhat how the people of Jericho felt about Zacchaeus. He was not only a publican, he was the chief of publicans. The publicans had become experts in fraud. The riches they amassed were gotten at the expense of other people. Zacchaeus was a thief. You can see him lying awake at night, lonely, staring at his tapestries that should have been in someone else's house, and wondering whether his emptiness would ever end. Then Zacchaeus somehow heard of Jesus, who accepted everyone who came to Him, who befriended publicans and sinners. A hope began to grow in his heart that perhaps he too could find peace. Then Jesus came to his town.

It sort of strikes your funny bone to see Zacchaeus, the director of the internal revenue service, running to climb up into a tree with the street urchins. But he did. This demonstrates one big thing. When there's a life-and-death matter at stake, you forget your inhibitions, your false dignity, and everything else. It proves that Zacchaeus was really at the end of his own resources, recognizing his need of the help that only Jesus could give. When we realize our need of Christ, nothing else will seem important enough to prevent us from coming to Him.

ZACCHAEUS COMES OUT OF HIS TREE

I dwell in the high and holy place, with him also that is of a contrite and humble spirit. Isa. 57:15.

When Jesus came to Jericho, Zacchaeus had reached the point of giving up on a life centered on himself. He was tired of his life of fraud and cunning, tired of running away from the Holy Spirit, and ready to accept the rest that Jesus had to offer. When he heard that Jesus was to pass that way, he ran ahead of the crowd and climbed into the branches of a sycamore tree in order to see Jesus.

When Jesus came to the place, He looked up and saw him— Zacchaeus, the one who thought he was going to be hidden from view. Jesus saw him and said unto him, "Zacchaeus." He knew his name. We understand He'd never met him. But He knew his name.

Jesus never passes anyone by. He is no respecter of persons. He has an equal regard for everyone. No one should feel that he has been left out or passed by. Jesus has passed your way. He passes everybody's way.

And Jesus said, "Make haste, and come down; for to day I must abide at thy house" (Luke 19:5). Zacchaeus was up a tree in more ways than one. He was out on the limbs of the tree not only physically but spiritually. We often try to compensate for our smallness of stature spiritually by making up for it with some external maneuver.

It is a law of the spiritual life that you have to come down in order to go up. Zacchaeus received Jesus joyfully. And, of course, whenever that happens, there are always some in the crowd who begin to complain and gripe. When they saw it, they all murmured that Jesus was gone to be a guest with a man that was a sinner. Why did Jesus have to choose to go and eat lunch with this wretch? Why didn't He choose someone in high esteem in the town of Jericho? But there's the gospel again, in one phrase: Jesus went to be the guest of someone who was a sinner. Jesus receives sinners. If it weren't for the fact that He does, there'd be no hope for you or me. Aren't you glad He is willing to be a guest with people who are sinners? That's good news. The good news of the gospel of Christ.

NOW IS SALVATION COME

And Jesus said unto him, This day is salvation come to this house, forsomuch as he also is a son of Abraham. Luke 19:9.

Zacchaeus stood and said unto the Lord; Behold, Lord, the half of my goods I give to the poor; and if I have taken any thing from any man by false accusation, I restore him fourfold" (Luke 19:8). What was Zacchaeus doing here? Well, some people will say he had been saved by giving to the poor or by restoring 400 percent. But Jesus' reply to his apparent beating of his own moral drums is very interesting. "And Jesus said unto him, *This day* is salvation come to this house." Don't miss that! *Today* this man receives salvation. Can't he receive salvation when he begins to mend his ways and to cover his tracks and to restore? No, there's no salvation in giving to the poor; even if you give 50 percent of your income, that is not what saves you. There is no salvation in restitution. If I have taken from any man by false accusation, to restore him 400 percent sounds like a pretty good restitution, doesn't it? But there is no salvation in that.

"It is true that men sometimes become ashamed of their sinful ways, and give up some of their evil habits, before they are conscious that they are being drawn to Christ."—*Steps to Christ*, p. 27. What's really happening? They are being drawn to Christ. "But whenever they make an effort to reform, from a sincere desire to do right, it is the power of Christ that is drawing them."—*Ibid.* So let's allow that it was the power of Christ that had drawn Zacchaeus to give 400 percent and 50 percent. But that wasn't salvation. "An influence of which they are unconscious works upon the soul, and the conscience is quickened, and the outward life is amended. And as Christ draws them to look upon His cross, to behold Him whom their sins have pierced, the commandment comes home to the conscience. The wickedness of their life, the deep-seated sin of the soul, is revealed to them."—*Ibid.* Not just the acts, but their real condition. "They begin to comprehend something of the righteousness of Christ, and exclaim, 'What is sin, that it should require such a sacrifice . . . ? Was all this love, all this suffering, all this humiliation, demanded, that we might not perish?' "—*Ibid.* "It is when Christ is received as a personal Saviour that salvation comes to the soul."—*The Desire of Ages*, p. 556.

JACOB COMES TO JESUS

This is none other but the house of God, and this is the gate of heaven. Gen. 28:17.

Jacob was a religious man. His family were church members. At the time he lived at home, his spiritual experience was not all bad. He was interested in the birthright for more than material reasons. He wanted to be able to commune with God as Abraham did. We'll have to give him good marks for that. "But while he thus esteemed eternal above temporal blessings, Jacob had not an experimental knowledge of the God whom he revered. His heart had not been renewed by divine grace."—*Patriarchs and Prophets,* p. 178.

Jacob had some misunderstandings of how God worked. He had been promised the birthright, but God has this persistent habit of waiting until the last possible minute. (I used to get mad at Him for that. But don't forget that God is the safest one in the universe to get mad at. If you're mad at Him, you might as well tell Him so, because He knows it anyway. But He never gets mad in return.) So God waited until the last minute, and Jacob decided that He was asleep at the switch and that he needed to do something to help God fulfill His promises. He and Rebekah got their heads together and came up with a master plan.

You know the rest of the story. Jacob got the birthright by fraud. The result was that Jacob never did see his mother again. You see him taking off through the desert sands, alone and guilty and in trouble. The whole thing had backfired. "God had declared that Jacob should receive the birthright, and His word would have been fulfilled in His own time had they waited in faith for Him to work for them."—*Ibid.,* p. 180. But they decided to do something themselves. So you see Jacob fleeing in despair. Night comes on, and he lies down after finding a rock for a pillow, and he hardly dares to pray.

He thought that all was hopeless, but he had a dream. In his dream he saw a ladder reaching from earth to heaven. Angels were ascending and descending the ladder. The ladder represented Jesus. Jesus was the connection between heaven and earth. Jesus was still there. Jesus still loved him. Jesus had come to him in his time of need, as Jesus always does when one is ready to accept the grace He has to offer. That night Jacob was converted.

MAKING DEALS WITH GOD

Surely the Lord is in this place; and I knew it not. Gen. 28:16.

When Jacob slept with the rock for a pillow and saw the ladder reaching to heaven, the plan of salvation was presented to him; not fully, but in such parts as were essential to him at that time. Although his mind at once grasped a part of the revelation, its great and mysterious truths were the study of his lifetime and were unfolded to his understanding more and more.

Let's look at the story in Genesis 28:13, 14. God is telling Jacob that the promises made to Abraham were just as good for him. Verse 15 says, "Behold, I am with thee, and will keep thee in all places . . . , and will bring thee again into this land; for I will not leave thee, until I have done that which I have spoken to thee of." Doesn't that sound like good news? And Jacob awakened and said, "Surely the Lord is in this place; and I knew it not." He was afraid. He set up a stone marker and called the place Bethel.

Verse 20 records how he slipped into something that was characteristic of his philosophy of religion at that time. "And Jacob vowed a vow." Look carefully at his vow. "If God will be with me, if He will keep me in the way I'm going and will give me food and clothing, if God will bring me back to my father's house in peace; *then* shall the Lord be my God." He's trying to make a deal with God. "You scratch my back, and I'll scratch Yours." Is the plan of salvation based on that? It's obvious that there was some misunderstanding on Jacob's part of how God works. He makes a vow. Salvation is not based on our making vows to God; it is our accepting the vows that God has already made to us. Genuine faith continues to love and trust God regardless of what happens to us. God has promised only strength for the day, not skies always blue. If Jacob had gone hungry, genuine faith would have said, "I still love You and trust You regardless."

Jacob continued making deals with God all the way to the brook Jabbok. Finally, he was found alone. It was there that he gave up on doing it himself and surrendered totally to the control of God.

WINNING BY LOSING

And he said, Let me go, for the day breaketh. And he said, I will not let thee go, except thou bless me. Gen. 32:26.

It is interesting to learn that salvation by faith is taught just as strongly in the Old Testament as in the New. This is not just a New Testament teaching. We have noticed that one of the stories that teaches some of the deepest lessons is the story of Jacob found in Genesis 32. In the previous chapter we find that Jacob has stolen away from his uncle, in the dark of night, taking his two wives and his flocks and herds, and is headed for home.

The closer he gets to home, the more nervous he gets. He hears that there are 400 soldiers coming. The enemy is coming. Esau is on the warpath. And Jacob gets scared. So he comes up with some clever strategy. He divides his company into two groups, thinking that if one group gets attacked, the other group can escape. He does everything he can think of to secure his own safety, to do his own thing. He thinks that God helps those who help themselves. Finally, in desperation, he goes by himself in the darkness of night by the brook Jabbok to pray. Genesis 32:24-28: "Jacob was left alone; and there wrestled a man with him until the breaking of the day. And when he saw that he prevailed not against him, he touched the hollow of his thigh; and the hollow of Jacob's thigh was out of joint as he wrestled with him. And he said, Let me go, for the day breaketh. And he said, I will not let thee go, except thou bless me. And he said unto him, What is thy name? And he said, Jacob. And he said, Thy name shall be called no more Jacob, but Israel: for as a prince hast thou power with God and with men, and hast prevailed."

From this story we learn two major things. First, conversion and absolute or constant surrender do not necessarily come at the same time in one's experience. In fact, they seldom do. The second point is that the end of self-effort requires a struggle that none of us are going to get by without recognizing we've been through it. Jacob came forth from this experience crippled. And we understand that he was crippled the rest of his life. We will know when such an experience happens. You may not know when you were converted. But you are going to know when you go through the kind of crisis that Jacob did at Jabbok.

TOUCHED BY GOD

I have seen God face to face, and my life is preserved. Gen 32:30.

After Jacob's final effort to secure his own safety, he had gone alone to the brook Jabbok. He had done everything he could do to save himself. It hadn't worked. He probably didn't think praying would work, either, if all his strategy and planning hadn't, but he wasn't going to take any chances. Then God came near to answer Jacob's prayer. He placed a hand on his shoulder. The night was dark, and Jacob was afraid. When he felt the touch of God, he thought it was the hand of an enemy. And so he fought Him. It took him all night, until the dawning of the day, to discover that God had come near to impart rich blessing.

This was a parable of his entire lifetime. For 20 years, whenever God placed His hand on his shoulder, he fought Him. He thought it was an enemy. God wanted to be in charge of his life, and Jacob wouldn't let Him. He wanted to be in charge of himself. That's the crisis of surrender. And it took pain for the day to dawn. But when the day finally dawned, then Jacob, instead of fighting God, clung to Him.

Our greatest strength is realized when we feel and acknowledge our weakness. Christ connects fallen men and women, in their weakness and helplessness, with the source of infinite power. What was it that dawned on Jacob's mind that night? He had been doing that which God did not expect or ask him to do. For 20 years Jacob had been trying to live up to the promises he had made to God at Bethel. Then he discovered that what he needed was to accept the promises God had made to him. He discovered that the effort God requires is not the fight to change one's life, not the fight to do what God has promised to do for us, but only the fight to maintain connection with Heaven, with God. There is something for us to do to secure salvation. We must come to Jesus. "Him that cometh to me," says Jesus, "I will in no wise cast out" (John 6:37).

It was by self-surrender and faith that Jacob gained the victory he had failed to gain in his own strength. It will be by surrender of self and by trust in God that we can gain the victory in our lives. When God places His hand on our shoulder, wouldn't it be wonderful to recognize Him as a friend rather than as an enemy?

WHEN THE LIGHT DAWNS

And Jacob was left alone; and there wrestled a man with him until the breaking of the day. Gen. 32:24.

There are several things that were characteristic of Jacob before his experience at Jabbok. First, the sin of his deception of his father was ever before him. It had been 20 years, but for 20 years he had been struggling with guilt over the fraud. Something else had continued in his mind. He was aware that the angels were protecting him, but Jacob still thought that he had to do something to secure his own safety. He didn't believe that God could fulfill His promises made at Bethel without his help.

Have you ever considered what *one* angel can do? What about the camp of the Assyrians, 185,000 strong? You know that story: "And when they arose early in the morning, behold, they were all dead corpses" (2 Kings 19:35). It was the work of one angel walking through the camp. Jacob knew that there were two companies of angels, one before and one behind. He even named the place after the two companies, but he must not have known much about the strength of angels or the power of God to fulfill His promises. He still thought he had to do something. This is characteristic of the unsurrendered stance, thinking I have to do something myself.

"This . . . will prove the ruin of many souls in our day. Thousands are making the same mistake as did the Pharisees whom Christ reproved at Matthew's feast. Rather than give up some cherished idea, or discard some idol of opinion, many refuse the truth which comes down from the Father of light. They trust in self, and depend upon their own wisdom, and do not realize their spiritual poverty. They insist on being saved in some way by which they may perform some important work. When they see that there is no way of weaving self into the work, they reject the salvation provided."—*The Desire of Ages*, p. 280.

We are told that Jacob came from that night of wrestling by the Jabbok a different man. This was 20 years after his conversion. Self-confidence was finally uprooted at Jabbok. Absolute dependence upon God was discovered by Jacob that night. From that point forward, the early cunning was no longer seen. His life was marked by simplicity and truth. He had learned the lesson of simple reliance upon heavenly power.

THE CRISIS OF SURRENDER

And whosoever shall fall on this stone shall be broken: but on whomsoever it shall fall, it will grind him to powder. Matt. 21:44.

Day by day God instructs His children. By the circumstances of the daily life His is preparing them to act their part upon that wider stage to which His providence has appointed them. It is the issue of the daily test that determines their victory or defeat in life's great crisis."—*The Desire of Ages,* p. 382. So there may be a series of little events, all based upon one issue: Am I going to do it myself, or am I going to trust God to do it? If I fail and continue to fail day by day, I can plan on a big wrestling with the angel some night by the brook Jabbok.

It happened to Jacob. It happened to Joseph. He must have failed a number of little crises, such as thinking he was pretty big in comparison to his other brothers. But you see him bound as a slave, on his way to Egypt, crying his eyes out. Peter found himself clutching the ground and grinding his face in the dirt in Gethsemane, wishing he could die because he had failed the crisis on the lake, failed again in the discussion about the Temple taxes. Not until after he realized his weakness, by the fire, as he saw the pain he had brought to the One he loved the most, did he experience absolute dependence upon Christ.

If conversion got by you imperceptibly, and you're one of those people who could never point to a time or date, or even year; if you've just been a good church member all your life, remember that absolute surrender is not going to come easily. "The warfare against self is the greatest battle that was ever fought. The yielding of self, surrendering all to the will of God, requires a struggle."—*Steps to Christ,* p. 43. The crisis of surrender, the being broken, the falling on the Rock, is a big crisis in the life of the Christian.

We are not indicating that you have to be totally transformed to be *accepted* by God. Jacob was accepted by God at Bethel. We are talking about the transforming work of the Holy Spirit.

Whatever form that great crisis takes in your life, just remember that when the hand of God is placed on your shoulder it's not the hand of an enemy. It's the hand of the best Friend you will ever have.

NOT MY WORK, BUT HIS

Now to him that worketh is the reward not reckoned of grace, but of debt. Rom. 4:4.

When a person first begins to understand that God offers a life of freedom, peace, and fulfillment through righteousness by faith in Jesus, the devil gets nervous. He has worked for as long as possible to keep everyone away from any interest in God whatever. He doesn't want anybody to come to Jesus and find rest. The further away we stay, the better he likes it. But if he fails to keep us from being drawn, to keep us from searching into the things of God, he still has other tactics.

The first of these is to try to get us to work on righteousness. It is possible to spend years of futile effort working hard on the externals, trying to make yourself good enough to be accepted by God.

Finally, the realization comes that righteousness is by faith in Jesus alone. We learn that external goodness is insufficient. We see that our hearts are evil and we cannot change them, even if we are successful in improving our behavior. At this point the devil comes in with another clever sidetrack. He tries to get us to work on our faith. He brings in all his arguments in favor of positive thinking and urges us to concentrate on making ourselves believe. He tries to get us more interested in claiming promises than in the One who made the promises. When we pray primarily for answers, and we don't get the answers we expect, he can then destroy our faith in God while professing to be exercising it.

When we realize that we cannot develop either righteousness *or* faith by our own efforts, the devil makes his final attempt to keep us from coming to Christ. *"Now* you've got it right," he says. "What you need to do is give up. You must try hard to give up."

It has been good news for many of us who have tried time and time again to make ourselves surrender, that surrender is a gift also, as surely as righteousness and faith are gifts. "No man can empty himself of self. We can only consent for Christ to accomplish the work."—*Christ's Object Lessons*, p. 159.

Every gift that God has to give us, righteousness, peace, faith, victory, eternal life, and even surrender, is available in only one way—by coming into relationship with the Giver, through a personal communication with Him.

YOU CAN'T CRUCIFY YOURSELF

He that findeth his life shall lose it: and he that loseth his life for my sake shall find it. Matt. 10:39.

Whenever Jesus spoke of the cross, He always referred to it as *our* cross, never as His. "He that taketh not his cross, and followeth after me, is not worthy of me" (Matt. 10:38). "If any man will come after me, let him deny himself, and take up his cross daily, and follow me" (Luke 9:23). It was on our cross, in our place, that Jesus suffered and died.

If you were to decide to take your own life, there would be many routes available. You could put a pistol to your head and pull the trigger. You could take an overdose of any number of drugs. You could jump off a high bridge or building. But there is one thing you can never do. You cannot crucify yourself! If you are going to be crucified, someone else must do it for you.

"The yoke and the cross are symbols representing the same thing—the giving up of the will to God."—*The SDA Bible Commentary,* Ellen G. White Comments, on Matt. 11:28-30, p. 1090. The very symbol used by Christ to represent complete surrender demands that this be accomplished by someone other than ourselves. No matter how hard we might try to crucify ourselves, we simply cannot do it. No matter how hard we might try to surrender ourselves, we can't do that, either. We can only consent for Someone else to do the work for us.

If we cannot crucify ourselves, if we cannot surrender ourselves, then it is inevitable that we cannot set up the timing, either. Every event in Christ's life moved according to God's timetable. Christ did nothing to hasten or delay the crisis, nor did He attempt to escape when the crisis came. He accepted God's plans for His life on a daily basis, and did not try to work out His own plans.

So it must be with us. Jesus Himself allowed room for growth. "First the blade, then the ear, after that the full corn in the ear" (Mark 4:28). Our effort toward hastening either growth or surrender is fruitless. We can only seek to know Jesus, seek personal fellowship with Him, and trust Him to finish the work He has begun in our lives. He will lead us on to complete surrender to Him.

VICTORY FROM SURRENDER

O my Father, if it be possible, let this cup pass from me: nevertheless not as I will, but as thou wilt. Matt. 26:39.

Surrender always requires a struggle. The basis of every temptation is to go it alone in some way, and depend on self instead of on God. Jesus was constantly tempted to go it alone. As His inherent abilities were greater than ours, so much greater was His temptation to rely on self instead of on His Father. In Gethsemane He faced the final struggle of surrender. If Satan failed here, his kingdom was forever lost.

Notice the basis of the final temptation. "He [Jesus] *seemed* to be shut out from the light of God's sustaining presence."—*The Desire of Ages,* p. 685. (Italics supplied.) Christ had spent His entire life on earth in fellowship with His Father. Never once had He broken from that abiding dependence upon God. He had done nothing on His own, only through His Father's will. But now, "so dreadful does sin appear to Him, so great is the weight of guilt which He must bear, that He is tempted to fear it will shut Him out forever from His Father's love."—*Ibid.*

Do you see the temptation? Satan made it appear that the only way Christ could save humanity was to break from His relationship with His Father. He had tried for 33 years to get Christ to rely on His own power. Now it *seemed* that the only way Christ could save us would be by going on His own, for if He took our sin it would separate Him from God. Satan said, "If You don't rely on Your own power now, You won't be able to save humans as You came to do. Sin is too offensive to God. He can't help You now. You've got to do it Yourself, Jesus, or fail in Your mission to save humanity."

But notice that the separation was only in *feelings*—in reality Jesus was *not* alone. "God suffered with His Son. Angels beheld the Saviour's agony."—*Ibid.,* p. 693. God separated from Jesus every beam of light, love, and glory. *But He was still there!* And it was in surrender to the will of His Father that Jesus was conqueror. In Gethsemane, and upon the cross, Jesus relied upon the evidence of His Father's love already given. "As in submission He committed Himself to God, the *sense* of the loss of His Father's favor was withdrawn. By faith, Christ was victor."—*Ibid.,* p. 756. (Italics supplied.) Surrender is the only way to victory.

THE NAME ABOVE EVERY NAME

That at the name of Jesus every knee should bow . . . and that every tongue should confess that Jesus Christ is Lord, to the glory of God the Father. Phil. 2:10, 11.

All power in heaven and earth centers in the person of Jesus. Everything we need in this world and in the world to come is found in Him. Without Him no one can hope to succeed. With Him failure is impossible.

What, other than the name of Jesus, can cause people to live in peace? He was born in a stable and cradled in a manger. Yet around that manger and that precious Babe the whole world gathers and stops and listens to the angels' song of peace on earth and good will to men, and all the world becomes tender and is drawn closer together.

Out of the dimly lighted stable of Bethlehem comes a Light that makes the hearts of people glow with a warmth that inspires them to the loftiest acts of which they are capable. The poor and the hungry are fed and the homeless are given shelter and the naked are clothed. Even the hard-fisted people wake up and become unselfish, sending good cheer into the desolate homes of the unfortunate. It happens as once more *we* gather around that stable and sing songs of peace on earth and good will toward men.

What, other than the name of Jesus, can cause people to die in peace? Millions of people have passed into the valley of the shadow with the name of Jesus on their parched lips. And for them the valley has been transformed with light and glory and the shadows have fled away as the Sun of righteousness has lighted up their last moments with the resplendent colors of the setting sun.

Jesus! How wonderful and precious is the name! He is the Prince of Peace, the mighty God, and the coming King. When we think of Him who was born in a stable and died upon a cross; who divides the centuries in two, and about whom all history revolves; who lifted empires off their hinges, turning the stream of time out of its course; and who at the same time binds up the brokenhearted and speaks peace to the troubled heart, may we not exclaim:

> All hail the power of Jesus' name!
> Let angels prostrate fall;
> Bring forth the royal diadem,
> And crown Him Lord of all!

NOT PEACE BUT A SWORD

Think not that I am come to send peace on earth: I came not to send peace, but a sword. Matt. 10:34.

The Baby and His parents were obviously poor. Dedications were common happenings in the Temple, and the priest who performed the service was unaware of anything unusual. But there were two aged people in the Temple that day, Simeon and Anna, who had looked longingly for the Messiah to come, and they had not looked in vain. Simeon took the Baby from Mary, and as he held Him he blessed the family and said to Mary, "Behold, this child is set for the fall and rising again of many in Israel; and for a sign which shall be spoken against" (Luke 2:34).

The prediction of Simeon was fulfilled in the life of Jesus. The gospel that Jesus presented never left people the same. They became either patriots or traitors to His cause. This polarization was steady, and increased in severity every day of His life, until the final showdown at Calvary. Although the idea that Jesus saves is beautiful, and we love to sing about it, Jesus also divides. He comes not to bring peace, but a sword. Jesus shakes people up.

We also notice here in this scripture that Jesus was set for the fall and rising again of many in *Israel*. We are not talking here about the Greeks and the Romans. Jesus came, and was set, for the polarizing, the decision making, of people already in church pews. As a result of Jesus' coming, people within the church polarized, went one way or the other. We notice again and again throughout the Gospels that there are only two ways to go. As the old song says, "Two ways for travelers, only two ways." There is no third option. We can never be in charge of ourselves. We can choose only who will control us. Either we accept His grace, we believe in Him, or we perish.

The lifting up of Jesus and Him crucified, the focusing on His life, will bring the same results today as when He was here on earth. The elements of human nature that were present at the time of Christ are still present today. As we come to a true knowledge of Jesus, we will also be compelled to choose to submit to His control or to refuse it. We cannot remain neutral.

JESUS, THE GREAT DIVIDER | **MAR 2**

Every valley shall be exalted, and every mountain and hill shall be made low. Isa. 40:4.

One of the first groups that fell at the coming of Jesus (who was "set for the fall and rising again of many in Israel") were the holders of tradition. Jesus said of those who came to Him accusing His disciples of transgressing the traditions of the elders, "In vain they do worship me, teaching for doctrines the commandments of men" (Matt. 15:9). The Christian church has often had problems with tradition. In all ages there have been customs kept alive, as doctrine, that have no Bible base. We often speak of the antichrist in this connection, but let's face it, tradition can be a problem for every church.

A second group of people who fell, and fell hard, under Jesus' polarizing presence was a group we might call the externalists. They were preoccupied with how they washed, the borders of their garments, long prayers, tithes on infinitesimal things, and the flies in the soup or the gnats in their water. Jesus faced them squarely in Matthew 23 when He told them that while they were apparently clean on the outside, inside they were filthy.

A third group who fell in the presence of Jesus were the self-righteous. How could they have missed the parable of the Pharisee and the publican as recorded in Luke 18? As we look back on it, it seems that it would have been inevitable that the self-righteous would have seen themselves pictured and admitted their need. But they held out against Him, and they fell.

A fourth group were the wise. The people who tried to trick Jesus. Again and again the doctors were put to confusion by simple questions that Jesus asked them, questions that even children should have been able to answer. They realized the truth that "he taketh the wise in their own craftiness" (1 Cor. 3:19). Liberals also fell in His presence. Jesus divided the broad church as well as the high church. The high church depended on its ritual, the broad church on its easygoing theology. And from all groups, those who relied on their leaders for their answers fell in the presence of Jesus, the Great Divider. Jesus' being set for the fall of many in Israel was a reality in His lifetime. The hills and mountains were laid low.

DOWN IS THE WAY UP

The Lord upholdeth all that fall, and raiseth up all those that be bowed down. Ps. 145:14.

When Jesus was here, His presence was the cause of polarization among all who met Him. He was "set for the fall and rising again of many in Israel." The worshipers of tradition, the self-righteous, the liberals, and those who depended on other people to determine truth for them fell hard when Jesus came. But there is a positive side to the picture also, which brings hope and courage to troubled hearts. The other part to Simeon's prophecy included the *"rising again* of many in Israel."

The story is told of someone who had fallen over the edge of a cliff, above the ocean. He hung on desperately and cried out for help. A voice above him said, "I will help you, but the first thing you must do to receive my help is to let go." Ouch! It is a surprise to some people to discover that at the point they let go, instead of crashing into the waters below they are surrounded by the gospel net. "They must fall who would rise again. We must fall upon the Rock and be broken before we can be uplifted in Christ. Self must be dethroned, pride must be humbled, if we would know the glory of the spiritual kingdom. The Jews would not accept the honor that is reached through humiliation. Therefore they would not receive their Redeemer. He was a sign that was spoken against."—*The Desire of Ages*, p. 57.

This is one of the reasons why people turn Jesus down. They do not want to enter into His kingdom through humiliation. He hath filled the hungry with good things and the rich He hath sent away empty. The problem of sin, our inability to meet the requirements of God's law, is what shows us our need and drives us to the Rock to be broken. For the backslider who wants to come back, for the teenager who is bound with guilt and sin, for the hopeless who thinks there's not a chance in the world, for *you,* comes this message: You *have* to be down before you can go up. The most dangerous position is not that of the one who is down, and knows it, but that of the one who feels that he is up and doesn't need to go down, the one who is living his spotless life independent of Jesus Christ. "They must fall who would rise again."

HARD TO BE LOST

Enter ye in at the strait gate: for wide is the gate, and broad is the way, that leadeth to destruction, and many there be which go in thereat. Matt. 7:13.

For a long time there have been people who have had the idea that the road to perdition is downhill all the way, paved with ice, and all you do is slip and slide your way right in.

One day I was visiting a lady in my local church. She was an older lady, approaching 80 years of age, tall, sophisticated, well educated. After we had visited for a while, engaging in typical small talk, I asked her whether there was anything I as her pastor could do to be of help or encouragement to her. She said, "Yes, if you could just get me out of this church and out of this religion, and away from this Bible and this God and this faith." And I said, "I beg your pardon?" She said, "I have been trapped. I grew up in a missionary's family, overseas. I had this whole business and routine of religion ingrained in me. I go to prayer meeting every Wednesday night. I can't help it. I don't want to. I go to church every week. I wish I didn't. I've tried to get away from the church and from God. I've tried to forget the whole business, but I can't." And she pleaded with me to help her escape! I assured her that this was not my responsibility as I saw it. She was an exaggerated case of one who has discovered that it's not easy to get away from God and salvation.

On the downhill road there are huge barriers and mountains and hurdles to cross that God Himself has been responsible for. God is determined that everyone possible will be saved. He will not violate our power of choice, but He has set up mighty agencies to make it as difficult as possible for anyone to be lost.

It is true that the way to life is described as a narrow way. "Yet do not therefore conclude that the upward path is the hard and the downward road the easy way. All along the road that leads to death there are pains and penalties, there are sorrows and disappointments, there are warnings not to go on. God's love has made it hard for the heedless and headstrong to destroy themselves."—*Thoughts From the Mount of Blessing*, p. 139. "The Lord is . . . not willing that any should perish, but that all should come to repentance" (2 Peter 3:9).

SALVATION FOR ALL

For the grace of God that bringeth salvation hath appeared to all men. Titus 2:11.

I'd like to take the position today that God is interested in the salvation of every person that He has created. "The grace of God that bringeth salvation hath appeared to all men." "The Spirit of God is freely bestowed to enable every man to lay hold upon the means of salvation. Thus Christ, 'the true Light,' 'lighteth every man that cometh into the world.' John 1:9. Men fail of salvation through their own willful refusal of the gift of life."—*The Great Controversy*, p. 262. Angels of heaven are passing through the length and breadth of the earth, seeking to comfort the sorrowing, to protect the imperiled, to win the hearts of men to Christ. Not one is neglected or passed by. God is no respecter of persons, and He has an equal care for all the souls He has created.

Away with the idea that because some church member in the Christian community let his canaries sing too loud, and I lost my sleep and got discouraged and bitter, that I am going to be lost. Away with the idea that a person can be lost because some church members let the Bermuda grass grow into his lawn. Away with the idea that someone who is sitting across the aisle from me didn't smile sweetly, and so I lost my experience. God's plan of salvation is far deeper and broader than the inadequacies of the Bermuda grass or the canaries or the person across the aisle. There are bigger issues involved.

God is determined that since He, not your parents, is responsible for having brought you into this world, that since He is a God of love and fairness and justice, He is not going to leave any stone unturned in your behalf.

At the time of Christ, the Jewish leaders opposed and rejected Jesus throughout His ministry. Constantly they sought for some way to trap Him, for some method of counteracting His influence with the people, for some way to stop His miracles and silence His teaching. "Still the convicting Spirit of God followed them, and they had to build up many barriers in order to withstand its power."—*The Desire of Ages*, p. 322. God does not change, and He is still determined to win each one of us today.

71

THE MOUNTAIN OF GOD'S WORD

The grass withereth, the flower fadeth: but the word of our God shall stand forever.
Isa. 40:8.

What are some of the mountains that God makes use of to fulfill His purpose, not willing that any should perish? One of the first is perhaps unique to civilized people, to those who have had a chance to know something of the things of God. It is the Bible.

Well, you say, what kind of deterrent is that? There are millions of people who buy Bibles, but they don't read them. It's still one of the best sellers, but not the best read! Yet the very fact of the existence of the Bible, when there have been thousands of skeptics and infidels who've tried to do away with it, says something, doesn't it? If these people who someday are going to want to see the Bible out of print and out of sight are going to fulfill their mission, they are going to have a monumental task. There are Bibles of all colors, shapes, sizes, and versions. How are they going to get rid of them all?

People go into a motel, somewhere, for a lost weekend. I daresay they've first got to get the Bible off the dresser top and into a drawer.

My brother and I went to hold some meetings one time in a town. The hall we wanted to rent was half of a double auditorium. We found that the left half was available on the nights we wanted for our public meetings, where we'd talk about the things of the gospel. However, the right half had dances going three nights a week. We pondered that a bit, and thought perhaps it would be a handicap. But on second thought we figured we might even get some deacons to pass out handbills to people as they went in to the dance. So we said we'd take it. But the manager said, "No, you can't have it." We wanted to know why not. He replied, "If people come to have a good time at the dance, and they see people going into the other hall at the same time with Bibles under their arms, it'll ruin the dance." So we didn't get the auditorium.

The very existence of the Bible is a barrier that God has erected to make it hard for us to be lost. That's good news. First Peter 1:23 says that the Word of God liveth and abideth for how long? Forever.

A MOUNTAIN OF GOSPEL SERMONS

For after that in the wisdom of God the world by wisdom knew not God, it pleased God by the foolishness of preaching to save them that believe. 1 Cor. 1:21.

The Bible, God's Word, is a barrier or mountain that would have to be crossed by one who would choose to be lost. A second great mountain that a person would have to get over would be the mountain of gospel sermons that he has heard. Paul said it, that it pleased God in His wisdom, by the foolishness of preaching, to save some. Yes, it seems foolish in a way. But God has seen some purpose in it for centuries.

I can remember gospel sermons that I heard when I was a boy that have stayed with me ever since. If I should happen to be so unfortunate as to decide that I wanted to be lost, I'd have to try to forget them. That's a big assignment. I remember a sermon one time at camp meeting—Jesus, my Saviour, my Lord, and my Friend. It was based on the scriptures that told of Him in those categories. I can still remember the main points of the sermon. How my heart was moved and touched. I must have been listening with a great need just then. Jesus, my Saviour, my Lord, my Friend.

I remember a sermon one time about blind Bartimaeus. The key phrase that ran through the sermon was, Jesus of Nazareth is passing by. Blind Bartimaeus didn't know it at first. He said, "What's the commotion?" They said, "Jesus of Nazareth is passing by." That is the last thing in the world Bartimaeus wanted to happen. He'd heard about Jesus. "Don't let Him pass by. Jesus, thou Son of David, have mercy on me." If I wanted to be lost, I'd have to forget that phrase. And there's a mighty agency of the Godhead that knows how to touch just the right part of my cerebrum to bring back the memory. Jesus of Nazareth is passing by. I don't want Him to pass by, do you?

I remember the sermons preached to me in song. Safe were the ninety and nine in the fold, safe, though the night was stormy and cold. But, said the Shepherd, when counting them o'er, one sheep is missing, there should be one more. God is not willing that any should perish. The message of the gospel, preached and taught and sung, is a mighty deterrent from continuing on the road to perdition.

THE MOUNTAIN OF COMMON SENSE | **MAR 8**

So teach us to number our days, that we may apply our hearts unto wisdom. Ps. 90:12.

The Bible and the preaching of the gospel in word and song are two great mountains that God has built up to prevent us from finding it easy to be lost. A third great mountain looming up is the mountain of your better judgment. Common sense. Jesus said it through the prophet: "Come now, and let us reason together" (Isa. 1:18). Let us reason together about what? Your sins! I have made provision for them to be white as snow, even though they are red like crimson. I've made provision for eternal life for you.

Well, now, someone may say, you can't prove that. If a person were to come to me and say, Prove to me that there is eternal life, I couldn't prove it. I don't have an instrument or scientific approach to prove eternity. But neither can the skeptic prove that there isn't any! Yet when people list the top questions they would ask if they knew they'd get the right answer, one question that always shows up in the top five—"Is there life after death? Is there something more beyond?" That's one big unknown, except by faith.

Frankly, if I'm just using my head and logic, just using human reason, I don't like the options offered by the person who does not accept God's way. It isn't eternal life in heaven versus eternal life in Las Vegas. It is eternal life in heaven versus dying at the end of threescore years and ten, and being dead for a long time, like forever. Right? That's not too impressive to me. I've heard people who feel self-satisfied and "mature" with the thought that they believe that all they have is this life, and when this life is over, that's it. They seem satisfied with that. I wonder what's the matter with their thinking!

I was talking to a man in the hospital who was chain smoking. He said, "Any coward can quit smoking. It takes a real man to die of lung cancer!" There's something wrong with his logic from the first word. Of course, he was being facetious. But with every cigarette he lighted, he had to cross the giant mountain of reason and common sense.

Better judgment is a mountain that God has designed to make being lost as hard as possible.

THE GREAT MOUNTAIN OF PRAYER

For this cause we also, since the day we heard it, do not cease to pray for you. Col. 1:9.

If at any time in your life you've heard anyone say, I'm praying for you, and I'm going to keep on praying for you, that's hard to forget! I believe in the effectiveness of prayer as a great mountain to keep us from sliding to perdition. If I wanted to be lost, I'd have to forget those moments as a child when I stumbled into my father's study at any time of the day or night and found him on his knees, and I knew at least one person he was praying for. Me! I read about a man named Peter. Jesus had said to him, "Satan wants to have you, but I have prayed for you that your faith will not fail." And suddenly, when Peter was cursing and swearing by the fire, those words came back. "I have prayed for you."

We had a long discussion in a midweek meeting one time, trying to figure out whether prayer was effective and how it worked. Finally we said, "Why don't we pray? Why don't we pray for an impossible case?" It just so happened that on that day I had been to see a returned missionary who had become discouraged, come home, and given up on God, the church, and everything. He and his family were bitter, and everyone knew it. As I had left that day, the man had said, "And don't pray for us, either!" His name was heavy on my mind at that meeting that night. I mentioned his name. A number of people knew him. We agreed that we couldn't find a more impossible case. We determined that we would pray every day that month, at home, and every Wednesday night, together, for this family. The following week his house burned down. At prayer meeting, I asked, "What have you people been praying for, anyway?" We prayed again. The next week he lost some valuable piece of equipment he needed in his business. The notice came out in the newspaper. We kept praying. We didn't understand what was going on. The devil? God? Who? All we knew was that at the end of the month, the last Sabbath, as the worship service was beginning, into the church walked this man and his family.

We ought to do more praying. Don't you believe that? We ought to. The prayers of loved ones are a giant mountain that makes it hard for us to be lost.

THE MOUNTAIN OF YOUR CONSCIENCE | **MAR 10**

And again he stooped down, and wrote on the ground. And they which heard it, being convicted by their own conscience, went out one by one, beginning at the eldest, even unto the last. John 8:8, 9.

The first four mountains that we have talked about that block our way downward, causing us to stop, realize, and think, are mountains that would be found primarily in civilized countries. The Bible, the sermons and songs that we have heard, our better judgment, and the prayers of our friends and loved ones who are Christians. The last four mountains would be perhaps more universal in application.

The first of these would be conscience. Conscience. Romans 2:15 talks about it. The Gentiles who had not the law of God found that their consciences witnessed to something. You can read about them. In lands where there has been no gospel preached, no education in spiritual things, no associates who have already accepted Christ, conscience speaks.

We have a hard time trying to define conscience. It's sort of nebulous. Sometimes we say it's the Holy Spirit. Well, no, it's more than that; or less than that—whatever. It's different from that. The Holy Spirit works through the conscience. Most of us know what it's like to be convicted by conscience. You see a group of men one day, planning to throw stones at a woman. Suddenly they stop, and with bowed heads and downcast eyes, slip away. Their consciences had convicted them. (See John 8.)

Conscience is present in the young, in the child. It is present in the old, if it hasn't been seared. And it takes a long time to sear a conscience. I remember telling a lie to my father when I was 4 years old. I've looked at my own children since. Four years old! How did I even know what a lie was, let alone tell one? I can still remember that lie. And for seven years it was on my conscience. Had anybody told me that I had a conscience? I didn't know much about a conscience at age 4. But something was convicting me. I'll never forget the peace the night I went into my father's bedroom at age 11, after he had gone to bed, and asked him to forgive me for the lie I had told at age 4. I dare say we all know what a conscience is all about. And the conscience is another mountain, another hurdle, that one would have to get past if he wanted to be lost.

THE MOUNTAIN OF TROUBLE

The way of transgressors is hard. Prov. 13:15.

Another great mountain that God uses to prevent us from sliding downward is a mountain that is not created by Him, but He does make use of it. He will take us wherever He can find us. It's the mountain of the sorrows and troubles of life. Tears, heartache, pain, parting, funeral trains, separation, hospitals, all have a way of somehow driving us to our knees. God is not responsible for sorrows and troubles; the devil is. But often in this area, the devil has met himself coming back. I believe firmly that if the devil had left me alone a long time ago, he could have had me. But he was so dumb that he kept needling me and trying to get me into the gutter, and this drove me to my knees. Have you ever had that happen? The devil is not happy just having people living apart from God; he wants them in the gutter, too. And in the process of trying to get some of us into the gutter, he drives us to find life with God. I don't like the world of sin in which I live. I don't like tears or pain or heartache. But sometimes when a person sings, "'He washed my eyes with tears, that I might see,'" it makes some sense, doesn't it?

I've met people in great sorrow who did not regret the sorrow in a sense, because through it they had found a meaningful relationship with the Lord Jesus. I'm not sure who brings the tears, but I am sure about who it is that makes us see. And I'm thankful for the sight that comes when we wake up to the realization that there is no place else to go. In John 6 Jesus said to His disciples, "Are you going to leave, too?" And they said, "We don't know where to go." There *is* no place else to go. Have you ever noticed, imprinted on the very countenance, the struggle and the fight that people who are trying to be lost are going through? Have you ever seen it? The furrowed brow, the lines in the face of the person who is trying to be lost.

Proverbs 13:15: "The way of transgressors is . . ." Easy? No. It's hard. I believe that if I wanted to be lost someday, I'd have to go to a great deal of effort and trouble to do it. I reject the idea that the road to hell is paved with ice. God has made it as hard as possible for each one of us to be lost.

77

PASSING MOUNT CALVARY

And thine ears shall hear a word behind thee, saying, This is the way, walk ye in it, when ye turn to the right hand, and when ye turn to the left. Isa. 30:21.

As we look at the mountains, the barriers, that are in the way of choosing to be lost, another great mountain that looms up is called the Holy Spirit. (See John 16:8-13.) When He is come, He will reprove how many? Just the Adventists? How many? Reprove the *world* of sin, of righteousness, and of judgment. The Holy Spirit is that still small voice. The Holy Spirit is working while you are sleeping. The Holy Spirit penetrated the body of a whale and talked to Jonah, who was down in the whale's stomach. The Holy Spirit can cross all boundaries and all barriers. The Holy Spirit can go to the darkest jungle, the remotest island. He is constantly working to draw men to God.

I've seen people who have shaken their fists at God and have said, "Leave me alone." I've heard of people who have prayed that the Holy Spirit would leave them. And once in a while that prayer seems to have been answered. But then I've met people, young people, even 10-year-olds, who are absolutely certain that they have committed the unpardonable sin.

I would like to take the position that the unpardonable sin is very difficult to commit. This in no way leaves the door open for license and procrastination. Not if we take a look at the next giant mountain that looms up. It is a mountain that looks something like a skull. It's outside the wall of Jerusalem. It has three crosses, and the center cross has friendly arms that still extend to every person, saying, "He that spared not his own Son, but delivered him up for us all, how shall he not with him also freely give us all things?" (Rom. 8:32).

How can you get past Mount Calvary? Even the heathen have a dim comprehension of the fact that someone must die to take the place of the sinner. God's Spirit is working to get through to every person. The story of the cross of Calvary is a giant mountain that pushes its snowcapped peak up into the blue. God cannot forgive sin, but because of the cross He can forgive *sinners*. If a person once gets a glimpse of that, how can he go past that giant hurdle into perdition?

GOD IS ON OUR SIDE

What shall we then say to these things? If God be for us, who can be against us? Rom. 8:31.

It is *hard* to be lost. God in heaven is not looking down with a spyglass, trying to find every spot or wrinkle that will give Him an excuse to exclude us from heaven. All the intelligences of heaven are united in the common purpose of trying to make it as easy as possible for us to be saved. "Jesus has made it as easy as He possibly can for His children."—Ellen G. White, in *Review and Herald,* April 29, 1890.

He holds out every enticement, every attraction, to direct our attention and affection to Him. He offers His love, communion with Him, peace, and a home with Him forever for all His children.

And if we ignore all of these, He still follows after us, reminding us through His Word, through His servants, through our own minds, through our loved ones who are His, through conscience, through the troubles of life, through the Holy Spirit, and finally through the greatest mountain of all, Mount Calvary. He reminds us that He is there, waiting, unwilling to lose any one of us, "not willing that any should perish" (2 Peter 3:9).

Listen, my friends, please don't ever believe the idea that it is hard to be saved and easy to be lost. If God is for us, who can be against us? I'm thankful for the giant mountains He has put in my way. Thankful that God has made every provision for everyone to be saved, eternally saved, to live with Him forever.

The clinching argument is this: If I am going to be lost, I have to fight God, and that's a lot to fight; I have to fight Jesus; and I have to fight the Holy Spirit. I have to resist the prayers and concern of all my Christian friends who are praying for me. I have to fight a two-thirds majority of the angels in this universe. If I choose to be saved, all I have against me is the devil and a one-third minority of angels, who screamed for mercy in the presence of Jesus when He was here, and who Jesus has promised He'll fight for me. No wonder it is hard to be lost!

"Love of Christ so freely given, grace of God beyond degree;
Mercy, higher than the heavens, deeper than the deepest sea."

HARD TO BE SAVED

Strait is the gate, and narrow is the way, which leadeth unto life, and few there be that find it. Matt. 7:14.

We have talked about the difficulty of being lost and how that the road downward is not a slippery, wide road with no obstructions. We noticed that God, through certain mighty agencies, has made it just as hard as possible for a person to be lost. But lest someone should get the impression that it is easy to be saved, we also need to consider how hard it is to be saved. Our text today has focused on Jesus' words concerning this. It is a narrow way, and a strait gate, that leads to life. How could it possibly be hard to be saved, if God is working so intently for the salvation of each one of us? How can it be true that only a few are going to find eternal life?

There are several texts that suggest that God is interested in everyone's being saved. John 3:17: "For God sent not his Son into the world to condemn the world; but that the world through him might be saved." It includes the whole world. First Timothy 2:4 reminds us that God would have all men to be saved. In Acts 2:21 there is a passage quoted from the Old Testament: "Whosoever shall call upon the name of the Lord shall be saved." And then, in the last book of the Bible, Revelation 22:17, it says that "whosoever will" may come. God is not in the business of trying to see how many He can keep out of heaven; He is trying to see how many He can get into heaven.

Now that doesn't sound as though it's going to be hard to be saved, unless it is hard to come to the Lord. If we come, He will give us rest. If we take His yoke, it's easy. So is it easy to be saved? Or is it hard to be saved? We could swing back and forth for a long time on that question. I would like to propose that if we come to Jesus, and continue coming to Jesus, it is easy. What makes it hard to be saved is *not* coming to Jesus and not continuing to come to Jesus for salvation. The thing that makes it so difficult and frustrating is that we continually find it hard to keep coming to Jesus. It is a fight to do this. But the Bible calls it a good fight, the good fight of faith.

DEVILS DON'T TRUST

Thou believest that there is one God; thou doest well: the devils also believe, and tremble. James 2:19.

Some people say you can't take the position that it would be hard to be saved when there are texts such as Acts 16:31 in the Scriptures: "Believe on the Lord Jesus Christ, and thou shalt be saved." Some people take the position that believing is all that's necessary. They say that if sometime during my life I have come to a decision to believe in the Lord Jesus Christ, then I am saved from then on—no problem, nothing to worry about, nothing to be concerned over, from that moment on.

Yet the Bible says that the devils do that much. They believe. They believe even a step further than some people believe. They believe that Jesus is the Son of God. They would even qualify apparently for John in his First Epistle, when he says that if you believe that Christ is come into the world, and that He is the Son of God, you will be saved (1 John 4:2). The devils in the days of Christ said, "We know who You are. You are the Holy One of God." (See Mark 1:24.) That's even a step further than some people go today, right? So there must be something more than simple believing in a surface understanding of the word.

What about the people who confess with their mouth that Jesus is in their life, and someday will even say, "Lord, Lord, we have cast out devils in thy name, and prophesied, and done many wonderful things" (see Matt. 7:22)? And they still aren't known by God. The person who will take Romans 10:9, 10, and say, "All you have to do to be saved is believe in the resurrection and confess that Jesus is Lord" still has to consider other scriptures.

Actually, the truth is that the deeper meaning of the word translated "faith" or "belief" is "trust." The devils believe, but they don't trust. And that's where the difference lies. It is possible for me to believe that there is a God and believe many things about Him, just as the devils do, but not trust Him. How wide can we open the strait and narrow gate? How much room can we make? Jesus says, "Come unto me, all ye that labour and are heavy laden, and I will give you rest" (Matt. 11:28). It is the coming to Him, and continuing to come, that develops the trust in Him. That is more than just a mental assent.

THE DO-IT-YOURSELF NATURE

For by grace are ye saved through faith; and that not of yourselves: it is the gift of God.
Eph. 2:8.

Man is an almost hopeless victim of do-it-yourself. Do-it-yourself is the label for man's nature with which he is born. Other labels would be self-centeredness and self-sufficiency. Even while we are small children this very principle is ingrained in our systems. I can remember trying to clean out our garage, and my 3-year-old wandering into the garage, wanting to help. He started to do something, and he was doing it wrong. I didn't intend for this thing to be placed there, or that to be picked up and put back from where I'd already moved it. And so I tried to correct him. What did he say? "Do it myself, Daddy, do it myself." Who taught that to him? Well, I may have helped. Mother may have helped. But he was born with that in his system. One of the most difficult things to tell a teenager who is just beginning to feel his wings and is leaving the nest is that he is a dependent creature and must depend upon God. How can a person satisfy his desire to be independent and self-sufficient and still be dependent upon God? Here is where we get into an extremely complex situation. This is the dilemma that makes it so hard to be saved. It is not only the dilemma of the child or the teenager but of everyone. It's man's nature.

Because we are born with this inherent do-it-yourself nature, and because we find it hard to surrender our independence, we have found that in religion a person often depends upon what he is able to do to earn and to merit his salvation. This is the basis of all the heathen religions. We easily become victims of works or of behaviorism as our hope of salvation. But Ephesians 2:8 and 9 tell us that by grace are we saved, through faith, and that not of ourselves. The grace is not of ourselves; neither is the faith of ourselves. Romans 12:3 tells us that faith is a gift, given to every person. And God has given us the Scriptures, by which faith grows. So faith is a gift, grace is a gift. We have to admit, if we are accepting God's Word, that we cannot look to ourselves for any hope of salvation whatsoever. We can only accept His gifts.

DON'T MEASURE YOURSELF

But unto every one of us is given grace according to the measure of the gift of Christ. Eph. 4:7.

One of the proofs that we are hopelessly hooked on the do-it-yourself approach is that often when a person begins to seek a relationship with God, he still measures whether or not he has a relationship by his behavior. Let's say that a person has been a victim of the disease of trying to work his way into heaven, and he discovers that we are saved by faith in Christ alone. So he begins to turn his attention toward Jesus and fellowship with Him. The first thing he tends to do is to look at himself the next day to see how much better a life he is living as a result of this relationship. Have you ever done this?

I was talking to someone one day who was having a terrible time trying to live life even in this world, let alone hope for eternal life. I tried to point him to Jesus, and gave him a few suggestions as to how he could become acquainted with Him, spending time with Him day by day. And then I said, "Now watch out. Because the first thing you are going to do if you spend time with God tomorrow is to try to decide whether you're succeeding by how life goes tomorrow. Life might even go worse tomorrow. It often does."

Have you ever discovered yourself living a more difficult life when you prayed harder? Have you ever discovered that when you made a determined effort to come into a closer relationship with Jesus, everything went wrong? Have you ever in all sincerity surrendered everything you knew to the Lord Jesus, and the next week everything went bad? Has that ever happened to you? I had a student say to me, "I've discovered I do better without God." And another student told me, "I quit being a Christian two weeks ago, and I haven't sinned since."

We should never judge our relationship by our behavior. That's God's business. God will judge every man according to his works. We are to judge no man, and if we are to judge no man, doesn't that include ourselves? It is possible for the Christian life to become unbearably hard because we constantly measure ourselves by ourselves, and look away from Jesus. We find it hard to look to Jesus, to accept that "there is none other name under heaven given among men, whereby we must be saved" (Acts 4:12).

IT'S HARD BUT IT'S EASY

Take my yoke upon you, and learn of me; for I am meek and lowly in heart: and ye shall find rest unto your souls. Matt. 11:29.

Another of the things that makes it hard to be saved is admitting that we need to renew our conversion again tomorrow, and the next day, and the day after. That is a cross to the human heart. Even the apostle Paul had a struggle with that. We are told that every day he found inclination at odds with God. Some people think that this was his inclination to do wrong things. Not so. The inclination that Paul found at odds with God was the inclination to be independent of God and to live life on his own steam again. That was his constant struggle. After all, he had done a pretty good job on his own, and could look back and say that touching matters of the law he was blameless. He had been a very successful Pharisee.

Through the converting power of God, our inclinations to do wrong things are transformed. "When we are clothed with the righteousness of Christ, we shall have no relish for sin; for Christ will be working with us."—Ellen G. White, in *Review and Herald*, March 18, 1890. But never, as long as life shall last here, will we lose the inclination to be independent of God. This is the constant struggle. To admit daily that we need God, to be crucified with Christ, is a painful work for the Christian. To say that this is easy, to say that coming to Christ and accepting His rest, which is offered as a gift, to say that taking His yoke, which is easy, is easy, is not correct. It is hard to come to Christ to rest. It is hard to continue to take His yoke, which is easy.

If only we could get it into our minds that everything valued by the world ends when Jesus comes again! There will be nothing of it important then, absolutely nothing! Houses, lands, cars, jobs, education, you name it. None of it is important when Jesus comes again. If only we could today think about that moment and say, Lord, help me to know what it means to come unto You and take Your yoke, which is easy. Easy? Yes. Easy in comparison with anything else the world has to offer. Hard for the stubborn human heart, but easy, considering eternity. May we today accept Jesus' invitation to come and find rest for our souls.

THE GOOD FIGHT OF FAITH

Fight the good fight of faith. 1 Tim. 6:12.

What is the fight of faith? Faith is trust. Whom do you trust? The one you know. So if you learn to know someone who is trustworthy, you will have faith. To know God results in trusting Him. When you get to know someone who is absolutely trustworthy, you can't help trusting him. Faith, therefore, is never worked up; it comes as a result of knowing God. And faith comes not to those who seek it, but to those who seek it not, who seek only Jesus. When we seek Jesus we learn to trust Him naturally, and when we learn to trust Him, this allows Him to do the work in battling the enemy that so many of us have tried with ill success. The fight of faith is nothing more than the effort required to come, every day, into close contact and personal relationship with the Lord Jesus Christ.

The fight of faith involves your daily devotional life. The fight involves momentary, hourly, contact with Jesus. And if we will fight the fight of faith, He has promised that He will fight the fight of sin. For a long time some of us became so involved in the fight of sin we had no time or energy left for the fight of faith. Have you ever been in that trap? One of the reasons that the Christian life is so deplorably hard is because we get involved in the wrong fight, the wrong battle, and we fight the battle where the battle isn't instead of where it is. The Christian life, and salvation, is summed up in relationship only, if relationship is properly defined and understood.

The premise of salvation through faith in Christ alone is that Christ is our total Saviour. Faith in Jesus is how we are saved, and our works are the result, never the cause, of our salvation. So God invites us to fight the right fight. How long has it been, my friend, since you sat down and exercised your mind in meditating, in grappling with the things of salvation? Or how long has it been since you watched four hours of TV and never knew where the time went? Whatever we contemplate, whatever we meditate on, is going to be exactly what we are in the end. "If the eye is kept fixed upon Christ, the work of the Spirit ceases not until the soul is conformed to His image."—*The Desire of Ages*, p. 302.

DAILY DEATH TO SELF

If any man will come after me, let him deny himself, and take up his cross daily, and follow me. Luke 9:23.

Jesus said, "If any man will come after me, let him deny . . ." What? *"himself."* Sometimes we read other things in there. Let him deny this or that or the other habit or practice or thing. I used to think that the cross was making myself not do something I really liked to do. I've heard other people say it too. "My cross is giving up my dancing. I can't dance anymore. I sure wish I could, but that's my cross." That is not what Jesus is talking about. No, the cross is to deny self. Let him deny *himself,* and take up his cross and follow Me.

Surrender is the surrender of ourselves, the giving up of ourselves. That's why the wrong understanding of surrender often leads to an escape, or substitute for the genuine. If I am big enough and strong enough and have enough backbone and willpower to give up this or that or the other thing, I can trick myself into thinking that I have surrendered myself. The truth is that I may have done just the opposite. If I think I can surrender my smoking, and I succeed in quitting smoking by myself, without the power of God, I may have created the atmosphere in which I will find my own damnation. Why? I may live a little longer without lung cancer, but during the time I am living longer, I am going to be ascribing glory and honor and credit to myself for having accomplished and succeeded, and will invariably want merit for my own achievement. Is this possible? The truth is that apart from Jesus I can give up my smoking or drinking or dancing only externally, anyway. Inside I'm still the same. The cross is not refusing to do something we would like to do. It's denying our*selves.*

This cross must be taken up how often? Once, at the beginning of my Christian life? No, daily. Listen to this: "Genuine conversion is needed, not once in years, but daily. This conversion brings man into a new relation with God. Old things, his natural passions and hereditary and cultivated tendencies to wrong, pass away, and he is renewed and sanctified. But this work must be continual. . . . No renewed heart can be kept in a condition of sweetness without the daily application of the salt of the word. Divine grace must be received daily, or no man will stay converted."—Ellen G. White, in *Review and Herald,* Sept. 14, 1897.

THE PERIL OF POSSESSIONS

*For a man's life consisteth not in the abundance of the things which he possesseth.
Luke 12:15.*

Jesus talked in Matthew 19 about the rich man, and presented His disciples with an insurmountable problem. They thought that a rich man must have been blessed by God in order to be rich, and that any rich man would be sure to make it into the kingdom of heaven. But in verses 23 to 26, Jesus said to His disciples, "Verily I say unto you, That a rich man shall hardly enter into the kingdom of heaven. And again I say unto you, It is easier for a camel to go through the eye of a needle, than for a rich man to enter into the kingdom of God. When his disciples heard it, they were exceedingly amazed, saying, Who then can be saved?" If a rich man can't make it, who's going to make it? But "Jesus beheld them"—He looked at them with kindness and patience—"and said unto them, With men this is impossible; but with God all things are possible."

Who was Jesus talking about? Only the rich who have the millions? Or was He talking about anyone who has anything that he will depend upon in place of God?

One time we discussed, with an academy group of young people, who would most likely be the best Christian on campus. And they said, If you're going to decide whether it's a fellow or a girl, it would most likely be a girl. Why? Well, girls need God more than the fellows do. Then we said, Suppose you take all the girls on campus, who would be the best Christian, the good-looking one or the not-so-good-looking one? Well, the one that's not so good looking. And of all the not-so-good-looking girls, who would be the best Christian, the one with lots of talent and the 4.0 grade point average or the one with little talent and a 2.0 average? They finally decided, on that basis, that the worst Christian on campus would be the best-looking fellow with the T-Bird and the trumpet and the beautiful voice and the expensive wardrobe and the 4.0 average. Which said, actually, that as long as a person has something he can depend on instead of God, he tends to do just that.

With men it is impossible, but not with God. How thankful we can be for a God who is doing all He can to open our eyes as to where our real dependence lies, to show us our need of Him, regardless of our external success.

THE GREATEST TRADE EVER

For he hath made him to be sin for us, who knew no sin; that we might be made the righteousness of God in him. 2 Cor. 5:21.

I have a ballpoint pen that I would like to trade with someone for a Cadillac Seville. Let me tell you about the ballpoint pen. It's not a bad one at all. Someone gave it to me. It's very nice. It's carved out of some sort of wood. It's quite expensive. There must be someone who likes to trade who would be interested in my offer.

When I was a boy back in Philadelphia, we used to trade bubble-gum cards and marbles. Three little ones for one big one. Later, in college, I remember one night in the boys' dormitory we had a necktie swap. It was one of the most fun things we ever did, getting rid of all the neckties we never wore and getting some better ones. My roommate started out with nothing and ended up with six beauties! Most of us have been involved in trading something. But if someone were to take me up on my deal with the ballpoint pen, I guarantee that he would qualify for one of two things. Either he would be stupid or he would really like me a lot. One of the two.

Today I would like to talk to you about the greatest trade ever. 2 Corinthians 5:21: "For he [God] hath made him [Jesus] to be sin for us, who knew no sin [referring to Jesus, of course]; that we might be made the righteousness of God in him." Let's paraphrase it just a little. For God hath made Jesus, who knew no sin, to be sin for us, that we, who knew no righteousness, might be made the righteousness of God in Him.

What would you do if Jesus Himself would today, in person, walk up to you as though you were the only one in the world? How would you feel if He would look into your face with His friendly eyes and open His arms as He did so long ago, saying, "My friend, I've come to trade you all of My righteousness for all of your sins"? Would you be interested? I have had people tell me that if He would do that, and if they could know that their eternal destiny was settled right there, it would be almost too good to be true. But it is true—the greatest trade ever leads to certainty in the Christian life and the assurance of our eternal destiny.

CERTAINTY OF ACCEPTANCE

And this is the will of him that sent me, that every one which seeth the Son, and believeth on him, may have everlasting life. John 6:40.

If you could approach God Himself with one question, what question would you like to ask Him? Some of us have taken surveys in various parts of the country, asking that question. It's probably a little self-centered, but the one question that always rises head and shoulders above all the rest is "Am I going to be saved?"

If Jesus came to you personally today and traded all His righteousness for all your sins, would there be any question concerning your eternal destiny right now? Would there? Some feel that this might be easier to accept if they had the advantage that the thief on the cross had. But most of us have to keep on living. Is your certainty in Jesus just as true today as it was 20 years ago when you first accepted the faith? Maybe we could accept that kind of trade *then*, but a lot of water has gone under the bridge since. Time has gone and some of you might even be thinking, I passed my 70 times seven long ago. We realize that God is wonderful in the forgiveness department, but we are afraid we have passed the limit. Perhaps you feel that you can't really accept this promise today. But I don't know of any date on this promise. I don't know of anyone for whom this promise is not made available.

I remember a man at a camp meeting who asked to talk with me. We went off into a corner, and he said, "It's too late, I've gone too far. I've committed the unpardonable sin; there's no chance for me." I invited him to open his Bible to John 6:37. He looked at it. Jesus' own words are recorded there: "Him that cometh to me I will in no wise cast out." I said, "What do you see in the margin?" He said, "I don't have a margin in my Bible." "Well, what do you see in the white space along the edge of the page? Is there a date on it?" "No." "Is there a name on it?" "No." "Then this promise is good for you, today." When Jesus says that He wants to trade all of His righteousness for all of your sins, the promise is still good today, as long as we accept it again today. We can have the assurance of acceptance with God each day, as we accept His trade anew.

Blessed are they which do hunger and thirst after righteousness: for they shall be filled.
Matt. 5:6.

Have you ever seen someone who was absolutely certain that he had committed the unpardonable sin? He was so worried about it! But the very fact that he was worried about it said something, didn't it?

I remember one camp meeting when each of the pastors took charge of a little group and conducted a testimony meeting. In my group, one elderly man who obviously had just come to Christ got up. His lip was quivering, and he was having a hard time keeping the tears back. He said, "For a long time God tried to get me, and He finally got me." And he sat down. I don't remember any of the other testimonies that were given that day, but I remember that one. I like it. I think God tries for a long time, don't you?

Provision has been made for Jesus to trade all of His righteousness for all of your sins. What is righteousness? We have some stock answers that we like to give. One of them is that righteousness is rightdoing. That's true. You can find an inspired statement to that effect. But let's not miss all the rest of them, too. Sometimes we become experts at taking sentences out of context and forgetting the rest. If righteousness is nothing more than rightdoing, then all you would have to do to become righteous would be to do what's right. Do you see the trap? Someone else says that righteousness is conformity to the will of God. That's true, and you can find an inspired statement for that. But there's also a trap there. You can be led, if you're not careful, to the idea that all you have to do is conform to the law of God. But that conformity can be merely external.

So as you go through the definitions, you can come to great frustration unless you face the only real live definition: righteousness equals *Jesus.* Romans 1:17: "Therein is the righteousness of God revealed," in the gospel of Jesus. The only kind of righteousness this world has ever known in a real live person was in the Lord Jesus Christ. The best single definition for righteousness is Jesus. When we read, "Blessed are they which do hunger and thirst after righteousness," what we're really saying is, "Blessed are they which do hunger and thirst after Jesus."

RIGHTEOUSNESS EQUALS JESUS

There is none righteous, no, not one. Rom. 3:10.

One of the major breakthroughs that come in the theme of salvation by faith is that you don't get righteousness by seeking righteousness. Righteousness comes by seeking Jesus. It is a trap of the devil for us to seek righteousness instead of seeking for Jesus. Righteousness is deeper than external actions.

The equation for righteousness is R = J, Righteousness = Jesus. If we're going to transfer it to our lives, it works like this: Mankind + Jesus = Righteousness. That's the equation for righteousness as far as we're concerned.

One day we were talking about this in class, and a math major in the back row with his pocket computer got this terrible look on his face and said, "Wait just a minute. We just came to the conclusion that Righteousness = Jesus. *Now* you say that Mankind + Jesus = Righteousness. But if Jesus = Righteousness, then Mankind = Nothing!"

I was conducting a Week of Prayer at a Christian medical school. That's a terrible experience. The medical students have brains bulging out of the sides of their heads. And you're supposed to try to say something! Part of the way through the week we got a reaction from some because we had talked about the fact that without Jesus we can do nothing. Some had gotten the impression that we were talking about being worthless. You don't tell people who have worked that hard toward their profession that they are worthless without getting some kind of reaction. There *are* people in the world who can do great things without God as long as God keeps their hearts beating in their chests. But God makes the hearts beat in the chests of those who curse Him.

Even though we are still helpless to produce righteousness, because righteousness is found only in Jesus, Jesus on the cross proved that every human being is *worth* the entire universe. We need to recognize that there's a big difference between being helpless and being worthless. When we accept the premise that we are nothing, we mean what Jesus said in John 15:5: "Without me ye can *do* nothing," in producing the fruits of righteousness. But without Him we *are* worth something; that's why He came—to show us that in Him all things are possible, and to prove the worth of a human soul.

RIGHTEOUSNESS FOR TODAY

O Lord, righteousness belongeth unto thee, but unto us confusion of faces, as at this day. Dan. 9:7.

C. T. Everson used to say that if we could take a giant scale, and put the world, weighing 6 sextillion tons on one side, and put one human being, even a baby, on the other side, the human would tip the scales. That's a good picture of how Heaven looks at one individual. We are worth everything, and the cross proves it. But we are still helpless to produce righteousness. The Bible premise is that when it comes to righteousness, we are totally bankrupt. We have none. Romans 3:10: "There is none righteous, no, not one." Isaiah 64:6: "All our righteousnesses are as filthy rags."

And yet we are invited to come to Jesus and trade our filthy rags for eternal life. There's nothing we can do to recommend ourselves in the eyes of Heaven. That's why we need to consider seriously this greatest trade ever that Jesus comes and offers to us today. Righteousness is found only in Jesus; as Daniel said, "O Lord, righteousness belongeth unto thee, but unto us confusion of faces, as at this day." "Sinful man can find hope and righteousness only in God; and no human being is righteous any longer than he has faith in God and maintains a vital connection with Him."—*Testimonies to Ministers,* p. 367.

In recent years there are some who have gotten the idea that all you have to do to have righteousness is to look up to heaven someday and say, "All right, I accept the fact that everything's taken care of." They believe that from that moment on, they are declared righteous and have nothing to worry about, and "everything's all right in my Father's house."

But please don't miss the fact that no human being will be righteous any longer than he has faith in God and *maintains a vital connection with Him.* That's why the Jesus movement of a few years ago faded away. There were so many who marched down the beach with their Bibles waving in the air like banners and the name of Jesus on their lips like a slogan, who stopped right there and never came into any closer fellowship with Jesus. The trade that Jesus offers, in exchanging His righteousness for our sins, is beautiful. But it's no good for tomorrow unless I accept it again tomorrow. It is only good for each today.

UNBROKEN CONNECTION WITH GOD

God is faithful, by whom ye were called unto the fellowship of his Son Jesus Christ our Lord. 1 Cor. 1:9.

I would like to tell you a parable. More than 20 years ago I fell in love with a beautiful girl. She lived in San Francisco; I lived in Los Angeles. The day came that we met in San Francisco where her parents were putting on the wedding, like parents of good brides do, and when the preacher asked me if I did, I admitted that I did. He pronounced us husband and wife. After the wedding she went home with her parents in San Francisco, and I went back to Los Angeles. Two years later someone came along and asked whether I was married. I said Yes. And they said, "We've never seen your wife." "I haven't either, for two years." "When was that?" "That was the day we were married." "You haven't seen her since? Do you write to her?" "No." "Do you telephone her?" "No." "And you're *married?*" "Yes, I said 'I do,' and I have a certificate to prove it." (I *did* tell you this was a parable, please!)

There were people who were baptized years ago, who apparently said I do, and have a baptismal certificate to prove it. But there's no such thing as any relationship continuing without communication.

As we continue the communication, the relationship, with Christ, then we have what is called righteousness. The Bible even calls us righteous. Are *we* ever righteous? 2 Corinthians 5:21: "For he [God] hath made him to be sin for us." Did He become sin for us? Yes. Did He ever become a sinner? *No!* Jesus became sin for us, but He never became a sinner. "That we might be made the righteousness of God in him." Does that ever make *us* righteous, any more than the first part made Him a sinner? No. We are righteous only in Him.

What does "in Him" mean? There's another text that might seem hard to understand. 1 John 5:12: "He that hath the Son hath life." Have you ever pondered what it means to "have the Son"? We say that we have a friend. I have a wife; you have a wife or husband. What does that mean? It means that you have a relationship with that person. When it says "he that hath the Son," it means having a relationship with Him. We are righteous so long as we are in Him.

93

DO YOU KNOW HIM?

That I may know him, and the power of his resurrection, and the fellowship of his sufferings. Phil. 3:10.

It came as a surprise to some of us to discover that the certainty and assurance of our eternal life is based upon being in relationship with Christ. That's why the question "Do you know Him?" is an important question. It's not a question of knowing *about* Him, but of *knowing Him.*

Romans 5 talks about the gift of righteousness. If we accept His gift today but don't stay with Him, then what happens to the gift? "No human being is righteous any longer than he has faith in God and maintains a vital connection with Him."—*Testimonies to Ministers,* p. 367. If God casts all our sins into the depths of the sea today, but between now and the time that Jesus comes we turn from Him, is He going to drag them up from the depths of the sea? Is His righteousness going to be taken back? And what about this statement from *Thoughts From the Mount of Blessing:* "'In His borrowed goodness good,' we may be perfect in our sphere, even as God is perfect in His"?—Page 77. Is His righteousness borrowed? Is it a gift? Or is it a trade? Which is it? Is it permanent or not?

I'd like to illustrate like this: Suppose I have a Cadillac Seville. But I'm single. And I would like to have someone nice to ride around in my Cadillac with me. This gets a little tricky, because how can I tell whether the young lady is interested in me or in my car? But finally one day I am convinced that a certain young lady likes me as much as she likes my Cadillac and she accepts my proposal. The day we are married, not only does she get me, but she gets the Cadillac as well. It comes with me. (Now don't confuse me with the marriage laws of your state. I have my own today.) Hopefully when she chooses me, she chooses me permanently. As long as she continues to choose me, she has the Cadillac. But if she ever chooses to separate from me, and no longer continue the relationship, no longer does she have the Cadillac.

Righteousness is never independent of Jesus Christ. There is no such thing as righteousness apart from Jesus.

FREEDOM THROUGH SLAVERY

Forasmuch as ye know that ye were not redeemed with corruptible things, . . . but with the precious blood of Christ. 1 Peter 1:18, 19.

In the old days, on the shores of the Mississippi, there was an auction block. Abraham Lincoln stood nearby one day and watched the tears flow and saw the heartache and pain of separation. He clenched his fists and said, "If I ever get a chance to hit this, I'll hit it, and I'll hit it hard." He did, and signed the Emancipation Proclamation with his own hand.

One day, before the Emancipation, old Joe, a slave, was on the auction block. He had seen too much, and he began to mutter under his breath, "I won't work! I won't work!" The bidders heard him, and bidding fell off. But one man continued, and paid good money for a slave who wouldn't work.

He led Joe to the carriage, and they drove out of town and down the road to the plantation. There, by a little lake, was a bungalow. It had curtains on the windows, and flowers, and cobblestones. The new master said, "Here's your new home, Joe." Joe could hardly believe it, but then he remembered and said, "I won't work." The master replied, "You don't have to work, Joe, because I bought you to set you free." I always liked that part, but that isn't the end of the story. Old Joe fell at the master's feet and said, "Master, I'll serve you forever."

I see another auction block. I see people who know what it means to have the tears flow, to have pain and heartache and separation. One day Someone from a far country looks down and says, "If I ever get a chance to hit that, I'll hit it, and I'll hit it hard." And He did. He signed the emancipation papers for the human race with His own blood. He bought us to set us free. But we look up at Him and say, "We won't work, because we *can't*." Have you ever tried it? We can't work. And He says, "*You* don't have to work. I bought you to set you free." When you catch that, you go to your knees at His feet and say, "Master, I'll serve You forever." And you discover that things you could never do before can now happen because Jesus lives His life within.

I understand He has some bungalows, by a lake that goes on and on, and looks like a sea made out of glass. There are cobblestones and curtains, and flowers like you've never seen. He has them all for you and me.

PEACE BRINGS RELEASE

Peace I leave with you, my peace I give unto you: not as the world giveth, give I unto you. Let not your heart be troubled, neither let it be afraid. John 14:27.

Here's a significant statement from the book *Steps to Christ,* page 49: "As your conscience has been quickened by the Holy Spirit, you have seen something of the evil of sin, of its power, its guilt, its woe; and you look upon it with abhorrence. You feel that sin has separated you from God, that you are in bondage to the power of evil." (Notice this is talking about a person who is in bondage to evil and *recognizes* it.) "The more you struggle to escape, the more you realize your helplessness." (Is this talking about a heathen, a rebel, or someone who is trying to live a right life?) "Your motives are impure; your heart is unclean. You see that your life has been filled with selfishness and sin. You long to be forgiven, to be cleansed, to be set free. Harmony with God, likeness to Him—what can you do to obtain it?" If I understand this correctly, this paragraph is describing a messed-up life, someone who is defeated, failing, discouraged. What can you do? The next paragraph gives the answer.

But do you know what I expected it to say? What you need is to try a little harder. What you need is to make more resolutions. What you need is to be more sincere, more dedicated, more consecrated. What you need, maybe, is more Bible study and prayer, or to get out and work for others. But instead, it says that what you need is *peace!* Sounds like a mistake! I thought that anyone knows that you can't have peace when you have a life that's mixed up like that. You have to get your life in order before you can have peace. But that's not what it says. It doesn't say that peace comes from victory, but that victory comes from peace. Can you fathom that? That is one of the greatest breakthroughs in the theme of salvation by faith.

It is known by the experts that the only way a child can outgrow his mistakes and failures is to know he's loved and accepted *while he's making them.* It is rejection that keeps a person in his sins and failures. It's knowing that you are accepted and loved that brings growth, that *transforms* your life. It is peace that brings release.

SALVATION BY FAITH ALONE

But of him are ye in Christ Jesus, who of God is made unto us wisdom, and righteousness, and sanctification, and redemption. 1 Cor. 1:30.

When the sinner realizes that because of what Jesus did on the cross he is accepted *just as he is,* this realization begins the transformation of his life. Sanctification therefore is based solidly on justification. If it isn't, it's going to end up misunderstood and confused. Sometimes we split theological hairs and try to decide which is the most important aspect of salvation—justification, sanctification, or glorification.

Which do you think is more important, getting married or staying married? I could recite some of the advantages to getting married. I also understand that there are some tremendous advantages to staying married once you have gotten married. Which of the two do you think is more important? Or is that a foolish question?

Which is more important, justification or sanctification? They are both important! For different reasons, maybe; but both are important. Both come in Jesus, and are by faith in Jesus, and are by faith alone in Jesus. We are not saying that works are not important, but we are talking about method, and the method for salvation is by faith alone.

"Let no man present the idea that man has little or nothing to do in the great work of overcoming; for God does nothing for man without his cooperation. Neither say that after you have done all you can on your part, Jesus will help you. Christ has said, 'Without me ye can do nothing.'"—*Selected Messages,* book 1, p. 381. "All that man can possibly do toward his own salvation is to accept the invitation, 'Whosoever will, let him take the water of life freely.'"—*Ibid.,* p. 343. That's all he can do. So there's something for us to do, but all we *can* do is to take the water of life freely. But that's an intangible. So what is the water of life? "In this *communion with Christ,* through prayer and the study of the great and precious truths of His word, we shall as hungry souls be fed; as those that thirst, we shall be refreshed at the fountain of life."—*Thoughts From the Mount of Blessing,* p. 113. (Italics supplied.) That's all we can do toward our own salvation—justification, sanctification, or glorification. Communion with Him. It's that simple.

THE ONLY WAY TO GET APPLES | **APR 1**

Ye shall know them by their fruits. Do men gather grapes of thorns, or figs of thistles? Even so every good tree bringeth forth good fruit; but a corrupt tree bringeth forth evil fruit. Matt. 7:16, 17.

Once upon a time there was to be a county fair. Special prizes were being offered for the best apples brought to the judging, and circulars had been sent all over the county to let people know about the contest.

Some of the people in the county weren't interested in apples at all. They threw away the announcements and forgot all about it. But the rest of them began to plan how they could produce a prize-winning apple.

Mr. Thompkins was a woodcarver. He chose a piece of pine and carved his apple out of wood. It was exactly the right shape, and when he had painted and polished it, it looked almost like a real apple.

Mrs. Jones hurried to town for some yarn. She knitted her apple. When she was finished, it didn't look *exactly* like an apple, but you could certainly tell right off that it was *supposed* to be an apple!

Some of the people made their apples out of plastic, some crocheted theirs, some stitched them in cloth. Some used clay or ceramics or glass.

Only a few took their apples off apple trees. Real fruit. When the day of the fair arrived, most of the apples looked pretty good on the outside. But when the judges tried to cut them open to see what they were like on the inside, all of the imitation apples were disqualified.

If you want to produce apples, the best thing for you to do is to find an apple tree, or plant one. And if you want to produce genuine fruit in the Christian life, the best thing for you to do is *to be* a Christian. An apple tree bears apples because it *is* an apple tree, never in order *to be* one. And a Christian does what is right because he *is* a Christian, never in order *to be* one. It's what's inside that counts. "The plan of beginning outside and trying to work inward has always failed, and always will fail. God's plan with you is to begin at the very seat of all difficulties, the heart, and then from out of the heart will issue the principles of righteousness."—*Counsels on Diet and Foods,* p. 35.

TO KNOW HIM IS TO TRUST HIM

The Lord is good, a strong hold in the day of trouble; and he knoweth them that trust in him. Nahum 1:7.

Many people are frustrated in living the Christian life because they are trying to do what is right in order to be Christians. It doesn't work! In John 6 the Jewish people came to Jesus with the question "What shall we do, that we might work the works of God? Jesus answered and said unto them, This is the work of God, that ye believe on him whom he hath sent" (John 6:28, 29).

The question is, How do we believe? If the work of God is that we believe, how do we do it? How do we get faith? How do we trust? Is it by trying hard to make ourselves trust?

In our relations with other people, there are two ingredients necessary to be able to trust someone. First of all, he must be trustworthy. Second, we must get to know him. Usually, we don't really trust anyone until we know him. Then, if he is trustworthy, we will trust him spontaneously. God is completely trustworthy. If you know God, you *will* trust Him, and you will trust Him naturally, spontaneously. If you don't know God, you will distrust Him.

Whenever you see a person who is giving evidence of distrust of God, he is advertising the fact that he doesn't know God. There are thousands of people in the world today who blame God for everything that comes along. Even the insurance companies do it. They call natural disasters "acts of God"! The only reason you distrust God is if you don't know Him.

So how do you learn to trust God? You learn to trust by getting acquainted with Him. God invites you to be more than simply a good liver. He invites you to know Him, to know His presence and power in your life. This is Christianity.

The majority of church members today are relying on what they do, instead of seeking personal acquaintance and friendship with God. According to recent surveys, only about one out of five are spending any time at all on a daily basis getting to know God. It's like trying to make apples apart from an apple tree. Apart from a continual connection with God, there can be no genuine trust, no fruit, and no real Christianity.

CHRISTIANITY IS KNOWING JESUS

I am the bread of life: he that cometh to me shall never hunger; and he that believeth on me shall never thirst. John 6:35.

Probably Jesus' greatest discourse on the close relationship of becoming acquainted with Him is found in John 6. The chapter cannot be read hastily. It's deep. But it has expressions such as these: "And Jesus said unto them, I am the bread of life: he that cometh to me shall never hunger; and he that believeth on me shall never thirst." "He that believeth on me hath everlasting life." "I am that bread of life. Your fathers did eat manna in the wilderness, and are dead. This is the bread which cometh down from heaven, that a man may eat thereof, and not die." "Except ye eat the flesh of the Son of man, and drink his blood, ye have no life in you." "He that eateth my flesh, and drinketh my blood, dwelleth in me, and I in him." "Many therefore of his disciples, when they had heard this, said, This is an hard saying; who can hear it?" "From that time many of his disciples went back, and walked no more with him."

Giving up on ourselves and becoming acquainted with God is the entire basis of the Christian life. But there are many professed Christians who will scrap it at that point and say, "No, thanks. I want a religion, a Christianity, in which I can manage my own life." It is an ego-deflating thing to come to Jesus and say, "Lord, You're right. I can't do it. I would like to turn my life over to You." But if you've had struggles and problems in your life that you'd like to face with the real answer, I invite you today to a personal acquaintance with God.

How do we come into a relationship with God, and stay in the relationship with Him? Here is the prescription for that: Take time, alone, at the beginning of every day, to seek Jesus through His Word and through prayer. This is how you receive of His grace. This is all you can do to become and to remain a Christian. If you do not have a relationship with God, you're not a Christian. There are many people in the church who don't know God and who don't care a whole lot about knowing the Lord Jesus. They are simply good livers. God invites us to something more. He invites us to know His presence and His power in our lives. This is Christianity.

EATING HIS FLESH AND BLOOD

Except ye eat the flesh of the Son of man, and drink his blood, ye have no life in you.
John 6:53.

At first glance the idea of eating Christ's flesh and drinking His blood may seem confusing. It seemed confusing to those who heard Jesus first speak these words in John 6. But we have been given a clear explanation of the meaning of this passage by the inspired commentary.

"The reception of the Word, the bread from heaven, is declared to be the reception of Christ Himself. As the Word of God is received into the soul, we partake of the flesh and blood of the Son of God. As it enlightens the mind, the heart is opened still more to receive the engrafted Word, that we may grow thereby. Man is called upon to eat and masticate the Word; but unless his heart is open to the entrance of that Word, unless he drinks in the Word, unless he is taught of God, there will be a misconception, misapplication, and misinterpretation of that Word.

"As the blood is formed in the body by the food eaten, so Christ is formed within by the eating of the Word of God, which is His flesh and blood. He who feeds upon that Word has Christ formed within, the hope of glory. The Written Word introduces to the searcher the flesh and blood of the Son of God; and through obedience to that Word, he becomes a partaker of the divine nature. As the necessity for temporal food cannot be supplied by once partaking of it, so the Word of God must be daily eaten to supply the spiritual necessities.

"As the life of the body is found in the blood, so spiritual life is maintained through faith in the blood of Christ. His is our life, just as in the body our life is in the blood. . . . By reason of the waste and loss, the body must be renewed with blood, by being supplied with daily food. So there is need of constantly feeding on the Word, the knowledge of which is eternal life. That Word must be our meat and drink. It is in this alone that the soul will find its nourishment and vitality. We must feast upon its precious instruction, that we may be renewed in the spirit of our mind, and grow up into Christ, our living Head."—Ellen G. White, in *Review and Herald*, Nov. 23, 1897.

IT TAKES TIME

But they that wait upon the Lord shall renew their strength; they shall mount up with wings as eagles; they shall run, and not be weary; and they shall walk, and not faint. Isa. 40:31.

Take time. Jesus' analogy is that the physical life and the spiritual life are sustained in the same way. From this we learn basic principles of how to have a meaningful relationship with Him. How fat would some of us be if we spent as much time eating our physical food as we spend alone with God?

"It would be well for us to spend a thoughtful hour each day in contemplation of the life of Christ."—*The Desire of Ages,* p. 83. This does not mean that you have to set a timer to make sure you spend exactly 60 minutes in communication with God every day. But it *is* going to have to involve something more than reading a text for the day while you have your hand on the doorknob. It will have to involve significant time, at least as much time as you spend eating your meals.

You say, "I don't have time." May I remind you that we find time for whatever we believe is important. The reason why many people do not spend time in relationship with Christ every day is simply that they don't believe that it's all that important. If they did, they would find the time available.

If I don't think it's important to spend the time to become acquainted with Christ, it must be because I think I can be saved in some other way than through knowing Him. And if one doesn't depend on Jesus, he is probably depending on himself. One of the major reasons why people do not spend time in beholding Christ and in relationship with Him is that they are still operating on the basis of trying to secure salvation by their own efforts.

It is true that the devotional life can become simply another "work." Spending time each day reading your Bible and praying will no more guarantee you a healthy spiritual life than daily eating and breathing will assure you a healthy physical life. But it's a sure thing that you cannot be healthy without it!

John 17:3: "This is life eternal, that they might know thee the only true God, and Jesus Christ, whom thou hast sent." Knowing God is what eternal life is all about, and is the purpose of the devotional life.

ALONE WITH GOD

Your fathers did eat manna in the wilderness, and are dead. This is the bread which cometh down from heaven, that a man may eat thereof, and not die. John 6:49, 50.

Jesus suggested the comparison between Himself, as the bread of life, and the manna that was given as bread from heaven to the people of Israel. Let's consider the story of the manna in Exodus 16 in relationship to the eating of the bread of life.

The manna had fallen the night before, and the children of Israel were wondering what it was. In fact, that's what they called it—"What is it?" That's what the word *manna* means.

"And Moses said unto them, This is the bread which the Lord hath given you to eat. This is the thing which the Lord hath commanded, Gather of it every man according to his eating" (Ex. 16:15, 16). What does it mean, "according to his eating"? Well, the primary reference here was to the number of the people in each family, but there's another principle we can apply from this, as well.

When I was living in Glendale, not too far from where Elder H.M.S. Richards lived, I went over to visit him one day. He was talking about the reason for lack of power today in the Christian ministry. And he said, "You know, there are very few of us ministers who spend even four hours a day alone with God. This is one of our problems!" And I said, "What? Oh, uh, . . . yes, that's really too bad, isn't it?"

What would you do if you decided to spend four hours alone with God tomorrow morning? Could you do it? What would you do during the four hours? Have you heard about people praying all night, and wondered what they found to pray about?

"Gather of it every man according to his eating." A thoughtful hour alone with God—can you do that? What about half an hour? Or will the time be different according to the growth and maturity of your Christian life? Is it possible that the beginning baby Christian may not know what to do with five minutes alone with God? It is possible that the mature Christian won't be able to find time enough? "And the children of Israel . . . gathered, some more, some less" (verse 17). But even those who gathered less still gathered!

YESTERDAY'S MANNA

And they gathered it every morning, every man according to his eating: and when the sun waxed hot, it melted. Ex. 16:21.

The children of Israel followed the instructions of Moses, gathering of the manna, the bread from heaven, according to their personal needs. "And Moses said, Let no man leave of it till the morning." What can we learn here to guide us in establishing a meaningful devotional life?

May I propose that one of the reasons why people have a hard time in trying to live the Christian life is that they are trying to rely on something that happened yesterday for today? It doesn't work. The Christian life operates on the trolley-car principle, not the battery principle! We cannot store up religion.

Some of the Israelites who didn't heed Moses' instructions and left the manna until the following morning found that it "bred worms, and stank"! Is it possible to have a Christian experience like that?

Yesterday's experience is no good for today. Here is where so many people have gone astray. They have heard that a devotional life, a relationship with God, is important. They "try" it for a day or two, then skip a week, then try another day. On again, off again; on again, off again. They say, "It doesn't work." Of course it doesn't work! It is possible to have just enough religion to make you miserable but not enough for a meaningful relationship. The consistency of the daily contact and communion with God is extremely important. Jesus said, "If any man will come after me, let him deny himself, and take up his cross *daily*" (Luke 9:23).

So the people of Israel gathered the manna "every *morning*, every man according to his eating: and when the sun waxed hot, it melted." Have you ever depended for your devotional life upon a prayer at night just before you fell into bed? Many people have discovered that when they changed the time of their praying and study from the last thing at night to the first thing in the morning, it made a big difference, and also changed the content of their prayers from simply "God, forgive me for all my sins and failures of today," to real fellowship and communion with Heaven. Take time, alone, *at the beginning of every day,* to seek Jesus through His Word and through prayer.

MAKING NO PLANS FOR YOURSELF

It is not in man that walketh to direct his steps. Jer. 10:23.

Have you ever considered how much Jesus, in His life here on earth, depended on His relationship with His Father? "Christ in His life on earth made no plans for Himself. He accepted God's plan for Him, and day by day the Father unfolded His plans. So should we depend upon God, that our lives may be the simple outworking of His will. As we commit our ways to Him, He will direct our steps."—*The Ministry of Healing*, p. 479.

If Jesus got His plans on a day-by-day basis from His Father, it would have had to be the first thing in the morning! It would be ridiculous to picture Jesus coming to His Father at the close of the day and saying, "Now what are Your plans for Me today?" That wouldn't make sense.

Wouldn't you like to live so close to the Lord that He would be able to flash His plans to you individually for the day? This doesn't mean that you don't make plans. But it does mean that if you have made plans on your own, you are always willing to have your plans interrupted. *Steps to Christ*, page 70: "Consecrate yourself to God in the morning; make this your very first work. Let your prayer be, 'Take me, O Lord, as wholly Thine. I lay all my plans at Thy feet. Use me today in Thy service. Abide with me, and let all my work be wrought in Thee.' This is a daily matter. Each morning consecrate yourself to God for that day. Surrender all your plans to Him, to be carried out or given up as His providence shall indicate. Thus day by day you may be giving your life into the hands of God, and thus your life will be molded more and more after the life of Christ."

As we grow more and more into the likeness of Jesus, we will be more and more sensitive to what His plans are, so that the plans we make will more often be His plans instead of simply our own.

The devotional time isn't for the purpose of just getting our time in, just being able to say we've spent an hour with God. It is for the purpose of getting to know God, learning to trust Him, knowing His will, and accepting of His sacrifice for us again for the new day. Do you know God today? Will you seek to know Him tomorrow morning as well?

ONE TO ONE WITH GOD

My voice shalt thou hear in the morning, O Lord; in the morning will I direct my prayer unto thee, and will look up. Ps. 5:3.

May I share with you the one method that I have found far better than any other for a meaningful time of fellowship with Christ day by day? I have tried a lot of other methods, and I've found some good ones, but none of them has ever surpassed this one.

Take the book *The Desire of Ages,* on the life of Christ. Begin with a short prayer for the guidance and enlightenment of the Holy Spirit, and then choose one chapter. At the bottom of the first page of each chapter it says something like, "This chapter is based on Matthew so-and-so." Look up the Scripture passage and read it carefully. Then read the chapter.

As you read it, try to consider it as something more than a history lesson. You're not just thinking of Nicodemus, who lived 2,000 years ago; you're not just thinking of some leper from the distant past, or of the disciples away back there. Put yourself in the picture with Christ. Nicodemus—that's you. The leper—that's you. Peter being asked by Jesus, "Do you love Me?"—that's you. Get yourself into the picture, so that it's you and God. You aren't reading the chapters for information, but for communication. (That's why you can go back and start the book over when you've finished—you're reading for communication.)

When you've finished reading, and pondering what you have read, then pray about what you've read. You can say, "Lord, I read today about Nicodemus. I realize that that's me. I would much rather discuss religion than be born again. But, Lord, I need to be born again. I don't understand all about it, but please accomplish that for me today. Take my heart, my life." You can talk to Him about what you've read. This way, every morning you have something new to pray about, because you have read something new.

If you will take time, alone with God, beginning each day with Him in fellowship and communication, and if you stay with Him, regardless of what happens, you will find the rest and peace that Jesus promised when He said, "Come unto me, all ye that labour and are heavy laden, and I will give you rest."

THE FIGHT OF FAITH

So then faith cometh by hearing, and hearing by the word of God. Rom. 10:17.

If you fight the fight of faith with all your will power, you will conquer."—
Testimonies, vol. 5, p. 513. What is this fight of faith? Paul talks about it:
"Fight the *good* fight of faith. Lay hold on eternal life" (1 Tim. 6:12).

If you fight the fight of faith with all your willpower, you won't have
any willpower left over for anything else! If it is true that "every failure on
the part of the children of God is due to their lack of faith" (*Patriarchs and
Prophets,* p. 657), then where should we put our effort and attention?
Strangely enough, it isn't toward faith, either! No, it's toward the object of
faith, the source of faith, which is Jesus. This is why it is so important to
take time day by day for knowing Jesus.

Without spending time in communication, in fellowship, there will be
no faith, no trust. Faith is best defined as trusting God (*Gospel Workers,* p.
259). There is no such thing as building a relationship of trust without
spending time together. No one gets acquainted with anyone else without
time for communication.

Relationships cannot live without communication any more than we
can live physically without eating. My dad used to tell me about a man
who trained his horse not to eat. It was more economical that way.
Unfortunately, just when he got him trained, he died!

If I quit feeding my physical life, I may be able to go along for a while
on the basis of what I have already eaten. I might live for a while on stored-
up fat. But sooner or later I am going to fall in a little heap on the sidewalk, and that will be the end of it. And the person who has initially
become a Christian and who has experienced the beginning of spiritual life
may be able to go for a little while without taking time to feed his soul; but
sooner or later he is going to end up in a pitiful little heap on the spiritual
sidewalk. Only by continual eating of the Bread of Life and drinking of the
Water of Life will our spiritual lives be strong and healthy.

THE SOURCE OF JESUS' POWER

And in the morning, rising up a great while before day, he went out, and departed into a solitary place, and there prayed. Mark 1:35.

When we consider the importance of spending time in personal communion and fellowship with God, we have Jesus' own example during His life here on earth. Did He spend time alone with His Father? We are told that often the early-morning hours found Him on the mountainside alone with God.

"It was in hours of solitary prayer that Jesus in His earth life received wisdom and power. Let . . . [us] follow His example in finding at dawn and twilight a quiet season for communion with our Father in heaven."—*Education*, p. 259. "Daily beset by temptation, constantly opposed by the leaders of the people, Christ knew that He must strengthen His humanity by prayer. In order to be a blessing to men, He must commune with God. . . . Thus He showed His disciples where His strength lay. Without this daily communion with God, no human being can gain power."—*Counsels to Parents and Teachers*, p. 323. "From hours spent with God He came forth morning by morning, to bring the light of heaven to men."—*Christ's Object Lessons*, p. 139.

If Jesus needed this communication with His Father in order to live the life of faith, how much more do we need it? Genuine faith comes only through the relationship with God, studying His Word, and in prayer. "Faith cometh by hearing, and hearing by the word of God" (Rom. 10:17). Without the ongoing relationship with God, we will not grow in grace. The relationship with God is an absolute necessity.

I used to think that the way to be a Christian was to try hard to live a good life. Then, if I had any time left over, I was to read the Bible and pray a little bit. But in order to have an ongoing, vibrant, healthy Christian life, we must take time for fellowship with Christ. It's that simple. This is where we must put our effort. It is not an option in the Christian life, but the vital basis.

When we come to God initially and accept the offer of His righteousness in exchange for our sins, our spiritual life begins. With the daily renewing of our acceptance, with time spent daily in beholding Him, we keep the reality of our acceptance with Him, and spiritual life continues.

TRUST ONLY IN GOD

Blessed is that man that maketh the Lord his trust. Ps. 40:4.

I was having a Week of Prayer one time with a group of medical students. One question that was turned in asked, "Could you please tell us how to live the Christian life in a practical, down-to-earth way? Not this Bible-study-and-prayer-and-witnessing bit, but instead give us something that's really practical."

Bible study is compared in Scripture to the eating of the Bread of Life, drinking the Water of Life. Prayer is called the breath of the soul. And witnessing is compared to exercise. So we could rephrase the question by saying, "Doctor, could you please tell us how to live a healthy physical life? Don't give us this eating-drinking-breathing-and-exercise bit, but something really practical!"

It's easy for us to miss it, because it is so simple. There is no substitute for private communication with God day by day. Family worship is significant, public worship is significant. But we must also have time alone with God for feeding our own souls.

One time a fellow minister told me that he felt that the average layman was so busy making a living, keeping body and soul together, that he could not be expected to take time alone with God, that the minister would have to do this for him, and would have to pass on what he had gained. Do you accept that? I could not.

I'd like to propose that one of our biggest problems in the Christian religion today is that people are constantly depending on people. It's nice to have people around that are on the same wavelength, the same frequency. But my relationship with Christ should never be dependent upon who is in town and who isn't. I cannot depend on other people to do my thinking and my studying and my praying for me. I must do it for myself.

The devotional life is not something that we rope off, locking God in a box, leaving Him and going on without Him the rest of the day. The focus of the devotional life day by day is to help me establish the practice of the presence of God all day long. To know God's presence moment by moment, hour by hour, throughout the day, is our goal, and His.

LOST AND FOUND

But they, supposing him to have been in the company, went a day's journey. Luke 2:44.

Jesus was 12 years old the first time His parents took Him along with them to the yearly Passover feast. When they returned from Jerusalem, Jesus stayed behind. Joseph and Mary didn't know it. Supposing Him to be in the company, they went a day's journey without Him. But when night came on, they noticed that He was not there. They sought for Him among their kinfolk and acquaintances. But when they found Him not, they returned to Jerusalem, still seeking Him. On the third day they found Him in the Temple, sitting in the midst of the doctors and teachers of the law, both hearing them and asking them questions. "And when they saw him, they were amazed: and his mother said unto him, Son, why hast thou thus dealt with us? behold, thy father and I have sought thee sorrowing. And he said unto them, How is it that ye sought me? wist ye not that I must be about my Father's business?" (Luke 2:48, 49).

There is a tremendous lesson for us in this story. It's possible to lose Jesus and not know it. *The Desire of Ages,* page 83: "In our association with one another, we should take heed lest we forget Jesus, and pass along unmindful that He is not with us. When we become absorbed in worldly things so that we have no thought for Him in whom our hope of eternal life is centered, we separate ourselves from Jesus and from the heavenly angels. These holy beings cannot remain where the Saviour's presence is not desired, and His absence is not marked. This is why discouragement so often exists among the professed followers of Christ."

It is possible today to lose Jesus in *one* day, supposing Him to be in the company. When it began to get dark, Joseph and Mary discovered their loss. Then they began to seek for Him among the kinfolk. But they couldn't find Him. Finally they headed back to Jerusalem, and found Him where they had lost Him. That's where you always find Jesus— where you last saw Him. Go back to where you separated from Him.

It's wonderful to have friends and relatives who know Jesus. But don't depend on *their* relationship with Him. You must seek Him for yourself. We can stay with Him only through personal fellowship with Him day by day.

LOST THROUGH NEGLECT

How shall we escape, if we neglect so great salvation? Heb. 2:3.

If Joseph and Mary had stayed their minds upon God by meditation and prayer they . . . would not have lost sight of Jesus. By one day's neglect they lost the Saviour; but it cost them three days of anxious search to find Him. So with us; . . . we may in one day lose the Saviour's presence, and it may take many days of sorrowful search to find Him, and regain the peace that we have lost."—*The Desire of Ages,* p. 83.

When we have lost sight of Jesus, the devil has a way of working to keep us from finding Him again, doesn't he? When my attention is away from Jesus, Satan comes in with his big guns blazing, and I fall and fail and sin. Then he says, "Well, now, God is probably mad at you. You'd better behave yourself for a couple of weeks, while you give Him a chance to cool off, before you try coming back again." After 10 days he hits me again, and I fall once more. Then he insists I have to wait another two weeks! This kind of waiting can go on and on. We can have the experience of losing Jesus at camp meeting, supposing Him to be in the company, and taking a whole year to find Him again. Why? Because He's lost? No, because of neglect on our part.

"Many attend religious services, and are refreshed and comforted by the word of God; but through neglect of meditation, watchfulness, and prayer, they lose the blessing, and find themselves more destitute than before they received it."—*Ibid.*

Have you ever observed a reformation that was followed by a deeper apostasy? Have you ever seen a revival on a campus or in a church, and discovered after it was over that things were worse than before it came? What is the problem? Neglect of meditation, watchfulness, and prayer.

Had Joseph and Mary done as Jesus did, and been about *their* Father's business, they would not have lost sight of Jesus. That was their business. And that's my business today—to stay close to Jesus.

The principle involved in salvation by faith is the trolley-car principle, not the battery principle. There is power no longer than there is connection with the line above. None are living Christians unless they have a daily experience in the things of God.

111

SAVED FOR FELLOWSHIP

I will dwell in them, and walk in them; and I will be their God, and they shall be my people. 2 Cor. 6:16.

There are those who say that our salvation is totally dependent upon the work of Christ, and that when we come to Jesus initially, we are just as saved as we will ever be. This is true. The thief on the cross was just as saved the day he came to Christ as he would have been 40 years from then, had he lived. But he had the advantage of dying right away, which most of us haven't had!

But although our salvation is based upon the work of Christ, none of us are saved any longer than we continue an ongoing relationship with Christ. "Sinful man can find hope and righteousness only in God; and no human being is righteous any longer than he has faith in God and maintains a vital connection with Him."—*Testimonies to Ministers*, p. 367.

It was the entrance of sin into the world that made our salvation a necessity. And what was sin? Sin was a broken relationship, separation from God. No longer could God walk with man in the cool of the day, no longer could He communicate with us face to face. It was to restore this broken communion that Jesus came to live and die for us. Through Jesus we are restored to fellowship with the Father. The purpose of salvation is not just that we can live eternally, free from sorrow, in the mansions prepared for us in heaven. The purpose of salvation is to restore us to the fellowship with God that was severed when sin came.

We are not saved by the devotional life. We are saved by our initial, *and* continuing, acceptance of Christ's sacrifice in our behalf, by coming to Him day by day. But for what are we saved? We are saved to be the friends of God that we were created to be, saved for fellowship and communion and relationship with Him.

This fellowship with Him gives us assurance of eternal life. Through this friendship with Christ, through beholding Him, He is also able to work the change in our lives that will bring us into harmony with Himself. Through the relationship with Christ comes victory, power for obedience, faith, the fruits of the Spirit, and empowering for service to others.

FELLOWSHIP IN SPITE OF FAILURE

That which we have seen and heard declare we unto you, that ye also may have fellowship with us: and truly our fellowship is with the Father, and with his Son Jesus Christ. 1 John 1:3.

John was known as one of the sons of thunder. For three years he walked with Jesus, personally. He knew what it was like to eat with Him, to travel with Him, to touch Him, to help Him with His necessities. And for three years John bickered and argued with the other disciples about who was going to be the greatest. For three years he still remained a son of thunder. For those who think that conversion and walking in fellowship with Jesus always changes one overnight, and if it doesn't happen, one doesn't have a genuine experience, consider James and John and the other disciples.

They fought and argued right up to the end of their time with Jesus—in the upper room they were still bickering about who was going to be the greatest. They didn't "slip" into arguing! They spent hours walking along the road, debating the subject. And they were so aware of what they were doing that they lagged behind Jesus, and He would end up in town a quarter of a mile ahead of them!

And when they finally caught up to Him, He would ask, "What were you talking about?"

And they would change the subject. They were embarrassed to admit what they had been doing, but they didn't stop doing it.

Jesus treated them kindly, tenderly, and John continued to walk with Jesus even after Jesus left. Years later he wrote it down, "Truly our fellowship is with the Father, and with his Son Jesus Christ." He was speaking in the present tense.

As John had continued his walk with Jesus, continued to commune with Him day by day, he had been transformed. Now, instead of asking "Who's the greatest?" and seeking the highest place, he said, "Beloved, let us love one another, for love is of God."

The purpose of the devotional life is to come into fellowship with Jesus. The purpose of walking, talking, and communion with Him is for fellowship. And ultimately, through this fellowship, we will become like Him.

LOOKING TO JESUS

Look unto me, and be ye saved, all the ends of the earth: for I am God, and there is none else. Isa. 45:22.

In all our devotional experience, the need is to study for the purpose of communication or fellowship with Jesus. Time alone at the beginning of every day *to seek Jesus* is the goal.

If I am seeking fellowship with Jesus, am I going to spend more time studying the four Gospels or some point of history or prophecy? If I'm seeking fellowship with Jesus, would I choose a volume of rebuke and reproof or *The Desire of Ages*? Let's make a distinction here. There are many people who have turned away from Ellen G. White and her writings because someone has majored in what we might call the instructional writings. There are entire books that are primarily for the purpose of instruction, counsel, reproof.

There are other books that we might call inspirational writings. This doesn't mean that you can't find some instruction in the inspirational, and some inspiration in the instructional. But there are these two general types of writings.

A person who studies only in the instructional often becomes the type of person who goes around with a special testimony for his neighbor across the aisle. He has a reproof and rebuke for every occasion. Please don't misunderstand when we say that *Testimonies to the Church* can be a dangerous weapon in the hands of someone who does not know how to read *The Desire of Ages* and *Steps to Christ*. If a person doesn't know how to sit with Mary at the feet of Jesus, and know personally His love and kindness, he can use the Ten Commandments as a lethal weapon. The law and the gospel must go together.

The study of the instructional writings has its place. But for the time of relationship with Jesus day by day, in order to become close friends with Him, we must study His life. "It would be well for us to spend a thoughtful hour each day in contemplation of the life of Christ. We should take it point by point, and let the imagination grasp each scene, especially the closing ones. As we thus dwell upon His great sacrifice for us, our confidence in Him will be more constant, our love will be quickened, and we shall be more deeply imbued with His spirit."—*The Desire of Ages*, p. 83. It is by looking to Jesus, uplifting Jesus, that we are changed into His image.

CONNECTION WITH HEAVEN

And Jesus said unto him, No man, having put his hand to the plough, and looking back, is fit for the kingdom of God. Luke 9:62.

Those who will put on the whole armor of God and devote some time every day to meditation and prayer and the study of the Scriptures will be connected with heaven and will have a saving, transforming influence upon those around them."—*Testimonies*, vol. 5, p. 112.

"Those who will put on the whole armor of God." Have you read about the armor in Ephesians? Every facet of the armor has to do with the elements of a personal devotional life. Word of God, prayer, sword of the Spirit. Every one of them has to do with the things concerning the fight of faith. So if we will devote some time every day to prayer, meditation, and Bible study, we will be connected with heaven.

I have heard people say, "I've tried that. It doesn't work. I wasn't connected with heaven. Nothing happened to me."

And I reply, "How long did you try?"

"Three days."

The only conclusion that I can come to is that if we determine that from now on, we are going to spend quiet time alone with God every day for the purpose of getting acquainted with Jesus and keep in touch with Him all through the day, and if we continue to seek this fellowship until Jesus comes, we will be connected with heaven.

The person who does not stay with seeking God on a continuing basis is not going to be connected with heaven. Our sole purpose in the devotional life is to seek Jesus. We seek Him through His Word and through prayer, and we choose what material we read with this goal of seeking Jesus in mind.

This involves commitment. It involves effort. At times there is a spontaneous desire to seek Jesus. At other times, it requires a struggle. But it is only as we make this commitment, as we make this effort, and daily seek Him, that we are connected with heaven, that our spiritual lives are really alive, and that the fruits of the Spirit are developed in us. "If the eye is kept fixed on Christ, the work of the Spirit ceases not until the soul is conformed to His image."—*The Desire of Ages*, p. 302.

TALK ABOUT GOD

Jesus answered, Verily, verily, I say unto thee, Except a man be born of water and of the Spirit, he cannot enter into the kingdom of God. John 3:5.

There was a man of the Pharisees named Nicodemus, a ruler of the Jews. The same came to Jesus by night and said unto Him, "Rabbi, you're a great teacher. You are a great miracle worker. Let's discuss something." Nicodemus came to Jesus with the idea in mind of entering into a discussion with Him. In so doing, he identified himself immediately as a potential pseudointellectual—one who uses the Bible and religious topics primarily as a launching pad for discussion.

It is possible to keep God at an arm's length by talking *about* Him. There are people who are looking for a method of forgetting God that will pass as a method of remembering Him (*The Great Controversy*, p. 572). You can be a church member in good and regular standing, and yet be running from God through the pseudointellectual escape.

So Nicodemus came and said, "Let's have a discussion—let's dialogue."

And Jesus said, "What you need is to be born again."

Jesus allowed Nicodemus to lead the conversation wherever he chose, but whenever Nicodemus paused for breath, Jesus brought it back to the real issue: "You need to be born again."

"Except a man be born again, he cannot see the kingdom of God." Since the new birth, or conversion, gives us a new capacity for knowing God that we didn't even have before, it is only after the new birth that the relationship with God can really begin. Before that time we find the Bible uninteresting, except as a basis for information. But when God has done His converting work through the Holy Spirit, then we will find meaning in studying the Bible for communication with Him.

An understanding of Bible truth depends not so much on the power of intellect brought to the search as upon the earnest longing after righteousness. But who longs after righteousness? It would have to be the converted person. No one is going to long after righteousness unless he has been born again. Paul says the carnal mind is at enmity against God. So the new birth precedes a meaningful devotional life.

YOU CAN'T CONVERT YOURSELF

Marvel not that I said unto thee, Ye must be born again. John 3:7.

Anyone knows that if you want to go to sleep, there are a couple of things you need to do. You have to put your back against the mattress, as a rule (although I went to sleep one time working on a combine harvester). You should turn out the lights. You can turn your radio down to nothing, instead of 40 decibels. And it helps to close your eyes! When my daughter was small, I got into the bad habit of lying down with her until she went to sleep. The situation came to the place where she wouldn't go to sleep until I would lie down with her. Sometimes I would have some place to go, and I'd look out the corner of my eye and say, "LuAnn, close your eyes." She would, but the next time I checked, they would be wide open again. I knew this one thing: if I could at least get her to close her eyes, it would surely help!

In order to have a meaningful relationship with Christ, in order to find value in spiritual things, you have to come to the experience of being born again. You cannot convert yourself. But you *can* place yourself in the atmosphere where it can happen. You don't have to sit and wait forever for something to hit you. If you are running from God, and find at the same time that deep inside you want to come into the right relationship with Him, you can at least place yourself in a religious atmosphere where the things of God are being presented.

If you are a student on a campus and realize that you are unconverted, instead of skipping every meeting or trying to sleep or read your way through, you can at least go and listen when the gospel is preached.

If you have found that the Bible is a dull book to you, and have left it to gather dust on the shelf year after year, you could at least take a few minutes each day to consider deliberately some passage on the life of Jesus, inviting God to meet you where you are and do His work in reaching your heart.

The responsibility for meaningful communication with God has to be *His*, not ours. But we can *come* to Him. We can place ourselves in the atmosphere where He can get through to us most easily, and then invite Him to work His miracle of regeneration in our lives.

DON'T GIVE UP

I press toward the mark for the prize of the high calling of God in Christ Jesus. Phil. 3:14.

Sam was a college student. He had worked for quite a while to save enough money to be able to go to school. At first he had been so excited about finally being able to start preparation for his lifework that his studies had come easily. But as the weeks went by, it seemed that the teachers piled on more and more work. He became involved in more social activities. He started cutting down on his sleep to keep up, and one evening a terrible thing happened.

He was trying to study for a quiz the next day when he began to grow sleepy. He yawned, stretched, and finally arose from his desk and splashed cold water on his face in order to stay awake. He started the chapter over again. But the next thing he knew he was remembering how delighted a certain friend of his from the opposite side of campus had seemed when she accepted his invitation to the weekend program.

Sam was horrified. How could he benefit from studying when his mind wandered or when he was half asleep? He *had* wanted to become a lawyer. But what could he do? Sadly he checked out of school and returned home.

"We thought you were going to college," everyone said when they saw him back at his old job.

"Well, I tried it," Sam replied. "But my studies weren't interesting to me. I would get sleepy, and my mind wandered when I tried to study. Since I wasn't getting anything out of it anyway, I quit and came back home."

What happens when you are reading the Bible and your mind begins to wander or you get sleepy? Do you do as Sam did, and quit? Do you put the Bible back on the shelf for another six months? Or do you do as Sam should have done, and keep at it?

Probably very few people have actually quit school because their minds wandered when they tried to study. And yet many have quit trying to have a relationship with God on that basis. It doesn't make sense, does it? We should be willing to put at least as much effort into something that has to do with all eternity as we are into those things that have to do only with our threescore years and ten.

THE PRAYER OF HUMILITY

Humble yourselves in the sight of the Lord, and he shall lift you up. James 4:10.

Anybody knows that in order to get acquainted or *stay* acquainted with someone else, you have to talk to that person. That's what prayer is all about. If the entire basis of the Christian life is a relationship, then prayer is an absolute necessity. There is no substitute, there is no alternative. For a blind man, there might have to be some alternative to reading the Bible—but there is no alternative for prayer.

How can this communication with God through prayer become meaningful? We are told that "nothing is more essential to communion with God than the most profound humility" (*Testimonies*, vol. 5, p. 50). Consider the story of the Pharisee and the publican, recorded in Luke 18:11: "The Pharisee stood and prayed thus *with himself*, God, I thank thee, that I am not as other men are . . ." And he went on to list his good behavior. Now in what sense was he not like other men? Externally or internally? It would have to be outward actions he was referring to. But the publican, "standing afar off, would not lift up so much as his eyes unto heaven, but smote upon his breast, saying, God be merciful to me a sinner." And the publican went down to his house justified, rather than the other.

The Pharisee could, by his own strong willpower, make his outward life correct. But his heart remained unchanged. It is only those who, with the publican, recognize their inability to do anything toward making themselves right with God, except to come to Him and admit their desperate need of His grace, that are justified.

It is more than just a matter of saying the right words. "The lips may express a poverty of soul that the heart does not acknowledge. While speaking to God of poverty of spirit, the heart may be swelling with the conceit of its own superior humility and exalted righteousness. In one way only can a true knowledge of self be obtained. We must behold Christ. It is ignorance of Him that makes men so uplifted in their own righteousness."—*Christ's Object Lessons*, p. 159. If we desire communion with God, we can contemplate Christ and invite His Spirit to bring us to that humility essential for communion with Him.

GOD ANSWERS SINNERS' PRAYERS | APR 23

And the publican, standing afar off, would not lift up so much as his eyes unto heaven, but smote upon his breast, saying, God be merciful to me a sinner. Luke 18:13.

In Luke 18:13 the publican says, "God be merciful to me a sinner." But in John 9:31, in the story of the man who was blind from birth, we read, "God heareth not sinners." And Psalm 66:18 says that if we regard iniquity in our hearts the Lord will not hear us.

Suppose you happen to be one who is regarding iniquity in your heart. How are you going to get rid of that iniquity? Any ideas? You can't do it by yourself. The only way that anyone can get rid of iniquity is by coming to God, through prayer. If He won't hear me until I get rid of the iniquity, but I can't get rid of the iniquity without His help, then I'm stuck! Have you ever pondered this?

What was the context of "God heareth not sinners"? It was a healing—the performing of a miracle.

If I am regarding iniquity in my heart, the Lord may not hear me for special prayers for healing or miracles or all kinds of other special blessings. But He would have to be willing to hear me for my prayer to find power to stop regarding iniquity in my heart, wouldn't He? He'd have to hear me on that. At least that! Yet there are people who feel that their prayers aren't going any higher than their heads because they feel that they aren't perfect yet, that they are still falling and failing.

Read the story about the man with leprosy who was cleansed. It shows that God *always* hears sinners when sinners cry out to Him for deliverance and forgiveness from sin. It may not always be God's will to do some things we ask, but it is always God's will to "cleanse us from sin, to make us His children, and to enable us to live a holy life" (*The Desire of Ages*, p. 266).

Don't let the devil keep you away from the prayer-communion with God because of your faults and failings. Any sinner, regardless of how far he has wandered from God—whether he is near to the Father's house or still in the pigpen—is offered help. Whoever cries out to God for forgiveness and for the power of God to deal with the iniquity that he has been regarding in his heart is *always* going to be heard.

120

TALKING FOR THE SAKE OF TALKING

And the Lord spake unto Moses face to face, as a man speaketh unto his friend. Ex. 33:11.

Think for a few minutes today about one of your close friends whose companionship you enjoy, and with whom you are able to visit on a regular basis. How long has it been since you talked to this person for as much as 10 minutes at a stretch, without asking them to give you anything or to do anything for you? What did you talk about? Most people would probably have little trouble talking to one of their best friends for longs periods of time without asking them for anything.

But how about God? How long has it been since you talked to Him for 10 minutes and neither asked Him to give you anything nor asked Him to do anything for you?

If the primary purpose of the Christian life is for relationship with God, then the primary purpose of prayer is for communication. Yet how many Christians consider prayer as primarily a medium through which to get things—primarily for the purpose of getting answers. In fact, there are some who have wondered whether or not they are even Christians, on the basis of whether or not they received the answers they were seeking.

We understand in our human relationships that the primary purpose for our talking is not to get something from the other person, but rather just talking for the sake of talking—talking because we enjoy the other person's company.

While those who are close to us are often willing to *do* many things for us, and while we certainly hope that if we were to offend one of our earthly friends and ask their forgiveness, they would grant it, yet seeking these services from them is never the *basis* of any really lasting relationship. But how often in our attempts to communicate with God we limit our communication to requests for His help, and miss the blessing of talking to Him just for the joy of talking to One who loves and understands us and is interested in whatever we are anxious to share.

If your communication with God has been primarily on a "give me or forgive me" basis, try setting aside 10 minutes today to talk to Him without asking Him for anything at all. You may discover a whole new dimension to praying that you have missed before.

WAITING ON THE LORD

Wait on the Lord: be of good courage, and he shall strengthen thine heart: wait, I say, on the Lord. Ps. 27:14.

One of the greatest secrets that have helped some of us to a more meaningful prayer life is simply to stop being in such a hurry! God communicates with us in two ways. He speaks to us through His Word, but He also speaks to us through prayer. God has a way of guiding your thoughts, of bringing ideas or convictions to your mind, if you are willing to wait before Him to give Him a chance to do this. The sum of prayer is not to rush into His presence, say what we have on our minds, and then hurry away. "Many, even in their seasons of devotion, fail of receiving the blessing of real communion with God. They are in too great haste. With hurried steps they press through the circle of Christ's loving presence, pausing perhaps a moment within the sacred precincts, but *not waiting for counsel.* They have no time to remain with the divine Teacher. With their burdens they return to their work. . . . Not a pause for a moment in His presence, but personal contact with Christ, . . . this is our need."—*Education,* pp. 260, 261. (Italics supplied.)

When you have finished talking to God about what you have read in your time of devotions, and have presented your requests and petitions, and have finished your speech, stay there. Don't jump up and rush off to work or to class. Stay in His presence. Keep your mind open for the messages the Holy Spirit may be trying to bring you. Listen. Allow God an opportunity to bring thoughts to your mind that you may need for the day ahead. Give Him a chance to remind you of things that you might have otherwise forgotten. Allow Him to communicate to you directly, by giving Him a few quiet moments to get your attention focused on the things He sees that you need to consider.

To try to describe this concept is sometimes a little awkward, but I believe that it happens, and that if we would stay on our knees after we have finished saying our little speeches, we would discover that God can communicate with us in two ways, much more than we often allow Him to do. "Through sincere prayer we are brought into connection with the mind of the Infinite."—*Steps to Christ,* p. 97.

BELIEVING THAT GOD *IS*

The righteous shall be glad in the Lord, and shall trust in him. Ps. 64:10.

Have you ever been afraid to admit to God that you were angry with Him? or that you didn't understand His dealings with you? or that you weren't at all sure that He was going to do for you that which you were asking Him to do?

There's a big difference between having faith that God is going to answer your prayers according to your understanding, and believing in *God.* "He that cometh to God must believe that he *is,* and that he is a rewarder of them that diligently *seek him*" (Heb. 11:6). If we believe that God *is,* and that He will reward our seeking of *Him,* we have faith. We do *not* have to believe that He will reward our seeking of *things* in the exact way that we have asked. Faith is much more than positive thinking. "When we do not receive the very things we asked for, at the time we ask, we are still to believe that the Lord *hears* and that He will answer our prayers. We are so erring and shortsighted that we sometimes ask for things that would not be a blessing to us, and our heavenly Father in love answers our prayers by giving us that which will be for our highest good—that which we ourselves would desire if with vision divinely enlightened we could see all things as they really are."—*Steps to Christ,* p. 96. (Italics supplied.)

Consider the prayer of Moses recorded in Exodus 5:23. He had come at God's command to free the people of Israel from Egypt. He had done as God had instructed in dealing with Pharaoh. And instead of letting the people of Israel go, as Moses had expected, Pharaoh had increased their burdens. Moses' prayers for the deliverance of the people seemed unanswered. He went to God saying, "Since I came to Pharaoh to speak in thy name, he hath done evil to this people; neither hast thou delivered thy people *at all*"! Moses didn't understand God's plan—and apparently wasn't too happy with the results right then—but he still believed in *God,* and continued to communicate with Him, telling God how he felt. His faith was evidenced, not because of some pious words, but by continuing to come to God, regardless of what answers he received.

123

PERSISTENCE IN PRAYER

And behold, a woman of Canaan . . . cried unto him, saying, Have mercy on me, O Lord. Matt. 15:22.

Jesus apparently didn't even notice the woman who was following Him. He did not respond to her cries, and finally the disciples asked Him to get rid of her, because she was bothering *them*. When He finally spoke to her, He told her that His help wasn't for her, and when she persisted in her request, He made reference to dogs. But she continued to plead, and her request was granted.

You see a widow, penniless, ragged, and alone. She comes repeatedly before a judge who could relieve her distress in a moment if he would choose to do so. But he refuses. She comes before him again and again to urge her request. Finally, he grants her the help she needs.

Why are these stories in the Scriptures? We are told that "perseverance in prayer has been made a condition of receiving" (*Steps to Christ*, p. 97), but *why*? Is God unwilling to come to our rescue? Does He have to be talked into helping us?

In both of these examples, God is revealed *by contrast*, not by comparison. The Syrophoenician woman was treated by Jesus in the way that the Jews would have treated her. He desired to awaken sympathy for her in the hearts of His disciples, although at the same time the disciples were much more in sympathy with the feelings of the Jews for "outsiders," and almost missed the point. But the woman, who saw the compassion of Jesus that He could not hide, continued to press her petitions until she was rewarded.

The unjust judge is also a reverse example of how God deals with us. God is more willing to give good gifts to us than we are to give them to our own children. He points to the unjust judge and shows that if even an unjust man can be won over by persistence, *how much more* surely will He, who wants to help us from the start, respond to our cries.

How do we obtain this persistence? "It was Christ Himself who put into that mother's heart the persistence which would not be repulsed. It was Christ who gave the pleading widow courage and determination before the judge. . . . And the confidence which He Himself had implanted, He did not fail to reward."—*Christ's Object Lessons*, p. 175.

SATAN'S PRAYER TRAP

Then they cried unto the Lord in their trouble, and he delivered them out of their distresses. Ps. 107:6.

If it is true that the relationship with Jesus is the entire basis of the Christian life, and that prayer, direct communication with God, is vital to that relationship, then it stands to reason that Satan will do everything in his power to prevent us from seeking God through prayer.

One of his most effective traps has always been to entice us to sin. He causes us to fall and fail, and then tells us that it's hopeless, that there is no point in seeking God any longer. Satan is much more interested in the use he can make of our bad behavior to cause us to break off our relationship with God, than he is in any of the bad things we do in themselves.

When we really believe that there is nothing we can do of ourselves to commend ourselves to God, nothing we can do to earn or merit God's salvation, then we will continue to seek the faith relationship with God, regardless of what happens in terms of our falling and failing and sinning. "When we feel that we have sinned and cannot pray, it is then the time to pray. Ashamed we may be and deeply humbled, but we must pray and believe."—*Thoughts From the Mount of Blessing*, p. 115.

There is power in prayer. It is only through prayer and communion with God that we will ever have strength to overcome the devices of Satan. The more we understand the importance of prayer, the more we will pray. We have been promised that "not one sincere prayer is lost. Amid the anthems of the celestial choir, God hears the cries of the weakest human being. We pour out our heart's desire in our closets, we breathe a prayer as we walk by the way, and our words reach the throne of the Monarch of the universe. They may be inaudible to any human ear, but they cannot die away into silence, nor can they be lost through the activities of business that are going on. Nothing can drown the soul's desire. It rises above the din of the street, above the confusion of the multitude, to the heavenly courts. It is God to whom we are speaking, and our prayer is heard."—*Christ's Object Lessons*, p. 174.

WE PRAY BECAUSE WE LOVE

Which of you shall have a friend, and shall go unto him at midnight, and say unto him, Friend, lend me three loaves; for a friend of mine in his journey is come to me, and I have nothing to set before him? Luke 11:5, 6.

The subject of intercessory prayer can raise many questions in the minds of those who are seeking a relationship with God. What place in our Christian life does praying for others have? What value is it? What results from it? The parable of the one seeking loaves at midnight gives some insights into these questions.

Notice, first of all, that *we* have nothing to set before those in need. We must go to some other source for our supply. If we are to minister to others we must ourselves go to our Friend, who is the Bread of Life, to gain that which is needed to share with others. And if we are concerned for the welfare of those around us, we will not mind the inconvenience involved in ministering to their needs. Even though it was midnight, the one in the parable was willing to go to find the help required. He was willing to persist in seeking until the help was granted.

The question is sometimes asked, How long shall we continue praying for our loved ones? When should we give up? I would like to propose that this is a question that love never asks! When we pray for those we love, we keep on praying because we cannot help praying. When John Knox prayed "Give me Scotland, or I die," he prayed because he loved Scotland, and true love *must* pray. When Moses continued to plead for Israel, even when God tried him by suggesting that He destroy them and start anew with Moses to build a nation, it was because his love for Israel was so great that he could not do otherwise. And Moses was but an example of the love that Jesus, our Intercessor, has for each of us.

Perhaps the greatest promise of this parable is the surety of God's response. The one who prays is given "as much as he needeth." "Never will one be told, I cannot help you. Those who beg at midnight for loaves to feed the hungry souls will be successful."—*Christ's Object Lessons*, p. 148. Prayer for others brings results! And our own relationship with God deepens as we join Him in reaching out to the ones for whom He gave His life.

GIVING IS LIVING

For whosoever will save his life shall lose it; but whosoever shall lose his life for my sake and the gospel's, the same shall save it. Mark 8:35.

When a person has begun a relationship with God, there springs up in his heart a spontaneous desire to share the love of God with others. "No sooner does one come to Christ than there is born in his heart a desire to make known to others what a precious friend he has found in Jesus."—*Steps to Christ*, p. 78.

The area of Christian witness is the third vital ingredient for a relationship with Christ. We talk to Him, we listen to Him talk to us, and we go places and do things with Him—that's Christian service. It is by working together, doing things together, traveling together, that we become better acquainted with others. This is also true of our friendship with Christ. As we work with Him, we enter more into sympathy with Him. "And the effort to bless others will react in blessings upon ourselves. This was the purpose of God in giving us a part to act in the plan of redemption."—*Ibid.*, p. 79.

In the physical world, if we eat and drink but never exercise, we will lose our power to act; similarly, the Christian who will not exercise his God-given powers not only fails to grow up in Christ but loses the strength he already has.

When someone who has begun a relationship with God and found meaning for a time later finds everything going sour, in nine cases out of ten the reason is lack of involvement in outreach and service for others.

God is constantly giving. His giving is the power that keeps the universe in existence. His watchcare and love for each of us have been unceasing. We cannot behold Him and become like Him, unless we, too, become involved in giving to others as we receive from Him. If we refuse to unite with Christ in service, we are in reality refusing further relationship with Him. And the relationship that we have already had will die away or become a mere form. As we talk of Jesus and share His love with those around us, our own love for Him will deepen, and our relationship with Him will continue to grow.

WHY THINGS GET WORSE

Though he slay me, yet will I trust in him. Job 13:15.

When the day came for the heavenly beings to appear before the Lord, Satan was there among them. The Lord asked him, 'What have you been doing?' Satan answered, 'I have been walking here and there, roaming around the earth.' 'Did you notice my servant Job?' the Lord asked. 'There is no one on the earth as faithful and good as he is. He worships me and is careful not to do anything evil.'

"Satan replied, 'Would Job worship you if he got nothing out of it? You have always protected him and his family and everything he owns. You bless everything he does, and you have given him enough cattle to fill the whole country. But now suppose you take away everything he has—he will curse you to your face!'

"'All right,' the Lord said to Satan, 'everything he has is in your power, but you must not hurt Job himself.' So Satan left" (Job 1:6-12, TEV).

Why is it that people often discover things going worse when they are seeking God more? When a person begins a meaningful devotional life day by day with God, he may find that everything goes wrong.

Now, of course, that makes sense from the devil's viewpoint; he knows that the communion with God is where the power is. Of course he will do everything he can do to discourage the person who is seeking that communion. But the question that perplexes us is, Where is God? Isn't He big enough to keep this sort of thing from happening?

This question has a fascinating answer, recorded in the book of Job. Don't look at Job's story as just a history lesson. It has practical application to us today. In the life of every person, in one way or another, the experience of Job is repeated. Satan knows that if he can just get us to break from our dependence upon God, his success is certain. If he can cause things to go wrong and thereby get us to scrap the whole business of seeking God, then not only has he succeeded in his aim to separate us from communion with Him but he also has proved that we were seeking God only for selfish reasons in the first place. Our only safety lies in determining to continue seeking God, regardless of what happens in our lives. If we do this, Satan's plans will be defeated.

THE DEVIL AND MRS. JOB

The Lord gave, and the Lord hath taken away; blessed be the name of the Lord. Job 1:21.

Satan was sure that the only reason Job was serving God was because of God's protection and blessing. God saw fit to give Satan permission to try to prove his point. He hurried from the presence of the Lord and destroyed all of Job's property.

Job misunderstood. He thought it was God who had taken away everything that he had. But in spite of his misunderstanding, he still maintained his trust in God. Satan secured permission to afflict Job further, by bringing pain and sickness to him. But still Job maintained his integrity.

Mrs. Job, however, did not. Job lost everything he had except his wife, and perhaps she should have been the first to go! But the devil knew that she would be a useful tool in his hands. As soon as he got Mrs. Job, he must have smiled, and reminded his evil angels that if they kept at it, they would surely get Job as well.

Satan doesn't care what he causes us to do or not do, as long as we are self-centered. Often he gloats not so much over what we do wrong as over what we *don't* do wrong through our *own* strength. He evidently arbitrarily chooses to leave some people in luxury while he pushes others into the gutter. He gets just as much mileage out of a Pharisee as out of a demoniac. A person can be just as lost while glorying in his successes as while wallowing in his failures. The one thing that causes Satan deep concern is when a person chooses to come into fellowship and communion with God, for he knows that that is what will vanquish him.

When a person becomes interested in knowing God, Satan shakes his fist at God and makes the same charge he did with Job. Sometimes the Lord sees fit to allow him to try us—to prove whether or not our seeking of Him is prompted by selfish motives, or whether we will love and trust God regardless of circumstances. This is the reason why things often seem to go worse, for a time, when we begin to seek a meaningful relationship with God. If we understand this, we will continue our communication with God, continue to trust Him no matter what happens, and then Satan is defeated.

JOB, PART II

Put on the whole armour of God, that ye may be able to stand against the wiles of the devil. Eph. 6:11.

Often a person who begins a relationship with God will find that things go worse, for a time, than they did before he began. And he wonders what is wrong. We can learn from the experience of Job that Satan is the one responsible, and that God permits him to work his will for a while in order to prove to God, to Satan, and to ourselves whether or not Satan's charge that we are seeking God for selfish reasons is correct.

Satan says to God, "You see that person there, seeking You? He's only interested in himself. He wants to get to heaven, and get over his problems, and he wants that peace that he hears others talk about. He wants victory over his sins, and to get rid of his ulcers. He's not seeking You because he loves You—he's seeking You because of what he can get from You." It's the same charge the devil made against Job.

Satan comes at us with all guns blazing. It's Job, Part II. All four tires go flat on the car on the same day. There's physical trouble. Perhaps you live a worse life than before. Suddenly you fail over things you thought you had the victory over long ago. What do you do? Do you say, "This relationship with God doesn't work—tomorrow morning I'll sleep in"?

So the next morning you *do* sleep in. Guess what happens? You have a good day. The air goes back into the tires! Your troubles seem to be over. At the end of the day you congratulate yourself on what a fine life you lived that day. And the devil and his angels have a laugh-in. They don't care what you do or don't do as long as they can keep you from your knees.

Well, you would think that when this happens, the devil would be smart enough to leave it at that. And he does, for a short time. He may leave us alone for a couple of weeks, even though he has us because we're not seeking God. But then he comes and brings trouble again—just for the fun of it this time. And it drives us to our knees!

What is the secret in the story of Job? When Job proved before the universe that he was serving God not for selfish reasons, but because he loved God, and that he would trust Him regardless, then God could come in with His blessings and cause the devil to flee.

130

FOR ALL THE RIGHT REASONS

Great and marvellous are thy works, Lord God Almighty; just and true are thy ways, thou King of saints. Rev. 15:3.

Do you realize how fairly God has been conducting this great controversy? Do you realize that the day is going to come when every knee is going to bow, and every tongue confess that God has been fair and just? Even Satan is going to kneel down and admit that God has never overstepped Himself.

You can almost see it as you read the description in the book *The Great Controversy.* You can almost see Satan himself lifted up above the rest of the millions of people who are meeting for the first and last time. And they look, and say, "Is this the man that made the nations to tremble and opened not his prison house?" There, before God's throne and the Holy City, Satan, by his own choice, goes to his knees and admits that God has been fair. Then he hates himself for it, and rushes to do battle.

In order for God to be proved fair and just before the universe, there are times when He sees that it will be best to allow Satan to have his way in bringing trouble to us for a time. And often Satan is correct in claiming that we were seeking God only for what we hoped to gain from Him, and that if things were to stop going smoothly, we would stop seeking God.

"We are often led to seek Jesus by the desire for some earthly good; and upon the granting of our request we rest our confidence in His love. The Saviour longs to give us a greater blessing than we ask; and He delays the answer to our request that He may show us the evil of our own hearts, and our deep need of His grace. He desires us to renounce the selfishness that leads us to seek Him. Confessing our helplessness and bitter need, we are to trust ourselves wholly to His love."—*The Desire of Ages,* p. 200.

When we understand this, we will understand why Satan comes at us with all his guns blazing when we begin a relationship with God, and we will also understand why God has to let him. God is big enough to keep him from it. But in order to be fair, God has to let him work. As we see our problem and choose to come to Jesus day by day regardless of what happens, we will find the grace of heaven to change our selfish motives, and to enable us to seek Jesus for the right reasons.

SEEKING JESUS FOR JESUS' SAKE |

For our light affliction, which is but for a moment, worketh for us a far more exceeding and eternal weight of glory. 2 Cor. 4:17.

The person who quits seeking a relationship with God when trials and troubles come into his life is the one who was seeking God for selfish motives to begin with. But often we are led to seek Jesus for selfish reasons. It is only by getting a glimpse of the love of Jesus that we are enabled to seek Him for *His* sake instead of our own.

A mature Christian is less concerned about his getting to heaven and more concerned about someone else's getting to heaven. Remember Moses, who was willing to throw his own eternal life in the balance in order to intercede for people who would just as soon have crushed his head with rocks and left his body in the desert sands?

We can't produce this kind of unselfish love. But God can. Love begets love, and as we go to our knees and see the issues involved, we can ask God to change our motives. We can ask Him to enable us to follow the example of Job, and love and trust Him regardless of what happens to us—even at the cost of our very lives. Outward difficulties will cease to affect the consistency of our relationship with God. We will continue to seek Jesus for Jesus' sake, because of His love for us.

It was God's contention that Job loved Him, that he served Him and trusted Him—and that whether or not things went well was beside the point. Job proved God right. It is our privilege today to prove God right again. We can keep in communion with heaven because of our love for God, and because of what Jesus has done for us at the cross. When we do that, then the rest of the story of Job can be fulfilled in our lives.

One day you see God coming to the devil and saying, "How are things going?" And the devil says, "I'm giving him everything I have." And God says, "I know. I've been watching. He's still seeking communion with Me, isn't he?" And the devil begins to fidget. God says, "Could it be possible that this person is seeking Me out of love, because of what My Son has done? That he loves Me?" And the devil flees. He has nothing further to say. Will you join me today in choosing to continue seeking God day by day, until He comes again, regardless of what happens?

YOU CAN'T MAKE YOURSELF BELIEVE |

Now faith is the substance of things hoped for, the evidence of things not seen. Heb. 11:1.

The story is told of a country church that had called a special prayer meeting to pray for rain. There had been no rain for some time, and the crops were drying up. One little girl who came to the meeting brought her umbrella. The people smiled at the faith of a little child. But it rained. Now let me ask you something: Did it rain because she brought her umbrella? Or did she bring her umbrella because she knew it was going to rain? The way you interpret this story may show quite a bit about how you define faith.

What about Peter and John at the gate Beautiful? They said to the lame beggar, "In the name of Jesus . . . rise up and walk." Apparently the lame man needed a bit of additional encouragement, for it says in Acts 3:7, 8, "And he [Peter] took him by the right hand, and lifted him up." But he was healed, and he "leaping up stood, and walked, and entered with them into the temple, walking, and leaping, and praising God."

Did this man receive healing because Peter and John had enough courage to walk up to a strange beggar and command him to be healed? Or did they have enough courage to do what they did because they already knew that God was going to heal him?

Perhaps the most common misunderstanding of faith is that it is something you work on—something you work up. That the way to have faith is to try hard to make yourself believe something is going to happen, and that if you succeed, it will happen. But the greatest evidence of genuine faith is that it is totally spontaneous. It comes naturally, as a result of something else. If we get that one point straight, it will save us from a great deal of difficulty. Ephesians 2:8 says that by grace are we saved through faith, and *that* not of ourselves. It is the gift of God. If faith is a gift that comes from God, then the only way to obtain genuine faith would be to come into a relationship with God in order to receive His gift. We don't *work* to receive a gift. We simply come to the one who is giving and accept it. So it is by coming to God that we receive His gift of faith.

THE GIFT OF FAITH

God hath dealt to every man the measure of faith. Rom. 12:3.

I grew up in a preacher's home. My father used to borrow measuring cups from my mother's pantry—a big quart measuring cup, and a little one-cup measure. He'd take them to his evangelistic pulpit, and he would say, "Suppose that God gave me *a* measure of faith, and gave you *a* measure of faith. And suppose He gave you this size, and He gave me this other size. It wouldn't be fair, would it?" The Scripture says God has given to everyone *the* measure of faith! He has given us all enough faith to get started with. He has given us all the ability to believe in something not seen.

But this is not saving faith. In order to have saving faith, we have to have more than God gave each of us to begin with. This is well explained in that further comment found in *Education,* pages 253, 254: "Faith that enables us to receive God's gifts is in itself a gift, of which some measure is imparted to every human being. It grows as exercised in appropriating the word of God. In order to strengthen faith, we must often bring it in contact with the word."

Have you ever thought that the way to exercise faith was to ask God for hard answers? Have you ever thought that the way to exercise faith was to make yourself claim promises, whether you really believed them or not? Have you ever heard that exercising faith is getting yourself into a tight spot and then waiting for God to bail you out? Not so. According to Scriptures, the exercise of faith has to do with getting often in contact with the Word of God. That's the way you exercise faith. "Faith cometh by hearing, and hearing by the word of God" (Rom. 10:17).

As we come in contact with God's Word, what happens? We get in touch with a Person—the Man of the Bible. All through the Bible, in every book, there is the Man. His name is Jesus. As we get to know more about Him, we begin to experience a saving relationship with Him. Genuine faith comes from the faith relationship. There is no such thing as genuine faith without a relationship. Faith immediately involves two parties—one party trusting the other. As we come to know the love of Jesus through communion with Him in His Word, faith in Him springs up spontaneously.

SPONTANEOUS FAITH

He that trusteth in his own heart is a fool. Prov. 28:26.

Saving faith comes only through the faith relationship with Christ. Perhaps the best single definition for faith is trust. "Faith is trusting God."—*Education*, p. 253. And if faith is trusting, then the moment you have faith, you have at least two parties. There's no such thing as faith and only one person. Faith has a subjective element—one depending on another.

How do you learn to depend on another? Well, there are two things needed. You must have someone who is trustworthy, and you must get to know them. If you have someone who is *not* trustworthy, getting to know them will not develop trust—it will develop distrust! If you become acquainted with a person who is untrustworthy, you won't have to work to distrust them—the distrust will be automatic. The opposite is also true. If a person is absolutely trustworthy, all you have to do to learn to trust them is to get to know them, and you will trust them naturally and spontaneously.

Saving faith is always the result of something else. It is the result of a relationship with the One who is trustworthy.

So, how do you develop a relationship? By becoming acquainted through communication. That's the way to have a relationship with anyone. How do you communicate with God, with Jesus? Through the Bible—that's how God talks to us. And through prayer—that's how we talk to Him. And through going places and doing things together—that's Christian service. Through these simple means that God has given, relationship can exist. When we get to know Him we will trust Him spontaneously, and when we trust Him we have faith.

Therefore, faith is never something we work on. It's the devil's idea to try to get us to work on our faith, because he knows that if he can get us to work on our faith, he can keep our attention from Jesus, the source of faith. By getting us to work on our faith, he focuses our attention inward on ourselves—and if he succeeds in that, there is no chance for real faith.

So if I want to have genuine faith—the kind that really counts, saving faith—I must learn to trust God. In order to do that, I must get to know Him. I can get acquainted with Him through the simple avenues of communication, and when I know Him I *will* trust Him spontaneously.

TRUSTING HIM

The fool hath said in his heart, There is no God. Ps. 14:1.

A man came to me one time and said, "I'm through with God. I'm through with faith. I'm through with religion. You can have it."

"What's the matter?" I asked him.

"My wife just died. I read in Scripture that 'Whatsoever you ask, believing, you shall receive.' For two years I have asked and believed that my wife wouldn't die. I told her every day, 'Don't worry—you're not going to die.' And now she's dead. There is no God. Forget it."

This misconception of faith has caused futile effort and discouragement for thousands of people. There are whole churches, whole religions, that are built on this idea of self-generated faith. They believe that if you can think positively enough, it will make things happen.

Faith is nothing more than trusting God. Trusting that He is love, that He wants to bring us the greatest happiness. Jesus is completely trustworthy. If you don't believe that, you don't know Him yet. The person who is not quite sure that he can trust Jesus is the one who has no relationship with Him.

I went into a dry-cleaning shop one morning in a town in the Northwest. There had been an automobile accident the night before, and the mother of four small children had been killed. The lady at the cleaners said, "Some people want to die, and ought to die, and they don't. Others don't want to die, and shouldn't, and they do. I don't think God knows what He's doing."

I asked, "Do we blame God for this kind of thing?" And she got mad at me and went into the back room and wouldn't talk anymore.

This lady was advertising the fact that she didn't know Jesus. Trust isn't a matter of believing that God will do everything we ask of Him in exactly the way, and at the time, that we expect. He even allows death to come, sometimes at a time that seems wrong to us. But if we know Him, we will not be found turning away from Him when trials come, but rather continuing to walk with Him because we know Him and trust Him.

FAITH AT THE BEDSIDE

And he said unto me, My grace is sufficient for thee: for my strength is made perfect in weakness. 2 Cor. 12:9.

During the first year of my ministry someone called me to the bedside of a dying man. I thought that if someone could believe strongly enough, and work up enough nerve, to take the man by the hand and tell him to be healed in the name of Jesus, it would happen.

After we had prayed and anointed him, I looked around among the older people to see who would have the courage to do such a thing, and guess where they were all looking? At *me!* And everything went black. I couldn't do it. I mumbled some pious clichés to the effect that God doesn't always answer prayer immediately, that sometimes it's later on, and I beat a hasty retreat. The man died. And I thought I had killed him!

There is probably no other time in the work of a minister when his personal relationship with God is called into account as closely as when he is asked to pray for healing for someone in need. Many of us have held the opinion that the determining factor in whether or not a person is healed lies almost entirely in the faith of the one making the request. We have felt that if a request for healing is denied, it is most likely because the faith of the intercessor is somehow lacking.

Perhaps this idea has come from the few instances in the life of Christ where He commended the person healed for his or her faith. But we need to remember that faith is trust in a Person, not in *answers* we expect to receive.

The apostle Paul asked three times that the Lord remove his affliction, yet it was not removed. It wasn't because Paul was short on faith; it was because God saw that greater benefit and blessing would come if Paul were given opportunity to find God's strength as the answer to his weakness.

Moses' faith in God was strong—yet God refused continued life for him, and laid him to rest. God had bigger purposes for Moses. And Moses is in heaven today as a result. "Not Enoch, who was translated to heaven, not Elijah, who ascended in a chariot of fire, was greater or more honored than John the Baptist, who perished alone in the dungeon."—*The Desire of Ages,* p. 225. Genuine faith in God trusts Him just as much in the good times as in the bad.

IN MY HAND NO PRICE I BRING

Not by works of righteousness which we have done, but according to his mercy he saved us. Titus 3:5.

Ten men came to see Jesus. Nine of them were Jews and one was a Samaritan. But they had at least one thing in common. They all had leprosy. Jesus sent them to show themselves to the priests, and on the way to the Temple they realized they had been healed. All 10 began running— nine toward the Temple, and one back toward Jesus. The Samaritan returned to say Thank You. We are told that the other nine had hearts "untouched by the mercy of God" (*The Ministry of Healing*, p. 233).

Simon the Pharisee also had had leprosy, and was also healed by Jesus, "but he had not accepted Him as a Saviour."—*The Desire of Ages*, p. 557. Simon didn't feel his need for Jesus' healing of his soul until at the feast when Jesus told the parable of the two debtors. *Then* he accepted Jesus as Saviour.

Twelve disciples were sent out as evangelists. One of the 12 was Judas. Jesus "endowed him with power to heal the sick and to cast out devils. But Judas did not come to the point of surrendering himself fully to Christ."— *Ibid.*, p. 717.

How much it would please our human natures if stories like these were omitted from the Bible record. We would much rather have a God who rewards *our* great faith, and *our* great righteousness, with His blessings. We are sometimes uncomfortable with a God who causes rain to fall on the just and the unjust (Matt. 5:45). But God's gifts to us stem from His goodness and His desire to bless us according to our needs.

As you study the record of Bible healings, you find examples of the healing of people of great faith, such as the centurion. Jesus marveled at his faith. You also find people healed who had no genuine faith in God at all. Some were righteous, some were unrighteous. The only common denominators were their great need, which only Jesus could meet, and their coming to Him with nothing to recommend them to His favor. The Pharisees suggested Jesus heal the centurion because he had built them a synagogue. But the centurion himself said, I'm not worthy. As we come to know the love of Jesus, we will come to Him with our need, not with our supposed merits, and trust Him to respond in the way He sees best.

BEHAVIOR OR RELATIONSHIP | **MAY 12**

This is the work of God, that ye believe on him whom he hath sent. John 6:29.

Our purpose today is to point out that faith is something more than the ordinary understanding of the word *belief.* In John 6 the Jews came to Jesus and asked, "What shall we do, that we might work the works of God?" Jesus answered, "This is the work of God, that ye believe on him whom he hath sent."

What is involved in "believing"? We are told that the faith in Christ that saves the soul is not what it is represented to be by many people. Believe, believe, is their cry. Only believe in Christ and you will be saved. (*The Seventh-day Adventist Bible Commentary,* vol. 6, p. 1063). One of the popular ideas of faith is that it is simply nodding your head, simply saying Yes to the fact that Christ exists, and that's all there is to it. Coupled with the rising emphasis on the theme of salvation by faith in Jesus alone, comes the immature, naive, license-ladened cry, "All you have to do is believe. Just believe." Well, you'll find there's something far deeper than that if you study the word *believe* and the context in which it is used in God's Word.

When the question came to Jesus, obviously the Jewish leaders at that time were hung up on the usual idea that you must deserve heaven and work your way in. And so their question is sort of a behavior-based question. "What shall we *do,* that we might work the works of God?" What they were really saying was, "What can we do to deserve heaven?" Jesus immediately shifted their attention from behavior to relationship when He said, "This is the work of God, that ye believe on him whom he hath sent." Immediately you have a clue. In the first place, belief is not based on *what,* it is based on *whom.* It isn't what set of doctrines or creeds you consider to be correct. I know in *whom* I have believed—not in *what* I have believed.

James says that even the devils believe—they believe and they tremble (James 2:19). But the devils obviously don't have saving faith. They don't trust God. An intellectual assent to certain Bible truths will always be insufficient. Even the devils believe to that extent. But the belief that is saving faith refers to the deeper trust, which comes only from a personal relationship with Jesus Christ.

UNDERSTANDING TRUE FAITH

Nevertheless when the Son of man cometh, shall he find faith on the earth? Luke 18:8.

One of the great reasons why people don't believe, why there are so many unbelievers, as we call them, is because the devil keeps a constant misunderstanding of God before us, to prevent us from having faith in Him. Although, as Hebrews 12:1, 2, tells us, Jesus is both the author *and* the finisher of our faith, even the faith of which He was the author fades away if you don't do more about it than just nod your head.

Jesus said in our text for today that when the Son of man comes, He is hardly going to find faith on the earth. We are told that in the last days the earth is going to be almost destitute of true faith (*Spiritual Gifts,* vol. 3, p. 94). There will be people everywhere who will be saying, Believe, believe, only believe. But this is not genuine faith. Genuine faith comes as a gift from God, and grows as it comes in contact with God's Word. "Faith cometh by hearing, and hearing by the word of God." So the first necessity for faith of the deeper hue is a knowledge of God and His Word. Yet even this knowledge is not enough. There must also be an understanding and accepting of God's Word.

One day Jesus walked with the disciples on the road to Emmaus. He saw that they had a problem with their understanding. They had been like people with veils over their eyes. Jesus opened their understanding, that they might understand the Scriptures (Luke 24:45). It would be worthwhile for us, rather than merely reading the Bible for knowledge, to pray for understanding as well; to pray that the misunderstandings of God that Satan is constantly urging upon us will be recognized in their true character.

The third ingredient for genuine faith, which comes as a result of the knowledge plus the understanding, is trust or confidence in God. As we see Jesus, who came to reveal God, and as we spend time in seeking Him, in coming in contact with His Word, in order to become acquainted with Him, we will see through the devil's deceptions regarding the character of God. Our misunderstandings of God will be corrected, and we will come to have the confidence and trust in God that is genuine faith.

FAITH IN THE CRISIS

And they said one to another, Did not our heart burn within us, while he talked with us by the way, and while he opened to us the scriptures? Luke 24:32.

One day on the road to Emmaus walked two men who did not believe. Their faith had been shattered. They were miserable. They talked to a Stranger who walked along with them, saying, "But we trusted that it had been he which should have redeemed Israel: and beside all this, to day is the third day since these things were done" (Luke 24:21).

These men had evidently been among the followers of Jesus, among the disciples who had been told repeatedly that Jesus would go to Jerusalem, be delivered into the hands of sinners, be put to death, and rise again the third day. They had heard Him say it, yet they hadn't heard Him say it! The Jewish leaders had remembered what He said. That's why they had gone to Pilate and insisted on a guard to place around the tomb. Mary Magdalene had heard what Jesus said. That's why she had anointed Jesus' feet with spikenard. But these followers had not heard. And so when a crisis came, it revealed the true nature of their faith.

We experience crises in our lives. Sometimes when these come, we wonder and are dismayed. But it is a blessing to have shaking experiences before the great final shaking. It is a real advantage to have the small winds blow before the big ones come. It is an advantage to learn to run with the footmen before you must contend with horses.

The reason a crisis is not all bad is because even though a crisis doesn't change you, it does reveal to you the direction in which you are already headed. And if there is time after a crisis to change, it can be a means of showing you your need. Disciples who were discouraged, fearful, and doubting, when they finally discovered the secret of their burning hearts on the road to Emmaus, were able to come back with allegiance and trust and faith that they had not known before. The crisis didn't produce the change—but it did give them an insight into their own hearts, which motivated them to change afterward. Crises bring understanding of our condition, so that we recognize our need and can turn to Christ before the final crisis, after which there is no opportunity for change.

FAITH OUT THE WINDOW

And Jesus answering saith unto them, Have faith in God. Mark 11:22.

A small boy was on a bus on his way home from Sunday school. The day was warm. The windows were open. The boy had received a motto on a card, "Have faith in God." As the wind swept through the bus, his card went flying out the window. He shouted, "Stop the bus! My faith in God just went out the window."

Now the truth is that faith, if it's genuine, does not go out the window. The only kind of faith that really goes out the window is the kind that's on a card, only surface faith. I'd like you to notice today that there's a time coming when everybody's faith is going to be tested to find out just how real it is, and that although everyone may look the same now, at that time there will be two distinct classes.

We read in Amos 8:11, 12, about a time coming when there will be people running from sea to sea, looking for faith. The context shows that it has something to do with the end of time, as well as with the days of Israel, because it talks about the sun and moon and dark days. It is well for us to evaluate *now* the extent of our faith. In Matthew 7 we find some tests as to whether a person really has genuine faith or not.

Matthew 7:21-23, in Jesus' own words: "Not every one that sayeth unto me, Lord, Lord, shall enter into the kingdom of heaven; but he that doeth the will of my Father which is in heaven. Many will say to me in that day, Lord, Lord, have we not prophesied in thy name? and in thy name have cast out devils? and in thy name done many wonderful works? And then will I profess unto them, I never knew you: depart from me, ye that work iniquity." Then He proceeds to tell the story of the wise man and the foolish man. Both of them built houses. However, one house was on the rock and the other was on the sand. It wasn't until the storm came that the real difference became apparent. Then the difference between the two houses and their foundations was easily seen.

Whether a person has genuine faith or not may not be that apparent when things are going well. But when the wind blows, when the storm comes, it is only genuine faith that can withstand the crisis.

142

BUILDING ON THE ROCK

For other foundation can no man lay than that is laid, which is Jesus Christ. 1 Cor. 3:11.

Jesus told the story of a wise man who built his house upon a rock. "And the rain descended, and the floods came, and the winds blew, and beat upon that house; and it fell not: for it was founded upon a rock" (Matt. 7:25). But there was also a foolish man in the parable, who built his house upon the sand. "And the rain descended, and the floods came, and the winds blew"—a great crisis, obviously—"and beat upon that house; and it fell: and great was the fall of it" (verse 27). Notice that the house did not change foundations. It fell.

Today there are crises of wind and flood and rain—crises of tragedy and grief and sorrow, which come into our lives. It is when these crises come that we are revealed for what we really are, instead of what we might appear to be. There is a sort of spiritual schizophrenia possible in the realm of the Christian religion, where a person can look good on the outside but be bad on the inside. We see it among the disciples of Jesus—there was one who looked good, who appeared to be as loyal as the rest, but when the crisis came, the separation was quite clear. Judas was able to cast out devils and heal the sick. He was one of Jesus' closest companions. But when the crisis came, it was discovered that inside he was quite different.

You see a tree out in the woods. It looks good on the outside, but it's rotten on the inside. Nobody knows—until the storm breaks, and it goes crashing to the ground. The storm doesn't change the tree from being rotten. Nor is it the storm that causes the tree to be rotten. The storm merely reveals the tree's true condition.

So it is when the storms come. A house does not change foundations. The house goes down. If it is not based on solid rock before the flood comes, it goes down when the flood comes—every time. It's just that simple. A crisis doesn't change anybody. If we are going to have a faith that will withstand the storms of life, this faith must be developed by becoming personally acquainted with Christ before the crisis hits. It is only the house that is founded upon the Rock *before* the storms come that stands.

THE CRISIS OF DEATH

Satan hath desired to have you, that he may sift you as wheat: but I have prayed for thee, that thy faith fail not. Luke 22:31, 32.

My brother and I were at Grandma's house. We were playing out back near the woodshed. We both looked and acted the same—quiet and calm—until a yellow jacket stung my brother. He began to carry on in a way that I thought was foolish—until the yellow jacket's brother stung me! And what looked at first to be foolishness turned out to be the first duet that my brother and I ever sang!

Our reaction in a crisis does not represent any kind of change. It merely reveals what was there, inside, all along. Usually a crisis will speed a person in the direction in which he was already headed. If you are walking up a mountain, and trip and fall, when you rise again you are usually a step or two beyond where you fell. And if you are going down the mountain, and you fall, when you rise again you are usually several steps below where you fell. The crisis of falling simply puts you farther along the path on which you were already headed.

God wants us to clearly understand when we are headed in the wrong direction. When a crisis comes and not only reveals our direction but even increases our momentum in that direction, we can be brought up short by the mercy of God and seek for His power to change our direction. Any change that comes will come *after* the crisis is over.

This is why death-bed repentances are seldom, if ever, genuine. If there is anything that is a crisis, it's death, when time and eternity somehow meet. And if a crisis simply reveals what you are, but does not change you, and if there is no time afterward for change, then how could you allow for death-bed repentances, save in the extreme exception?

"Courage, fortitude, faith, and implicit trust in God's power to save, do not come in a moment. These heavenly graces are acquired by the experience of years."—*Christian Experience and Teachings*, p. 188. It takes time to transform the human into the divine. This shows us another picture of the love of God, that He allows the smaller winds to blow, that we may see ourselves and have opportunity to prepare for the greater winds to come, seeking a relationship with Him that is not based on fear but rather on love.

THE CRISIS OF TEMPTATION

My brethren, count it all joy when ye fall into divers temptations; knowing this, that the trying of your faith worketh patience. James 1:2, 3.

A crisis doesn't change us or our direction. It merely reveals to us where we were headed before it came along. It is interesting to notice that even temptation is a crisis. Every time the enemy hits us with a temptation, it is a mini-crisis—or sometimes a maxi-crisis! But a crisis, nonetheless. Every temptation that comes to us reveals to us, by its results, our direction at the time the temptation came.

If a person is not surrendered to God at the time of a temptation, there is little chance of surrendering then. What happens if we are apart from God at the time of the temptation is that we are then dependent upon our own backbone or willpower. The strong overcome, externally, on their own steam, while the weak don't make it at all. But internally, where it really counts, both are equal. Both give in to the temptation, because the devil is stronger than we are, and we will lose every battle with him that we attempt to fight in our own power.

In Hebrews 4 we are reminded of our great High Priest, and invited to come boldly before His throne of grace, that we may obtain mercy *and* find grace to help in time of need. There is a sequence. We come boldly before His throne of grace *now*, that we may find grace to help in time of need, when that time comes. The person who comes before the throne of grace only in time of need will fail. When the time of need, the time of temptation, comes, it reveals whether or not that grace has been obtained. "We may keep so near to God that in every unexpected trial our thoughts will turn to Him as naturally as the flower turns to the sun."—*Steps to Christ*, pp. 99, 100. If trial comes, and we shake our fist at God and charge Him with dealing harshly with us, this reveals to us that we must have been walking some distance from Him. We do not know our own hearts. Some people who have thought that they could weather the storms on a thousand seas have drowned in the bathtub. We are so deceived concerning our own hearts. So, because of His love, God allows trials and temptations to come, that we may see things as they really are.

THE DAY OF THE GREAT CRISIS

They shall run to and fro to seek the word of the Lord, and shall not find it. Amos 8:12.

At the very end of time, just before Jesus comes, there is going to be a great crisis. People at that time will have revealed that they are going one way or the other—fast. The difference between this great crisis and the smaller ones preceding it is that when the winds really blow with hurricane force, there is no time to change direction. The changes will need to have been made before the storm. If that's true, then God would be exceedingly anxious to have us understand ourselves before that time ever came. In Amos 8 is a prediction of the day coming when people will be running from sea to sea, from coast to coast, looking for a faith that they have neglected and that they can no longer find. They will realize that nothing counts except this, and they will throw their riches to the moles and the bats, desperate, panicky, seeking with fear that which they could have had earlier but refused.

How can we know if we are safe from the storms that are about to blow? There are two clues as to how to know whether you are going in the right direction. Matthew 7:21, are you doing the will of God, and Matthew 25:12, do you know Him? "When we know God as it is our privilege to know Him, our life will be a life of continual obedience."—*The Desire of Ages,* p. 668. This places knowing God as the cause, and doing God's will as the result. Both are equally significant and important, but one is completely the cause of the other. How can I know if I am going toward God, if I am going up the mountain instead of down? The important factor is, Do I have a personal, meaningful relationship with God day by day?

When I know Him as it is my privilege to know Him, my life *will be* a life of continual obedience. If I am having trouble with the continual obedience, it isn't because I'm not trying hard enough to obey. It's because I don't know God as it is my privilege to know Him. That's where the trouble is. If I will continue to seek fellowship with God, continue to take advantage of the privilege given me to know Him, then He will complete the work that He has started in my life, and bring me into the final great crisis with security and assurance.

COURAGE FOR THE CRISIS

Cast not away therefore your confidence, which hath great recompence of reward. Heb. 10:35.

There was a vision given a long time ago, recorded in one of the first books that was given to this church by the special gift that God provided. It's found in the book *Early Writings*, page 269 and onward. It was a vision of what would take place in the lives of people just before Jesus comes.

We have sometimes spent a lot of time studying and discussing what is going to happen politically and internationally at the very end. But it is even more interesting to notice what happens internally and experientially to the people of God. You may want to study the whole chapter, entitled "The Shaking," on your own. But notice parts of it here.

"I saw some, with strong faith and agonizing cries, pleading with God." What kind of faith? Strong faith! Don't miss that. "Their countenances were pale and marked with deep anxiety, expressive of their internal struggle. . . . Large drops of perspiration fell from their foreheads."

This description can be extremely encouraging. Have you ever had the idea that people who are experiencing deep anxiety and internal struggles were people who were far from God? Have you ever thought that anxiety and struggle were signs of *lack* of faith? That if you had strong faith, you would never experience this sort of agony? Not so. You can be strong in faith and still have deep anxiety!

Then it says, "Now and then their faces would light up with the marks of God's approbation." When? All the time? No, only now and then. "And again the same solemn, serious, anxious look would settle upon them. Evil angels crowded around, pressing darkness upon them to shut out Jesus." Notice their main purpose—to shut out Jesus from the believers' view. "As these praying ones continued their earnest cries, *at times* a ray of light from Jesus came to them, to encourage their hearts." Not all the time, but only at times.

When the heavens are as brass over your head, take courage. It is not an evidence of defective faith on your part. You don't have to add to the struggle and anxiety that you experience by berating yourself for your lack of faith. As you continue to seek Jesus, and continue your earnest pleading with Him, rays of light from Jesus will again come to encourage your heart.

THE FINAL TEST

But now they desire a better country, that is, an heavenly: wherefore God is not ashamed to be called their God: for he hath prepared for them a city. Heb. 11:16.

Over in England during the second world war, there was a camp where many of the Allied espionage agents received their training. The methods were rigorous. The trainers would take those who were going into espionage, and change their environment, their food, their habits, their practices, their customs. They dressed them in German uniforms, gave them German names. It was the objective to transform them completely so that they would consider themselves Germans.

The success of the program was determined by a final test. They took the soldiers on an extended march. Finally, in the middle of the night, they allowed them to crumple into pathetic little heaps in their pup tents. After they were sound asleep, they were roughly awakened, with spotlights shining in their eyes, and asked, "Who are you?"

Now if you were one of these agents, and as you awakened you said, "I'm Henry Smith," and then to the questions "Where are you from?" and "Where are you going?" replied, "Canada," and, "I'm going home to mother," it would be a long time before you went home to mother! But if you said, "Mein Name ist Heinrich Schmidt [or something like that]," and, "I am from Frankfurt, and am going to Berlin," then before long you would be in Berlin.

Some of them passed the test. But I think I see a different scene. I see a Master Teacher who deals not simply with food and clothes and outward actions. He deals with minds, and hearts, and motives, and tastes, and desires. When you have been trained in close connection with this Master Teacher, who is your best friend, you are transformed within and without. Someday the spotlight comes on. You are shaken, as from a deep sleep. There are voices saying, "Who are you?" And you say with great assurance, "I am a follower of Jesus Christ, who died in my place." "Where are you going?" "I look for a better country, a city that has foundations, whose builder and maker is God."

Thank God for the little crises that precede the big ones. Thank God for the opportunity to know, before it is too late, whether our faith in Him is based solidly on Christ.

COME AS YOU ARE

Whosoever will, let him take the water of life freely. Rev. 22:17.

The story is told of a man whose horn on his car wouldn't work. So he went to the garage in town to have it fixed. When he got there, it was raining, and he found that the door to the garage was closed. On the door was a sign that said, "Honk for service"! Have you ever felt that repentance was something like that?

I'll never forget trying to convert my boy. I was worried about him. There were problems in the town where we were living at the time. Kids were being jailed for dealing in street drugs. I was afraid he would become involved. I talked until I had talked too much, and finally realized that I'd better stop talking and begin praying.

Then some kids that he admired from the academy invited him down to a discussion at the Bible teacher's house. He decided to go and ask some hard questions. He liked to ask hard questions. So he went and began to play his game. But about halfway through the evening he began listening. He didn't know until later that some of those other kids were praying for him. But before the evening was over he heard something that he had never heard before—although I can assure you that he *had too* heard it before! It had simply never registered. He heard that we never change our lives in order to come to Jesus. That we always come to Jesus just as we are, and He is the one who changes our lives.

He came home about ready to speak in tongues! He was so excited. He came to me and said, "Listen, Dad, listen to this! We don't change our lives in order to come to Christ. We come just as we are. *He* changes our lives!"

I didn't want to spoil it for him, so I said, *"Really?"* And the very blood in my veins began to sing. The next morning I passed by the door to his room and saw him reading his Bible. The day before, he couldn't have cared less about the Bible. Now he couldn't put it down. Before the week was out, he had an "evangelistic" meeting in the living room with some of the other academy kids, trying to share his new insights.

When one realizes for the first time that we really can come to Jesus just as we are, it makes all the difference in the world.

REPENTANCE IS A GIFT

For godly sorrow worketh repentance to salvation. 2 Cor. 7:10.

Jesus loves to have us come to Him just as we are. Repentance is not our work, not a condition for acceptance with Him. We are told that this is "a point on which many may err, and hence they fail of receiving the help that Christ desires to give them. They think that they cannot come to Christ unless they first repent."—*Steps to Christ*, p. 26. But repentance is a gift. We *receive* this gift when we come to Christ.

In Revelation 3:19 the Laodicean church is admonished to be zealous and repent. For those of us living during this time in the earth's history who are at least potential Laodiceans, it is of utmost importance that we understand the nature of true repentance. It is not a matter of working hard, trying to make yourself sorry. Acts 5:31 tells us, "Him hath God exalted with his right hand to be a Prince and a Saviour, for to *give* repentance to Israel, and forgiveness of sins." "Repentance is no less the gift of God than are pardon and justification, and it cannot be experienced except as it is given to the soul by Christ."—*Selected Messages*, book 1, p. 391. So if I want repentance for today, I can go to my knees and ask God for it, because it is a gift and He delights to give good gifts to His children. Notice all of 2 Corinthians 7:10: "Godly sorrow worketh repentance to salvation not to be repented of: but the sorrow of the world worketh death." Where do you get godly sorrow? From God! You don't work it up yourself.

We need to understand what it is that Laodicea needs to repent of. It is *not* primarily immorality. Laodicea is quite moral. Laodicea is known for its external goodness. But in spite of that, the Saviour is standing on the outside, knocking, seeking admission. What Laodicea needs to repent of is its morality, its many good works *apart from Jesus*. Is it possible that Jesus can still stand outside the great churches and institutions we have built, still knocking for entrance?

We need to repent of living a life whose center and focus is anything other than Christ. Is Jesus the central focus of your home, your life, your relationships? Is He the theme of your thoughts, your conversations? Or do you need to come to Him for repentance for having kept Him knocking on the outside of your heart?

150

THE GOODNESS OF GOD

Him hath God exalted with his right hand to be a Prince and a Saviour, for to give repentance to Israel, and forgiveness of sins. Acts 5:31.

My brother and I used to be roommates in college. This was rather unexpected because we had spent much of our time up until then fighting with each other. Our parents used to worry that we would never live to grow up. But we found out when we got to college that we were very close. Psychologists tell us that you have to love someone in order to fight with them—that if you didn't love them, you wouldn't waste your time! Maybe that was the underlying cause of all of our arguments. But when we were roommates we got along very well.

We used to clean the room every Friday, for Sabbath. But one week I was behind on some of my studies, trying to finish a term paper before the deadline. When my brother came in, I was still typing away. "Quick! Hurry!" he said. "We've got to do the room."

And I said, "You do it. I can't. I'm too busy." And we began to teeter on the edge of the combat precipice again.

But then he relaxed and said, "That's all right. That's perfectly all right. I understand. You must be under terrible pressure. It must be mighty hard for you. I'll clean the room. I'm happy to clean the room. I'll do it all by myself. You go ahead and work on your paper."

And he broke my heart! I put down my paper and I helped clean the room. We used that approach on each other many times after that. It was a different approach; it was only in fun. But it was a simple illustration of the fact that when someone doesn't act against you, but rather gives evidence of loving acceptance, this wins you—right? The "goodness" of my brother led me to help clean the room.

The Bible says in Romans 2:4 that it is the goodness of God that leads us to repentance. But when we talk about the goodness of God, it's real. It's not faked. It's the only kind of real goodness there is. Are you seeking for genuine repentance? As you come to Christ, study His life, contemplate His character and mission, and understand His great love and acceptance for you, you will be brought to repentance.

BROKEN LAW
AND BROKEN HEART

But he was wounded for our transgressions, he was bruised for our iniquities. Isa. 53:5.

When I was in seventh grade I attended a school in Michigan that had one room with 13 students in eight grades. Our teacher was only 17 years old. It was her first year of teaching. She loved us and did the best she could for us. She knew how to teach, but she had a problem keeping law and order. In fact, about halfway through the school year the school board met to consider seriously whether to allow her to finish the year.

The students seemed gradually to lose respect for her. Students like to know what their limits are, and they began to criticize her instead of thinking of all that she had done for us. One day after school as I was starting home, I met some students below the classroom window, talking about how they didn't like the teacher and hoped that she would leave. When everyone else is talking about how they don't like the teacher, guess what you do? Have you ever been in that situation? Peer pressure, they call it. So I chimed right in. "That's right, she's no good. I don't like her either." Just as I said it, I looked up through the open window above. Our teacher was standing behind the piano where she didn't think she could be seen. Her face was pointed downward, and the tears were dropping to the floor. I'll never forget the look of hopeless despair on her face that day.

I tore myself from the scene and headed home. I kept seeing that face. The disappointment of someone who had done the best she could for me was too much. I didn't sleep well that night. I kept remembering how at Christmas time she had bought every one of us a worthwhile gift. She had gone out of her way to be friends with each of us. She loved to read stories after lunch. She had done so many things for me, and I had disappointed her. The next day I had to sit down and write a note telling her I was sorry. I really *was* sorry. Why? Because I had done something more than break a rule. I had broken someone's heart. There's a difference, isn't there?

Genuine repentance comes only in the setting of a one-to-one personal relationship with the Lord Jesus. When the reality of that friendship is recognized, and we see that our sins have broken His heart, then it is that our own hearts break.

NO RIGHTEOUSNESS BY CONFESSION

He that covereth his sins shall not prosper: but whoso confesseth and forsaketh them shall have mercy. Prov. 28:13.

One of the first steps in coming into a meaningful relationship with God is to admit that we are sinners, to admit that we have a sinful nature, and that, apart from Christ, that sinful nature is going to control us. Until we face our problem, we will not realize our need of Christ. We must recognize that we are sinners by nature. Whether we are lying, cheating, or stealing is beside the point. When we see our need and come to Christ, He gives us repentance. It is only when we have accepted this gift of repentance that confession can be genuine.

Notice what is necessary to precede genuine confession: "If we have not experienced that repentance which is not to be repented of, and have not with true humiliation of soul and brokenness of spirit confessed our sins, abhorring our iniquity, we have never truly sought for forgiveness of sin; and if we have never sought, we have never found the peace of God."—*Steps to Christ,* p. 38. It is important to understand that repentance precedes confession. Repentance comes after we have come to Christ, not before. And confession *follows* repentance. This is one of the reasons why so many people have problems with confession. We have gotten the idea that confession is the way to get to Christ, or that we get repentance by confession.

Have you ever had the idea that there is a certain merit in confession? Have you ever felt that if you were sure to have all your sins confessed every night before you went to bed, you would be sure of salvation? There is no such thing as "righteousness by confession"! It is pointless to try to confess if you haven't repented, because you will end up with confession as a system of merit, a way to try to work your way into God's favor. Confession comes as a *result* of genuine sorrow for sin. It is not the cause (*Steps to Christ,* p. 39).

Confession includes two aspects. It is not merely a listing of our specific shortcomings and mistakes and failures. Genuine confession also acknowledges our continuing condition as sinners, and in brokenness of spirit admits our need of Christ and our dependence upon Him.

153

NO EXCUSES IN CONFESSION

If we confess our sins, he is faithful and just to forgive us our sins, and to cleanse us from all unrighteousness. 1 John 1:9.

It is only when we have experienced genuine repentance that we can make a genuine confession. Perhaps one of the best ways to test the genuineness of a confession is to realize whether or not there is any excuse added to the confession. If I come to you and say, "I'd like to ask you to forgive me. I am sorry that I lied about you, but if you weren't such an ugly person I wouldn't have lied in the first place," you can know immediately that I have not had genuine repentance!

The problem of self-justification began in Eden. Adam blamed Eve for his problems, and Eve blamed the serpent. We are told that "when sin has deadened the moral perceptions, the wrongdoer does not discern the defects of his character . . . and unless he yields to the convicting power of the Holy Spirit he remains in partial blindness to his sin. . . . To every acknowledgment of his guilt he adds an apology in excuse."—*Steps to Christ*, p. 40.

There is no chance whatever for genuine reformation apart from repentance. Have you ever had someone tell you to "say you're sorry"? Did that make you sorry? Have you ever told someone else, perhaps your children, "Tell them you're sorry"? Does that make them sorry? Unless we *are* truly sorry, our confessions will be worthless, and no reformation will result. We all know by experience that we cannot reform ourselves, but as we get a glimpse of Jesus, and see the disappointment on His face, and see His love for us and His long-suffering, then we will experience true sorrow for sin.

It is only as we accept the mercy and the compassion of Jesus that He can, through us, pass on His mercy and compassion to others. Jesus is the only One who can give you peace. He loves you. He gave Himself for you. He will not judge you unfairly. His heart of love is touched with the feelings of your infirmities. As we come to understand His love and how much pain we have brought to His heart by our sins, we will be truly repentant, truly sorry for what we have done to hurt Him. The confession that springs from sorrow for hurting One who loves us will not give excuses, but will be heartfelt. And the result of that will be reformation.

AN HONEST CONFESSION

Confess your faults one to another, and pray one for another, that ye may be healed.
James 5:16.

Have you ever wondered how to know whether or not to confess a particular sin to God or to other people? Have you ever pondered what to confess and what not to confess, wondering where to draw the line? We have evidence that we should be very careful in our confessions. "In many of our religious awakenings mistakes have been made in regard to confession. While confession is good for the soul, there is need of moving wisely."—*Testimonies*, vol. 5, p. 645. The question of how and to whom sins should be confessed is one that demands careful, prayerful study. We must consider it from all points, weighing it before God and seeking divine illumination (*ibid.*, pp. 645, 646).

So when the question comes, To whom should I confess my wrongs? there are several guidelines we have been given. First of all, don't neglect to confess your faults to your fellowmen when they have a connection with them (*Fundamentals of Christian Education*, p. 239). Second, as a general rule, confess the sins of a private nature to Christ (*Counsels on Health*, p. 374).

If I have a valid relationship with God, I do not have to sit down and take inventory of my life and try to figure out how many I have wronged, and lie awake at night making a list and checking it twice. God, in the setting of my relationship with Him, has ways of impressing me with what to confess.

The responsibility for convicting us of what we need to confess belongs to God and the Holy Spirit. Our part is to respond to Him immediately, not to wait. If we have sins to confess, we should lose no time in making them right. It's hard to admit that you are wrong. But when we understand that lack of confession and making things right is blocking our continuing relationship with Christ, when we see the close connection that confession has with our growth in the Christian life, it appears not quite so difficult.

We all have struggles on this subject. But we can be thankful for the lovingkindness of Jesus today. He is still big enough to communicate to us, in our relationship with Him, just what to confess and how to go about it.

"SAY YOU'RE SORRY!"

Now I rejoice, not that ye were made sorry, but that ye sorrowed to repentance.
2 Cor. 7:9.

When I was in the third grade, we were playing outside at recess time. When we came in, hot and dusty, to clean up in the boys' washroom, we forgot to do it quietly. Suddenly the teacher from the room next to us burst into the washroom and said, "What's the matter with you? You sound like a bunch of wild Indians!"

Well, in the first place, I didn't think she had any business coming into our washroom. And in the second place, I didn't like what she said. So I replied sassily. She thought I was acting a little big for my britches and told my teacher about it. My teacher told me to tell her I was sorry.

But I wasn't sorry. So I didn't go and apologize. The next day when I arrived at school, my teacher stopped me and said, "Did you tell her you were sorry?" I was in a tight place. I said, "Yes, I did." But she had the goods on me. She had already checked with the other teacher. She replied, "I was just talking to Miss Brown, and she said you didn't."

Now I was in bigger trouble. So I said, "But I did! She must not have heard me." My teacher dropped the matter.

We finished the school year, and my family moved to another town. But every time I opened my Bible I'd remember the lie I had told my teacher. To convict of sin is the Spirit's work, and He does a pretty good job of it, doesn't He? Finally, I sat down and wrote a note to my teacher, confessing the lie I had told. But I still wasn't sorry about Miss Brown!

I told this story at a camp meeting, and after the meeting there was a lady waiting to see me. It was Miss Brown! More than 30 years had gone by. I still wasn't sorry! We talked for a little while, and when I got home, there was a letter from Miss Brown. *She* was sorry! But when she was sorry, then I was sorry! I've thought about it many times since. Why wasn't I sorry earlier? Well, I didn't know her very well. About the only contact I ever had with her was that day in the washroom. If our only contact with God is a casual, once-in-a-while kind of meeting, we will never come to the place of being sorry when we hurt Him. It's when we see His love and know He is our friend that we are led to genuine repentance.

UNLIMITED FORGIVENESS

Then came Peter to him, and said, Lord, how oft shall my brother sin against me, and I forgive him? till seven times? Matt. 18:21.

The disciples came to Jesus and asked how often they should forgive one another. The Pharisees said three times and you're out. The disciples wanted to show that they had learned *something* about the kind of forgiveness that Jesus offered, so they upped it to seven times. But Jesus said, "I say not unto thee, Until seven times: but, Until seventy times seven" (Matt. 18:22).

Which is easier to forgive: the first time someone offends you, or the tenth time that same person offends you? How about the hundredth time? Usually in our dealings with one another, we feel quite self-righteous in forgiving the first time. But if the offense is repeated and repeated, it isn't long until we come to the conclusion that the repentance on the part of the offender isn't genuine anyway.

In Luke 17:4 the lines are drawn even closer. Jesus said that if your brother trespasses against you "seven times in a day, and seven times in a day turn again to thee, saying, I repent; thou shalt forgive him. And the apostles said unto the Lord, *Increase our faith*"! It takes a lot of faith to give that kind of forgiveness! But what is Jesus really saying in these instructions? True, He intends that we be forgiving toward those who sin against us. But this is simply another example of the kind of love and forgiveness that God has toward us.

In our relationships with one another, if we offend someone but we have a long track record of good behavior, we could almost feel that they owe it to us to forgive us just this once. But by the time we have offended someone seven times in a day, and seven times in a day turned again saying, I repent, we no longer feel that we *deserve* anything. And if we are forgiven we can understand clearly that it is not because of *our* goodness, but because of the love and goodness of the one who has forgiven us.

This is the kind of love and goodness that comes only from God. He is the author of it, and it is good news that John 6:37 has no date on it. Today, again, regardless of how often you have failed, how often you have sinned, if you come to Him, you will be accepted, you will not be cast out.

157

FORGIVEN MUCH—LOVE MUCH

Wherefore I say unto thee, Her sins, which are many, are forgiven; for she loved much: but to whom little is forgiven, the same loveth little. Luke 7:47.

There was a feast at Simon's house. Simon was worried that Jesus' acceptance and forgiveness were being dispensed a little too freely. So Jesus told him the parable of the two debtors. One of the debtors owed a great deal. The other's debt was small. Both were forgiven. Jesus asked, "Which of them will love him most? Simon answered and said, I suppose that he, to whom he forgave most. And he said unto him, Thou hast rightly judged" (Luke 7:42, 43).

To our human understanding, the freely offered forgiveness could be dangerous. It looks as though it would lead to license. It seems that somewhere there must be a limit to the number of times we can repent, or we would continue choosing to sin and repent forever. But love is the great safeguard against license. Because the ones who have been forgiven much know better than anyone how great is the love of the One who has forgiven them, they love the most in return. "Those to whom He has forgiven most will love Him most, and will stand nearest to His throne to praise Him for His great love and infinite sacrifice. It is when we most fully comprehend the love of God that we best realize the sinfulness of sin."—*Steps to Christ*, p. 36.

As we know that we are loved, unconditionally, we are freed to respond with love of our own. It is as we know and believe the love of God to us that we are led to repentance, and the more we know of His love, the more our repentance will deepen.

If we love Him we *will* keep His commandments. It is only as we love Him that we *can* keep His commandments. "All true obedience comes from the heart."—*The Desire of Ages*, p. 668. When we come to Jesus each day, just as we are, we realize His acceptance of us. When He gives us His gift of repentance, we come to understand something of the love that is great enough to offer repentance and forgiveness, even to those of us who need to be forgiven "much." And love for Him springs up in our hearts. As we love Him, we desire to obey. God's forgiveness, so freely offered, not only does not lead to license but it is the only basis of true obedience that there is. Romans 2:4 tells us that it is the goodness of God that leads us to repentance.

ACCEPTED BECAUSE OF JESUS

But God commendeth his love toward us, in that, while we were yet sinners, Christ died for us. Rom. 5:8.

One time, at an airport, I ordered a sandwich between flights, and made the mistake of going off and leaving it sitting there on the counter. I had other things on my mind, so had to go back to get my sandwich. But suppose I went to a dealer to buy a Mercedes. There's little chance I would go off and leave *that*. The more we pay for something, the more we value it.

The infinite, priceless gift of God in Jesus Christ makes it certain that we are accepted, because Jesus' sacrifice has been accepted. God will not forget us or leave us alone after having paid such a price for our salvation. We can praise God anew for that today.

According to Romans 4:5, God justifies the ungodly. God accepts sinners when they come to Him just as they are. This is one of the most important and significant truths as we begin to understand the theme of salvation by faith. We do not wait for some point when we have become good enough for God to accept us. He loves to accept us just as we are when we come to Him. This is true when we come to Him initially, and the promise is good for today, as well. We can come to Him again today, just as we are, and He accepts us.

It is only people who understand that they have already been accepted by God who can safely talk about obedience. If I am not sure of my acceptance, it is extremely hazardous for me to study the subject of obedience, because it will be nothing but discouraging.

When a sinner responds to the convicting power of the Holy Spirit, he comes to God just as he is, and because of Jesus he is put right with God.

Nothing that man can do can possibly add to this salvation. No work of man has merit or value in itself. Our obedience is not what makes us right with God; it is not what causes our salvation. But for the Christian who understands this clearly, who is looking to the merits of Christ for his assurance and pardon, rather than to his own works, the subject of obedience is still extremely important. Once we have our foundation for salvation clearly understood, then we are ready to begin to build walls on that foundation.

THE JUST SHALL LIVE BY FAITH

Now the just shall live by faith: but if any man draw back, my soul shall have no pleasure in him. Heb. 10:38.

The group of God's people who live just before Jesus comes are going to be known by two characteristics, according to Revelation 14:12. They are going to keep the commandments of God, *and* have the faith of Jesus. What is meant by "keeping" the commandments? It would have to mean something more than believing in the commandments of God. It would have to include more than thinking that the commandments of God are nice. It isn't just to be in favor of the commandments.

Perhaps you have heard that it is true you will be keeping the commandments but that you won't be keeping them perfectly. Let's read it that way: "Here are they that keep the commandments of God, but not perfectly." Do you want that added? That isn't what it says. I would like to take the position that if you don't keep the commandments of God perfectly, you don't keep them at all. Either you do or you don't.

The final issue in the great controversy is not going to be over whether Jesus died or not, or over whether or not His blood is sufficient. The *last* great issue, just before Jesus comes, is whether we can obey or whether we continue to disobey. That's the final conflict. (See *The Desire of Ages*, p. 763.)

Can we obey? Or can we not obey? Does this subject seem incompatible with the theme of salvation by faith in Jesus? Does it sound as though we're headed straight for legalism? Or is it possible that the subjects of obedience and of salvation by faith alone can be found to harmonize?

When we accept as the foundation of our hope of salvation that we can come to Jesus just as we are, and are accepted because of what He did for us at the cross, we are then able to understand obedience correctly. Paul says, "For I am not ashamed of the gospel of Christ: for it is the power of God unto salvation to every one that believeth; to the Jew first, and also to the Greek. For therein is the righteousness of God revealed from faith to faith: as it is written, The just shall *live* by faith" (Rom. 1:16, 17).

Perhaps it is a new thought to some that we *live* by faith, as well as come to God by faith initially. Obedience is by faith, plus or minus nothing else. Obedience is by faith alone.

160

THE METHOD OF OBEDIENCE

As ye have therefore received Christ Jesus the Lord, so walk ye in him. Col. 2:6.

When we come to Jesus for pardon, because of the sacrifice He made for us at Calvary He is able to accept us just as we are. And each day, as we come to Him anew, He continues to accept us and assure us of salvation. Once we have come and accepted His salvation, we must recognize that the method by which we stay with Christ and grow in grace is the same method by which we received Him at first—that the just shall *live* by faith.

What does it mean to live by faith? In order to understand this, we have to remember what is involved in genuine faith. Faith is something far deeper than a mere mental assent to truth. It involves trust in a Person, in someone we have come to know personally and discovered to be completely trustworthy. Faith is always spontaneous, and is the natural result of a relationship with Christ.

This is not to say that obedience is not necessary. Obedience is required. It is important. It is essential. In the life of the Christian both faith and works will *exist*. But we must understand how this is to be accomplished. We need to consider what is meant by the word *by*. When we are talking about living *by* faith, what do we mean? The usual understanding in the English language of the word *by* refers to method. I travel to New York *by* plane. I make my living *by* working.

The Bible truth is that those who have been justified by faith shall *live* by faith, as well. Living the Christian life is accomplished through the same means by which the Christian life was begun. "As ye have therefore received Christ Jesus the Lord, so walk ye in him." It is only through faith that we are able to keep God's commandments. Obedience by faith is the only kind of true obedience that there is. "When we know God as it is our privilege to know Him, our life will be a life of continual obedience."—*The Desire of Ages*, p. 668. Notice the condition—when we know God.

It is not our trying hard to make ourselves acceptable to God that makes us acceptable. Nor is it our trying hard to obey that makes us obedient. Both acceptance and obedience come as a gift from God, and are received only by faith, through the continued relationship with Him.

WE CAN'T OBEY

For as by one man's disobedience many were made sinners, so by the obedience of one shall many be made righteous. Rom. 5:19.

The method by which we live the Christian life is the same method by which we began it—by faith alone. Our justification is by faith alone—our acceptance with God is based totally on our receiving the merits of Jesus in our behalf. And we are to live by faith, as well.

One of the first reasons why obedience *has* to come by faith only is because of the nature of sin and sinners. We are all sinners, whether we have ever done anything "wrong" or not. It is not sinning that makes us sinners. It is getting born that makes us sinners. "For as by one man's disobedience many were *made* sinners, so by the obedience of one shall many be made righteous" (Rom. 5:19). We are sinners because we are born in this world of sin, and whether we ever sin or not is beside the point. We *are* sinners. "Our hearts are evil, and we cannot change them."—*Steps to Christ,* p. 18.

There are many texts that remind us of this fact. "There is none righteous, no, not one" (Rom. 3:10). "If we say that we have no sin, we deceive ourselves" (1 John 1:8). We are "by nature the children of wrath" (Eph. 2:3). "I know that in me (that is, in my flesh,) dwelleth no good thing" (Rom. 7:18). We are all sinners, and were all *born* sinners.

Perhaps the clearest passage on this subject is found in John 3. Christ tells us that in order even to see the kingdom of God, we must be born again. If this is true, then there had to be something wrong with our first birth. All of us who are born into this world are born with a problem—we are born separated from God. That is the basic issue in being born sinners. We would remain so forever had it not been for the cross. But because of the cross, we do not have to remain separated from God. God gives every person the option of being born again.

The reason for studying this point in connection with the subject of obedience is this: If our hearts are evil and we cannot change them, then how could we ever obey? If in our flesh dwells no good thing, then how could *we* ever obey? *We* can't! It is only as we come to Jesus, admitting our helplessness, and accepting Him by faith, that makes obedience possible.

Oh that you would
Bless me indeed and
enlarge my territory
that your hand would
be with me and that
you would keep me
from evil that I may
not cause pain

SINFUL BY BIRTH

If we say that we have no sin, we deceive ourselves, and the truth is not in us. 1 John 1:8.

All of us who are born into this world are born separated from God. Jesus provided a way by which we can be brought back into the relationship with God that was severed when Adam sinned.

The first symptom of being born separated from God is that we are born self-centered. That's the problem. We are all self-centered. From this self-centeredness springs everything that we call sin. And apart from God this condition will continue. Perhaps it would be well to remind ourselves of this premise: "None of the apostles and prophets ever claimed to be without sin. Men who have lived the nearest to God, men who would sacrifice life itself rather than knowingly commit a wrong act, men whom God has honored with divine light and power, have confessed to the sinfulness of their nature."—*The Acts of the Apostles,* p. 561. We are sinners by nature, and will remain so until Jesus comes again.

Please notice that we are sinners by birth, and that we will continue to be sinners by nature, until Jesus comes again, *whether we're sinning or not.* When the apostles and prophets admitted and confessed the sinfulness of their nature, they weren't saying that they were continuing to sin. When Paul said that he was the chief of sinners, he didn't mean that he was sinning all the time. Even before Paul was converted on the Damascus road, his behavior was above reproach. He was one of the best livers around. His conversion didn't result in a sudden moral decline. But as he drew closer and closer to Jesus, he realized more and more the sinfulness of his nature. "The closer you come to Jesus, the more faulty you will appear in your own eyes; for your wisdom will be clearer, and your imperfections will be seen in broad and distinct contrast to His perfect nature. This is evidence that Satan's delusions have lost their power."—*Steps to Christ,* pp. 64, 65.

It is only through union with Christ, through relationship with Him, and dependence upon Him moment by moment, that we are enabled to be truly obedient, in spite of the sinfulness of our natures.

TREES OF RIGHTEOUSNESS

That they might be called trees of righteousness, the planting of the Lord, that he might be glorified. Isa. 61:3.

We are born sinners, and we sin because we *are* sinners. We are not sinners because we sin! One of the evidences that we are all sinners is that we all die. You can't argue with that, can you?

I was speaking about this subject one time and a university professor spoke up from the back, "Birds die! Are they sinners? Cats die. Are they sinners?" Yes, they are! And I heard a couple of sinners fighting in the woods behind my house just last night! They had four legs and fur. But what was their problem? They were self-centered. The taint of sin has permeated every level of creation. We live in a world that carries the burden of sin, and so do we.

If this is our condition, if our hearts are self-centered and if we are sinners by birth and by nature, how can we ever hope to obey? Jesus talked about it in Matthew 7:16-18: "Do men gather grapes of thorns, or figs of thistles? Even so every good tree bringeth forth good fruit; but a corrupt tree bringeth forth evil fruit." If a good tree cannot bring forth evil fruit, and a corrupt tree cannot bring forth good fruit, then how can we ever hope to obey?

There is a beautiful text on this found in Isaiah 61:3: "To appoint unto them that mourn in Zion, to give unto them beauty for ashes, the oil of joy for mourning, the garment of praise for the spirit of heaviness; that they might be called trees of righteousness, the planting of the Lord, that he might be glorified."

So the Bible speaks of trees of righteousness that the Lord Himself plants for His own glory. This gives us hope. There is a possibility for bad trees to bring forth good fruit if the miracle of what Jesus is suggesting in these words of Scripture is a reality. Because of another tree, the tree on which Jesus offered up His life for our sins, we are given the offer of becoming trees of righteousness, the planting of the Lord. And as we unite ourselves to Him, we are enabled to do the deeds of righteousness as well, and to bring forth good fruit—fruit to His glory.

BAD GOODNESS

But we are all as an unclean thing, and all our righteousnesses are as filthy rags. Isa. 64:6.

B ecause we are born separated from God when we come into this world, we are all partakers of the common problem of self-centeredness. Sometimes people look at a newborn baby and ponder, How could such a tiny person be a sinner? He has never had a chance to break the commandments. How could he be a sinner? But if you recognize that sin's number-one manifestation is self-centeredness, it is a little easier to understand. Newborn babies are certainly self-centered! They're the most *openly* self-centered people around! Never mind if mother is sleeping or eating or trying to do something else. When baby wants something, he wants it now!

Another problem people sometimes face is how they can be sinning by continuing to live their life on their own, apart from God, so long as they are good, moral people. We have tended to define sin in terms of doing bad things, and if we are strong-willed enough to refrain from doing bad things, we think that we have righteousness.

The apostle Paul admitted that he was the chief of sinners. Did that mean that his life was immoral, that he was the chief of criminals? No, it meant that he had come close enough to the Lord Jesus to recognize his true condition. He recognized that the only righteousness he had came from Jesus, and that apart from Him he had none at all.

It is a hard thing to realize that even our good deeds can be sin if we are living apart from the faith relationship with Christ. It is difficult to admit that "all our righteousnesses are as filthy rags." The text doesn't say that all our filthy rags are as filthy rags, or that all our iniquities are as filthy rags. That we could accept more easily. No, all our *righteousnesses,* all our rightdoing, all our so-called obedience, that is done apart from Christ, is still filthy rags, is still sin.

It is the motives and desires on the inside that God looks at, not our outward appearance. We may mow the widow's lawn, in itself a good deed, but apart from Christ it is sin, because our motive will inevitably be a selfish one. True obedience is always from the heart, and comes only through a relationship with Christ.

CHRIST'S OBEDIENCE IN US

I am crucified with Christ: nevertheless I live; yet not I, but Christ liveth in me: and the life which I now live in the flesh I live by the faith of the Son of God, who loved me, and gave himself for me. Gal. 2:20.

Since we are sinners by birth and by nature, and because there is no such thing as righteousness apart from Jesus, we can come to only one conclusion. In order to be trees of righteousness, the planting of the Lord, we must have accepted of His grace and forgiveness initially, and we must continue the relationship and communion with Him. "Sinful man can find hope and righteousness only in God; and no human being is righteous any longer than he has faith in God and maintains a vital connection with Him."—*Testimonies to Ministers,* p. 367.

The real issue in sin is not in doing bad things, but rather in living our lives, good *or* bad, apart from Christ. Our deeds, whether outwardly good or bad, are done for selfish reasons if we are not in dependence upon Christ and abiding in Him.

Since we are sinners by nature, *we* of ourselves are never going to be able to produce any obedience. If *we* are the ones doing the living in the Christian life, we can produce only thorns and thistles. If *we* are the ones who are working the works, what we produce will always be imperfect.

Which brings us to a crucial question. In the Christian life, do *we* do the living, or does Christ do the living in us? The Bible teaches plainly that Christ wants to live in us, to work in us, "to will and to do of his good pleasure" (Phil. 2:13). It is possible for Christ to dwell in our hearts by faith (see Eph. 3:17).

If we are depending on our own obedience we can never hope for anything but imperfect obedience. But if Christ is living in us, His work in us will not be imperfect. Through His indwelling presence and control, we can obey perfectly. We obey, yet it is not us, but Christ living in us.

The just shall *live* by faith. If those who have been pardoned and justified through the righteousness of Christ are living by faith, they *can* obey. As we live the daily Christian life by faith in Jesus only, and with Him dwelling in us, we can have obedience that is real.

OBEDIENCE COMES FROM PEACE

Great peace have they which love thy law: and nothing shall offend them. Ps. 119:165.

It is an amazing fact that it is God's forgiveness, His mercy, and His peace that changes our lives. Peace was purchased at the cross. Because of the cross, the good news is out again today: "Him that cometh to me I will in no wise cast out" (John 6:37).

If you are looking for victory and longing for true obedience, the very first prerequisite is that you understand the unconditional love and acceptance of God for you. We don't get peace by getting victory, we get victory by getting peace. The only person who can ever obey is the one who already has the peace of acceptance with God.

When we consider the subject of obedience, and try to learn how obedience fits in with the subject of salvation by faith alone, there are two dangers. The first is that we will focus only on the obedience. We will consider obedience only in terms of outward actions, behavior, morality. When this happens, we begin to try to make ourselves obey in order to find favor with God. If we are strong-willed and succeed, we become proud of our success and more self-centered than ever. If we are weak, we do not succeed even outwardly, and we give up in discouragement.

The second danger is that we will conclude that obedience is neither necessary nor possible. We forget that obedience or disobedience is the great issue to be decided at the very end of the great controversy (see *The Desire of Ages*, p. 763). We forget that whether or not obedience was possible, or necessary, was the initial issue in the great controversy, when Satan fell from heaven and accused God before the universe of creating laws that were impossible to obey. The great controversy is not yet finally settled, and the question of whether or not obedience is possible is still being debated. God says it is essential. Satan says it is impossible. And each of us must decide whom we are going to believe.

As we come to God, admitting our helplessness to save ourselves or to make ourselves obey God's law, He gives us peace. And peace brings release. Peace brings victory. Peace brings obedience—the only kind of true obedience that there is.

OBEDIENCE FROM WITHIN

For therein is the righteousness of God revealed from faith to faith: as it is written, The just shall live by faith. Rom. 1:17.

Obedience comes only by faith. Obedience is by faith alone. Those who have been counted just shall *live* by faith as well. One of the reasons that obedience can come only by faith, and by faith only (and if you don't think I'm trying to say that more than once, you've missed the point), is found in the Sermon on the Mount. There Jesus teaches that you don't have to commit adultery to commit adultery. And you don't have to kill someone to be guilty of murder. If you have lust or anger in your heart, you are guilty already.

If this is true, then much of what we would like to call obedience is actually sin. If I want to cheat on my income tax, but I don't do it, I am still a cheat. If I find the idea of robbing a bank appealing, even if I have never stolen a dime in my life, I'm still a thief. In fact, if I crave unhealthful foods, even if I am strong-willed enough to refuse to eat them, I can still be a glutton! Notice this comment in *Counsels on Diet and Foods,* page 35: "Men will never be truly temperate until the grace of Christ is an abiding principle in the heart. All the pledges in the world will not make you or your wife health reformers. No mere restriction of your diet will cure your diseased appetite. . . . Christianity proposes a reformation in the heart. What Christ works within will be worked out under the dictation of a converted intellect. The plan of beginning outside and trying to work inward has always failed, and always will fail. God's plan with you is to begin at the very seat of all difficulties, the heart, and then from out of the heart will issue the principles of righteousness."

Let me ask you a question. If God has wrought His work in your heart so that you have begun to see sin as He sees it; so that your tastes, inclinations, ambitions, and passions are brought under His control (*Selected Messages,* book 1, p. 336); so that your feelings, thoughts, purposes, and actions are in harmony with God's will (*Steps to Christ,* p. 61)—if that has happened, will you have to try hard to obey? Why, you'd have to try hard not to! Through the ongoing faith relationship with Jesus, we *can* be changed into His image, so that we are obedient—from the inside out.

SURRENDER OF SELF, NOT THINGS

Whosoever believeth on him shall not be ashamed. Rom. 9:33.

If we are sinners, and cannot produce genuine obedience apart from God, then all we can do regarding ourselves is to surrender ourselves—give up on the idea that *we* can ever produce genuine obedience.

The word *surrender* doesn't show up in the Bible. The closest thing is the word *submit,* found in Romans 9:30 to 10:4. "What shall we say then? That the Gentiles, which followed not after righteousness, have attained to righteousness, even the righteousness which is of faith. But Israel, which followed after the law of righteousness, hath not attained to the law of righteousness. Wherefore?" (Or why?) "Because they sought it not by faith, but as it were by the works of the law. For they stumbled at that stumblingstone." The stumblingstone is Jesus.

"Brethren, my heart's desire and prayer to God for Israel is, that they might be saved. For I bear them record that they have a zeal of God, but not according to knowledge." They're ignorant about something. What is it that they're ignorant about? "For they being ignorant of God's righteousness, and going about to establish their own righteousness, have not *submitted* themselves unto the righteousness of God. For Christ is the end of the law for righteousness for every one that believeth."

Well, someone says, what kind of righteousness is this talking about? Imputed? Or imparted? It makes no difference! There is no such thing as righteousness apart from Jesus. Whether it's imputed or imparted is beside the point. The person who stumbles and does not know righteousness in either sense is the one who is trying to do it himself. Notice that they have not submitted *themselves*—it isn't talking about surrendering things, but surrendering self. There can be a big difference between surrendering things and surrendering self.

The strong-willed person who quits his smoking, drinking, and dancing, apart from Christ, may become a "good" church member. But who really did it? He did. And thus even his good behavior is still sin, because he is living apart from Christ. The only kind of obedience we can ever produce on our own is merely outward. And it isn't real. True obedience comes only from Christ, through the relationship with Him.

169

ESCAPE FROM SURRENDER

For they being ignorant of God's righteousness, and going about to establish their own righteousness, have not submitted themselves unto the righteousness of God. Rom. 10:3.

A strong-willed person can use giving up his wrong deeds as an escape from true surrender, giving up on him*self*. Even the strong-willed person must come to the realization that although he might be able to give up the external wrong actions, within he is still the same. Only God can deal with the problem of sin on the inside.

Perhaps some speaker tells our young people that the devil has something to do with rock music, and they get rid of their rock records. But those who have given up their rock music for any reason other than a love for Jesus, and letting Jesus come into their lives, have not really given up their rock music. When the unclean spirit is pushed out by the person, and the place is left swept and garnished, seven other spirits will come and take its place. Sin is never really pushed out by the person. Sin is always crowded out by the Lord Jesus coming in. And whenever a person tries to push out sin by his own backbone and willpower, he is going to end up in a worse condition than before. He may or may not go back to rock music. But he may go into deep pride because of his accomplishments. And pride is the worst of all sins.

So, you see, the question of surrender can be very tricky if we think that it has to do primarily with giving up things. Surrender is giving up on ourselves, and accepting Jesus' own words in John 15:5, "Without me ye can do nothing." This is not talking about the things that God has given everyone the ability to do as long as He keeps their hearts beating. Without Jesus, you can still take out your garbage. Without a relationship with God, you can still make a million, it has been proved. Without God, you can be a sharp businessman or a mathematician or a doctor. Without God, you can even curse God. Because of His love for people, and His respect for their power of choice, He will even keep the heart beating in the chest of the man who curses Him. But without God, even the strongest person in the world cannot produce the fruits of righteousness. That's what John 15:5 is talking about. Without Him, there is no such thing as genuine obedience.

THE FRUIT OF THE FRUIT OF THE FRUIT

But now being made free from sin, and become servants to God, ye have your fruit unto holiness, and the end everlasting life. Rom. 6:22.

If obedience or disobedience is the last issue to be decided in this world (see *The Desire of Ages,* p. 763), but if, because I am a sinner by nature and cannot obey, then there is only one possible thing for me to do. That is to give up on myself, admit that I cannot do it, and realize that the only way obedience can happen is through faith and trust in the One who *does* have the power to change me from the inside. "We cannot keep ourselves from sin for one moment. Every moment we are dependent upon God. . . . Christ lived a life of perfect obedience to God's law, and in this He set an example for every human being. The life that He lived in this world we are to live through His power. . . . The Saviour took upon Himself the infirmities of humanity and lived a sinless life, that men might have no fear that because of the weakness of human nature they could not overcome. Christ came to make us 'partakers of the divine nature,' and His life declares that humanity, combined with divinity, does not commit sin."—*The Ministry of Healing,* p. 180.

Right here many people become nervous. When we look to ourselves, we realize how far short we come. But we are not to look to ourselves, but to the power of God. This is how it works: the relationship with God, based on communication with Him day by day, results in the fruit of faith. Faith results in the fruits of the Spirit. And the fruits of the Spirit result in obedience. All of them spring from the relationship of personal fellowship with the Lord Jesus. Jesus lived His life in this world through the power of His Father, the power that came from above—not from the power that came from within. In so doing He became our greatest example of how to live the life of faith.

We will never *be* just like Jesus. Jesus was sinless from the start—we weren't. Jesus was the Son of God—we aren't. Jesus never needed a Saviour—we do. But just because we will never *be* exactly as Jesus *was* does not mean that we cannot obey as Jesus obeyed. There is a difference. By depending on Jesus as He depended on His Father, we can have victory.

171

CHOOSING TO LET GOD CHOOSE | **JUN 14**

And if thy right eye offend thee, pluck it out. Matt. 5:29.

Jesus referred to the problem of surrender in very interesting words. He said, "If thy right eye offend thee, pluck it out, and cast it from thee: for it is profitable for thee. . . . And if thy right hand offend thee, cut it off, and cast it from thee: for it is profitable for thee." Have you ever pondered this passage? I'm thankful for the insight given in *Thoughts From the Mount of Blessing,* page 61: "It is through the will that sin retains its hold upon us. The surrender of the will is represented as plucking out the eye or cutting off the hand."

Someone says, "If I'm supposed to give up my will, that sounds to me as though I'm going to go through life maimed and crippled." For the high achiever, the capable person, this seems disconcerting. Sometimes they even become angry at it. "God made us in His image," they say. "He's not going to take away our wills. He's not going to make automatons out of us."

I'd like to invite you to read *Steps to Christ,* page 47, very carefully before this day is over. Within the context of that page, *will* is defined as our power of choice. Every time you read the word *will,* substitute *power of choice,* and see what you come up with. You can conclude nothing else than that surrender is giving up our power of choice.

"Oh, but I'll be crippled!" Well, if God invites me to give up my power of choice, can't I leave the question of whether or not I'm going to be crippled up to Him? God invites us to surrender our will toward everything except the continuing relationship with Him. We are always free to choose whether to continue seeking Him. We never lose our power of choice there.

Let's get more practical about it. Say I have a problem: smoking. And God says, "If you will give up your power of choice toward everything except your relationship with Me, an entire change can be wrought in your life." Is the victory gained by choosing not to smoke? No, it doesn't work that way. Instead, I give up my power of choice to Him, and exercise my power of choice toward the faith relationship. Jesus then comes in and lives His life in me, and *He* chooses not to smoke! Obedience comes only by faith, because we are invited to give up on ourselves and allow Christ to control us and choose for us, as we surrender more and more constantly to Him.

HOPE FOR THE WEAKEST

Who through faith . . . out of weakness were made strong. Heb. 11:33, 34.

One time I was talking to the husband of one of my church members. He was an alcoholic. Looking at me through bleary eyes, he said, "I *admire* the Seventh-day Adventists. It takes a strong person to be a Seventh-day Adventist." Do you agree with that? Or is it possible for a weak person to be a Seventh-day Adventist, as well?

For too long, religion has catered to the strong-willed people. We have tended to attract that kind of members to the church. At any time that Jesus as our only hope of salvation, and our only power for obedience, is not emphasized as the dominant theme, it is inevitable that we are going to end up with some sort of do-it-yourself system.

When we realize that God wants us to surrender *ourselves* to Him, to give up on ourselves and on the idea that *we* can ever produce genuine obedience, we begin to understand what Paul meant when he said, "It is no longer I who live, but Christ who lives in me" (Gal. 2:20, RSV). Through the power of an indwelling Christ, the weakest person in the world, as well as the strongest, is assured of victory.

It was the strong-willed people who crucified Jesus when He was here. They were threatened by His acceptance of weak people. They didn't want to hear about surrendering themselves, giving up their will, their power of choice, to God. A group of them attended Matthew's feast one day, and *The Desire of Ages*, page 280, describes their response to Jesus' teachings. When they discovered that there was no way of weaving themselves into the plan of salvation, they rejected it. There are thousands of people who want a religion that allows them in some way to weave themselves into the picture. They want to earn a part of their way themselves. And when they discover that there's nothing they can do but fall at Jesus' feet in humility and admit that they cannot produce anything of value apart from Him, this becomes too heavy a cross to bear.

It is crucifying to admit that we cannot overcome sin, that we cannot obey, that we cannot produce righteousness, but that Jesus must do all of this for us. But it is only in taking up the cross daily that we follow Him.

173

NO ADVANTAGE FOR THE STRONG |

He giveth power to the faint; and to them that have no might he increaseth strength.
Isa. 40:29.

The good news of salvation by faith in Jesus is not merely good news for the strong person. It is good news for the weakest person as well. This is true for obedience as well as for eternal life. Because genuine obedience always comes from within, and because the strongest person, apart from Christ, can produce only outward obedience, none have an advantage in overcoming.

But what about the relationship with Christ? The effort involved in the fight of faith, in coming to Christ initially and in continuing to come, does not always happen spontaneously. And if that faith relationship with Jesus is the entire basis of the Christian life, then doesn't the strong person have an advantage after all?

Have you ever read that "when it is in the heart to obey God, when efforts are put forth to this end, Jesus accepts this disposition and effort as man's best service, and He makes up for the deficiency with His own divine merit"?—*Signs of the Times,* June 16, 1890. Sometimes we have read this sort of statement and concluded that it is talking about putting forth effort in trying hard to obey the commandments. But if you check the context, if you read the whole article from which it was taken, you will find that it is referring primarily to the effort put forth in seeking the *relationship* with God, from which all genuine obedience springs. It is talking about having the desire in the heart to obey God by opening the door and inviting Him into your life. It is talking about the effort involved in reserving that quiet corner of the day for fellowship and communion with Him, so that He will be able to go with you all through the day. When you do that, then Christ with His own divine merit will make up for deficiencies in the constancy of dependence that the growing Christian feels.

The weakest person, who can't stop his drinking or smoking or anything else, who also fears that he cannot enter into a meaningful private life with God, has hope too, because God will meet him more than halfway. But when it comes to overcoming sins, God doesn't meet me more than halfway—He has to do it *all.*

GOD PLANTS SEEDS, NOT TREES

So is the kingdom of God. . . . First the blade, then the ear, after that the full corn in the ear. Mark 4:26-28.

It would be wonderful if it were true that from the first time we were brought to the place of giving up on ourselves and surrendering our will to Christ we had uninterrupted victory. But we must face reality. A growing Christian does not experience constant dependence upon God's power. When God plants a tree, He plants a seed. When He plants corn, first comes a blade, then the ear, and after that the full corn in the ear. So there's no need for discouragement when we realize that our obedience is not perfect all the time.

In the first place, God doesn't accept us because of our obedience. He accepts us when we come to Him, presenting the merits of Jesus in dying in our place. Our acceptance before Him, and the certainty of our salvation, is already settled, as we *continue* to accept what Jesus did for us at the cross. And second, God Himself allows for growth.

The only way to victory and obedience is to look to Jesus, and what He has done and wants to do in our lives. As we grow as Christians, our trust and our total dependence upon His power is going to be inconstant. At times we will remember that we cannot overcome Satan in our own strength. We won't even try. We will look to Jesus for victory, and He will give it to us. At other times we will think that we can manage things ourselves, and we will fall and fail and end up in defeat. But this is not reason for discouragement. God has provided power for us to obey, and also forgiveness and pardon for sin.

There is a statement that I think should be written in the flyleaf of every Bible: "There are those who have known the pardoning love of Christ and who really desire to be children of God, yet they realize that their character is imperfect, their life faulty, and they are ready to doubt whether their hearts have been renewed by the Holy Spirit. To such I would say, Do not draw back in despair. We shall often have to bow down and weep at the feet of Jesus because of our shortcomings and mistakes, but we are not to be discouraged. Even if we are overcome by the enemy, we are not cast off. . . . As we come to distrust our own power, let us trust the power of our Redeemer."—*Steps to Christ,* p. 64.

ONLY TWO MASTERS

No man can serve two masters. Matt. 6:24.

Obedience can come only by faith, first of all, because of the nature of mankind. We are sinners. We will be sinners until Jesus comes, and sinners cannot produce obedience. Second, obedience can come only by faith; because since we are sinners and cannot produce obedience apart from God, all we can do is give up ever hoping to produce any real obedience. The only thing we can do is surrender, give up on ourselves, submitting totally to the control of Jesus Christ.

What does it mean to be controlled by God? I used to think that there were three choices as to who could be in control of my life. I thought that we could either be under the control of God, or we could be under the control of Satan, or we could be in charge of ourselves and run our own lives. There are many young people, teenagers especially, who would like the option of being able to be in control of themselves. They have experienced the thrill of breaking from the nest, and are eager to do their own thing.

It comes as a surprise to discover that there's no such thing as being in control of ourselves. We are either under the control of one or the other of two powers—that's all. The only control we have is to choose which power is going to control us. Had it not been for the cross, we would have been hopelessly under the devil's control, with no other option. But Jesus at the cross made it possible for God to give us another choice—the choice to come under His control.

Being under the control of Satan brings the most abject slavery. Choosing to come under God's control brings the greatest freedom. But it's still control. "Know ye not, that to *whom* ye yield yourselves servants to obey, his servants ye are to whom ye obey; whether of sin unto death, or of obedience unto righteousness. But God be thanked, that ye were the servants of sin, but ye have obeyed from the heart that form of doctrine which was delivered unto you. Being then made free from sin, ye became the servants of righteousness" (Rom. 6:16-18). The question here is whether I'm a servant of sin and Satan or a servant of Jesus. There is no other choice. Jesus Himself talked about only two masters, and you can't serve both. It's always one or the other. The choice is open to each of us today to choose who will control our lives.

CONTROLLED BUT FREE

Neither yield ye your members as instruments of unrighteousness unto sin: but yield yourselves unto God, as those that are alive from the dead, and your members as instruments of righteousness unto God. Rom. 6:13.

An instrument is something that is used and controlled by the artisan or the soldier. An ax in the hands of a 4-year-old will not bring down a giant tree in the forest. But an ax in the hands of an experienced woodsman will bring down the tree. The law, being weak through the flesh, is never going to be kept by people apart from Christ. But when a person becomes an instrument in the hands of Christ, then obedience is possible.

An instrument is a passive thing, but many of us are afraid of the word *passive.* Someone asks, "Do you mean that I am to yield up my will to God, and be controlled by Him, so that I won't even choose what color of wallpaper to put on the wall? I won't even choose what color of socks to wear, or what dress to put on?" Well, I'd like to ask you a question: What's so frightening about that? You know, I have chosen the wrong wallpaper a few times. I would just as soon have a little help with the wallpaper! Especially with hanging it! But if you don't want to go that far, then go at least this far: We are absolutely dependent upon God's control for obedience to His law.

We don't have to be afraid of becoming puppets, of losing our power of choice, or our individuality. If it is the Creator who invites us to come under His control, why does the matter seem so scary? Our Creator is the One who wanted us in His image, with individuality and power of choice, to begin with. The idea of making us "free moral agents" was His in the first place. Can't we safely leave the rest of the road in His hands, and respond to His invitation to yield ourselves to His control?

My son used to like to jump off the piano bench into my arms. It wasn't his idea at first. I thought it up! I put him up there and said, "Jump. I'll catch you." Without a moment's hesitation, he jumped. And I caught him. Why? Because he trusted me. If I trust my heavenly Father, and He invites me to come under His control, to surrender myself to Him, will I not be safe in His hands? Trusting Him is the only kind of real freedom there is.

GENUINE OBEDIENCE

Know ye not, that to whom ye yield yourselves servants to obey, his servants ye are to whom ye obey; whether of sin unto death, or of obedience unto righteousness. Rom. 6:16.

Every soul that refuses to give himself to God is under the control of another power. He is not his own. He may talk of freedom, but he is in the most abject slavery. . . . While he flatters himself that he is following the dictates of his own judgment, he obeys the will of the prince of darkness."—*The Desire of Ages,* p. 466. "Unless we do yield ourselves to the control of Christ, we shall be dominated by the wicked one. We must inevitably be under the control of one or the other of the two great powers that are contending for the supremacy of the world."—*Ibid.,* p. 324.

Everyone in this world, everyone in the church, is under the control either of God or of Satan. As we choose to enter into the faith relationship with God, this enables Him to be in control of our *direction,* and our direction will be upward, in spite of the occasional misdeed. If we do not choose to have a relationship with God (and there are too many church members who have not), then our direction is controlled by Satan, and it will be downward, in spite of the occasional good deed.

God's ultimate goal for us is that not only will He be in control of our direction but that we will continue this relationship until He is able to lead *us* to be under His absolute control all of the time. He will hold over us absolute sway—by our own choice. And we will be possessed by the Holy Spirit. Don't tell me that that kind of person would be unable to obey!

The devil's purpose is that we will stay apart from a relationship with Jesus so that he will have control of our *direction,* until he reaches his goal for us. His ultimate goal is to have us under *his* absolute sway, and have *us* possessed by him. And, please, devil possession can be manifested in more ways than just frothing at the mouth and rolling in the dirt. The Pharisees in the days of Christ were possessed by the same evil spirit as the demoniac in the Temple.

When we realize our condition as sinners, and surrender ourselves to the control of God, He brings us to the point of obedience—obedience by faith in Him alone. To be controlled by God is the only route to genuine obedience.

POSSESSED BY THE SPIRIT

I have loved thee with an everlasting love: therefore with lovingkindness have I drawn thee. Jer. 31:3.

When the soul surrenders itself to Christ, a new power takes *possession* of the new heart. . . . A soul thus kept in possession by the heavenly agencies is impregnable to the assaults of Satan."—*The Desire of Ages*, p. 324. Does that sound like good news? We may not understand exactly all that is meant by having Christ living in us, controlling us, and willing and doing in us. But we can be thankful that we have that choice. Frankly, I'm not too happy with my performance apart from Him. I *am* thankful for the victory, power, and obedience available as we place ourselves under His control, aren't you?

"In the change that takes place when the soul surrenders to Christ, there is the highest sense of freedom. . . . The only condition upon which the freedom of man is possible is that of becoming one with Christ."—*Ibid.*, p. 466. How is it possible to be free and at the same time to be controlled? The secret is found in the key word, *love*. The control of love causes a person to do what he couldn't have done otherwise—and like it! Not only like it, but be thrilled with it.

I was shaving one morning when my 4-year-old came up to me and said, "Daddy, I *need* a white kitty with blue eyes." Now, I don't like cats—I don't like the way they come up and rub against me without even being invited. They fight with each other in the woods at night and keep me awake. But my daughter hadn't yet noticed what horrid animals they are! I replied, "Where would you keep a white kitty?" She said, "In my room." And I saw an escape. "You can't keep a cat in your room—there isn't any *place* for a cat the way you keep your room!" She disappeared, and I thought I had had the last word.

But before I had finished shaving, she was back. She took my hand and led me to her room. I'd never seen it so tidy. I still don't know what she did with all the stuff in such a short time. But her room was spotless. In a final attempt to save the day I said, "LuAnn, did you clean up your room because you want a white kitty with blue eyes, or because you love your daddy?" And she said, "Because I want a . . . because I love my daddy!" Our home has had a white kitty with blue eyes ever since! The control of love makes all the difference.

HOW SIN BECOMES HATEFUL

I delight to do thy will, O my God: yea, thy law is within my heart. Ps. 40:8.

The program that most of us have operated on at some time, at least, in our Christian lives is this: we think we will always love sin, but we will grit our teeth and stay away from it because we love God. The usual concept in Christian circles is that in living the Christian life we refrain from evil and do what is right because we love God, even though we would like to do wrong. "I love to dance. I always did. I probably always will. But I won't do it, because I love Jesus." "I love pork. Pork was always one of my favorites. I'd love to have some right now. But I've given it up—that's my cross for Jesus, and I'll bear it for Him." I do not believe that this is genuine obedience.

"All true obedience comes from the heart. It was heart work with Christ. If we consent, He will so identify Himself with our thoughts and aims, so blend our hearts and minds into conformity to His will, that when obeying Him we shall be but carrying out our own impulses. The will, refined and sanctified, will find its highest delight in doing His service. When we know God as it is our privilege to know Him, our life will be a life of continual obedience. Through an appreciation of the character of Christ, sin will become hateful to us."—*The Desire of Ages*, p. 668.

Don't work on obedience—put your attention toward knowing God, and obedience will come. Isn't that clear? Yet how many of us have wasted countless time and energy working on obedience, instead of seeking to know God.

We understand the working of cause and effect in many other areas of our lives. Even children know that if they want to grow, the thing to do is eat—not try hard to grow. Good doctors know that it is essential to discover the cause of an illness, not merely to treat the symptom. Is it any different in our spiritual lives? God knows that if He can gain possession of our hearts, our behavior will be changed naturally and spontaneously. He knows that if He can somehow let us see sin as He sees it, and understand His love sufficiently so that we will trust Him with our happiness, we will come to hate sin as He does. And if we hate sin, if we find sin repulsive, as Jesus did, will not obedience naturally follow?

ON AGAIN, OFF AGAIN

My little children, these things write I unto you, that ye sin not. And if any man sin, we have an advocate with the Father, Jesus Christ the righteous. 1 John 2:1.

When we study the subject of God's control we are faced with a practical problem. As we are growing in our Christian lives and in our relationship with Christ, sometimes we depend on Him and sometimes we depend on ourselves. Sometimes we allow Him to control us; at other times we take the control away from Him and are again controlled by Satan. While it is exciting to realize that it is possible to be, at any given moment, completely under God's control and have all the obedience and victory that He has for us, we still must realize that we take advantage of this possibility only part of the time.

Remember Peter? In the sixteenth chapter of Matthew we see this principle of part-time control working in his life. Jesus asked the disciples who they said He was. Peter answered, "You're the Christ." And Jesus commended him for his answer, telling him that it was the Spirit of God that revealed that to him. But just a few moments later, when Jesus began to speak of His coming sufferings, Peter rebuked Him and said, "No, this isn't going to happen to You." And Jesus said, "Get thee behind me, Satan." Obviously, one moment Peter was under the control of God, and the next moment he was under the control of Satan. The thought of the sufferings to come caused him to take his eyes off God's power and focus on himself, and he fell.

Martha is another example. When Jesus came to visit her and her sister after the death of Lazarus, she met Him with strong faith, not doubting His power and His love even in the face of death. But moments later, when He told her to roll away the stone, her thoughts turned to self, and she doubted His word. Part-time control by God, part-time control by Satan.

This fact is recorded in Scripture time and time again. The disciples, who at the foot-washing were "all clean," forsook Jesus and fled when the mob arrived at Gethsemane. Zacharias, looking for a moment to the weakness of humanity, doubted the angel's word, and was unable to speak until the birth the angel foretold. Each of us today, as we grow, can experience the same thing. But God leads us as quickly as possible to His control *all* the time.

181

PASSIVE CAN BE ACTIVE

And what shall I more say? for the time would fail me to tell of Gideon, and of Barak, and of Samson, and of Jephthae; of David also, and Samuel, and of the prophets. Heb. 11:32.

In surrendering to God's control, some are afraid that their individuality and personality will be destroyed. They are afraid that they will become puppets. What we need to understand is that there are only two possibilities for who is to control our lives—God or Satan—never us. And which is more likely to end in the destruction of our individuality and freedom? The control of God or the control of Satan?

God *does* know how to preserve our individuality, even as He controls us. He is the One who created that individuality to begin with. If there was ever a stubborn person it was the apostle Paul. Before he came to Christ, he was stubborn for himself and his own ideas. After he came to Christ, he was stubborn for God and His cause. Before Andrew came to Jesus, he was quiet and retiring. After he came to Jesus, he was still the same, but always *quietly* bringing someone from the sidelines to Jesus.

Are you worried about becoming a passive instrument in the hands of God? Didn't you ever sing, "'Have Thine own way, Lord! Have thine own way! Hold o'er my being Absolute sway'"? Did you mean it? Or are you bothered by the word *passive?* Just don't forget how active passive can be!

Jonathan was apparently out of his mind. He took his armor-bearer and went climbing up a mountain to wipe out an entire enemy army by himself. But he was being controlled by God. He was a passive instrument in God's hands. And the enemy went running.

Gideon went to war with pitchers and candles. He had sent home 95 percent of his army, keeping only a handful. They attacked, and the enemy fled. He was being controlled by God.

Moses led more than a million people from bondage in Egypt to the Promised Land. Joshua, under God's control, led the people of Israel on to possess the land. Paul traveled from one city to another, starting either a revival or a riot wherever he went. The control by God will make us the most active we've ever been. But we are still simply instruments in His hands. Are you willing for Him to control you today?

OBEDIENCE—THE FRUIT OF FAITH

Abide in me, and I in you. As the branch cannot bear fruit of itself, except it abide in the vine; no more can ye, except ye abide in me. John 15:4.

Obedience can come only by faith, because obedience is the fruit of faith. Faith is always the spontaneous result of something else. Jesus said, "Abide in me, and I in you. As the branch cannot bear fruit of itself, except it abide in the vine; no more can ye, except ye abide in me. I am the vine, ye are the branches: He that abideth in me, and I in him, the same bringeth forth much fruit: for without me ye can do nothing" (John 15:4, 5).

John 15 is probably one of the most outstanding passages in all Scripture concerning how obedience comes, and teaching us that genuine obedience is natural and spontaneous. It is not forced. Let's look at this passage phrase by phrase for a moment. "Abide in me, and I in you." What does that mean? To be "in Christ" simply means to be in *relationship* with Him, to be in fellowship and communion with Him. And what does the word *abide* mean? If you do a careful study in the Bible on the word *abide*, you will discover that it simply means "to stay." The two men on the way to Emmaus said to the Stranger, "It is late in the day; abide with us. Stay with us."

There are two things that are equally necessary for the Christian life. One is to get with Jesus in the first place, and the other is to stay with Him. Getting with Him is no good unless you stay with Him, and obviously, you can't stay with Him unless you first get with Him. And how do we stay with Him? In the same way as we got with Him. All by faith, and the ingredients that result in faith, the methods of communication.

Then the chapter says that the branch cannot bear fruit of itself unless it abides in the vine. When we talk about fruit, we talk about the fruit of the *vine*. It's not the fruit of the branches. But God doesn't produce anything apart from us. He produces fruit through us. If we are branches and try to produce fruit apart from the vine, we're not going to get any fruit at all. We're going to get nothing. Never forget that the fruit is always the fruit of the vine. God works through us; He doesn't bypass our faculties. Working through us, He produces the genuine fruit of obedience.

FRUIT TO HIS GLORY

Herein is my Father glorified, that ye bear much fruit. John 15:8.

Jesus said in John 15 that if we abide in Him, we will bring forth much fruit, but without Him we can do nothing. We can do nothing toward what? The context of the passage is that we can do nothing toward producing fruit. We all know that we could do nothing, period, if God didn't keep our hearts beating. But He was talking to people whose hearts were already beating. And He says, "Even though your heart is beating, you cannot produce fruit apart from Me. You can produce nothing."

If you want a mini-course in salvation by faith in Christ alone, there are two texts that sum it all up. John 15:5: "Without me ye can do nothing." And Philippians 4:13: "I can do all things through Christ." Put the two together. If without Him we can do nothing, but with Him we can do all things, then that leaves the final answer to the question of human effort. The only thing left for me to do is to get with Him. And stay with Him. That's all I can do.

It is through the process of getting with Christ in communion and fellowship that we abide in the vine. That's the way we come to Him in the first place, through studying His Word and through prayer; and that's the way we stay with Him in the second place. It is as we stay with Him, and continue our relationship with Him, that we bear fruit to His glory.

There's nothing more spontaneous than fruit. If you read the chapter in *The Desire of Ages* on the vine and the branches, you find these words: "The Saviour does not bid His disciples labor to bear fruit. He tells them to abide in Him."—Page 677. Where is the labor? To abide in Him. *Steps to Christ*, page 61, says that obedience is the fruit of faith. So if one is the result and the other the cause, you put your attention toward the cause, never toward the result.

That's why some of us have taken the position that genuine obedience is natural. Natural obedience comes as a result of the faith relationship. It is by beholding that we become changed. As we deliberately choose to spend time each day in beholding Christ, in contemplating His life, in communing with Him, the fruits of the Spirit, and the fruit of obedience, will be seen in our lives.

HOW TO KNOW YOU'RE FOR REAL

For of the abundance of the heart his mouth speaketh. Luke 6:45.

Would you like to know for sure whether or not you are a Christian? Would you like to know for sure whether you are a genuine follower of Christ? "Oh," someone says, "the proof of it is if you are living a good life." No, that doesn't prove a thing. There are many people who live good lives apart from Jesus. They are externally obedient, apparently good moral people. There are good moral people who would give you the shirt off their back, and curse God at the same time. You know that. Morality can come from all sorts of bad motives. We can put on a good performance because we want others to think well of us, because we want to stay out of jail, or even because we're just too afraid to do anything else!

So how are we supposed to know whether we are really Christians? *Steps to Christ* gives two tests. Of whom do you love to talk, and of whom do you love to think? (See page 58.) If you find yourself often thinking of Jesus and wanting to talk about Him, this is probably as close as you are going to get to a test of whether or not you are a genuine Christian.

The early Christians were called "Christians" because Christ was all they could talk about. "Christ did this. Christ said that. Christ did the other." And finally the people who listened said, "We might as well call them *Christians*." What would you be called if people chose your name on the basis of what you talk about the most? If you are a Christian, you will love to think and talk of Jesus.

As we continue to focus on Jesus day by day, and look at His love and mercy, and understand more of the sacrifice that He made in living and dying for us, we will be changed. As Jesus becomes the center and focus of our lives, our conversation will reveal the fact. Our thoughts will center upon Him. And our behavior will more and more be genuinely obedient, as a result of seeing what Jesus has done for us and how great is His love for us. It is by dwelling upon Jesus and His love that our lives are changed.

He that saith, I know him, and keepeth not his commandments, is a liar, and the truth is not in him. 1 John 2:4.

Jesus is the greatest example of obedience that we have, and He did it all by faith, through dependence upon His Father, even as He now invites us to depend on Him and His Father. The example of Jesus is the greatest reason why we may understand that obedience comes only by faith. Jesus was never our example in justification. He didn't need any justification. But He was our example in sanctification, in living the Christian life, for He lived His entire life through faith in another power.

In the opening of the great controversy, Satan had declared that the law of God could not be obeyed. That's been his charge all along. He also claimed that should the law be broken, it would be impossible for the sinner to be pardoned. Please don't forget who it is that says that the law of God cannot be obeyed. When men broke the law of God, Satan exulted. But by His life and death, Jesus proved that God's justice did not destroy His mercy. He proved that sin could be forgiven and that the law could be obeyed perfectly. "It was because the law was changeless, because man could be saved only through obedience to its precepts, that Jesus was lifted up on the cross. Yet the very means by which Christ established the law [justification] Satan represented as destroying it. Here will come the last conflict of the great controversy between Christ and Satan."—*The Desire of Ages,* p. 763. There are even champions of the cross in our church today who say we can't obey the law of God.

Until the end of time, obedience or disobedience is the question to be decided by the whole world. So this is a pretty big issue. And it is very "Adventist." If we don't continue to maintain our understanding of why we are Seventh-day Adventists, we are going to lose out in the end.

Jesus came to die for us; He also came to give us an example of how to live. He said, "The Father that dwelleth in me, *he* doeth the works" (John 14:10). Jesus was so surrendered to His Father's will that the Father alone appeared in His life. Jesus, who was God, lived as a man, through dependence upon His Father. By His example we see that we can live the same life of obedience, through dependence upon Him.

POWER FROM ABOVE

I in them, and thou in me, that they may be made perfect in one; and that the world may know that thou hast sent me, and hast loved them, as thou hast loved me. John 17:23.

One of the most beautiful truths in the whole theme of salvation by faith is that Jesus came not only to die for us but to show us how to live, through dependence on the power that is above us, not the power that is within us. Jesus said in John 5:19 and 30, "I can do nothing of Myself."

It is almost a comedy that, while Jesus, who *had* power within Him that He could have used, constantly depended upon the power above Him and never used the power He had within, we, who have no power within to produce anything in terms of obedience or righteousness, constantly try to depend upon the power that we don't have! Jesus, who was God, lived as a man, through dependence upon God. And we who are men try to live as God. It simply can't be done. This is one of the most conclusive reasons why obedience can come only by faith.

Jesus not only proved that the law of God could be kept but He makes provision for each one of us to keep it if we will depend on God as He did. Jesus had no advantage over us (*The Desire of Ages*, p. 119). Not even by a thought did Jesus yield to temptation. So it may be with us (*ibid.,* p. 123). We can obey as Jesus did (*ibid.,* p. 309). We can overcome as Jesus did (*Thoughts From the Mount of Blessing,* p. 17). Through grace, the law of God can be perfectly obeyed by every child of Adam (*ibid.,* p. 49). Jesus' life in you will produce the same as in Him (*ibid.,* p. 78). Satan claimed that it was impossible for man to obey God's commandments. In our own strength it is true that we cannot obey them. But Christ in the form of humanity, by His perfect obedience, proved that through Him we can obey every one of God's precepts (*Christ's Object Lessons,* p. 314).

Obedience is possible. Obedience is necessary. Obedience is important. If we depend upon Jesus as He depended upon His Father, we will have Him dwelling in us, and obedience will come naturally, spontaneously. "The life that Christ lived in this world, men and women can live through His power and under His instruction. In their conflict with Satan they may have all the help that He had. They may be more than conquerors."—*Testimonies,* vol. 9, p. 22.

OBEDIENCE BY FAITH

Chosen and destined by God the Father and sanctified by the Spirit for obedience to Jesus Christ and for sprinkling with his blood. 1 Peter 1:2, RSV.

Truth should never be judged by our experience. If the Wright brothers had done that, they would have continued making bicycles. But they said, "There's something possible that we haven't seen yet." And today we have a Boeing 747 that is longer on the inside than was the Wright brothers' first flight.

The fact that obedience is possible, and that obedience is necessary, and that obedience is God's goal for each of us, should not be discouraging. Perhaps you are aware, as I am, and painfully so, that you are not obeying perfectly all of the time. But whether we fall or fail has nothing to do with the truth of the fact that God has the power to keep us from sinning.

Obedience is possible. It is possible only through faith. This is true because faith is not just mental assent but trust based on relationship with One who is trustworthy. It is true because of our nature as sinners. Because apart from Jesus we have no righteousness, and only through connection with Him are we partakers of His righteousness. Obedience is only by faith because of the nature of surrender. When we are faced with our helplessness as sinners, our only option is to give ourselves up to the control of God. Obedience is only by faith because of the fact that until we have given up to God's control, we are being controlled by Satan. There is no middle ground where we run our own lives. We are under either God's control or the control of the enemy. Obedience is only by faith, because obedience is a fruit of faith, and fruit is always spontaneous, always a result of something else. Fruit is never obtained by working hard on producing fruit. Fruit comes by being united to the vine. And, finally, obedience is only by faith because of Jesus' example. As we depend on Him, in the same way as He depended on His Father, the obedience that was manifested in His life will be seen in our lives as well.

Obedience is not the cause of our salvation, even though it is a condition. It is the result. As we behold the love of Jesus day by day, we are changed into His image.

SALVATION AND YOUR WILL

So then it is not of him that willeth, nor of him that runneth, but of God that sheweth mercy. Rom. 9:16.

One of the major breakthroughs in understanding how to live the Christian life is to learn how the will operates in sanctification. We were told a long time ago that we would be in constant danger until we understood the right action of our will in living the Christian life, and that through the proper understanding of the will, an entire change could be made in our lives (see *Testimonies,* vol. 5, p. 513; *Steps to Christ,* p. 47).

It all has to do with the question of whether sanctification is by faith alone or whether it is by faith plus works. The question of divine power and human effort is still awaiting our careful study. Many people accept the premise that *justification* is by faith alone, but find it hard to turn loose of the idea that there is something we can do to save ourselves in the process of *sanctification.* Some consider it dangerous to give up the idea that the *method* of living the Christian life is by faith plus works. "The third angel's message will not be comprehended, the light which will lighten the earth with its glory will be called a false light, by those who refuse to walk in its advancing glory. . . . In the manifestation of that power which lightens the earth with the glory of God, they will see only something which in their blindness they think dangerous, something which will arouse their fears, and they will brace themselves to resist it."—*Selected Messages,* book 1, p. 372.

The problem is that if we do not understand how to use the will properly, we are likely to use it improperly. That's where the danger is. If we put our effort and our willpower toward that which is impossible for us to do, then we will end in defeat. If we don't understand properly how our will and human effort operate in living the Christian life, the devil is going to have a ready-made method of discouraging us, and short-circuiting the whole relationship with God. We will lose the assurance that we gained when we first accepted Christ, because we will not understand how to maintain that assurance by keeping our attention directed away from ourselves to Jesus. Genuine faith and trust in His merits is our only hope at the beginning and all through the Christian life.

THE USE OF YOUR WILL

For I know that in me (that is, in my flesh,) dwelleth no good thing: for to will is present with me; but how to perform that which is good I find not. Rom. 7:18.

The question of the will, how our will and our willpower operate in living the Christian life, is a vital one. The two major texts, from Paul, on the subject of the will are Romans 7:14-21 and Philippians 2:12, 13. Romans 7 talks about the frustration of the converted Christian who has not yet learned to depend upon God's strength, and is trying to depend on his own strength. The predominant word in this passage is *do.* That which he wants to *do,* he doesn't *do.* And that which he doesn't want to *do,* he does. And right in the middle, verse 18, he says, "For to will is present with me; but how to perform that which is good I find not." The person whose emphasis is on doing what is right is not going to find how to perform.

In Philippians 2:12, 13 we are told to "work out your own salvation with fear and trembling. For it is God which worketh in you both to will and to do of his good pleasure." It is God that does *both* the willing and the doing when it comes to performance in the life of the Christian. God does *not* do both the willing and the doing in the life of the Christian when it comes to seeking the faith relationship. Is there a difference? It is *not* God that does the willing and the doing in the fight of faith. It *is* God that does the willing and the doing in the fight of sin. God has promised to fight sin and the devil for us, if we will allow Him to do so (2 Cor. 10:4, 5). And the way we allow Him is by doing the willing and the doing in the area of relationship and fellowship with Him, which He can never do for us.

There is a part in the Christian life, at the beginning and in the continuing process, where there is something we have to do. Admittedly, faith is from God's initiative all the way along. But there is still a point at which we must choose to respond to His initiative. And the proper use of the will is in choosing to respond to God's knocking at the door for relationship with Him. If we will choose that, and continue to choose that, God will demonstrate in our lives, more and more unto the perfect day, that He can do the willing and the doing through us concerning the fight of sin.

THE SIMPLICITY OF THE GOSPEL

For it is written, I will destroy the wisdom of the wise, and will bring to nothing the understanding of the prudent. 1 Cor. 1:19.

But God hath chosen the foolish things of the world to confound the wise; and God hath chosen the weak things of the world to confound the things which are mighty; and base things of the world, and things which are despised, hath God chosen, yea, and things which are not, to bring to nought things that are: that no flesh should glory in his presence. But of him [of God] are ye in Christ Jesus, who of God is made unto us wisdom, and righteousness, and sanctification, and redemption: that, according as it is written, He that glorieth, let him glory in the Lord" (1 Cor. 1:27-31).

I'm glad today that we have been promised wisdom, because the simplicity of the gospel is a hard subject to understand. One of the reasons it is so hard to understand is because it is so simple. For a long time we have been looking for something deep and theological, when the truth is, it is simple. And God sometimes has to help us realize how simple it really is.

We had a teacher in college who used to tell us that "great art conceals art." He had to explain that to us. He said that many things that are so profound are profound in their simplicity. At first glance, that which is really great may be so unobtrusive that it doesn't appear great.

I'm thankful that Jesus is our wisdom. Please notice that there is no such thing as wisdom apart from Jesus. We are not given wisdom as an entity in itself—wisdom is in Jesus. *He* is made unto us wisdom.

Jesus came into this world and depended upon His Father for wisdom. *God* was *His* wisdom. The wisdom we see demonstrated in His life came from His Father. That same wisdom is available to us today, through connection with Jesus. It is wisdom that enables us to understand in its completeness the theme of salvation by faith in Jesus. It's hard, because there is something about the human mind that resists the idea that there is no way in which we can save ourselves. But the truth is that all we can do is to come to Jesus just as we are, and continue to come to Him day by day, in order to continue the experience of salvation. There is wisdom from above to help us understand and accept this simple gospel.

191

JESUS IS OUR WISDOM

If any of you lack wisdom, let him ask of God, that giveth to all men liberally, and upbraideth not; and it shall be given him. James 1:5.

If you want to know the difference between Christianity and other religions, you don't need to go buy a book on world religions or take a course on the subject. You need to take a look at just one factor. Religions other than the Christian religion are based upon the premise that man can in some way save himself. The Christian religion alone says that mankind needs a Saviour, that he's not big enough to save himself. But we need wisdom from above us to be able to grasp that fact, *and accept it.*

1 Corinthians 1:30 says that Jesus is our wisdom. Some say that this text is referring to Christ's imputed work, not imparted. Do you have it clear in your mind the difference between these two terms? Perhaps a memory device might help. In the middle of one word is the word *put*—im*put*ed. It refers to that which is *put* to our account in heaven. In the middle of the other is the word *part*—im*part*ed. It refers to that which becomes *part* of our lives. Is God's promised wisdom referring to something imputed, wisdom put to our account? That wouldn't be worth much, would it? Our text today says, "If any of you lack wisdom, let him ask of God, that giveth *to all men* . . . and it shall be given *him.*"

This is an important point because of the next three gifts mentioned in Corinthians. Christ Jesus is "made unto us wisdom, *and* righteousness, *and* sanctification, *and* redemption." They aren't simply put to our account either. They include the work of God *in* us as well. Just as wisdom comes to us in Christ, so do righteousness and all the rest.

Jesus is our wisdom for the purpose of understanding the great aspects of salvation, righteousness (or justification), sanctification, and redemption, which includes the whole spectrum of salvation, including glorification when Jesus comes again. Justification is experienced when we get with Jesus in the first place, sanctification is experienced as we stay with Jesus, and glorification will take place as we go with Jesus when He comes again. All three are included in salvation, and all come as gifts from Jesus as we continue the faith relationship with Him.

NO CONDEMNATION

For God sent not his Son into the world to condemn the world; but that the world through him might be saved. John 3:17.

Justification, which includes freedom from the guilt of our past sins, prepares us for sanctification, which includes ultimate freedom from our present sinning. If you don't have justification straight, you will be confused on sanctification as well. In order to be able to accept the power of God over our present sins, we must understand that He does not condemn us for our sins of the past. When we come to Him for justification, not only does He forgive us but we stand before Him as though we had never even sinned. It is this freedom from guilt and condemnation that allows us to experience the growth and victory in our lives that come from knowing that we are at peace with God.

In *Steps to Christ,* page 49, the first paragraph talks about a failing and discouraged life. It then says, "It is peace that you need." Have you thought that in order to have peace you had to get your life fixed up first, and have victory over your sins? No, it is the peace with God that gives you the power for your life to be changed. Peace doesn't come from victory— victory comes from peace. It is feeling that you are rejected that keeps you in your sins and failures. Loving acceptance paves the way for growth.

Satan has triumphed time and time again by getting religious people to believe that when they fall or fail, they are condemned. But Romans 8 says it is God that justifies. Who is he that condemns? You know who condemns. It is Satan! John 3:16 is a well-known text—but have you learned verse 17? "For God sent not his Son into the world to condemn the world; but that the world through him might be saved."

Have you ever heard discussions about which is more important, justification or sanctification? I'd like to remind you that the question is a foolish one. Sanctification must be based solidly on justification. They are both important! It's like asking which is more important, getting married or staying married. They are both important! They are important for different reasons, but they are both important. What God has done for us and what He wants to do in us are *both* good news. They are both included in salvation.

ALL THAT WE CAN DO

For it is God which worketh in you both to will and to do of his good pleasure. Phil. 2:13.

One of the probing questions that has frustrated Christians for years is the question of how the will operates after conversion. There have been debates and questions concerning the will, but most of the discussions have dealt with the use of the will before conversion—whether man is free to be saved or not. Very little has been done on the use of the will after conversion. But there are several classic statements on the subject, from inspiration.

What can *we* do in this whole business of salvation from our sinning? *Selected Messages,* book 1, page 381, says: "Let no man present the idea that man has little or nothing to do in the great work of overcoming; for God does nothing for man without his cooperation. Neither say that after you have done all you can on your part, Jesus will help you. Christ has said, 'Without me ye can do nothing.'" "All that man can possibly do toward his own salvation is to accept the invitation, 'Whosoever will, let him take the water of life freely.'"—*Ibid.,* p. 343. So let's nail it down—there is something for us to do, and that is to take the water of life freely.

But that's an intangible. Where is the water of life? The same author defines what it is in *Thoughts From the Mount of Blessing,* page 113: "In . . . communion with Christ, through prayer and the study of the great and precious truths of His word, we shall as hungry souls be fed; as those that thirst, we shall be refreshed at the fountain of life." So, how do we partake of the water of life? By communion with Christ, through prayer and the study of His Word.

One of our problems in trying to live the Christian life is that we often are found trying hard to do that which God has told us we cannot do—fight sin and the devil. And we do not put forth effort to do that which He has invited us to do, that is, seek communion with Him. This does not mean that works are unimportant, but we are talking about method. And the method of knowing God's gifts is by faith alone. As we put forth our effort to come to Jesus, and to keep coming to Jesus, He will fulfill His promise to work in us, to will and to do of His good pleasure.

FIGHTING THE RIGHT FIGHT

Thou blind Pharisee, cleanse first that which is within the cup and platter, that the outside of them may be clean also. Matt. 23:26.

When the devil comes to tempt us, he doesn't knock on the door and say, "Good morning. I am the devil. I have come to tempt you today." He knows it wouldn't work that way. If he did that, we would say, "We've heard of *you;* forget it!" and slam the door in his face.

So he comes at us instead through our weaknesses, through our problems. The devil is stronger than we are. He is smarter than we are. He knows that the best way to tempt us is to get us to concentrate on our faults and weaknesses, trying to overcome *them,* instead of looking to Jesus and depending on His strength. There is a big difference between the fight of faith, which the Bible invites us to fight, and the fight of sin. If we try to fight sin and the devil in our own strength, we will lose the battle every time.

Jesus gave the Pharisees instruction as to where to put their effort. He told them that if they would clean the inside, the outside would be clean as well. This is one of the most important truths in understanding how to live the Christian life. It is essential to realize where our human effort must be directed, and where our human effort is totally useless. We are told that if we will fight the fight of faith with all our willpower, we will conquer (see *Testimonies,* vol. 5, p. 513). What is the fight of faith? It is the life of relationship with God, the striving to set aside time day by day for the purpose of getting acquainted with the Lord Jesus. This fight of faith is the only fight for the Christian spoken of in the Bible. As we direct our energies and efforts toward *that,* Jesus will fight sin and the devil *for* us as He has promised to do. "May the God of peace himself sanctify you wholly; and may your spirit and soul and body be kept sound and blameless at the coming of our Lord Jesus Christ. He who calls you is faithful, and *he will do it*" (1 Thess. 5:23, 24, RSV).

"Man is not able to save himself, but the Son of God fights his battles *for him,* and places him on vantage-ground by giving him His divine attributes. And as man accepts the righteousness of Christ, he is a partaker of the divine nature. He may keep the commandments of God, and live."—Ellen G. White, in *Review and Herald,* Feb. 8, 1898.

GOOD CHOICE, BAD PERFORMANCE

For the good that I would I do not: but the evil which I would not, that I do. Rom. 7:19.

Suppose I decide that I want to be a great singer. I rent a concert hall, and advertise in all the papers: "Come and hear the concert." I've made a good choice. I want to sing like one of the greats. Nothing wrong with that choice. So the crowd turns out. The time comes for the concert to begin. I go out onto the platform, and the piano gives the introduction. I open my mouth. To will is present with me, but now I've got to perform. And how to perform I find not! My voice squeaks and cracks and fades away, and above the shouts of laughter and derision, I make my way offstage. I have chosen to be a great singer, but I can't perform.

Suppose I choose to live the Christian life. Nothing wrong with that choice. I watch to see how it's done, and then I try. But although I've made the right choice, when it comes to performing, I'm finished. Paul discovered the same thing. Even Paul, with his tremendous intellect, who apparently was such a strong person, had discovered his weakness within. He knew the right choices, and he chose correctly—but then he couldn't perform. He talks about it in Romans 7. Right in the middle of his frustration, expressed by all those would nots and do nots, we find this verse: "For I know that in me (that is, in my flesh), dwelleth no good thing: for to will is present with me; but how to perform that which is good I find not" (verse 18).

When I decide that I want to do right, that I would like to keep God's commandments and be obedient to Him, I've made the right choice. But if I'm trying to fight sin and the devil myself, I can never succeed, because the problem of sin is on the inside, and even strong people can control only the externals.

In order to have the proper understanding of how to use your will (your power of choice), and your willpower (your power to follow through with your choice), you must understand the role of human effort in living the Christian life. God has never promised to seek Himself for us. He has never promised to do our Bible study and our prayer and our witnessing for us. But He *has* promised to fight Satan for us (see Rom. 8:37). As we put forth our effort toward knowing Him, He will give us victory.

196

WHEN ALL THINGS ARE NEW

Therefore if any man be in Christ, he is a new creature: old things are passed away; behold, all things are become new. 2 Cor. 5:17.

This text doesn't say that some things are to become new, but that *all* things *are* become new. Have you ever wondered when this was going to happen in your life? Many young people have expected that as soon as they were first converted, everything was supposed to be different, and they would have no more problems or failures from that point on; and that if they did, they probably weren't converted in the first place. This has discouraged many people.

We must understand that the new heart that is promised to us *leads to* a new life (see *Steps to Christ*, p. 18). We have a Bible full of case histories of people who have demonstrated the fact that when a person is born again, there still is the race to run, the battle to fight. Godly people didn't go from being sinners to saints, in terms of performance, overnight. Some people get nervous here and say that if we talk that way, we will open the door for license. But let's face reality. It is because we haven't faced reality that we have a lot of discouraged people. The disciples bickered and argued for three years about who was going to be the greatest. They knew that what they were doing was wrong. On their last trip to Jerusalem, when the Samaritans refused them hospitality, they wanted to call down fire from heaven. But Jesus didn't ask to start over with a brand-new twelve. He made allowance for struggling, growing Christians.

Let's make allowance for growth, but let's not leave all the victories God has in mind for us until just before we die or are translated. 2 Corinthians 5:17 is not just for the end of the line somewhere.

The truth is that at any time when we are depending on God's strength instead of our own strength, we can know complete victory, *now*. And at any time we depend on our own strength, we fail. As growing Christians we fluctuate between depending on His strength and on our own. That's the painful swing that we all experience. However, the growing Christian, even the baby Christian, can understand victory in the ultimate sense, *so long as* he depends upon God's power for obedience. It is when he depends upon his own power that he is defeated.

SO LONG AS

Whosoever abideth in him sinneth not. 1 John 3:6.

As we are growing in our Christian lives, at any time that we are depending totally on God's power, instead of our own, we experience victory. At any time we depend on our own power, we fall and fail. There is no middle ground. Either we are 100 percent surrendered, or we are 0 percent surrendered. The part-of-the-time victory, and the part-of-the-time defeat, is not a result of being partly surrendered, but rather of being 100 percent surrendered only part of the time.

This is what 1 John 3:6 is saying: "Whosoever abideth in him sinneth not." So long as we are abiding in Him, we are new creatures. And then so long as we are in the stance of abiding dependence upon His power, we do not commit sins. In order for the enemy to cause us to fall or fail, he first has to get us to break from the abiding dependence upon God.

Steps to Christ, page 62, describes the experience of justification. "If you give yourself to Him, and accept Him as your Saviour, then, sinful as your life may have been, for His sake you are accounted righteous. Christ's character stands in place of your character, and you are accepted before God just as if you had not sinned." That's justification. Then it continues, *"More than this . . ."* (You mean there's something more than justification? Yes!) "More than this, Christ changes the heart. He abides in your heart by faith. You are to maintain this connection with Christ by faith and the continual surrender of your will to Him; and *so long as* you do this, He will work in you to will and to do according to His good pleasure." (Italics supplied.) *So long as!* Three key words. Don't miss that phrase! Have you been so-long-as-ing it lately? "So long as you do this, He will work in you to will and to do according to His good pleasure. . . . With Christ working in you, you will manifest the same spirit and do the same good works—works of righteousness, obedience."

This obedience and victory for the Christian is not reserved for just before he dies or is translated. It is available the first week of the baby Christian. As we look away from our performance, to Christ, we are given the victory; and we continue to have victory *so long as* we continue to abide in dependence upon His power.

SPONTANEOUS VICTORY

Thine, O Lord, is the greatness, and the power, and the glory, and the victory.
1 Chron. 29:11.

So long as we are in the relationship of abiding dependence on God's power, sin has no dominion over us. The experience that we know of sometimes being defeated and sometimes having victory comes about because we don't depend on God's power all the time. We are painfully aware of these times when we fall and fail and are overcome by the enemy. We tend to become preoccupied with the one time that we lost our temper during the day, and conclude that we have had no victories.

The Desire of Ages, page 668, tells us that when we know God as it is our privilege to know Him, our life will be a life of continual obedience. Sin will be hateful to us. Is it possible that when we are in the close relationship of knowing God, and depending on and trusting in Him, that we may not even *notice* some of our victories, because they come naturally? If there is victory and obedience in the Christian life that is natural and spontaneous, then much of it could happen without our especially noticing it. Why is this? Because when those kinds of victories come, where is our attention? It is on Jesus. It is when our attention is on ourselves that we are so aware of how we are doing—and it is when our attention is on ourselves that we experience defeat!

Because of this, it is Satan's constant effort to get us to take our eyes off Christ, so that He won't be able to work His will in our lives. He knows that if he can get us to look away from Jesus and to ourselves, he has us. And he can succeed in diverting our attention from Christ by drawing our attention either to our defeats *or* to our victories! Have you ever been defeated because Satan came to you and said, "Look at how well you've been doing lately"?

But we have been told, "Not even by a thought did He [Jesus] yield to temptation. So it may be with us. Christ's humanity was united with divinity; He was fitted for the conflict by the indwelling of the Holy Spirit. And He came to make us partakers of the divine nature. *So long as* we are united to Him by faith, sin has no more dominion over us."—*The Desire of Ages,* p. 123. As we continue to look to Jesus day by day, we will learn to depend more constantly on Him.

CHOOSING GOD'S CONTROL

Choose you this day whom ye will serve. Joshua 24:15.

The person who has the abiding relationship with Christ, that is, daily fellowship and communion, with the devotional life as its base, has chosen to put God in charge of his *direction*. Within this relationship, as God leads us upward, we are at any moment either depending totally upon His power or we are depending 100 percent on ourselves.

Satan is constantly trying to distract our attention so that we will not stay locked in on the abiding dependence upon God's power. When we begin trying to fight Satan in our own strength, when we begin to concentrate on our behavior and performance, our attention is away from Jesus, and our dependence upon His power is broken. This can happen even though the relationship with Him may be continuing day by day. Whenever our attention is on our sins and weaknesses and problems, we are overcome.

If a person chooses to have the abiding relationship with Christ, his *direction* will be upward. God controls it, bringing him just as quickly as possible to abiding and depending upon His power all the time. But as we grow, there are times when we look to Jesus, and times when we look away from Jesus to ourselves, even in the course of a given day.

The beautiful thing is that God does not judge our character by the occasional good deed and misdeed that come as a result of that pattern. He looks at the tendency, the direction of the life. If we deliberately choose to place ourselves under His control day by day, by seeking the relationship with Him, *He* will lead us to total dependence upon His power all the time. The growth in the Christian life is basically the growth in learning to stay in dependence upon Jesus more and more constantly.

If we do not choose to have the relationship with Christ day by day, if we do not understand the proper use of the will, and where to put our human effort, and if we continue to seek to fight sin and the devil on our own, then our direction will be downward. Anyone who does not have a continuing relationship with the Lord Jesus, whether he has once become a Christian or not, is giving Satan control of his direction.

Our part is to choose the ongoing relationship with Christ, until ultimately we can be led to total dependence on Jesus' power all the time.

THE WELL HAS BEEN DUG

If any man thirst, let him come unto me, and drink. John 7:37.

Ed didn't feel very well. His mouth was dry, his lips were cracked, and he was so dizzy that he often fell down. And whenever *that* happened, he really got discouraged.

One day he decided to go to the doctor. Surely he didn't have to be like this the rest of his life. After the doctor had listened to his symptoms, he nodded his head. "Ed, your problem is that you are thirsty! It's a common enough problem." Ed felt relieved. "What should I do?" he asked.

The doctor leaned back in his chair. "First you should decide what bothers you the most. Is it the dry mouth, the cracked lips, or what? Let's say, for example, that your cracked lips bother you the most. Work on them until they are healed up. Then go to work on something else. Use your willpower. That's the key."

Ed went home, but after several days of saying, "I choose not to have cracked lips," he was in worse shape than ever. He tried another doctor. The second doctor was sympathetic when he heard Ed's story. "I can't imagine why the other doctor didn't tell you!" he exclaimed. "What you need when you are thirsty is water!"

"Water?" asked Ed faintly. "That does sound good. Where can I get some?"

"It comes from a well," replied the physician.

Ed hurried off—and began trying to dig a well. In a short time he collapsed. It was apparent that he would die before he could dig deep enough. But then he heard the good news. There was a well already dug. All he had to do was to go to the owner of the well, and he would be given all the water he needed. Ed went to the well and accepted the free gift. Now he's jogging around the countryside telling everyone the good news.

How many of us in our Christian life have spent fruitless time trying to overcome the symptoms of sin and trying to gain for ourselves the water of life. When we understand that the proper use of our will is to come to Christ, who issued the invitation "Let him that is athirst come. And whosoever will, let him take the water of life freely," we will find the victory that we sought in vain in our own strength. We don't need to dig the well—it has already been dug. All we need to do is to come and to accept the riches of His grace.

201

ULTIMATE VICTORY NOW

Nay, in all these things we are more than conquerors through him that loved us.
Rom. 8:37.

When we talk about the obedience of faith, we are not talking about an effortless life. We are talking about effort that comes naturally, instead of forced. We should be afraid of a religion that simply sits and waits and does nothing. There was a group of people known as Quietists who were legitimately charged with that. They expected God to do *everything*. But there is something that God cannot do for us. He cannot respond to Himself for us. We have to respond to Him ourselves. This is the way we cooperate with Him.

Some of us have had the idea that we will spend most of our lives struggling and fighting and gritting our teeth in an attempt to refrain from sin, and that somewhere down at the end of our Christian life, just before we die, we will find our efforts rewarded by no longer having sin appealing to us. But it is good news that this ultimate victory is available *now*.

When I was a teenager, I thought that probably by the time I reached my 20s I would be experiencing this sort of victory. Late in my 20s, I decided that it must happen in my 30s. But toward the end of my 30s, I was still flunking the course. And I moved it ahead to the 40s. I wouldn't want to tell you where I've had to move it now! But does the experience of being a new creature in Christ have to wait? Do we have to wait until we are so old that we couldn't sin anymore if we wanted to, because we are too feeble? Do we believe in righteousness by senility?

I've had grandmothers and grandfathers tell me that they are still looking for *all* things to become new. Age is not the determining factor. The thing that makes the difference between the old creature and the new is being in Christ and depending on Him. That is the big if—"If any man be in Christ."

At any time we are in Christ, in relationship with Him and in dependence upon His power, we will be new creatures. It is when we leave the dependent relationship with Jesus, and try to manage our own affairs, that we lose the battle with Satan and fall and fail. But to be new people is our privilege today, so long as we depend upon Christ's power.

INSIDE OUT

Woe unto you, scribes and Pharisees, hypocrites! for ye make clean the outside of the cup and of the platter, but within they are full of extortion and excess. Matt. 23:25.

Most of us have tried harder to clean the outside than the inside, and that's our trouble. That was the trouble of the Pharisees in the days of Jesus; He told them that if they would clean first the inside of the cup and platter, the outside would be clean. He didn't tell them to first clean the inside and then go to work on the outside. Being a new creature comes as a result of being in Christ. But most of us have spent years in fruitless effort trying hard to be new creatures, new people—from the outside. And we have spent little or no effort on being in Christ.

1 John 3:6 says, "Whosoever abideth in him sinneth not." This is another cause and effect. Should we put forth effort to abide in Him, or should we put forth effort to "sin not"? Most of us spend our time and energy in trying not to sin rather than directing our time and energy toward abiding in Him. Some say that this verse is talking about habitual sin. But when does a sin become a habit? Is it a habit if you do it once a year? How about six times a day? How about twice a week? It is difficult to say definitely when sin becomes a habit.

Look at *Steps to Christ,* page 61: "If we abide in Christ, if the love of God dwells in us, our feelings, our thoughts, our purposes, our actions, will be in harmony with the will of God as expressed in the precepts of His holy law." Please don't miss this point. Our feelings, our thoughts, our purposes—not just actions—will be in harmony with God's will. And it will happen when we abide in Christ, and His love dwells in us.

Have you ever heard someone say, "I haven't taken a drink for twenty years, but I haven't felt like drinking for three days"? But if we abide in Christ, our feelings as well as our actions will be in harmony with God's will. God doesn't give victory by changing simply the outward actions, and doing nothing about the feelings, thoughts, and purposes—the inside. God works from the inside out. And if our feelings, thoughts, and purposes are in harmony with God's will, would we have to try hard to obey, and to overcome temptation? No, it will come spontaneously to the one who abides in Christ.

ALL OR NOTHING

Doth a fountain send forth at the same place sweet water and bitter? Can the fig tree, my brethren, bear olive berries? either a vine, figs? so can no fountain yield both salt water and fresh. James 3:11, 12.

There are only two choices in the Christian life when it comes to abiding. We can either be abiding in Christ, or we can be not abiding in Christ. We can be depending upon Christ, or we can be depending upon ourselves. There are no other options. We cannot depend partly upon Christ, and partly upon self. It's all or nothing.

If when we first came to Christ we had locked in on God's power, and stayed there ever since, we should never have disobeyed or sinned again (1 John 3:6). But most of us are willing to admit that we have not had continual, unbroken victory in our Christian life, from the day we first came to Jesus to this very moment. Instead we admit to falling, and failing, and having to come to God for His forgiveness again and again. In the Christian life we experience a swing between abiding dependence upon Christ and depending upon our own power. This is why we have the interrupted victory we have known. If sin gets through to me at any moment, it is because I was not united to Christ by faith at that point.

We are told repeatedly that Jesus hated sin. Every sin was torture to His spirit (see *The Desire of Ages*, p. 111). He hated sin with a perfect hatred (see *Selected Messages*, book 1, p. 322). Contact with evil was unspeakably painful to Him. He could not witness a wrong act without pain that was impossible to be disguised (see *The Desire of Ages*, p. 88).

When we are united to Him by faith, sin will be hateful to us, as it was to Jesus. We will have no relish for sin (see *Messages to Young People*, p. 338). We will look upon sin with abhorrence (see *The Great Controversy*, pp. 649, 650). The renewed heart will have hatred for sin (see *The Great Controversy*, p. 508). "The prevalence of a sinful desire shows the delusion of the soul."—*Thoughts From the Mount of Blessing*, p. 92.

When we find sin to be appealing, we may know that we have somehow turned from the abiding dependence upon God and are depending upon ourselves. It is when we have done this that temptation has power over us. But victory comes spontaneously when we depend upon Him.

OUR ONLY SAFETY

Watch and pray, that ye enter not into temptation. Matt. 26:41.

Satan is well aware that the weakest soul who abides in Christ is more than a match for the hosts of darkness. . . . Therefore he seeks to draw away the soldiers of the cross from their strong fortification."—*The Great Controversy,* p. 530. Satan knows that he has to do this in order to get us. He knows the power of abiding in Christ.

If one who is abiding in Christ is more than a match for the powers of darkness, and if one who is abiding in Christ does not sin (1 John 3:6), and if one who is abiding in Christ doesn't even *feel* like sinning, but rather finds sin repulsive (see *The Great Controversy,* p. 508; *Thoughts From the Mount of Blessing,* p. 92; *The Desire of Ages,* p. 668), then how could Satan manage to tempt us?

On pages 71 and 72 of *Steps to Christ* there are five ways listed that he comes to bring temptations to us *when* we are abiding in Christ. "When the mind dwells upon self, it is turned away from Christ, the source of strength and life. Hence it is Satan's constant effort to keep the attention diverted from the Saviour and thus prevent the union and communion of the soul with Christ." So his constant effort is to get us to look away from the abiding dependence upon God's power to ourselves. Then we end up trying to fight sin in our own power. *Steps to Christ* then lists the ways he accomplishes this separation. (1) The pleasures of the world. These would have to be innocent pleasures, but things that could divert our attention from God if we focused on them. (2) Life's cares, perplexities, and sorrows. We have all had our share of these, and know how difficult it is at times to continue trusting God when troubles come. (3) The faults of others. Have you ever had your mind turned away from Christ because of the faults of others? (4) Your own faults and imperfections. This one is especially effective for those who are the most conscientious! And finally, (5) anxiety and fear as to whether or not we shall be saved.

It wouldn't work for Satan to come to one who is abiding in Christ and tempt him to break one of the commandments. Sin is repulsive to the one who is abiding in Christ and Christ in him. So Satan comes instead with whatever will get our attention off Jesus. It is only through abiding in Christ and keeping our eyes fixed upon Him that we have victory.

JESUS TAKES AWAY OUR SINS

And ye know that he was manifested to take away our sins; and in him is no sin. 1 John 3:5.

Someone wrote a book about how to live the victorious Christian life. The author is listed on the cover as "the Unknown Christian." When I saw that, I wondered what he was trying to tell me. How to live the victorious Christian life, by the unknown Christian. Who's done it? Can anyone do it?

When we talk about living the victorious life, we are not talking about overcoming unknown sin. That would have to be totally God's department. How could we possibly do anything with sin that we don't even know about? And we are not talking about what is going to happen to the sinful nature. Whatever happens to our sinful nature would also have to be handled totally by Christ. The one thing that we are talking to and can be aware of is how known sin is overcome. We are not talking about absolute perfection, but simply the question of overcoming known sin. This is possible, this is necessary, and this is God's plan for us in our lives today.

Can sin be overcome? The answer is Yes. One Person did it. His name is Jesus. According to Hebrews 4:15, He was tempted in all like as we are, yet without sin. 1 Peter 2:22: He did no sin, neither was guile found in His mouth. John 16:33: He said of Himself, "I have overcome." 1 John 3:5 tells us that in Him is no sin. But the same verse also tells us that He came to take away *our* sins. Did Jesus live His sinless life by being God? Or was it through the power of God, united to His human nature in the same way that is available to each of us?

Jesus lived His life as a man, not as God. He was born God. But He did not use that power to live His life. When He said, "I can of mine own self do nothing," He was telling us that He is our example. He came to show us how to live in dependence upon another power. The power that He had for living His perfect life came from above Him, rather than from within.

I don't have to be told that I don't have any power within me apart from Jesus. I have been beaten down too many times. But if His power is available to me as well, then it is possible for me to live today as He did, and be more than conqueror through Him that loves us.

LIVING WITHOUT SINNING

To him that overcometh will I grant to sit with me in my throne, even as I also overcame, and am set down with my Father in his throne. Rev. 3:21.

Can anyone live without sinning? Yes. Jesus did. Can *we*? No. Romans 8:7 says the sinful mind is not subject to the law of God, neither indeed can be. Romans 3:23 says that all have sinned. Until we realize our desperate condition, there is no chance for our presuming to handle the question of living without sinning. We *are* sinners, and we're going to remain sinners until our nature is changed.

So we come to a strange enigma. Psalm 1:6 says that the Lord knows the way of the righteous. Well, we are called righteous because of Jesus. But is that all that's involved? 2 Corinthians 5:21 says that Jesus was made sin for us, that we might be *made* the righteousness of God in Him. If that's true, then whatever can be accomplished in our lives in living without sinning is going to be accomplished through connection with Jesus, never independent of Him. So when we ask whether or not anyone can live without sinning, the answer is Yes. One did. His name was Jesus. We can't, apart from Him. There's no way. But we can and we will, in connection with Him.

You don't have to read very far into the book of Revelation to find the "he that overcometh" phrases. Overcoming sin and sins is one of the last things we glimpse as we study the Bible. It is one of the last realities concerning those people who live before Jesus comes.

When Jesus said to the woman that was dragged to Him, "Go, and sin no more," when He said to the man who was healed, "Sin no more," was this idle talk? *Could* they obey His command? Was it possible through His power? Of course!

Let's not get bogged down in trying to figure out who's done it, either. It's none of our business who's done it. Trying to decide truth on the basis of who has done it is very dangerous business. Jesus is our example, and it is to Him that we are to look. If we abide in Him as He did in His Father, we will be overcomers, in the same way that He was. It is only in looking to Him, not in looking to others around us, or in looking to our own lives and trying to measure ourselves, that we find victory.

KEEP LOOKING TO JESUS

Be sober, be vigilant; because your adversary the devil, as a roaring lion, walketh about, seeking whom he may devour. 1 Peter 5:8.

One of Satan's favorite activities is to club us over the head with our failures, shortcomings, and mistakes. There are probably many reasons for this. First of all, when we are feeling guilty we are miserable, and he enjoys making us miserable. Second, if he can keep our attention focused on the failures we have made, we're more likely to make more, because our attention will be taken off Jesus. And third, if he can lead us into such discouragement that we will give up in despair and scrap the whole relationship with Christ, and even give up on trying to be Christians, then he has accomplished his main purpose.

Whenever we look away from Christ, then the devil immediately gets us preoccupied with how we are doing. If you have been depending on Christ all day long, except for a few minutes when you lose your temper and throw the frying pan through the kitchen window, what stands out in your mind at the end of the day?

And which kind of victory do you remember longer? The victory that came when you were depending on Christ, and because of that the temptation seemed hateful and repulsive to you? Or the one that you struggled with for three days, wanting desperately to give in, but finally managing not to because you knew it was wrong? Victory from the inside out is the only real victory there is. When we find sin desirable and appealing then we have *already sinned*, internally, whether we ever commit the wrong action or not. When we understand this, then we know that the victory for which we struggled for three days was likely just external in the first place, and not real victory at all. But we still remember it better than the spontaneous, genuine victories that come when we are looking to Christ.

This is why it is never safe to look to our own performance as a measure of our Christian growth. If we take our eyes off Jesus and look at ourselves, we will inevitably be taken in by either pride or discouragement, depending on how we think we are doing. But as we continually look to Jesus, and think and talk of Him and His love for us, we will be more and more constantly abiding in Him, and depending on His power.

OVERCOMING THE WORLD

For whatsoever is born of God overcometh the world: and this is the victory that over-cometh the world, even our faith. 1 John 5:4.

If we could all overcome sin, it would surely cut down on the tragedies we experience in this world, wouldn't it? I am interested in overcoming sin, aren't you? And we know that it will happen only as we focus on Jesus. The Bible has some things to say about sin and how to overcome it.

God has only one kind of victory over any kind of sin, and that is natural and spontaneous victory, for the one who is abiding in Christ. All of the forced victories are the ones that we do ourselves. And what we call victory in that case is only external. The Bible definitely has made it clear that God has power that He wants to *give* us to keep us from sinning. He has also made provision to forgive those who fall and fail while they are growing. We can be thankful for both truths today.

The righteousness of Christ includes both God's forgiveness *and* His power to overcome. However, we need to remind ourselves that anyone who overcomes sin is not going to go around advertising it, and is not going to be claiming that he is sinless. In 1 John 1:8 we read that anyone who says he *has* no sin (or sinful nature) is deceived. But this doesn't do away with the Bible truth that we can overcome sin.

Have you ever heard anyone say that you won't stop sinning as long as you live on this earth, but so long as you hate it, everything is OK— that's all God expects? Do we say this to the murderer? Do we tell him to do the best he can not to kill too many people, but that so long as he hates what he's doing, there's no problem, that's the best God expects of him? Do we give that advice to the thief or the drunkard or the adulterer? Then should we take comfort in that idea for our "little" sins?

In 1 John 5:4 we find one of the key factors in overcoming sin: "This is the victory that overcometh the world, even our faith." When we learn that faith is a byproduct of the faith relationship with Christ, that faith is trust in someone whom we know is trustworthy, then it becomes clear that the way to victory is through ongoing fellowship and communion with Christ. This is the avenue that He uses to bring us to true obedience.

For what the law could not do, in that it was weak through the flesh, God sending his own Son in the likeness of sinful flesh, and for sin, condemned sin in the flesh. Rom. 8:3.

Sin is never overcome apart from the faith relationship with Christ. But within that relationship with Him, there are several steps that God leads us through to overcome sin in our lives. The first is to admit that sin *is* sin. If you have been struggling with a problem, and have had no victory, this could be one of your difficulties. Have you come to the place of admitting that it is sin, or are you still trying to excuse it? Has the Holy Spirit brought conviction to you on this point, or are you trying to go on what your parents said about it, or what your neighbors or pastor thinks? Victory never comes until we ourselves realize a thing is sin.

Once we have acknowledged that something is a sin, we must realize that we are helpless to do anything about it ourselves. The strong person may control his outward actions, but he hasn't overcome the sin. Sin is always from within, and is overcome only by God's power.

When we have come to the point of recognizing sin, and admitting our helplessness to battle with it, we then must realize where the battle *is*. In Romans 8:3 it says that what the law could not do, in that it was weak through the flesh, God, sending His own Son in likeness of sinful flesh, and for sin, condemned sin in the flesh, that the righteousness of the law might be fulfilled *in us* who walk not after the flesh but after the Spirit. If you are trying to overcome in your own strength, you will find nothing but weakness. But if you come to Christ, and allow His Spirit to work in you, you will overcome. If we direct all of our willpower toward seeking the faith relationship with Christ, we will have none left to fight sin and the devil. And that's how it should be, for Christ has promised to do this for us.

Another step is to recognize that God does not condemn us. God sent not His Son into the world to condemn the world. As we see the love of Jesus, and realize God's loving acceptance of us, it will break our hearts and transform our lives. And, finally, as we see what sin did to Jesus on the cross, this will become a mighty shield from temptation.

GOD'S LOVING PRESENCE

He that hath my commandments, and keepeth them, he it is that loveth me: and he that loveth me shall be loved of my Father, and I will love him, and will manifest my-self to him. John 14:21.

As a shield from temptation and an inspiration to purity and truth, no other influence can equal the sense of God's presence."—*Education*, p. 255. Are you having problems with sin in your life? One of the real reasons behind that could be that you don't sense God's presence, for if we did sense His loving presence, we would have a mighty shield against temptation.

Perhaps it sounds mystical, ethereal, that Jesus can be more real to us than He was to the disciples when He walked the dusty roads of Galilee. But it is true. John 14:21 makes it very clear that He loves us and will manifest Himself to us. And this sense of His presence is our shield against temptation and sin. As we make the deliberate choice to continue the daily relationship with Jesus, He will then lead us more and more into the constant realization of His presence.

I used to come home from school and head for the cookie jar. Have you ever done that? (I think they were molasses cookies with wheat germ!) Of course, I'd go for the cookie jar because I was hungry. Now I'm paying for my past because I have children of my own that I have had to try to keep out of the . . . apple bin! But when Mother was in the kitchen, with her loving presence, I suddenly had no problem keeping out of the cookie jar. However, Mother could be in the kitchen only sometimes. She wasn't there when she was in the basement or out in the yard or upstairs. But God, through His angels and His Holy Spirit, can be everywhere present. There's not a place where we can flee, but God is present there. If only we realized this every moment, it would make all the difference, wouldn't it?

And it's God's *loving* presence that is constantly surrounding us. It isn't a condemning presence. Fear will keep you from robbing a bank when the policemen are there. Fear will keep you from impropriety with your friend in the park, when the moon is shining and Father and Mother drive up behind you. Fear will prevent many things. But the presence of God that shields us is His loving presence. It's real. It is the loving presence of Jesus that gives power for overcoming and victory.

SIN LEADS TO SINS

Whosoever committeth sin transgresseth also the law: for sin is the transgression of the law. 1 John 3:4.

There is a difference between temptation and temptation*s*. It is the same difference as that of sin and sin*s*. Sin is living apart from God. Sin*s* are the results of that—the doing of wrong things, the acts of transgressions. Jesus never lived a life apart from God, although there was evidently some appeal to Him to be independent and trust to His own power. As a result of His not living life apart from God, but living a life of constant dependence upon God, sin*s* or temptation*s* had no appeal to Him. He was repulsed by them.

If we are in total dependence upon God's power at any given moment, and Satan hits us with one of his temptation*s* to sin*s*, we are repulsed by it, just as Jesus was. The victory comes spontaneously, because we don't even find the offer appealing. We don't find the wrong act desirable.

But when we are depending upon ourselves, we *will* find ourselves responding to Satan's temptation*s*, at least internally. Temptation*s* come in the following sequence. First, the temptation is presented. There is no sin in being tempted. Then we recognize the temptation, and have a chance to consider it. This still is not sin, for Jesus in the wilderness recognized that He was being tempted, and knew what the issues were.

The third step in temptation*s* comes only for those who are not depending upon God's power at the time of the temptation. That is, they consent to it in their minds. There is an inward response of "Yes, that sounds like fun!" It's sort of like an inward jack-in-the-box getting its lever pushed, and up pops the little man. But for the one who is in dependence upon Christ, this inner response, this finding the temptation desirable and appealing, does not take place.

At any time that we give inward consent to a temptation, we have already sinned. Because sin*s* always begin on the inside (whoever hates his brother is a murderer, whoever looks on someone with lust is an adulterer). For the one who is depending upon his own strength, this consent is given every single time. It is only when we are depending upon God's power that we are enabled to have the victory even at the point of desire.

WHEN TEMPTATIONS BECOME SIN

But every man is tempted, when he is drawn away of his own lust, and enticed. James 1:14.

Jane had a problem with honesty. Or should we say she had a problem with *dis*honesty? Well, anyway, she was a crook. She was a thief. She was a cheat. But one day she met Someone who had made a thief His last friend on earth, and she began to get acquainted with Him. She was convicted about her stealing, but more than that, she was convicted that she had been living her entire life apart from God. She began to understand something of God's love and acceptance, even for thieves, and she realized her need of Him. She surrendered to Him, and was converted.

One day Jane was in the grocery store. As she came around the corner by a soap display, she saw that someone had left her shopping cart untended, and her purse was within easy reach, gaping open, with a nice fat wallet right on top. A temptation. Now it is no sin to come upon an unwatched purse. So far, Jane was all right.

Jane immediately recognized that this was a temptation. She realized that she had an opportunity to steal someone's money. But she still hadn't sinned. Recognizing temptation is not sin. Jesus recognized when He was being tempted, and He never sinned. So she was still all right.

Now there are only two possibilities of what could happen next in this story. If Jane is depending upon God's power at that moment, and controlled by Him, she will be repulsed by the idea of stealing. She will find it unappealing. And she will be given victory spontaneously at that point.

If she is depending upon her own power at that moment, however, she will respond inwardly. "What an opportunity!" She will consent in her mind to the temptation. She will probably plan it. "Let's see, is there really no one in sight? Now if I just grabbed it and put it under my coat . . ." Whether or not she follows through on those plans will depend largely upon how strong-willed she is, and how much self-control she can muster. But she has *already* sinned, when she consented to it in her mind. Regardless of what *action* she takes, she has already sinned. True victory comes only from the inside, where God is dwelling, when we are in dependence upon His power instead of our own.

BEING GOOD BY NOT BEING BAD? | **JUL 26**

But I say unto you, That whosoever looketh on a woman to lust after her hath committed adultery with her already in his heart. Matt. 5:28.

If it is true that the thoughts and intents of the heart are as much brought into account as the actions, and that when we have inwardly consented to a sin, we have already sinned, whether we ever go ahead and commit the action or not, then why not go ahead with the action? If we have sinned already, and lost the battle, why not follow through with impure actions?

Well, first of all, there may be some good moral reasons why *not* to follow through with the sinful action that have nothing to do with God or victory or spiritual life. If we have enough willpower to keep from killing someone we are angry with, we will be able to stay out of jail, and that's a plus. And there would be some real benefits for the person we are angry with, too! There are all kinds of moral benefits to be reaped from positive behavior. But it's still not *victory* in God's sight. And there is another reason, besides the moral benefits, that make it a good idea not to follow every inward sin with an outward manifestation of it. There is power available to turn back to Jesus and His power before the inner failure is worked out.

When we understand that we have already sinned when we have given inward consent to wrong, and if we no longer call that victory, then we have the choice of turning to God for repentance *before* we follow through on the action. We can realize that our eyes have somehow been attracted away from Christ, and will not even attempt to fight the enemy in our own strength, but admit our helplessness and turn to Him.

For the growing Christian, there may be many times when we will find ourselves depending upon our own strength, and giving in inwardly to temptation. Because of the moral benefits to be reaped, we may be forced to grit our teeth and use our own backbone to keep from following internal defeat with external sinning. But *we should not call this victory!* If we are unwilling to admit that we are walking apart from Christ, it will be much longer before we are willing to turn and come again under His power. But when we admit that we *have sinned already,* and turn to Him again for repentance, He is able to give it to us.

VICTORY FROM WITHIN

But I say unto you, That whosoever is angry with his brother without a cause shall be in danger of the judgment. Matt. 5:22.

One day as I was teaching a college Bible class, I noticed that two of my students on the back row were kissing. I was insulted. I was angry. I lost my temper. In the first place, I didn't think it was a very proper thing for them to do. In the second place, it reflected on my abilities as a teacher. They should have been so fascinated with my presentation that they wouldn't have had time to kiss! *In my mind,* I went back to where they were sitting and banged their heads together. (It wouldn't have been that easy to do—I mean, there wasn't that much *room* between their heads!)

However, I *didn't* follow through and actually do it. I was tempted. I recognized the temptation. And because I was not depending upon God's power at that moment, even though I was right in the middle of teaching a *Bible* class, I sinned. I consented to the temptation. I thought it was a good idea. I responded to the suggestion in my mind. And I planned it. But I didn't act it. I was able to keep myself from getting violent. In fact, I controlled my temper so well that so far as I know, no one in the class ever knew that I was upset. I didn't follow through on the action because I didn't think the administration would be too impressed with my techniques if they heard about it. And I wasn't sure that it would add to the rapport with the rest of the class. But still I had sinned. In God's eyes, I *had* banged their heads together! I had not experienced victory, even though I was able to control my external actions.

When we talk of the necessity for victory to be internal as well as external, in order to be victory at all, we are not encouraging people to go around doing whatever they feel like doing while waiting for God to change the inside. But in a sense, this is probably not a danger anyway, because there are enough self-centered reasons for good outward behavior. If someone is strong enough, he will not choose to end up in jail or ruin his reputation, regardless of the question of victory in God's sight. But it is still important for us to realize that the only victory that is real is that which comes from within. Then we will realize our need of dependence upon Him, which comes as a result of our relationship with Him.

THE SEARCHER OF HEARTS

The heart is deceitful above all things, and desperately wicked: who can know it? Jer. 17:9.

Thus saith the Lord; Cursed be the man that trusteth in man, and maketh flesh his arm, and whose heart departeth from the Lord. For he shall be like the heath in the desert, and shall not see when good cometh; but shall inhabit the parched places in the wilderness, in a salt land and not inhabited. Blessed is the man that trusteth in the Lord, and whose hope the Lord is. For he shall be as a tree planted by the waters, and that spreadeth out her roots by the river, and shall not see when heat cometh, but her leaf shall be green; and shall not be careful in the year of drought, neither shall cease from yielding fruit" (Jer. 17:5-8). Here is a contrast between the one who trusts in the Lord and the one who trusts in flesh, or himself. The book of Psalms says that he who trusts in his own heart is a fool.

Today's text says that the heart is deceitful—even as to whether we are trusting in God or ourselves. Have you ever *thought* you were trusting in God but found that you were trusting in yourself and didn't know it until you had a horrible fall, showing how deceitful your heart really was? God has made provision to search our hearts and test our minds.

"God leads His people on, step by step. He brings them up to different points calculated to manifest what is in the heart. Some endure at one point, but fall off at the next. At every advanced point the heart is tested and tried a little closer. . . . Here they have opportunity to see what is in their hearts that shuts out Jesus."—*Testimonies*, vol. 1, p. 187.

A person who is abiding in Christ's strength experiences the power of God so that sin has no dominion over him. "He [Christ] abides in your heart by faith. You are to maintain this connection with Christ by faith and the continual surrender of your will to Him; and *so long as* you do this, He will work in you to will and to do according to His good pleasure."—*Steps to Christ*, pp. 62, 63. (Italics supplied.) It is not our part to keep examining ourselves moment by moment to see whether we are abiding in His strength. We may not be able to judge correctly. Our part is to continue our relationship with Christ by faith, through daily communion with Him, and He will bring us to victory.

THE REAL ISSUE IN TEMPTATION

The name of the Lord is a strong tower: the righteous runneth into it, and is safe.
Prov. 18:10.

Those who realize their weakness trust in a power higher than self. And while they look to God, Satan has no power over them. But those who trust in self are easily defeated."—Ellen G. White, in *Review and Herald*, Dec. 16, 1902.

If Satan has no power over us, we will not find the promptings of sin appealing. We are not saying that the sinful nature will be eradicated. But so long as we are in possession by the Holy Spirit, we will not respond to the promptings of sin, even though we are tempted.

Temptation when you are not finding the suggestion of sinful *things* appealing is the temptation to pull away from the control and possession by the heavenly agencies, and depend upon your own strength. This was Jesus' great temptation.

At those times when we are in the stance of total dependence upon God, we have the victory over all sins. But the growing Christian is easily distracted from that stance.

Joshua was one of the most godly men who ever lived. He was one of the two, out of the vast multitude, who had enough faith in God to be able to make the trip all the way from Egypt to the Promised Land. He experienced the power of God to such an extent that he could direct his army so that the enemy found them impregnable. By faith they crossed over the Jordan into the Promised Land. By faith the walls of Jericho fell down. But we see Joshua depending upon his own strength to handle the little village of Ai, and his forces were defeated overnight.

So the growing Christian is easily distracted. "Satan is well aware that the weakest soul who abides in Christ is more than a match for the hosts of darkness. . . . Therefore he seeks to draw away the soldiers of the cross from their strong fortification."—*The Great Controversy*, p. 530. James talks about it in James 1:14: Each one is tempted when he is carried away and enticed by his own lusts. And when lust has conceived it brings forth sin, and when sin is accomplished, it brings forth death. There is a drawing away in temptation that results in temptations for all sorts of other things. But as long as we are in dependence upon God's power we cannot be overcome.

217

OUR WEAKNESS, HIS STRENGTH

But let patience have her perfect work, that ye may be perfect and entire, wanting nothing. James 1:4.

Satan knows that so long as we depend upon God's power and keep our eyes upon Jesus, we are impregnable to his temptations. So he works to distract us and to get our attention focused on ourselves, for if he can do that he can overcome us. The cruel fact is that we often do not know when we have been distracted. Have you ever had the experience of having a meaningful devotional time with Jesus in the morning, and sometime during midday being absolutely vanquished by the enemy on some particular weakness, and you didn't even know at what point you had turned away from Jesus?

God in His kindness, in His merciful and loving way, is interested in revealing to us how easily we are distracted from dependence upon Him. He helps us realize just as soon as possible that we have been turned from Him, and He wants to help us realize what will keep us from that. So we come to the testing and proving process to reveal to us our characters. James 1:2-4 tells us to greet the testing process with joy, for it brings about growth and patience. God does not bring the temptations and trials, but He is able to use them to reveal to us our need of Him.

God brings us to one point after another designed to show to us what is in our hearts. This is described in *The Ministry of Healing,* page 470: "Many who sincerely consecrate their lives to God's service are surprised and disappointed to find themselves, as never before, confronted by obstacles and beset by trials and perplexities. They pray for Christlikeness of character, for a fitness for the Lord's work, and they are placed in circumstances that seem to call forth all the evil of their nature. . . . Like Israel of old they question, 'If God is leading us, why do all these things come upon us?'"

God's purpose is to reveal to us, step by step, point by point, just where it is that we are tempted to depend upon our own strength, and turn away from His power. As we endure the test and continue to seek the daily fellowship with Him, He will lead us just as fast as possible to the place of total dependence upon Him, and total possession and control by Him, all the time.

THE LIGHT THAT DOESN'T BLIND |

But the path of the just is as the shining light, that shineth more and more unto the perfect day. Prov. 4:18.

Have you ever wondered why it is that the big sins seem to be overcome more easily than the "little" sins? The answer lies in the fact that we can overcome *all* sin *so long as* we are depending upon God's power, and that we cannot overcome *any* sin when we trust to our own power. But before we are willing to trust to God's power, we must come to the place of *dis*trusting our own power. We find it easier to understand that we cannot overcome on the "big" sins, but much harder to understand that we are helpless to fight the devil ourselves in regard to the "little" ones. It is because we ourselves try to handle the areas of "little" sins that we are overcome.

Imagine yourself in a dark room, and you have become accustomed to the darkness. There is a closed Venetian blind at the window. If someone were to go to the cord at the side of the blind and yank it up all at once, the sudden sunlight would blind you. God, in His love, opens up the Venetian blind one slat at a time. He does not tell us all that He has to reveal to us at once. He begins with the big issues, the obvious sins. As we learn to trust Him on those, He goes on to the "little" sins.

If you approach a man on death row and talk to him about salvation, you don't begin by telling him not to polish his shoes on Friday night. There is a sequence that God Himself recognizes. In Exodus 23 the Lord is talking about overcoming the enemy for His people. He promises to make all their enemies turn their backs. He says He will send hornets, which are extremely effective weapons! But then He adds, verses 29 and 30, "I will not drive them out from before thee in one year; lest the land become desolate, and the beast of the field multiply against thee. By little and little I will drive them out from before thee, until thou be increased, and inherit the land."

God knows that if He tried to change us all at once, and reveal to us every weakness that we have at one time, it would destroy us. So He takes it slowly, at a pace that we, in our weakness, can endure. But so long as we continue to seek fellowship with Him day by day, the work that He has started in our lives He will carry forward to completion (Phil. 1:6).

THE NONWITNESS

Verily, verily, I say unto thee, We speak that we do know, and testify that we have seen. John 3:11.

Imagine with me a court scene. The prisoner is brought in. The prosecuting attorney and the defense attorney take their places. The judge enters, and the court is in session. The first witness is called to the stand. He is sworn in, and takes his seat. The questioning begins.

"Where were you on the night of the twenty-seventh, at about 10:00 p.m.?"

Silence.

"I said, where were you on the night of the twenty-seventh?"

More silence.

And the judge demands, "Why aren't you answering the question?"

"Well," the witness speaks at last, "I feel that being a silent witness is enough. It should be apparent to all, by my mere presence here in this courtroom, how I feel about this case, and I think that should be sufficient. I'm not that comfortable answering questions. I might give a wrong answer or something. I prefer to be simply a silent witness."

The judge sends the first "witness" out of the room and calls in another witness. The second witness is sworn in, and takes his seat on the witness stand. The trial continues. "Where were *you* on the night of the twenty-seventh, at about 10:00 p.m.?"

"At home in bed."

"Did you hear or see anything unusual?"

"No, I was not only in bed but the drapes were shut, my radio was playing soft music in the background, the lights were out, I had a pillow over my head, and I was asleep. I couldn't see or hear a thing!"

"And you're a *witness?*"

The majority of Christians today are like one of these two witnesses. They are either determined to remain silent witnesses or else they have nothing personal to tell. And because of this, their witness for Christ is ineffective. It is only when we have become personally involved with the Lord Jesus, and have personal testimony to give, and then *give* it—by our influence, yes, but also by our words—that we become effective witnesses for Him.

WHY REVIVAL FADES

For whosoever will save his life shall lose it: but whosoever will lose his life for my sake, the same shall save it. Luke 9:24.

Do you believe that witnessing is always spontaneous? If you really have gotten a glimpse of the love of Jesus, will you be able to keep still about it? Or will it be automatic for you to talk of the things of the gospel? Look at two sentences in *Steps to Christ*. The first one says, "No sooner does one come to Christ than there is born in his heart a desire to make known to others what a precious friend he has found in Jesus."—Page 78. So let's nail that point down. If you have become involved in the things of the gospel, you will have a desire to tell others about the friend you have found in Jesus. The other sentence says, "The Christian who will not exercise his God-given powers not only fails to grow up into Christ, but he loses the strength that he already had."—Page 81.

When you put these two together, you have this conclusion: In the first enthusiasm of accepting the gospel, I have something to tell. But if I don't tell, I will lose whatever I have. You will have to conclude, then, that it must be possible not to tell. Witnessing must not always be spontaneous. If telling was always an automatic thing, then it would be irrelevant to include the second thought, that if you don't tell, you will lose what you have already. So although the initial impulse to tell is spontaneous, the deliberate action may not be that spontaneous.

It is possible to sit in your closet and meditate and read the gospel, and become excited about it for only so long, and then it will go sour unless you begin to share with others. If you try to hide it, you will end up in greater darkness than before you started.

"Should we give our lives up to prayerful meditation, our lights would grow dim, for light is given to us that we may impart it to others, and the more we impart light, the brighter our own light will become."—*Selected Messages,* book 1, p. 139. Those who have known great revival, but failed to become involved in sharing, will find that the revival will fade and darkness will return.

Do you know what it means to speak to someone specifically about the things of the gospel, and what Jesus means to you? It is as we share the love of Jesus with others that we draw nearer to Him ourselves.

SURRENDERED FOR SERVICE

Then said Jesus unto his disciples, If any man will come after me, let him deny himself, and take up his cross, and follow me. For whosoever will save his life shall lose it: and whosoever will lose his life for my sake shall find it. Matt. 16:24, 25.

Earlier in this passage, Jesus had asked His disciples whom they said that He was. And Peter had said, "Thou are the Christ, the Son of the living God." Jesus commended him for his response. Then Jesus began to talk about going to Jerusalem, where He would be delivered into the hands of evil men, and crucified, and buried, and rise again the third day. Peter, I suppose still riding high on his recent achievement, thought he would come through again with the right answer. And he began to rebuke Jesus, saying, "Be it far from thee, Lord: this shall not be unto thee." You recall what happened next, verse 23. Jesus turned and said to Peter, "Get thee behind me, Satan: thou art an offence unto me."

Then Jesus proceeded to try and straighten out their thinking. He said, "Look, I'm going to Jerusalem and the cross. And if you will come after Me, then deny yourself and take up *your* cross, and follow Me. There's a cross for you, too."

What is our cross? It is submitting ourselves to Jesus. It is submitting our wills to Christ. It has to do with surrender, and giving up on ourselves. It has to do with living for Christ rather than living for self. The cross, the yoke, and the surrender of our will are all the same. And the yoke is placed upon the oxen for the purpose of service.

Jesus said in Luke 9:23, "If any man will come after me, let him deny himself, and take up his cross *daily,* and follow me." So step one is to surrender our lives totally to Jesus, and step two is to become involved in co-operation, through a life of service for Him.

What does Jesus mean when He invites us to follow Him? He is inviting us to a life of outreach and witness. "Follow me, and I will make you fishers of men." When we stop trying to save our lives, and begin to seek first the kingdom of God, we will become involved in service to others, and will be following Jesus, who lived His entire life for the purpose of blessing and helping others.

TO GIVE IS TO LIVE

Neither do men light a candle, and put it under a bushel, but on a candlestick; and it giveth light unto all that are in the house. Matt. 5:15.

We spend so much of our lives trying to build up enough security for a rainy day, trying to plan, and save, and accumulate, to be protected against loss, and all the time the facts keep staring us in the face. He that tries to save his life is going to lose it. It is the one who has been willing to lose his life who finds it.

We have been told that in the great judgment day, those who have not worked for Christ, who have drifted along thinking of themselves, caring for themselves, and ignoring the needs of others, will be placed by the Judge of the whole earth with those who did evil. They will receive the same reward (see *The Desire of Ages,* p. 641). We know, if we have studied it at all, that to give is to live, and not to give is to die. We must impart in order to receive, and the one who stops imparting is going to stop receiving. Even our capacity to receive is maintained only by giving. This is why many Christians never grow, and why many churches never grow. The only way that God can save us is by allowing us to work with Him. "The effort to bless others will react in blessing upon ourselves. This was the purpose of God in giving us a part to act in the plan of redemption."—*Steps to Christ,* p. 79.

The biggest single need of the church, and of the individual Christian, is to accept the challenge of getting involved in outreach and service. Witnessing is not primarily a matter of going out and knocking on doors, trying to convince total strangers of their need of Christ in five minutes or less so that you can rush on to the next house. Witnessing must become a way of life in order to be really meaningful.

It is impossible to witness unless you have something to tell. The relationship with Christ must be the basis for any outreach to others. But it is equally impossible to be a witness and never tell anything. A candle gives no light unless it is lighted, but if, as soon as it is lighted, it is covered up so that its light cannot be seen, it will soon go out. It is only as we share our light with others that we ourselves can grow.

HOLY GROUND

And he said, Draw not nigh hither: put off thy shoes from off thy feet, for the place whereon thou standest is holy ground. Ex. 3:5.

Moses had been in the wilderness for 40 years, herding sheep. They weren't even his own sheep—they belonged to his father-in-law. One day as he was traveling along through the desert sands, he saw a bush that was on fire. He went closer to investigate. The Lord spoke to him from the bush and said, "Put off thy shoes from off thy feet, for the place whereon thou standest is holy ground."

What was it that made the ground around the burning bush holy ground? Oh, you may say, it was God's presence. But hadn't God been present with Moses, in his desert wanderings, *before* the burning bush? Yes. So what made the difference now? It was that Moses *realized* in a special way that God was there.

Jesus came to earth for only 33½ years Thirty of those years He spent in the carpenter shop. We are told that Jesus was serving God just as much in the carpenter shop as during the 3½ years of His public ministry (see *The Desire of Ages,* p. 74). Jesus, while working as a carpenter, realized God's presence there with Him, and the carpenter shop became holy ground for Him.

Wherever we work, wherever we spend our days, can be holy ground for us if we realize the Lord's presence there. We don't have to go to some temple or holy mountain. He is always with us and as we discern His presence, the ground whereon we stand becomes holy ground. It makes no difference if you are a sheepherder, like Moses, or a carpenter, like Jesus, or a teacher or businessman or housewife or salesman. It makes no difference if your place of business is "the backside of the desert" (Ex. 3:1), as was Moses', or in the crowds of the city. The office, the home, the place of business, can become holy ground as you realize that the Lord is with you there.

Witnessing for Christ is not something that is limited to Sabbath afternoons. It is rather a way of life. Perhaps the broadest field of witnessing you will ever have is to be found in the place where you earn your livelihood, for it is there that you spend so much of your time. If you dedicate your place of business to the Lord, to be holy ground, He will be present there.

FREE TRIP TO THE HOLY LAND

Even as the Son of man came not to be ministered unto, but to minister, and to give his life a ransom for many. Matt. 20:28.

M any feel that it would be a great privilege to visit the scenes of Christ's life on earth, to walk where He trod, to look upon the lake beside which He loved to teach, and the hills and valleys on which His eyes so often rested. But we need not go to Nazareth, to Capernaum, or to Bethany, in order to walk in the steps of Jesus. We shall find His footprints beside the sickbed, in the hovels of poverty, in the crowded alleys of the great city, and in every place where there are human hearts in need of consolation. In doing as Jesus did when on earth, we shall walk in His steps."—*The Desire of Ages,* p. 640.

God's purpose for His church as a body, and for each of His children as individuals, is that they walk in the footsteps of Jesus in service for others. It is the law of life throughout the entire universe that to give is to live. Heaven itself has initiated this giving, and it is only as we in turn give to others that we can have life and growth.

We see this principle demonstrated in the physical world. No matter how fresh and clean the air we breathe, once we have breathed in, we must then breathe out again. Trying to add air to lungs that are full is impossible. And to hoard what air we have inhaled will result in death.

We see this principle of giving demonstrated in the natural world. All of nature is interacting to produce life. It is only through constant giving, and receiving, and giving again, that the things of nature are able to grow and flourish.

The angels of heaven are engaged in constant ministry. They work unceasingly to bring help to those who are inferior to them in every way, and for the purpose of bringing us to a closer relationship with God than they themselves can know.

And the greatest Example of giving is found in Jesus. He came not to be ministered unto, but to minister. Yet how many of us, as His professed children, try to hoard the gifts of His grace, and refuse to become involved in working for others. The Christian life was designed to be an opportunity for giving. Let us follow the steps of Jesus in reaching out to others.

THE HAPPIEST PEOPLE

*In thy presence is fulness of joy; at thy right hand there are pleasures for evermore.
Ps. 16:11.*

We understand that the people who would not be happy in heaven won't be there at all. One of the most outstanding truths that we know about heaven is that people are happy there. Have you ever wondered what makes heaven a happy place?

Now I'm sure that the boys and girls will find time for playing in heaven. For instance, I'm sure that the children will find a lot of pleasure in playing with all the animals there. It will be fun for the children, and even for some of us older ones as well, to be able to fly without having to get into an airplane first. It will be fun to try hang gliding without the hang glider, or parachute jumping without the parachute! Maybe we can even do some scuba diving in the river of life, without all that heavy equipment. And the opportunities for travel will be unlimited.

But the primary fun and happiness of heaven is not going to be in getting your own "kicks." Notice *Steps to Christ,* page 77: "The spirit of Christ's self-sacrificing love is the spirit that pervades heaven and is the very essence of its bliss." The reason people are happy in heaven is because they are involved in reaching out to others. And that is the secret of happiness here on this earth as well.

The happiest person in the world is the one whose life is the most centered in others, and the most miserable person in the world is the one who is the most self-centered. The person whose main interest in life is trying to figure out what he can do or try next to get the most, to have the most fun, is a miserable unhappy person. Have you ever gone to some amusement center and watched the faces of the people there, waiting in line to "have fun"? The majority of them are pretty unhappy looking. And the children who could hardly sleep the night before while waiting for the big day of "fun" are invariably grouchy all the way home.

If you are looking for happiness and fun and enjoyment, the best place to look—the only place to look—is to service, to sharing, to trying to bring the greatest happiness to those around you. This is the source of joy in this life, and will be the source of happiness in the life to come.

CONCERN FOR THE FATHER

For how shall I go up to my father, and the lad be not with me? lest peradventure I see the evil that shall come on my father. Gen. 44:34.

For how shall I go up to my father, and the lad be not with me?" Judah was pleading for his younger brother Benjamin. Judah had been the one whose idea it was to sell Joseph into slavery. Judah had been part of the plot to kill a young sheep and dip Joseph's coat in its blood, and present it to his father to make him think that Joseph had been killed. But now we see him pleading for his brother's life and willing to take the place of his brother in prison, if only his father might be spared further grief. There's been a change of heart somewhere, a complete change. I like what has happened to Judah, don't you?

Previously, Judah hadn't cared for his father's feelings. Now he is concerned about them. Before, he thought only of himself. Now he is thinking of the welfare of others as more important. He used to be dishonest; now he is honest. Judah's life had been changed. He has taken the responsibility of becoming surety for Benjamin. Judah had voluntarily become surety for him. He had taken that responsibility upon himself by choice.

When a couple decide to have children, they have made the choice to become surety for those children. When one chooses to become a teacher or pastor, he is choosing to become surety for those under his charge. These are voluntary responsibilities, not ones that are laid on us by another.

The day is soon coming when we will go up to our Father (1 Thess. 4:16, 17). We can be thankful today for a God who cares, and who will do everything possible that when we go up to our Father and His Father, those we love will be with us. Aren't you thankful for the One who, like Judah, stepped forward and said for you, and for those you love, "I will be surety for them. Let Me take their place"? Aren't you thankful for the burden of the parent or teacher or friend that you knew, who became surety for you? Won't you join me today in determining not to bring sorrow to the heart of our Father by not being there when all His children are gathered home? Won't you join with Judah in that plaintive appeal made in the court of one of the mightiest nations of the land, "Let me be surety. For how shall I go up to my father, and the lad be not with me?"

227

WITNESSES FOREVER

For ye know the grace of our Lord Jesus Christ, that, though he was rich, yet for your sakes he became poor, that ye through his poverty might be rich. 2 Cor. 8:9.

Can you imagine, one day in heaven, your angel coming to you and saying, "How would you like to take a journey?"

And you respond, "Of course. Where are we going?"

"There's a little planet, way out on the rim of the universe, where they want to hear what it's like to have been ransomed from a lost world," your angel says. "*I* can't tell them. But I'll show *you* how to get there."

Would you be interested? The law of giving is the law of the universe. And although the doctors will be out of a job in heaven, and the funeral directors will be unemployed, and many of the other jobs we have here on this earth will be no more, the Christian witness will go on forever. Angels never felt the joy that our salvation brings. And if giving is the essence of heaven's bliss, then it wouldn't hurt to get started on it right here and now, would it?

If my primary motive in being a Christian is to try to get myself to heaven, then it is possible that I'm not a Christian at all. The one who has truly become a partaker of the spirit of Christ is more concerned about someone else's salvation than his own.

Remember Judah, when he had become surety for his brother Benjamin? When he thought that Benjamin would be kept in Egypt as a slave, and thought of the grief it would bring to his father, he offered to take Benjamin's place.

Remember Moses, when he was leading the Israelites out of Egypt? God offered to destroy the ungrateful rebels, and start over again with Moses to make a great nation. Moses was willing to put his own eternal life in the balance in order to save the people he loved.

And Jesus, the greatest Giver of all, did not count heaven a place to be desired while we were lost, but came on the long, expensive journey, risking His own eternal life, in order to secure a place for us in heaven. It is His spirit of unselfish giving that was shown in Judah, in Moses, and in all heaven. It is this willingness to spend and be spent for others that is our need today.

LOVE KNOWS NO END

How shall I give thee up, Ephraim? how shall I deliver thee, Israel? Hosea 11:8.

If you ever have any doubt about the love of our heavenly Father, look at Jesus, who came to reveal Him. You see Him riding on a donkey, down toward the gates of the city. He looks over the brow of the hill toward the city below, and, convulsed with sobs, He cries, "O Jerusalem, Jerusalem. How can I give you up?" When we catch a glimpse of the One who loved us so much, then we can begin to understand the pain and longing of the question "How can I give you up?" And our hearts are drawn out in love and service to those around us, to try to bring as many as possible of them to accept God's salvation.

As we look at those we love who are struggling, and realize the tremendous price that has been paid for them, if we really see it, then it makes no difference how good or bad or obnoxious they are. It makes no difference if they are easy to get along with, or difficult. It's like the two men who met in town one day. The first man had a son who had been into all kinds of trouble. And the second man said, "If that had been my son, I would have disowned him a long time ago."

And the first replied, "I would have too, if he had been *your* son. But not *my* son." You simply cannot walk away from those you love. There are many parents, teachers, relatives, and friends today who can identify with this truth.

Sometimes we say to people, You are responsible for someone, but they may not feel responsible at all. Sometimes we try to lay a heavy load upon people in terms of spreading the gospel. We say, Now you be surety for everyone in your block. You are responsible for this one or that one. If they are lost someday, their blood will be required of you. But this only makes people feel guilty when they don't get involved in the gospel work.

Once in a while someone asks, "How long do I have to pray for someone to be saved?" That is a foolish question. Love never asks it. Love continues to plead and to intercede because it can do nothing else, because it is unable to bear the thought of giving up on the one who is loved. Love does not know "it is enough."

FISHERS OF MEN

And he saith unto them, Follow me, and I will make you fishers of men. Matt. 4:19.

In John 21 you have the story of the disciples who had decided to go fishing. Jesus asked them, "Have you any fish?" But they had worked hard all night and taken nothing. Then He told them to cast their net on the right side of the ship, and their nets were filled. He made it clear that if you are going fishing, you must fish on the right side of the boat. The wrong place to fish is on the wrong side of the boat.

We don't do injustice to Scripture when we transfer the fishing story to real life today and apply it to fishing for men, because Jesus Himself is the One who made the analogy. He said, "Follow me, and I will make you fishers of men." So what can we learn from the story of the fish and Jesus' encounter with the fishermen-disciples?

We know what it's like to toil all night and to take nothing. Have you ever had that experience? There's many a Christian who has. He has tried to respond to duty, tried to witness, and was unsuccessful. It is discouraging to have doors slammed in your face. It is a miserable thing to fish all night and take nothing. What drudgery it is to try to do God's work with man's tools, and to splash the water and make a great many waves, only to catch a few small ones that slip away back into the sea again. This is par for the course in the experience of many Christians.

We need to realize that this failure can be a prelude to the miracle of the fishes. It's not so bad to toil all night and accomplish nothing if it brings us to our knees. Our problem is that sometimes we have done as the disciples did, and gone fishing *by ourselves.* Sometimes we plan and work and go to a great deal of expense and preparation. But we fail, because we are fishing from the wrong side of the boat.

What is the wrong side of the boat? It is the side of self-effort. The right side was the side that Jesus was on. "Jesus had a purpose in bidding them cast their net on the right side of the ship. On that side He stood upon the shore. That was the side of faith."—*The Desire of Ages,* p. 811. It takes faith to become involved in fishing for souls. It is as we unite with Christ and follow His instructions that we are enabled to be fishers of men.

LIONS IN THE STREET

The slothful man saith, There is a lion without, I shall be slain in the streets. Prov. 22:13.

The slothful man is really saying that he doesn't want to go out into the streets because he might get hurt. He would be taking a chance if he went out. He'd rather stay home where it's warm and comfortable and safe. Have you ever felt like this man when you were invited to become involved in the Christian witness? Is it possible in that sense to stay in the house because we are afraid there are lions out there, and we might be hurt?

One reason many find it so comfortable to stay inside by the fire is because of spiritual uncertainty in their own lives. They realize deep down that their religion is just a habit or facade. They shrink from having it closely examined by others. So they stay away from witnessing because they aren't that sure of their own standing with God.

Another lion in the street is the fear of being pushed into a theological corner by someone asking hard questions. Have you ever wanted to stay inside by the fire because of that reason? We have a tendency to let the professionals do the witnessing for us, to let them face the lions in the street in our behalf. We figure that they are lion tamers! They are supposed to have all the right answers, and know how it's done.

A third lion in the street is the fear of failure. Have you ever tried to witness to someone, perhaps given Bible studies or whatever, and felt you failed? Have you been afraid that it was your fault that the people to whom you witnessed did not decide for God?

To deal with these lions in the street, I'd like to remind you that for the spiritually uncertain, to come into Jesus' presence is a motivating experience. When we know Jesus as our friend, and realize His loving acceptance, we will no longer be afraid of that particular lion. Second, the primary Christian witness is to tell others what Jesus means to us. And we can always admit that we don't know a theological answer, but are willing to search for it. And third, we have never been asked to weary ourselves over success. The results of our work are to be left in God's hands. God invites us today to become involved in active service for Him, and He will deal with the lions.

WHY GO TO CHURCH?

Let us hold fast the profession of our faith without wavering; (for he is faithful that promised;) and let us consider one another to provoke unto love and to good works. Heb. 10:23, 24.

What is the worst reason you can think of for going to church? What is the best reason you can think of? As I have pondered why people go to church, and why I go to church, I think that the worst reason I as a preacher could possibly have for going is because it's my job. But here from the Bible are three *good* reasons for going.

The first is because God tells us to. Hebrews 10:25: "Not forsaking the assembling of ourselves together as the manner of some is; but exhorting one another: and so much the more, as ye see the day approaching."

The second reason is because the church is a body, and there is no complete body without all of the members together. This truth is found in 1 Corinthians 12:27: "Now ye are the body of Christ, and members in particular." Paul goes on to give a parable of how the physical body teaches us important truths about the body of Christ, His church. The body needs every member, even the ones who are considered insignificant. It takes all the different parts to make the whole, and a body is a body only if it hangs together.

The third reason for going to church is because Jesus went to church. It was His custom. But if anyone ever had an excuse for not going to church, it was Jesus. Have you ever attended church and had the other members become so upset with you that they took you out afterward and tried to push you off a cliff? Jesus did. But He didn't stop going to church.

Sometimes people come to me and say, "I don't need to go to church. I get more of a blessing just being out in nature." Notice the emphasis: "I *get.*" And when someone tells me that, I remind them on the basis of case history and on the basis of God's Word, that they are going to die. It is a fact. If you cut off your foot and send it out for a walk in the woods, it isn't going to live very long. They tell me that you can cut off a lizard's tail, and it keeps wiggling for little bit. But not for long. And although a lizard can grow a new tail, a tail can't grow a new lizard. No member of the body can live for long without the rest of the body. Union with the body is essential for life, for growth, and for usefulness.

FAITH AND REASON

And as Moses lifted up the serpent in the wilderness, even so must the Son of man be lifted up. John 3:14.

There are at least three types of people who go to church. There is the committed Christian, who loves to see Jesus lifted up. He goes to church because he wants to. Nothing can keep him away. He has been solidly converted. He desires nothing so much as communication with the Lord Jesus. He has a meaningful prayer life and studies God's Word. He loves to share with others. He has learned to trust in God, and when God says go to church, he says, All right, if God says it, I'll do it. If he had been present when Moses said for the people to look at the snake, he would have looked at the snake without question. He believes that God knows what is best for him.

For the committed Christian it is pointless to talk about reasons for going to church, because that's where he desires to be. The committed Christian goes to church because he loves to. But in almost any so-called Christian group, there are some who are *not* committed Christians.

There is another group of people who go to church who are simply regular church members. Somewhere along the line they got baptized. It may or may not have meant something to them at that time, but they have no current relationship with the Lord Jesus. They go to church because it is a habit. They are stuck. They have a beaten path between home and church, and can't get out of the routine. They go for the sake of their reputation, or for some other selfish reason. If this sort of person had been alive at the time of Moses, he would have probably insisted on knowing a good reason before he looked. God is not against reason. It's not wrong to have some understanding, so long as we don't insist on having everything completely clear before we are willing to act on God's Word.

The third type of person who comes to church is actually hostile to religion. He comes to church because he is forced to come. Not only would he be uninterested in looking at the snake, but he wouldn't care about reasons for it, either. This type is not interested, period. But for all three types, God, through His Holy Spirit, is present in His church. He will meet the needs of any who come to Him. He will do all that He can do to reach each one.

THE ORGANIZED BODY

For as the body is one, and hath many members, and all the members of that one body, being many, are one body: so also is Christ. 1 Cor. 12:12.

Can you imagine a human body disorganized? What would happen if the brain, instead of telling the hand to open the door, decided to do away with organization? The face would get smashed. I'm thankful that the body is organized. And organization is meaningful for the church body as well.

A body cannot live without eating. But what is it about the body that eats? Is it the mouth? No. If you cut out the mouth, and tell it to eat, it's not going to eat. Is it the stomach that eats? No. It's the mouth *and* the stomach and all the rest of the body, clear out to the tiny cells, that absorb nourishment from the bloodstream. The whole body eats. And eating is one of the things the church body does. John 6 talks about it. We eat the bread of life and drink the water of life.

A body cannot live without breathing. Here again, it's the whole body that breathes, not just the nose or the lungs. Prayer is the breath of the soul. And the church body, when it meets together, is involved in breathing—communion with God. Eating and breathing are both essential to life.

But a body must also exercise. 1 Timothy 4:7, 8, refers to this. Exercise, in the spiritual sense, is outreach and service for others.

There are two reasons that we can have for coming to church and meeting with the other members of Christ's body. We come to church to get, and we come to church to give. If your primary reason for coming to church is to get, then you find it easy to skip it, and go for a walk in the woods. But to *give* is the greater purpose for attending church. There are ways that we can give as a corporate body that would be impossible for us individually. Which one of you, by yourself, has ever sent out a missionary to a foreign field? But think of the hundreds that have been sent out by the church!

When we go to church to give, as well as to receive, we will see the importance of meeting together with the body of Christ. There may be those who have just been rescued from the Jericho road who need our help. And the great Good Samaritan says to those who are willing to give to others, "Take care of them. And when I come again, I will repay you."

JESUS WENT TO CHURCH

And he came to Nazareth, where he had been brought up: and, as his custom was, he went into the synagogue on the sabbath day. Luke 4:16.

We give public confession of our allegiance and our worship of Jesus when we attend church. Matthew 10:32 says that if we confess Jesus before men, He will confess us before His Father. Jesus went to church, giving us an example to follow. He went to church to announce to the world His connection with His Father, and His allegiance to Him. He went to church to give, and kept on going to church, in spite of the difficulties He encountered.

Jesus stood up at the synagogue one Sabbath in Nazareth, and read from the book of Isaiah. He read that He was sent to preach the gospel to the poor. Why? Because those who are rich and increased with goods and in need of nothing cannot understand the gospel. He said He was sent to heal the brokenhearted. Why? Because it is when the heart has been broken and emptied of self that it feels its need. He was sent to preach deliverance to the captives. Why? Because all of us are captives to sin, and only those who realize their bondage are open for the Son who can set them free. He was sent to bring recovering of sight to the blind. Why? Because without spiritual eyesalve, we can't see our need of Christ's righteousness. He came to set at liberty them that are bruised.

Have you been beaten and bruised by the devil? Have you been discouraged because of your sins? Have you felt condemned, and guilty, and afraid that Jesus wouldn't accept you? There is good news. Jesus accepts you just as you are. Poor? Brokenhearted? Captive to sin? Blind? Bruised and bleeding? Yes. He loves to accept you just as you are.

Jesus went to church for the purpose of sharing the good news. And He knew where it would lead Him. It led Him down the rocky, rugged path to the cross. But all through His life He went to church, and gave, and continued to give and serve and reach out to others.

I invite you to make it your custom to go to church, for the purpose of giving to others, at least the influence of your presence. I invite you to join in sharing the good news of the gospel with those who are in need, by going to church to give rather than merely to get. To give is far bigger, far better, than to receive.

235

HEAVEN IS REAL

Beloved, now are we the sons of God, and it doth not yet appear what we shall be: but we know that, when he shall appear, we shall be like him; for we shall see him as he is. 1 John 3:2.

Would you like to live your life over again? Most people say, "I surely would. There are a lot of things I'd do differently." No. Would you like to live life over again just the way you have lived it, without changing any part of it? The more one has seen of what life has to offer in this world, the quicker comes the response, "No, thanks."

Since this is true, then one of the greatest hopes that we have here is for heaven. To accept the salvation that God has provided, and to help others accept it, is our biggest purpose for being here. Aren't you thankful today that we believe in heaven?

There are many people who do not believe that heaven is a real place. But the doctrine of heaven, as a real place, is a Bible doctrine in which Seventh-day Adventists believe strongly. If heaven seems unreal to you, perhaps it is because Jesus seems unreal. A skeptic once said to a little street urchin who believed in heaven, "But what if you get to heaven, and Jesus isn't there?" And the boy replied, "Where Jesus is, that *is* heaven." If Jesus is real, then heaven is real.

Is Jesus real? Most people believe that He was real before His resurrection. Some have trouble believing He is real afterward. But the Bible teaches that Jesus is real postresurrection. Luke 24:39, the disciples thought they were seeing a ghost, but Jesus said, "Behold my hands and my feet, that it is I myself: handle me, and see; for a spirit hath not flesh and bones, as ye see me have." Thomas was the doubter, but Jesus told him in John 20:27, "Reach hither your hand. Touch me. Handle me." And Thomas exclaimed, "My Lord and my God." Jesus was just as real after He was resurrected as He was before.

Add to that 1 John 3:2: "But we know that, when he shall appear, we shall be like him; for we shall see him as he is." We are going to be like Jesus when He comes again. And since Jesus is real, when we see Him face-to-face we will be real. Heaven won't be some vague, mystical place; it will be real.

236

WHEN TIREDNESS ENDS

For our conversation is in heaven; from whence also we look for the Saviour, the Lord Jesus Christ: who shall change our vile body, that it may be fashioned like unto his glorious body, according to the working whereby he is able even to subdue all things unto himself. Phil. 3:20, 21.

Most of us could stand some changing, some working over. All of us can accept the need for change at the time of glorification. We will be made like His glorious body. It will be a real body, for Jesus is real, and when He comes again He will take us to a real place.

In the New Jerusalem, Jesus is preparing a place for His people. We are promised mansions to live in (John 14:1-3). We are told about what some of our activities will be. We will build houses and inhabit them. We will plant vineyards and eat the fruit of them. We will not labor in vain, but will long enjoy the work of our hands (Isaiah 65).

Jesus is also interested in our identity. The New Jerusalem has foundations, and on those foundations are the names of people. They are the same names that their mothers gave them when they were born. We will be known by our names, by our features, by our mannerisms. We shall know even as also we are known (1 Cor. 13:12).

Sometimes young people say, "Who wants to go to heaven—I'd get tired of living forever!" But stop and think for a minute about what it is in this life that makes you tired. We get tired of tears. But Isaiah 65:19 says that the voice of weeping will be heard no more, nor the voice of crying. Revelation 7:17 says that God shall wipe away all tears from the eyes of the redeemed. We get tired of sin. Revelation 21:27 says that nothing abominable will be in the New Jerusalem. We get tired of death, and of pain. Revelation 21:4 says there shall be "no more death, neither sorrow, nor crying, neither shall there be any more pain." We get tired of sickness. But Isaiah 33:24 says that "the inhabitants shall not say, I am sick." We get tired of being lonely. But Revelation 21:3 says that God Himself shall dwell with them, and be their God, and they shall be His people.

Jesus has offered us the choice to live forever. Heaven is a real place, and it was created with our highest happiness in mind.

GOD WANTS YOU THERE

But now in Christ Jesus ye who sometimes were far off are made nigh by the blood of Christ. Eph. 2:13.

Have you ever wondered whether heaven will be worth it? Have you ever thought that perhaps you don't need to live forever with God? But what about God? Is it possible that He needs you, that He wants you? Perhaps one of the greatest reasons for desiring heaven is just because He wants us there so very much.

The mansions, the streets of gold, the fruit of the tree of life, all have been prepared with your happiness in mind. The God who created every leaf and blade of grass and snowflake unique created only one you. Each individual is different. Each one is special. Each one is loved by God as if there were not another soul upon earth for whom Jesus gave His life. If you refuse His offer of salvation, and decide that the price of heaven is too great, throughout eternity you will be missed by His great heart of love.

Are you going to be there? Or do you say, "I've gone too far in sin. I'll never make it to heaven. There's not a chance in the world for me." A teenager told me one time, "If I got to heaven I'd be so surprised I don't know *what* I'd do."

"But now in Christ Jesus ye who sometimes were far off are made nigh by the blood of Christ." Have you been a long way off? Through the blood of Jesus you are made near. There is good news for you today. You can accept the gift of salvation and be brought near through the blood of Jesus. He invites you today to a saving relationship with Him, so that you can be assured of a home in heaven tomorrow.

"In the Bible the inheritance of the saved is called 'a country.' Hebrews 11:14-16. There the heavenly Shepherd leads His flock to fountains of living waters. The tree of life yields its fruit every month, and the leaves of the tree are for the service of the nations. There are ever-flowing streams, clear as crystal, and beside them waving trees cast their shadows upon the paths prepared for the ransomed of the Lord. There the wide-spreading plains swell into hills of beauty, and the mountains of God rear their lofty summits. On those peaceful plains, beside those living streams, God's people, so long pilgrims and wanderers, shall find a home."—*The Great Controversy*, p. 675.

HOPE FOR A SICK WORLD

And there shall be signs in the sun, and in the moon, and in the stars; and upon the earth distress of nations, with perplexity; the sea and the waves roaring; . . . for the powers of heaven shall be shaken. Luke 21:25, 26.

If I were a physician and had a patient as ill as this world is now, I would despair of being able to do anything to help him. A patient with a weak heart is not necessarily doomed to an early death. With good care and intelligent treatment, he has a good chance of living to a ripe old age. If, however, he is afflicted with cancer also, and tuberculosis and pneumonia, if he breaks out all over in a rash, and contracts typhoid, and in addition to all this has a stroke or two, his chance of recovery would be about nil.

This is the condition of the world today. Unrest is breaking out all over. The cancer of sin has permeated the whole social fabric. Vice and dissipation have broken down the constitution. False political and religious doctrines are poisoning the wellsprings of life. The air is contaminated with intolerance and hatred. The whole world seems on the verge of collapse. The first stroke came in the first world war, followed by a second and worse global war. To the astonishment of many, the patient rallied, and doctors are now frantically looking for a remedy that will prevent another stroke. Few believe that civilization will survive one more. It is three times and out. The only solution to the problem is Jesus Christ, and He is coming soon, to set up a kingdom that will last forever.

Seventh-day Adventists believe in the second coming of Jesus Christ. They have taught it and preached it and hoped for it for a long time. There was a time when those who believed in the end of the world were considered alarmists. Today they are considered realists. Even scientists and statesmen are concluding that we cannot go on much longer. But we have this hope—the hope that He that shall come will come. The hope that He will come with clouds, and every eye shall see Him. The hope that He is coming to gather His children home, and bring an end to sin and sorrow. The center of our hope is Jesus. It is Jesus who is coming back again. It is Jesus who has been preparing a home for us. It is Jesus who has the only answer for the dying world.

HIS GLORIOUS APPEARING

For as the lightning cometh out of the east, and shineth even unto the west; so shall also the coming of the Son of man be. Matt. 24:27.

Jesus was being held captive before Caiaphas. False witnesses were coming in to try and prove Him deserving of death. But Jesus held His peace. Finally, in frustration, the high priest said to Him, "I adjure thee by the living God, that thou tell us whether thou be the Christ, the Son of God" (Matt. 26:63). When Jesus was under oath, in this earthly tribunal, even though He had been holding His peace, He did not hesitate to reply. Not only did He answer the question, but He gave more than He was asked for. "Jesus saith unto him, Thou hast said: nevertheless I say unto you, Hereafter shall ye see the Son of man sitting on the right hand of power, and coming in the clouds of heaven." That could keep the high priest awake for many nights. He got that for which he did not ask. Jesus under oath promised that He would come again. How can you improve on that for proving that He's coming?

If there is anything the devil hates to hear about, it is the fact that Jesus is coming back to earth. He knows that when that happens, his power will be at an end. So he tries to deceive as many as possible by projecting onto Jesus his own manner of working. How does Satan work? He is sneaky! The devil doesn't come openly. He sneaks. So he has been working to convince people everywhere that Jesus is planning to sneak in and sneak out. But we are told that every eye will see Him (Rev. 1:7). He will come as the lightning. There is nothing secret about Jesus' coming except the day and the hour, which only the Father knows (2 Peter 3:10).

Why does Jesus come? The answer tells us something important about Jesus. Jesus finishes what He begins. Because we are slaves to the clock, it seems to us that there has been a long wait. We sometimes wonder whether He will finish His work. Scoffers have said it won't happen. But the time is fast approaching when "he that shall come will come."

During this waiting time our task is to seek to know Jesus and help others to know Him, so that when He comes we will be found of Him in peace. Those who have walked with Jesus here will be able to look up and say, "Lo, this is our God; we have *waited* for him, and he will save us."

GOD FINISHES WHAT HE STARTS | **AUG 22**

For yet a little while, and he that shall come will come, and will not tarry. Heb. 10:37.

Several years ago my father and my uncle were holding meetings in a certain city. My uncle had just started preaching one night when a man near the front of the auditorium jumped up and turned around and began shouting to the congregation. He said, "Don't believe what these Venden brothers are telling you. They are talking about the end of the world, and it's never going to happen. Things continue just like they always have and always will." He turned to my uncle and continued, "You can't show me one single proof that it's going to happen."

And my uncle said, "Yes, I can—you're the latest one I've seen!"

"What do you mean?"

And my uncle read from 2 Peter 3:3, 4: "There shall come in the last days scoffers, walking after their own lusts, and saying, Where is the promise of his coming? for since the fathers fell asleep, all things continue as they were from the beginning of the creation." And the man slumped into his seat. Exciting things happened back there on the sawdust trail! The Lord gave the right scripture at the right time.

God doesn't start something and leave it undone. It is a habit of people here in this world of sin to start things and never finish them. Parents try to teach their children to finish what they've started. But Jesus always finishes things. On the morning of the Resurrection He paused long enough to fold the grave clothes and put them neatly away. He was finished with them. He needed them no more. That tells you something about Jesus.

What is He going to finish when He comes again? He's going to finish the great plan of salvation, of redemption, of restoration. He has made provision to more than make up to us for being born in this world of sin. He is able to carry forward to the end the work He has started in our lives. He can follow through to the end, which is only the beginning of eternity.

Jesus *is* coming. He is coming openly, to be seen by all. He is coming to finish the work that He began in redemption. He is coming to deliver us from a world of sin, and to take us to live forever with Him in the homes He has prepared for those who love Him.

241

WHY ME?

Fear ye not therefore, ye are of more value than many sparrows. Matt. 10:31.

When tragedy strikes, one of the first questions asked by its victims is usually, "Why me? Why did this have to happen to me?" But after the first shock and pain is over, and we begin to become more aware of the sorrow and tragedy that is all around us in this world, the second phase is usually, "Why them? Why all these others around me that I see hurting, too?" Then we can begin to try helping others as best we can. The one who stays in the first stage, simply concerned with himself and why this had to happen to him, has problems that go on forever. The one who moves to concern for others discovers his problems diminishing.

We can see something similar in relationship to this whole world of sin. Have you ever asked why you had to be born here? When your eyes have been opened, and you see that you live in a world that has gone wrong, has your first reaction been, Why me? But God leads the poor sinner to look around him and discover that others are suffering also. His own misery changes into compassion as he looks out on a world of tragedy and asks, "Why them? Why *all* of them?"

But there is yet a bigger issue that we can be led to see, after our attention has been attracted away from ourselves. Why the universe? Why God? Why the broken heart of Jesus? Have you ever felt concern for them, up there?

We see a tiny fragment of the sorrow and pain of the world. We watch the news, see pictures flash past of a part of disaster—a few who are starving, one who has died. And we weep for the little we see. But God sees it *all*. He feels each pain with His infinite heart of love, which yearns after each of His children with a desire that would have made the sacrifice of the cross for even that one. His great heart of love is broken again as our hearts are broken. And His greatest sorrow comes from those that He longs to help, who refuse to come to Him for life.

True maturity in the Christian life is less concerned with one's personal salvation than with seeking to bring relief to others, not for *our* sake, and not even for *their* sake alone—but for the sake of the God we love.

THE DOOR IS STILL OPEN

Who shall not fear thee, O Lord, and glorify thy name? for thou alone art holy: for all nations shall come and worship before thee. Rev. 15:4.

Revelation 20 is the only chapter in the Bible where the thousand years, or millennium, is mentioned. Let's read the first six verses of the chapter. "And I saw an angel come down from heaven, having the key of the bottomless pit and a great chain in his hand. And he laid hold on the dragon, that old serpent, which is the Devil, and Satan, and bound him a thousand years, and cast him into the bottomless pit, and shut him up, and set a seal upon him, that he should deceive the nations no more, till the thousand years should be fulfilled: and after that he must be loosed a little season.

"And I saw thrones, and they sat upon them, and judgment was given unto them: and I saw the souls of them that were beheaded for the witness of Jesus, and for the word of God, and which had not worshipped the beast, neither his image, neither had received his mark upon their foreheads, or in their hands; and they lived and reigned with Christ a thousand years. But the rest of the dead lived not again until the thousand years were finished. This is the first resurrection. Blessed and holy is he that hath part in the first resurrection: on such the second death hath no power."

The beginning of the thousand years is the first resurrection. There is another resurrection at the end. The righteous are raised at the first resurrection, at the coming of Jesus. They are taken to heaven to live and reign with Christ. The wicked are in their graves until the second resurrection a thousand years later. Satan and his angels are bound to the earth.

When Jesus comes, the announcement will be made that he that is unjust shall be unjust still, and he that is holy will be holy still. In spite of how much Satan would like us to believe that there will be a second chance, the Bible teaches that there is only one. But until that time, the door is still open. We still have the option of choosing to answer Christ's knock at the door of our hearts, and to prepare to meet Him. There is hope for each person today, as well as for those who have fallen asleep in Jesus. Christ has the power to raise them from the dead.

GOD IS FAIR AND JUST

Blessed and holy is he that hath part in the first resurrection: on such the second death hath no power. Rev. 20:6.

What does the thousand years tell you about God, about Jesus? It tells you that God is absolutely insistent that the books are opened for everyone to see. He wants each one to understand clearly the nature of their own response to truth, and that of those around them. He is not going to do anything in secret or in hiding. He is anxious for everyone who is saved eternally to understand clearly why anyone is lost eternally.

Part of the rationale for this thousand years of investigation is the forever sealing of the universe against sin. The history of sin will be open before all, and all can see the causes and the results. We will be able to trace the working of sin, not only upon our own hearts, but upon all who ever lived on this earth. Will there be some heartaches during that thousand years? Probably so. Can God take care of that? He's big enough, isn't He? I'm not sure what will be going on, or how it's going to proceed, but I do know enough about God and about Jesus to trust Him to work it out. He knows what is best.

When the thousand years are finished, all the universe will realize that God has been fair and just every step of the way. He has never overstepped Himself. At the end of the thousand years, after the second resurrection, when the Holy City descends, and everyone who has ever lived or died meets for the first and last time, Jesus will be vindicated before all. Even Satan will admit that God has been fair and just in everything He has done.

Which side of the walls of that city would you like to be on? Do you know? Will you be watching from the inside, or will you be among those standing outside whom Satan tries to inspire for one final attack on the city? He will rush among the ones who have come forth from their graves in the second resurrection—criminals, generals of armies, sinners from every age. He tries to get them to attack the city of God. He reminds them that they are in far greater number than the ones inside. But his power is at an end. It has been proved to the entire universe that God can be trusted, and throughout the rest of eternity we will dwell in peace, for sin will never rise up the second time. None will ever again doubt God's great love.

JESUS REVEALED BY EVIL SPIRITS

I know thee who thou art, the Holy One of God. Mark 1:24.

L et's take a look today at how Jesus is revealed by evil spirits. It sounds almost sacrilegious to say it, but the premise is that every doctrine of the Bible in some way reveals Jesus. When Jesus was here on earth, He was confronted with evil spirits frequently. Look at Matthew 8:16, 17: "That evening they brought to him many who were possessed with demons; and he cast out the spirits with a word, and healed all who were sick. This was to fulfill what was spoken by the prophet Isaiah, 'He took our infirmities and bore our diseases'" (RSV).

In Mark 1:23 and onward we are told that "immediately there was in their synagogue a man with an unclean spirit; and he cried out, 'What have you to do with us, Jesus of Nazareth? Have you come to destroy us? I know who you are, the Holy One of God.' But Jesus rebuked him, saying, 'Be silent, and come out of him!' And the unclean spirit, convulsing him and crying with a loud voice, came out of him. And they were all amazed, so that they questioned among themselves, saying, 'What is this? A new teaching! With authority he commands even the unclean spirits, and they obey him'" (RSV). It is interesting to note that the first testimony recorded in Mark as to who Jesus was came from the Father Himself, in Mark 1:11. And the second as to who Jesus really was came from an evil spirit whose control over his victim was about to end. Maybe they know something that we don't know. After all, they dwell on a plane above that of mere humans. They understand the great controversy to a degree that we do not.

Satan's working is more than superstition, and is effective today as well as back in the days of Christ. Satan is not as smart as God is, but he certainly is smarter than we are. He has planned a very clever attack on God's people in these days. When we see what he is planning, it throws light on some very beautiful things about Jesus and what His plans are. Because the devil is smart he attacks God's people at the points where it really counts. The Lord has shown us specific areas where Satan is attacking so that we can see what God sees to be the most crucial issues. God does not want us to be taken unawares, but to have our eyes open, and flee to Him for protection from all Satan's devices.

YOU DON'T HAVE TO BE DECEIVED | **AUG 27**

Put on the whole armour of God, that ye may be able to stand against the wiles of the devil. Eph. 6:11.

The enemy in this world is not merely humanity. The real enemy is stronger than we are. "For we wrestle not against flesh and blood, but against principalities, against powers, against the rulers of the darkness of this world, against spiritual wickedness in high places. Wherefore take unto you the whole armour of God, that ye may be able to withstand in the evil day, and having done all, to stand" (Eph. 6:12, 13). Even though the enemy is stronger than we are, he is a defeated foe, so there is no reason for any of us to be defeated by him. The Lord has offered us an armor of truth that will protect us from Satan's attacks.

One of the truths about Satan is that he enjoys the spectacular. He likes to do flashy things. We are warned about this in Revelation 17 and 2 Thessalonians 2. Satan knows that people are impressed by the sensational, and this is one of his tricks. Sin doesn't make sense. Physical evidence will warn you that smoking produces lung cancer. Common sense will tell you that losing your temper isn't the best way to handle a problem. Rebellion simply doesn't make good sense. No one chooses Satan's way on the basis of logic and reason. So he plans his attack on another line—he tries to deceive us, to impress us with the supernatural. And if we trust our senses, we will be deceived.

Sometimes we have thought that the final issues will be very simple. Do you keep the Sabbath, or don't you? Do you belong to the remnant church, or do you belong to one that isn't? But it will not be simple. Satan is planning to deceive the very elect, if possible. The only way he could hope to do so would be to come up with a deception that was very close to the real thing.

It is an evidence of the love of God that He has given us warning in advance, that no one need to be taken in by the plans of the enemy. We have been warned against trusting to our senses, warned that we must trust only to the Word of God, and warned that without the vital relationship with Him we will be deceived. God has done everything possible to prevent our being lost, because in His great love He wants each of us to spend eternity with Him.

THE DEVIL IS A LIAR

If the Son therefore shall make you free, ye shall be free indeed. John 8:36.

Satan is come upon our world with renewed force in these last days. He knows his time is short, and he works with all his cunning to deceive God's people and to deceive the whole world. One of the hallmarks of his working is the supernatural. He enjoys putting on a good show—and there are millions who respond to their senses and follow his leading because it is so spectacular. Only a few are willing to deny their senses and follow the Word of God regardless of appearances.

From the very beginning, when Satan assured Eve that she wouldn't die, he has used as one of his greatest tools the concept that there is no death. Human beings don't find death that appealing, so they are willing to believe what he tells them. This opens the door for Satan to control lives.

Another of his most successful ploys is to tell us that we can live as we choose—that sin doesn't make any difference. He has been telling people since the beginning of time that God's law doesn't have to be kept. He comes to the world at large and says, If it feels good, do it. He offers momentary sensory pleasure in exchange for eternity, and millions accept his offer without hesitation. He comes to the church, and says, God's law is too big, too vast, too complex. We can never hope to obey it. Just let the blood of Jesus cover, and do your best to be a nice person, and that will suffice. And those within the church too often follow blindly along.

Jesus Christ offers us a different kind of life. He offers us the life of death to self. He offers us the indwelling, controlling power of His Spirit to keep us from sinning. In John 8:31 Jesus promised that if we continue in His love, and know the truth, the truth will make us free. He went on to explain that whoever sins is a slave to sin. The freedom Jesus brings is freedom from slavery, from sin, and from Satan's power.

Spiritism is not a distant issue—we will each be confronted by it in some form or another. It is only as Jesus sets us free and keeps us free that our minds will not be under the control of the enemy. The only power stronger than Satan is that of Jesus, whose voice can command him to leave, and he must obey. It is this power that gives us safety in these perilous days.

DOES GOD LOVE THE DEVIL?

How art thou fallen from heaven, O Lucifer, son of the morning! Isa. 14:12.

Do you think Jesus loves the devil? Think of what the devil has done to Him. Think of the eternity of peace that he destroyed. Think of the pain and sorrow and death for thousands of years. Think of how much the devil hates Jesus. Do you think Jesus loves the devil?

We have taken the position that crisis does not change character, that it merely reveals it. The entrance of sin into the universe, and the length to which God had to go to provide a way of escape, is the greatest crisis that Heaven has ever faced. And this crisis reveals His character of love as nothing else ever has or ever will. There is a very real sense in which the devil reveals Jesus. In the story of Satan the real hero is Jesus, and Jesus is therefore revealed in a way that is perhaps never revealed otherwise.

Second Corinthians 13:8 tells us that we can do nothing against the truth—only for it. And the one who has done the most in the entire universe against the truth ends up revealing truth in a way never otherwise revealed.

The first war came in heaven. This war did not catch God by surprise. But in spite of the fact that He knew in advance how Lucifer (who became Satan, or the devil) would respond, He created him, gave him positions of honor, and treated him with utmost fairness and love. He never discriminated against Lucifer. In fact, He is still treating Satan with fairness. We human beings cannot handle the foreknowledge that God has. If we knew in advance that someone was going to end up being our enemy, we'd start treating him like an enemy right now. But not God. He gave Lucifer every advantage.

We see this revealed again in the life of Jesus. Jesus knew in the beginning that Judas would betray Him. But Jesus treated him with love and respect, giving him no excuse for his treachery. Jesus did everything in His power to reach Judas.

God wanted only a service of love, made by a free choice. So God did not destroy Satan, but gave him opportunity to prove his point. By paying the terrible price of the cross, God was able to provide a universe ultimately free from sin forever, and still preserve the free choice of His created beings. What a motivation to us to choose Him and respond to His great love.

THE RISK OF FREEDOM

So God created man in his own image, in the image of God created he him. Gen. 1:27.

When God chose to allow Satan access to this world, to give him opportunity to prove his charges against the justice and love of God, He took a tremendous risk. God knew that by His very nature He Himself was limited to truth, righteousness, and fairness. He knew that Satan could deal in half-truths, deceit, pressure, and force. He knew that Satan would not be fair. God knew that many people would make the wrong choice. Why did He take such a chance?

As we look at the costliness of sin, it should tell us something about how much free choice means to God. He has a great respect for our freedom to think and choose for ourselves. He appeals only to our minds, to our good judgment, to our love for Him that is awakened by His great love for us.

Satan has taken full advantage of the freedoms that God allowed him. He spread rebellion among the angels, gaining almost half of them for his side. And he has worked to add to his numbers from this world ever since.

It says something important to us about the character of Jesus that He is willing to take risks. He knows that He will often be misunderstood—both by those in rebellion, who will accuse Him of cruelty in His dealings with them, and by those who are loyal, who will question His wisdom in permitting the rebels to continue. To allow men free choice is the greatest risk that God could take, but it was the only way He could preserve our freedom. God was willing to go the hard way—to pay the terrible price of freedom—that we may have a universe forever free from sin throughout eternity.

The price of freedom that God was willing to pay can never be comprehended by our minds. God was willing to send His Son to run the risk, along with each of us, of choosing rebellion. God was willing to stand weeping in the shadows as He watched His Son suffer and bleed and die, that we might have the choice to live. Jesus was willing to leave His place of honor and light and glory, finding heaven not a place to be desired if we could not be there with Him. The greatest accusation against God, by the greatest rebel of all time, was answered by the greatest love—and love triumphed, proving conclusively to the entire universe that God is love.

JESUS REVEALED BY DEATH

I am the resurrection, and the life: he that believeth in me, though he were dead, yet shall he live. John 11:25.

There's a long list of unpleasant words that begin with the letter *D.* There's *darkness* and *defeat* and *dismay* and *despair* and *doubt* and *discouragement* and *disaster* and *distress* and *discord* and *discontent!* How's that? Do you like those? But the most dreaded of all these is the word *death.*

Many people in the world at large believe that when you die, that's it. You're dead forever. There's nothing beyond the grave. Frankly, I'm not impressed with their theory, are you? It's not as if they were offering eternity in Las Vegas versus eternity in heaven. That might have at least a little attraction for some. But it's eternity in heaven versus nothing. I'm thankful today that death is *not* the end, and that God has bigger plans for us than eternal annihilation.

It is good news to realize that what we call death has never been any problem to God. Jesus called it sleep. We have read that the wages of sin is death—but the real wages of sin is the *second* death. The second death the Christian doesn't have to be concerned about. And what we call death, sleep, the moment of silence, is not something to be unduly concerned about either. *The Desire of Ages,* page 787, says, "To the believer, death is but a small matter. Christ speaks of it as if it were of little moment." Christ said, "If a man keep my saying, he shall never see death" (John 8:51).

When the Lord Himself descends from heaven with a shout, and the dead in Christ are called forth from their sleeping beds, it will be one of the easiest things God ever did. The only problem for Jesus is unbelief—the problem of trying to persuade our stubborn wills to yield to His control, to come to Him that we might have life. That's the problem!

When Jesus called death *sleep,* He was saying something wonderful, for sleeping carries with it the idea of the other end of the line—the waking up. When Jesus came to the damsel and said, "She's not dead, she's sleeping," He said that because He recognized that the waking-up time was coming. Because Jesus died, and rose again, each of us today has the choice of living forever. We may sleep—but we won't die. Jesus Himself will come to awaken us so that we may spend eternity with Him.

REAL CHRISTIANS NEVER DIE

Verily, verily, I say unto you, If a man keep my saying, he shall never see death.
John 8:51.

In the days of Jesus death was a dread mystery. People had a complete blank as to what death was all about. Multitudes approached the valley of the shadow with nothing but fear and foreboding. There were continuing arguments between the Sadducees and the Pharisees about the resurrection, and what happens to a man when he dies. The Sadducees didn't believe in the resurrection. That's why they were sad, you see! The Pharisees did believe, and so the arguments continued at great length.

Jesus came and said some very definite things about what we call death. In John 11:26 He said, "Whosoever liveth and believeth in me shall never die." And then He asked, "Do you believe this?" Let me ask you that. Do you believe this? Or do you believe that to say that the one who lives and believes in Christ shall never die is going too far? Well, it's what the Bible teaches.

Sleep is not all bad. I have seen people who were exhausted, overworked, and weary, who looked forward eagerly to being able to go to sleep. We have all experienced it. Adam lived for more than 900 years. Have you ever read his reaction when the time came for him to go to sleep? It's found in *Patriarchs and Prophets*, page 82: "Adam's life was one of sorrow, humility, and contrition. When he left Eden, the thought that he must die thrilled him with horror. . . . [But] though the sentence of death pronounced upon him by his Maker had at first appeared terrible, yet after beholding for nearly a thousand years the results of sin, he felt that it was merciful of God to bring to an end a life of suffering and sorrow." Adam was glad to be able to lie down and go to sleep.

We understand that for those who sleep, the passage of time is unnoticed. Can you imagine going to sleep, and awaking the next instant to see Jesus coming? Adam went to sleep after a life of toil and sorrow, and so far as his awareness is concerned, the next moment he'll be awakened. It is one of the blessings of sleep—to be unaware of the passing of time. It also shows the mercy of God today, that He does not prolong our lives in this world. Perhaps 60 or 70 years is about all we could take of this life. Then it's good to go to sleep, knowing that Jesus will awaken us when He comes again.

THE WAKING-UP TIME

But now is Christ risen from the dead, and become the firstfruits of them that slept. For since by man came death, by man came also the resurrection of the dead. For as in Adam all die, even so in Christ shall all be made alive. 1 Cor. 15:20-22.

The glorious truth of the gospel was spoken by Jesus at the tomb of Lazarus. "I am the resurrection, and the life: he that believeth in me, though he were dead, yet shall he live: and whosoever liveth and believeth in me shall never die" (John 11:25, 26). Perhaps at times Seventh-day Adventists have worked too hard to make sure that people were dead and in their graves. In spite of the fact that we do not believe in the immortality of the soul, in spite of the fact that we do believe that people are unconscious in their graves now, awaiting the resurrection, we still can believe that *Christians never die.* The only real death is the second death. The sleeping, the waiting in our graves for the voice of Jesus to call us forth, is not death. What we see in the funeral chapel of today is only sleep—and for the believer, it is not the end of the line. We as Christians have been given a fantastic hope.

When Jesus told His disciples, after waiting for two days, that it was time to go and awaken Lazarus, the disciples misunderstood. But Jesus was speaking of what we refer to as death. In His eyes it was only sleep.

For those who go to sleep, the story isn't over yet. The same One who awakened Lazarus, and proclaimed Himself the resurrection and the life, will awaken the sleeping saints. Jesus changed death to sleep.

This does not mean that we will not sorrow when our loved ones fall asleep. We may miss them sorely. We may shed tears. (We sometimes shed tears and miss our loved ones when they are gone on a long journey.) But it is not a matter of saying goodbye forever. Jesus is what makes the difference between sleep and death. If Christ be not raised, then is our faith in vain, and they also which are fallen asleep are perished. But Christ *has* risen, and we too shall rise to everlasting life. In Christ shall all be made alive. Death's sting has been taken away. The golden morning is fast approaching. Jesus soon will come. We have the promise today of the resurrection, of the waking-up time, of the reuniting with our loved ones, nevermore to part.

JESUS REVEALED BY THE SABBATH

And he said unto them, The sabbath was made for man, and not man for the sabbath: therefore the Son of man is Lord also of the sabbath. Mark 2:27, 28.

There is an astronomical reason for the length of the year. It is the time it takes for the earth to travel around the sun—365 days, 5 hours, 48 minutes, and 46 seconds. And it never varies. The month is based on the relationship of the earth to the moon. The day is based on the rotation of the earth on its axis. Have you pondered lately that there is no astronomical reason whatever for the week? The only reason for the week, in spite of the skeptics and the infidels, is Creation. Every time a person in this world, regardless of his thinking, his profession, or his religious beliefs, says, "Today is Monday, the second day of the week," he is admitting the Creation story!

You can discuss and argue science and religion until you are blue in the face, but as soon as the scientist says, "Well, I'll see you on Thursday," he has lost the argument right there! It can be shown by Scripture, and even by history, that the weekly cycle has never been broken from the very beginning of time. The God of heaven who was in charge of the whole idea in the first place has done His job in preserving this fact.

Jesus said that He is Lord of the Sabbath. It is a mark of His creative power. This is what made Him Lord of the Sabbath. It was given in honor of Creation. To say that the Sabbath was made for the Jews would be the same thing as saying that the world was made for the Jews! The world was made for man, and the Sabbath was made for man as well.

The Bible says to *remember* the Sabbath day. What does the Sabbath show us about Jesus, who is the Lord of the Sabbath? For one thing, it indicates that Jesus is a great liberator. The Sabbath was given anew to the Israelites when they were freed from slavery in Egypt (Deut. 5:15). *We* are carnal, sold under sin. But Jesus comes to us today and offers us freedom. He becomes our Liberator today. The Sabbath is a weekly reminder of that fact. When we accept the gospel, we are freed from being rebels. We may still fall and fail as we grow, but we are freed from our rebellion, and are given cause to celebrate the freedom that the Sabbath represents.

THE SIGN OF SANCTIFICATION

That ye may know that I am the Lord that doth sanctify you. Ex. 31:13.

Some believe that sanctification is something that will happen to you just before you die, but that is not so. Sanctification is the work of a lifetime, just as much as breathing is the work of a lifetime. At the very beginning of your acceptance of the plan of salvation, your sanctification took place. Sanctification in Bible usage is a finished, completed work, as well as a progressive work. It means that one is set aside for a holy purpose. It is God that does it in the beginning, and in the ongoing process as well. He says, "I am the Lord that doth sanctify you." He is active in your everyday life, and has promised to carry forward the work He has started.

The Sabbath is a symbol of sanctification. The Sabbath is a reminder of our liberation from bondage. It is a reminder that life has meaning now. It is a reminder that God is active in our everyday life, carrying forward His work of growth, of holy use, of purpose for our lives. The Sabbath is all of that and much more. The Sabbath was designed for spiritual growth and refreshment and rest. When Adam and Eve were created, their first whole day was a day of rest. Were they tired, so soon after being created? No, God wanted them to be reminded of the fact that the best man could do when he came on the scene was to rest, for the works were already done.

This is what Hebrews 4 is all about. "Let us therefore fear, lest, a promise being left us of entering into his rest, any of you should seem to come short of it." "For we which have believed do enter into rest." "For he spake in a certain place of the seventh day on this wise, And God did rest the seventh day from all his works." "For he that is entered into his rest, he also hath *ceased from his own works,* as God did from his." "Let us labour therefore to enter into that rest."

How do you enter into rest? By believing or trusting in the Lord Jesus Christ. And we must labor to enter into that rest. Isn't that a strange phrase? Have you ever labored to rest? Where is the labor? Jesus said, "Come unto me, all ye that labour and are heavy laden, and I will give you rest" (Matt. 11:28). The labor is in coming to Him for rest. Our labor is not to fight the devil and sin and temptation. God gave us the Sabbath to remind us of this fact.

GOD'S PRESENCE MAKES A DIFFERENCE

And hallow my sabbaths; and they shall be a sign between me and you, that ye may know that I am the Lord your God. Eze. 20:20.

There are times in God's relationship with His people when His presence is very noticeably felt. One of those times is in the Communion service, if you are open to sense it, and not worrying about being embarrassed by someone washing your feet. Another time when God's presence is uniquely sensed is at a baptism. There's something special then, and all heaven rejoices as some of the notes from the angel choir seem to echo in our hearts here. And then I believe that God is often very much present at a Christian funeral. Time and eternity seem to meet somehow, and God is able to communicate with us in a special way as we stop and think. And I believe that God is also especially present on Sabbath.

One time during the war a doctor and his family invited us to travel to the city with him for a concert. My father had been driving an old Dodge. It was hard to get new cars, and the engine in the Dodge had been rebuilt. I don't know how many times the speedometer had gone around. My brother and I used to long for a new car. The doctor had a brand-new Cadillac that he had managed to get from a patient of his who owned the dealership. The Cadillac just kind of glided along. When we returned to our '41 Dodge that night, everyone was tired and kind of quiet, until about the tenth time my father tried to get the emergency brake off, and then we all burst out laughing! This old Dodge was something else compared to the Cadillac. There was something different about the Cadillac. There was more power there!

When the Sabbath comes, and you sit and watch the sun sink, and you think on eternal things, and invite the Holy Spirit and angels to come close, they are there. There's something different about this day. "It [the Sabbath] was designed to bring men into communion with God."—*The Desire of Ages*, p. 286. And when Jesus comes 105 trillion miles and knocks on my door for a special appointment, I want to be ready and waiting for His arrival. I want communion and fellowship with Him on this special visit, don't you?

THE SEVENTH DAY

Keep the sabbath day to sanctify it, as the Lord thy God hath commanded thee.
Deut. 5:12.

Johnny left home one Sunday morning on his way to Sunday school. He had two dimes in his hand; one for the Lord, and one for ice cream on his way home. As he was crossing the street, he slipped, and one of the dimes rolled down into the gutter. He was regretting that the *Lord's* dime had gone down the drain, when a friend came by who *wasn't* going to Sunday school. It wasn't long before he agreed that his mother would never know, and they went fishing. But in spite of his efforts and proper timing, he got home a little late, and soon his mother had the whole story.

As a punishment, his mother sent him to his room to read the fourth commandment 50 times. Johnny began to read. "Remember the sabbath day, to keep it holy. Six days shalt thou labour, and do all thy work: but the seventh day is the sabbath of the Lord thy God." After the first few times he had it by memory. The words burned deep into his mind, and when he finished he was sure he would never again go fishing on Sunday.

Several weeks later his teacher at school asked for someone to give the days of the week in order. Johnny volunteered. He stood and recited, "Monday, Tuesday, Wednesday, Thursday, Friday, Saturday, Sunday." The teacher said, "That's fine, but you made one mistake. Sunday is the first day, and Saturday is the seventh. Try it one more time." Johnny hesitated a moment. "Monday, Tuesday, Wednesday, Thursday, Friday, Saturday, Sunday." Again the teacher asked that he begin with the first day, but he recited it the same as he had at first. The teacher told him sternly to stay after school. But Johnny said, "Teacher, if you had read the fourth commandment as many times as I have, you'd *know* Monday is the first day of the week, and Sunday is the seventh!" Obviously something was wrong. Someone had tried to change something.

It was predicted that the time would come when people would try to change God's holy day. But Jesus had a high regard for the Sabbath. It is because of this that Satan has tried so hard to produce a counterfeit. Luke 4:16 says that to worship on the Sabbath day was Jesus' *custom.* If we follow His example and teachings, it will become our custom as well.

256

TRUTH OR TRADITION

Howbeit in vain do they worship me, teaching for doctrines the commandments of men. Mark 7:7.

Jesus' custom was to keep the Sabbath (Luke 4:16). It had been His custom when He lived in Nazareth, working in the carpenter shop. It was a custom that He continued all through His life. He was the Creator, and yet we see Him resting on the Sabbath day as He Himself had commanded. Obviously, He was giving us an example that we can follow today.

Jesus warned the people against their traditions. He had no time for anything based simply on tradition when it came in collision with His Father's commandments. It's interesting to make a list of the traditions that we have today. Some of us think that it is sin to open our eyes during prayer! That's just a tradition. There's no basis in Scripture for that. Some people feel it's a sin to put anything on top of the Bible. That's a tradition. Some parents tell their children it's a sin to take part in the Communion service before they have been baptized. Another tradition. Should we throw out all traditions? No, you don't throw them out arbitrarily. Some of the traditions may have good reasons for them. But whenever tradition comes in collision with the truth of God, then the tradition goes. Jesus spoke to this point, "Howbeit in vain do they worship me, teaching for doctrines the commandments of men. For laying aside the commandments of God, ye hold the tradition of men. . . . Full well ye reject the commandment of God."

Any kind of false Sabbath or false day of worship that the world has gotten into the habit of observing is strictly a tradition, because you don't find it in Scripture at all. If you want to keep the Sabbath of the Bible, you are going to keep the seventh day, according to Scripture.

The most oft-given reason for keeping Sunday is that it is the day of Jesus' resurrection. It's a nice-sounding reason—but it has no Bible base. If you are going to follow the Bible teachings, you will keep the seventh day. For those who want to honor the Resurrection, we have the service of baptism. That's the *Scripture* memorial for the Resurrection. Jesus rested at the end of Creation, and rested again in the grave after He had finished His work on the earth. And today He invites us to rest in memorial of the works of creation and redemption He has accomplished for us.

THE BIRTHDAY OF THE WORLD

And God blessed the seventh day, and sanctified it: because that in it he had rested from all his work which God created and made. Gen. 2:3.

It was God who set aside the seventh-day Sabbath in the beginning in honor of Creation. Evidently the Creator realized the importance of having His creatures remember His creatorship and His creation every week. The Sabbath is in honor of the birthday of the world. You can't change anybody's birthday. When someone comes along with a pseudo-Sabbath, or another day to take its place, they are obviously false, because no one can change anyone's birthday, not even Abraham Lincoln's or George Washington's! We can change the official memorial holidays, but have we changed their birthdates? Of course not. We can decide to have our holiday on a different day, that's all. And why do we do this? Because Washington and Lincoln obviously don't mean that much to us anymore. We are more concerned with having a day off than with honoring Washington and Lincoln. Isn't that true? Why, I can prove it to you. On the last celebration of Lincoln's or Washington's birthday, how many of you sat around reading about Lincoln or Washington and meditating on them?

When you forget about the person whose birthday you are supposed to be celebrating, as time goes by you can find it easy to change it into simply a holiday. Don't miss this in relationship to the Sabbath. God Himself couldn't change the Sabbath, as long as it continues to be a memorial of what it is, because to change the day that was set aside in honor of Creation would be impossible even for God Himself.

But God is interested in sanctifying a people, not *just* a particular day (Heb. 13:12). People begin to experience sanctification the moment they are born again as new creatures in Christ. We can be thankful to the Creator for not only our first birth but the new birth as well. Thus the Sabbath becomes a reminder not only of the fact that God created us in the first place but of our redemption, through the blood of Jesus. The Sabbath has been given to us as a sign of our sanctification (Ex. 31:13; Eze. 20:12). *We* have been set apart for a holy purpose. The Sabbath is more than a matter of law. It is a matter of Christian life and experience.

CHANGING THE SABBATH

Moreover also I gave them my sabbaths, to be a sign between me and them, that they might know that I am the Lord that sanctify them. Eze. 20:12.

As the Jews departed from God, and failed to make the righteousness of Christ their own by faith, the Sabbath lost its significance to them."—*The Desire of Ages*, p. 283. Is it possible today that the significance of the Sabbath to you right now is meaningful for you in proportion to your experience of righteousness by faith? "In order to keep the Sabbath holy, men must themselves be holy. Through faith they must become partakers of the righteousness of Christ."—*Ibid.* The Sabbath was a token of separation from idolatry, which includes self-worship. Self-worship is the idea that we can save ourselves. When I pull away from idolatry, I am pulling away from the idea that I can save myself, and trusting only in the righteousness of Jesus. That's what the Sabbath represents.

The Sabbath is a symbol of our connection with God. If you are having trouble with the Sabbath, and are questioning its importance, you have deeper trouble somewhere else. If you find that the Sabbath is a drag, and are tired of the routine, and waiting impatiently for the sun to set, your trouble is not with the Sabbath but is far deeper than that. Your problem has to do with your relationship with the Lord Himself. Sometimes we sit around judging some prelate over in Italy who had the audacity to change the Sabbath. But if you have pulled away from a deep dependence upon Jesus Christ as your personal friend and Saviour, and you don't know Him today, then you yourself have changed the Sabbath, too. Long before the Sabbath was changed by Constantine and the council, it had already been changed experientially in the hearts of the people. And when it is changed experientially in the hearts of people, it is only a matter of time until it can be changed on the calendar as well. There is a close connection.

If you have trouble today with the Sabbath being a formal routine, may I suggest that instead of leaving the church you change the Sabbath back into what God intended it to be in the first place. This is done by turning to Jesus Christ as your Creator, toward Jesus as your Redeemer, and toward Him as your Sanctifier, in a daily, close connection with Him.

ONLY TWO CHOICES

Hurt not the earth, neither the sea, nor the trees, till we have sealed the servants of our God in their foreheads. Rev. 7:3.

We were holding some public meetings in central California, and had engaged the Voice of Prophecy quartet to come and sing for us. They wanted to know what the topic of the sermon was, so they could choose some appropriate music for the occasion. We told them it was the mark of the beast! Their faces went blank, and we suddenly realized that there are few songs on that subject. I suppose this indicates something. The only way you could come up with a song about the mark of the beast would be to stress the positive instead of the negative.

In Revelation 14:1-6 you see a group of people who live at the very end of this earth's history, who are on God's side. They are extremely loyal. It says that they follow the Lamb whithersoever He goeth, and that they are without fault before God's throne. This same group is also mentioned in Revelation 7:1-4. Notice in both passages that God's name is written in their foreheads.

Revelation 13:1-9 describes a second group. They worship the beast, and wonder after him. In verse 16 of the same chapter it says that this second group receives a mark also, some in their right hand, and some in their foreheads. So the contrast is that at the end of time there are two groups: one with the seal of God in their foreheads, and one group with a mark from the beast in their forehead *or* in their hand.

It is possible for this subject to become complex, with all the history and prophecy and dates and texts. But there should be some way to make it simple enough for even the boys and girls to understand. When Jesus comes again you will either have the name of God in your forehead or the mark of the beast in your forehead or hand. There are only two choices, or two groups. The middle ground that so many occupy today will have disappeared. This tells us something about Jesus. It tells us that He wants us to make decisions. He gives time and is patient and works with us. But He does not want us to sit forever on the fence. The time is coming when each one will be forced to decide either for or against Him. And on our choice depends our eternal destiny.

THERE SHALL NO EVIL BEFALL THEE

He that dwelleth in the secret place of the most High shall abide under the shadow of the Almighty. Ps. 91:1.

If you were to take the books of Daniel and Revelation out of your Bible and paste them together, you would have a history of the world from about 600 B.C. until the end of time. It would be a history of the world in advance—called prophecy. At the very beginning of this history are some exciting stories to keep the children's attention. For example, the three Hebrews in the furnace, Daniel in the lions' den, and the handwriting on the wall. In Daniel 2 is the table of contents of this history of the world. It tells of the great world empires clear through to the end of the world. Babylon, Medo-Persia, Greece, Rome, followed by ten kingdoms, followed by God's kingdom. Daniel and Revelation were designed for the time of the end.

Much of the detail has to do with the last of the world empires and the coming of Jesus. God is interested in each one of us knowing clearly and in advance what the issues are, so that we can choose intelligently which of two groups we would like to become a part of.

Until shortly before the coming of Jesus, there will be three groups of people living upon the earth—the cold, the hot, and the lukewarm (Revelation 3). But when Jesus comes, there will be only two groups. There will be only hot and cold. The lukewarm will have disappeared. There will be one group with the seal of God in their foreheads, and one group with the mark of the beast in their foreheads or hands. Two groups. Other Bible descriptions of these two groups are righteous and wicked, good and bad, wheat and tares, just and unjust, sheep and goats, and so on. But two clear groups.

Do you have any idea which group you would like to be in? Do you realize the alternatives? Do you realize that if you are in one group you will not be able to buy or sell? Do you realize that you will have the death penalty over your head? That's what happens to God's group. But the other group will suffer the seven last plagues, and will gnaw their tongues for pain, and the sun will scorch them with heat. It looks at first glance as though you are in trouble no matter which you choose! But God's people have been promised that there shall no evil befall them. We can hide in Him, and find safety there.

261

VICTORY OVER THE BEAST

And I saw as it were a sea of glass mingled with fire: and them that had gotten the victory over the beast, and over his image. Rev. 15:2.

There are eight distinguishing marks to identify the beast spoken of in Daniel 7 and Revelation 13. This beast gets his authority from pagan Rome. The beast blasphemes against God. It has political strength. It makes war on God's people, is a persecuting power. It rules for 1,260 years. It receives a deadly wound at the end of that time. It has a number that is applied to it, 666. And it has a mark that people can receive in either their foreheads or their right hands.

God has something that you can receive in your forehead—called the seal of God. But the mark of the beast can be received in either the forehead or the hand. You are aware that the book of Revelation is full of symbols. Symbolically, then, when something is received in the forehead, what would it refer to? That someone will come along with a branding iron and press it into your forehead? No, the suggestion is that you will receive it in your *mind.* It will be received intelligently by your reason and judgment. If you have the name of God, the seal of God, in your forehead, it means that it has entered into your mind, your thinking, your decisions.

What would the right hand signify? Work, action, activity. When you receive God's seal, it *has* to be in the forehead. But the mark of the beast can be either in the forehead or the hand. People are evidently going to accept the mark of the beast either in their thinking or simply through external pressure, outward compliance. God is interested only in intelligent worship. He looks on the inside—out of the abundance of the *heart* the mouth speaketh. Man looks on the outward appearance, but the Lord looks on the heart. The seat of worship to God is in the mind, not just actions.

What does a seal consist of? A seal of any government has at least three things. The name of the ruler, his title, and the territory over which he rules. The seal of God is found in the Sabbath commandment. It is the Sabbath of the *Lord.* The Lord made heaven and earth—He is our Creator. There's His title. And how much did He create? His territory includes heaven and earth and the sea and all that in them is. Because He is our Creator and Redeemer, He is the One we are to worship.

GOD OF EVERYTHING

If any man worship the beast and his image, and receive his mark in his forehead, or in his hand, the same shall drink of the wine of the wrath of God. Rev. 14:9, 10.

The seal of God in the people's foreheads at the very end has to do with the Sabbath, the day of worship in honor of the Creator. Therefore the mark of the beast must have something to do with a day of worship as well.

The mark-of-the-beast issue is far deeper than simply a day to go to church. The common thread going through all the three angels' messages is a warning against self-worship. The thing that is so tragic about this beast power is that it is an organized group for self-worship, that even thinks it can change God's laws. Daniel 7:25 predicted it. Revelation 13 and 14 give warning against this power, and its attempts to change God's laws and His times. You cannot go through those scriptures without being startled at how deeply God feels about the issues. There are many people who know that the Sabbath is the day of worship taught by Scripture, but they have not realized how God feels about it. The reason God feels this way is because He gave it in the first place in honor of Creation.

If I were the devil, and I saw a day given every week in honor of the Creator, the One who made all things, I would be so upset that I would have to do something about it. If there's anything greater than saying that God made a tree or a mountain or an ocean, it is that God made *everything*—"All that in them is." You can't get any bigger than that. So Satan had to do something about the day of worship in honor of that. God has sent us special information that this would happen, and when it would happen, and how God would feel about it, so that we would not be caught unawares. Jesus is revealed in this doctrine in His feelings about the day of worship, about His law, and about a group of people who go along with Satan's deceptions, and a group who stand loyal to Him to the very end. "I saw as it were a sea of glass mingled with fire: and them that had gotten the victory over the beast, and over his image, and over his mark, and over the number of his name" (Rev. 15:2). Don't you want to be in that group that has gotten the victory over self-worship, over independence, over trying to be God?

THE 144,000

And I saw as it were a sea of glass mingled with fire: and them that had gotten the victory over the beast, and over his image, and over his mark, and over the number of his name, stand on the sea of glass, having the harps of God. Rev. 15:2.

There will be a group of people at the end of time who will have gotten the victory over the beast and his power. They will have gotten the victory over self-worship. They will have gotten the victory over any idea that they can challenge their Creator or change His times and laws. They will have the victory over independence, pride, and selfishness. They will stand among the group on the sea of glass someday—the group of 144,000—and sing the song of Moses and the Lamb.

Have you ever wondered who the 144,000 are? It's very clear who they are. I know who they are, and you do, too! The only trouble we have is trying to figure out who the rest of the people are. The problem in Revelation isn't who the 144,000 are, it's who is the great multitude that no man can number—that's the mystery.

But it says about these people that they are not only blameless but faultless. It reminds us of Romans 8:29. Instead of the image to the beast, what do we see? "For whom he did foreknow, he also did predestinate to be conformed *to the image of his Son,* that he might be the firstborn among many brethren." It is important to understand about the beast, and the mark of the beast, and the image to the beast. But it is far more important to be sure we know Jesus, and are allowing Him to change us to His image. I would like to have more concern and interest and preoccupation with being conformed to the image of His Son than with conformity to this power that thinks to exalt himself above the throne of God.

The group that stands on the sea of glass and sings the song of Moses and the Lamb is made up of people who have the seal of God in their foreheads—God has written His name in their foreheads because they belong to Him. Their greatest ambition is to follow Him wherever He goes.

We need to remember that no one will be following the Lamb everywhere He goes throughout eternity unless he begins following Him on this earth. Those who have now been following Jesus day by day will be sealed by Him, and will have the privilege of following Him forever.

DON'T BE AFRAID

Fear none of those things which thou shalt suffer. Rev. 2:10.

Momentous times are just upon us. People are going to face death over a day of worship. Sometimes we wonder how it could ever happen. Do you think you could face death rather than be disloyal to God? Do you have a faith that can withstand pain and hunger and persecution?

Sometimes boys and girls, and even older folks as well, lie awake at night because they have heard too many gory details of what the time of trouble is going to be like. But don't forget Psalm 91. Don't forget that Huss and Jerome *sang* as they were martyred. Have you ever burned your finger on a hot stove? Did you sing? Not likely! Obviously martyrs were sustained by a power outside themselves in order to be able to do as they did. The courage of a martyr, however, is not supplied until it is needed. There's no point in trying to figure out whether you have enough courage right now to be martyred. You don't. It isn't sent until it is required.

Those who have the seal of God, those who are loyal to Him and to His day of worship, will be unable to buy or sell. But God has promised that our bread and water will be sure. "I have been young, and now am old; yet have I not seen the righteous forsaken, nor his seed begging bread" (Ps. 37:25). Those who remain loyal to God will have a death decree hanging over their heads, but the words of Jesus come to each of His children, "Be thou faithful unto death, and I will give thee a crown of life" (Rev. 2:10).

On the other hand, those who receive the mark of the beast will receive the seven last plagues. And they will ultimately end up in the lake of fire, with no hope of a future resurrection.

God is able to preserve those who are loyal to Him. Sometimes we have recited the promises of His Word as a routine. But it won't be a routine when you face the closing scenes of this earth's history. "He that dwelleth in the secret place of the most High shall abide under the shadow of the Almighty. I will say of the Lord, He is my refuge and my fortress: my God; in him will I trust. Surely he shall deliver thee from the snare of the fowler, and from the noisome pestilence" (Ps. 91:1-3). Notice that it's talking about the plagues. "There shall no evil befall thee, neither shall any *plague* come nigh thy dwelling" (verse 10). The promises are sure—you can't miss if you're on God's side.

DON'T KILL YOUR HUSBAND

Wherefore, my brethren, ye also are become dead to the law by the body of Christ; that ye should be married to another, even to him who is raised from the dead. Rom. 7:4.

There was a woman one time who was married to a nit-picking, perfectionist man. It was misery. She thought that everything would be all right to begin with, but the longer she lived with him, the more she realized that it was impossible to please him. If the potatoes were just a little bit too brown, it was dark-blue Monday. If the house wasn't exactly right, things got really heavy. His preoccupation with perfection was so unbearable that one night she was lying awake thinking about the problem, and she began to think of a way out. She had made a vow to live with him till death do us part. He was sleeping quietly beside her, and she thought how easy it would be to . . . well, that wouldn't be the thing to do. Then she thought maybe she should be the one to go. Even the possibility of dying herself seemed less unbearable than continuing to live in the way she was living.

But then she realized that the ideal situation would be for her to die, and thus be released from the marriage that was unbearable, but come back to life again and be able to marry another man.

Do you have any idea where we're going with this parable? Have you read about it in the Bible? It's found in Romans 7. No one likes to kill himself, but people have done it. If you want to kill yourself, you can jump off the Empire State Building. You can put a gun to your head or you can overdose on some drug. But you cannot crucify yourself. There is only one way for you to be crucified. Someone else has to do it.

Romans 7 talks about the perfectionist husband—the law. The law says you can't do this and you can't do that. And there's no way you can measure up. Death is the only way out. You can die to your old life. Jesus has made it possible that if we die with Him, and are buried with Him, we can rise again to walk with Him in newness of life. That's what the symbol of baptism is all about.

Jesus has offered us this new life if we will accept His sacrifice for us at the cross and allow our old natures to be put to death. We have the choice today to rise again, to walk with Him in freedom and peace.

ATTENDING YOUR OWN FUNERAL

Therefore we are buried with him by baptism into death: that like as Christ was raised up from the dead by the glory of the Father, even so we also should walk in newness of life. Rom. 6:4.

In the Old Testament there was a multitude of ceremonies. In the New Testament there are only three—marriage, baptism, and the Lord's Supper. Both marriage, which came at Creation, and the Lord's Supper, which began originally at the Passover, came from Old Testament times. Only baptism is added in New Testament times.

There are people who feel that something happens to a person at baptism, that the person is changed in some way by the ceremony itself. The Bible does not teach this, but rather indicates that in baptism we are simply acknowledging by an outward ceremony an experience that has already taken place within. The people who have felt that baptism would do something to them, in terms of changing their lives and freeing them from sin, have often been disappointed.

I went to visit a woman one time who said, "Don't talk to me about baptism. I've been baptized three times, and not one of them took!" She made it sound like a vaccination! Baptism was never designed to inoculate a person against sin and temptation. The ordinance of baptism is a symbol. Baptism itself is not a substitute for conversion or the new birth. The new life with Christ must have already begun, and baptism then becomes meaningful as an outward sign to announce to others what has already happened.

Seventh-day Adventists practice baptism by immersion, rather than another method adopted for the sake of convenience, as many Protestant groups have done. But this very inconvenience reminds us of something important about Jesus. It was not convenient for Him to come to this earth, putting on the robe of humanity. It was not convenient for Him to suffer, to die, for our sins. But He did not consult His own convenience.

When we realize the lengths to which Jesus went in His sacrifice for us, and when our hearts have responded to Him in love and surrender, we will be daily in relationship and contact with Him. Then it is very significant for us to choose to follow His example in baptism.

267

PREPARATION FOR BAPTISM

And now why tarriest thou? arise, and be baptized, and wash away thy sins, calling on the name of the Lord. Acts 22:16.

There are three prerequisites for baptism. First of all, a person must understand. Matthew 28:19, 20, says, "Go ye therefore, and teach all nations, baptizing them in the name of the Father, and of the Son, and of the Holy Ghost." Notice what happens first—teaching preceded baptism. So when a person is baptized, he is admitting publicly that he has been taught by God, taught by the Holy Spirit, and by His messengers, and that he understands.

There have been young people who have been bribed and persuaded by their parents or someone else to be baptized, who were taught nothing before baptism except that their parents wanted them to do it. They may have been given a few facts concerning doctrines, but they have not been taught of God. They have no relationship or fellowship with Him.

Mark 16:16 gives a second prerequisite. "He that believeth and is baptized shall be saved; but he that believeth not shall be damned." Don't miss the sequence—believing comes before baptism. Trust in God is what is needed. Eternal destiny is not decided primarily by baptism, for there are exceptions to the rule. The thing that brings damnation is not the absence of baptism but the absence of belief or trust in God.

The third prerequisite is found in Acts 2:38. Here on the day of Pentecost, Peter is preaching. He says, "Repent." Why did he say that? Because in the middle of his presentation the congregation interrupted him and asked, "Men and brethren, what shall we do?" They had been convicted. And Peter's response was, "Repent, and be baptized every one of you in the name of Jesus Christ for the remission of sins." So the third prerequisite is to repent. Repentance is sorrow for sin, and turning away from it. But there's only one way that can happen. It is as we see what our sin has done to Jesus, and are sorry for hurting our best Friend, that we are able to be genuinely repentant.

Jesus offers to us today the opportunity of coming to Him, to learn of Him, and to trust in Him. He offers us the gift of repentance. And as we respond to Him, He then invites us to follow the example He set, and be baptized for the remission of sins.

268

WHAT ABOUT REBAPTISM?

When they heard this, they were baptized in the name of the Lord Jesus. Acts 19:5.

In the first few verses of Acts 19 there is a definite Bible reason for being baptized a second time. It doesn't necessarily have to do with growth in the Christian life. It has to do with new light about Jesus that one didn't have before. It is something that, because a person didn't know of it, he has been neglecting. When the disciples spoken of in Acts 19 heard about the new truth that they hadn't been aware of, they were baptized a second time.

Our practice in the church has been to baptize people a second time if they have once been Christians but turned their backs on God and gone their own way. When they returned, they became convicted that they wanted to renew their public confession of Jesus Christ.

Occasionally someone will come who says, "I was baptized when I was 10 or 11, and I didn't know what it was all about. I was just baptized because the rest of the kids were. But since that time I have died, and no one attended my funeral. I have been born again, and no one has celebrated my birthday. So I'd like to be baptized for real this time." We don't hesitate when a person is convinced by the Spirit that he wants to make this decision.

There has been a certain stigma attached to rebaptism in the minds of some. Particularly if someone who has appeared to be a good church member seeks rebaptism, the question in the minds of many is, "I wonder what he did wrong!" Because of this, sometimes the one who is choosing to be rebaptized will meet with a few friends in some outdoor setting rather than in the church. But I liked the testimony of a couple who were rebaptized recently. They had been church members in good standing, but had only lately come to a personal relationship with the Lord Jesus. And they said, "I suppose that some of you are wondering why we have chosen to take this step. Perhaps you are wondering what we did wrong. Well, we did the worst—the very worst!" And you could have heard a pin drop. They continued, "We have done the worst. We have lived our good, upright, moral, religious lives apart from Jesus. And that's the worst." In order for baptism to be meaningful, whether a first baptism or a rebaptism, it must be an evidence of a life changed by relationship with Jesus.

THE GIFT OF PROPHECY

And he gave some, apostles; and some, prophets; and some, evangelists; and some, pastors and teachers. Eph. 4:11.

There were some longtime Seventh-day Adventists who were taking a trip with some new converts to their church. One of their stops was in Salt Lake City, Utah, where they toured the temple square and other points of interest. The new converts said, "We're glad that the Seventh-day Adventist Church doesn't have any of this prophet business." The Seventh-day Adventist friends sort of went hot and cold, and tried to think what to reply. Obviously, these new converts had been rushed into the church without sufficient preparation.

Not only does the gift of prophecy and prophets have something to do with God's church, but this gift has had something to do with God's people in all ages. According to God's plan, the gift of prophecy is scheduled to be in His church to the very end of time.

If you don't believe in the gift of prophecy, you don't believe in the Bible. And if you're having trouble with the gift of prophecy in the church, you're also having trouble with Scripture.

Most of us would deny ever seeing a real live prophet. But perhaps you have tried to imagine what it would have been like several years ago to have seen a prophet in person. And yet this is God's purpose in the church. Not only was it His purpose in regard to the Ephesians in the days of Paul, but you notice that in this passage, it is for the perfecting of the saints till we all come in the unity of the faith. Have we reached that yet? Has the Christian church today come to that place? Not yet!

Some people look back on the gift of prophecy and say that it was sent for the purpose of helping immature, naive people grow up. And once the church comes of age and matures, it no longer needs the gift. I don't believe it. It was given till we all come to the unity of the faith and the knowledge of the Son of God, to the measure of the stature of the fullness of Christ, that we henceforth be no more children tossed to and fro, carried about by every wind of doctrine. We have not arrived. We have not reached the full stature yet. The gift of prophecy is still meaningful for us today.

COMING BEHIND IN NO GIFT

Even as the testimony of Christ was confirmed in you: so that ye come behind in no gift; waiting for the coming of our Lord Jesus Christ. 1 Cor. 1:6, 7.

Evidently God has had a purpose for the gift of prophets or prophecy, which was designed to help the people of God stay in the truth. It was His purpose that this gift be always present so that people could have the advantage of detailed counsel that is relevant to the time and place in which they live.

According to Scripture, the gift of prophecy is for the church—so don't go looking for a true prophet of God outside the church. The gift is for believers (1 Cor. 12:28; 14:22). Paul made the analogy between the gifts to the church and the human body. In this analogy, the gift of prophecy can be compared with eyes. Evidently they saw it this way back in the Old Testament days (1 Sam. 9:9). In those days the prophet was called the "seer." The prophet was the eyes of God's people. Again from the same analogy, it's natural to expect prophets to have vision or visions. Numbers 12:6 says that God will reveal Himself through His prophets in visions and dreams.

It is God's purpose in the last days that the church come behind in no gift (1 Cor. 1:7). He doesn't want us to come behind in apostles or pastors or teachers or evangelists, neither in prophets. And I'd like to suggest that the gift of prophecy is designed to include more than one person. It did in Bible times, and evidently it will at the very end of time. According to Scripture, the gift of prophecy will be manifest in the church just before Jesus comes.

Well, a true prophet, whether in Bible times or at the end of time, is going to be counterfeited. The devil will see to that. This has always been one of his methods of operation. We have been warned, in Matthew 24:24, that there will be false prophets. But Matthew 7:20 says we can test them by their fruits. In 1 Thessalonians 5:21 we are invited to prove all things, and keep that which is good. God is very interested in giving us every benefit today, including the gift of prophecy, to make it as hard as possible for us to be deceived.

271

MORE THAN A PROPHET

Wherefore then were ye not afraid to speak against my servant Moses? Num. 12:8.

There are three manifestations of the gift of prophecy described in Scripture. First is the ability by the Holy Spirit's power to speak for God. Sometimes we confine the gift of prophecy to prediction and fulfillment. But it includes anyone who speaks God's truth for a particular time.

The second manifestation includes actual dreams, visions, and predictions. This is not seen so much today. But there is an even more rare function. This has to do with a special-messenger type of prophetic assignment that includes more than prophecy. There have been only three people in the history of God's people who have been known as *more* than prophets.

Numbers 12:6-8 tells of the first one. The Lord had come down in the cloud and spoken to the people, "Hear now my words: If there be a prophet among you, I the Lord will make myself known unto him in a vision, and will speak unto him in a dream. *My servant Moses is not so. . . .* With him will I speak mouth to mouth, even apparently, and not in dark speeches; and the similitude of the Lord shall he behold: wherefore then were ye not afraid to speak against my servant Moses?" Here God is indicating to Aaron and Miriam that Moses was not only a prophet but he was more than a prophet. God had a relationship with him and a function for him that included more than the term *prophet* signified.

The second instance is found in Luke 7:26-28. Jesus is speaking, "But what went ye out for to see? A prophet? Yea, I say unto you, and much more than a prophet. This is he of whom it is written, Behold, I send my messenger before thy face, which shall prepare thy way before thee." He was referring to John the Baptist, God's messenger to prepare the way for Jesus' first coming.

The third instance was a young lady in the past century who was told that she was God's messenger. *Selected Messages,* book 1, pages 34 to 36: "If others call me by that name [prophet], I have no controversy with them. But my work has covered so many lines that I cannot call myself other than a messenger. . . . My work includes much more than this name [prophet] signifies. I regard myself as a messenger, entrusted by the Lord with messages for His people."

THE VOICE OF GOD TO YOU

But what went ye out for to see? A prophet? Yea, I say unto you, and much more than a prophet. Luke 7:26.

There have been only three "more than prophets" in the history of God's church. Moses, who led the nation of Israel to the Promised Land; John the Baptist, who prepared the way for Christ's first coming; and Ellen White, who was sent with a special mission before Christ's second advent. I would like to suggest that it would be unlikely that we have another of this type of prophet before the end of time, although the evidence is that we will have again the manifestation of the gift of prophecy. It is quite possible that we will again see not only those who speak forth in God's name but those who predict or who are given special messages of warning, comfort, and guidance to God's church.

I believe in the work and writings and teachings of Ellen White. Anyone who knows the least thing about the history of Seventh-day Adventists should believe in them. And if they don't believe in them, they will have trouble with Scripture, too. I believe in them in spite of books written against them. Books can be written against everything and anything. If you are selective with your sources, you can build a case against the American flag or motherhood or apple pie.

I believe in the gift of prophecy given to the church in the past century, because I have found it to be the voice of God to my own soul. And if I have problems with it, I will also have problems with the Bible.

One of the reasons that I value this gift to the church is that it was through this gift I was led to an understanding of the righteousness of Jesus Christ. When I came into great trouble, and was about ready to give up, and cast about for some other kind of anchor, it was the description of the glories, the kindness, the beauty of Jesus, in books such as *The Desire of Ages,* that captured my attention. I have always been intrigued that this woman who wrote God's messages had the love of God as her favorite topic.

There are those who get the wrong impression of this gift. They think Ellen White was glum, gloomy, and morose. They think she dealt primarily in reproofs and rebukes. But if you will study her writings with an open mind, you will discover that Jesus is her central focus.

273

SATAN'S LAST DECEPTION

And the dragon was wroth with the woman, and went to make war with the remnant of her seed, which keep the commandments of God, and have the testimony of Jesus Christ. Rev. 12:17.

There are all kinds of winds blowing today, and all kinds of voices to be heard. There are shots from every direction being fired at the gift of prophecy given to this church. That is one of the greatest signs that Jesus' coming is right upon us, because that's the last thing that happens just before He comes.

"Satan is constantly pressing in the spurious—to lead away from the truth. The *very last* deception of Satan will be to make of none effect the testimony of the Spirit of God. 'Where there is no vision, the people perish' (Prov. 29:18). Satan will work ingeniously, in different ways and through different agencies, to unsettle the confidence of God's remnant people in the true testimony.

"There will be a hatred kindled against the testimonies which is satanic. The workings of Satan will be to unsettle the faith of the churches in them, for this reason: Satan cannot have so clear a track to bring in his deceptions and bind up souls in his delusions if the warnings and reproofs and counsels of the Spirit of God are heeded."—*Selected Messages*, book 1, p. 48.

We can take courage when we hear people questioning the validity of the Spirit of Prophecy, even though we feel sorry for those who are involved in trying to make the testimonies of none effect. We can take courage, for it shows without question that the coming of Jesus is soon.

I believe that the inspiration of the Spirit of Prophecy and the inspiration of the Bible are the same inspiration. While it is true that the Spirit of Prophecy writings are not canonical, it is still true that they are from God in a special sense. There is a truth and a power and an inspiration to be found there that is not to be found in the works of other great Christian writers. The Spirit of Prophecy writings are *above* the writings of other Protestant commentaries on the Scriptures.

But none of this opposition has come as a surprise to God. It was all predicted. And we can know that it will continue, thus giving us one of the greatest signs that we can see today of the nearness of the coming of Jesus.

JESUS REVEALED BY THE JUDGMENT

The kingdom of heaven is likened unto a man which sowed good seed in his field: but while men slept, his enemy came and sowed tares among the wheat, and went his way. Matt. 13:24, 25.

When the seed that was sown in this parable came up, the servants of the householder noticed that there were tares among the wheat. They came to their employer and said, "Sir, didst not thou sow good seed in thy field? from whence then hath it tares?" He recognized immediately the work of an enemy. But he did not respond as his servants expected, and ask them to root out all the tares. He told them instead to let them both grow together until the time of the harvest. Then they would be able to tell the wheat and tares apart without mistake, and could safely separate them.

This parable of Jesus is about the judgment. In the field of the world, which God had planted with good, an enemy came in and brought evil. The time of judgment is the time when the final separation between good and evil will be made.

One thing this parable shows us concerning what Jesus is like is that the wheat and tares are both allowed time to develop. They are both allowed time to make fully manifest, to themselves and to the rest of the world, what their character really is.

The servants could recognize the presence of weeds, of tares, in the field even from the beginning. But they did not have the insight to judge correctly in every case. So it is in the universe. The unfallen angels, and the rest of the watching creation, were able to see that there were problems when Satan was cast out of heaven. But in order for there to be no question as to which was wheat and which was tares, God allows them both to develop fully, so that their quality will be fully manifested. At the time that both good and evil are mature, there will be no question for any as to which is which, and as to the character and value of either.

Following the judgment, when the wheat and tares are identified because of their unquestionable character, the rewards of each are given. The tares are bound in bundles to be burned. But the wheat is gathered into the barn. The judgment reveals to all the universe the fairness and rightness of God, as well as His mercy, in allowing every opportunity for repentance.

275

JUSTICE *AND* MERCY

And as it was in the days of Noe, so shall it be also in the days of the Son of man.
Luke 17:26.

God called Noah to be His messenger. He instructed him to warn the world that a flood was coming. Noah was told to build an ark, and for 120 years he worked to finish his task. He faithfully gave the twofold message of warning and of hope that a way of escape was being provided. Not one who accepted the way of escape perished.

The wickedness of Sodom and Gomorrah was so great that God was moved to judgment. But before He sent the fire from heaven to destroy them, He came to Abraham with word of what He was about to do. Abraham pleaded with Him to give them a final chance. God answered Abraham's prayer, and sent angels with a message of warning to the city. But it was not merely a message of warning. They also offered Lot and his family a way of escape. In fact in the end, they had to take Lot and his family by the hands and lead them out of the city. Even then, Lot's wife turned back and refused the way of escape provided.

God told Jonah that judgment was coming upon Nineveh. Jonah was perhaps the most unwilling prophet of all time. He tried running away. When that didn't work, he grudgingly went to give God's message, that in 40 days Nineveh would be destroyed. All the people of Nineveh put on sackcloth and ashes, and repented. The crisis was averted. But Jonah was so angry that he wanted to die! He was more concerned with his own reputation as a prophet than with the lives of all the people in the city.

Whenever God becomes involved in the work of judgment, the ingredients of these Bible examples are always present. He sends someone with a message of warning, and He also provides a way of escape. This is true also for the final judgment that is soon to come upon the world. For centuries the Lord has been sending one messenger after another to give us warnings, so that none need be unprepared. The three angels' messages remind us that the hour of His judgment is come. God would have none of us caught by surprise.

But Jesus is revealed in the judgment. He is the way of escape provided. Because of His sacrifice, none need perish. There is hope. There is an ark of safety in Him for all who will accept the deliverance He offers.

JESUS REVEALED BY REPENTANCE

Repent ye therefore, and be converted. Acts 3:19.

Which comes first—repentance or forgiveness? Is repentance a condition for coming to Christ? Do we have to make ourselves sorry for our sins before God can accept us? Probably the most important truth to understand in the doctrine of repentance is that it is never to be a barrier between the sinner and Christ. We can always come to Him just as we are, and it is then that He gives to us the gift of repentance.

But notice that repentance comes *before* forgiveness, or justification. Acts 5:31 says that God has exalted Christ to give repentance to Israel, *and* forgiveness of sins. And *Steps to Christ* makes this comment on page 26: "Just here is a point on which many err, and hence they fail of receiving the help that Christ desires to give them. They think that they cannot come to Christ unless they first repent, and that repentance prepares for the *forgiveness of their sins.* It is true that repentance does precede the forgiveness of sin; for it is only the broken and contrite heart that will feel the need of a Saviour. But must the sinner wait till he has repented before he can come to Jesus? Is repentance to be made an obstacle between the sinner and the Saviour? The Bible *does not* teach that a sinner must repent before he can heed the invitation of Christ, 'Come unto me, all ye that labour and are heavy laden, and I will give you rest.'" (Italics supplied.)

So the sequence is that first we come to Christ, then we are given the gift of repentance, which we are to accept. And after that we are forgiven. Does this sound as though there is a condition to having our sins forgiven? Well, there is! But this truth teaches us a very beautiful thing about God. Jesus and His love is revealed in a unique way. Jesus accepts us just as we are, and He gives us the necessities for salvation.

Jesus already knows that we have no merit to recommend us to Him, so He doesn't even look for it or expect it. There are conditions for the blessing of salvation that He offers, but they are not conditions that *we* are able to meet. So when He comes to us, offering us life and salvation, at the same time He offers us as free gifts all the prerequisites for salvation. He has made every provision so that none except for those who stubbornly refuse His grace need fail of receiving the salvation He has provided.

CHANGE OF RAIMENT

He that overcometh, the same shall be clothed in white raiment. Rev. 3:5.

Once there was a very wealthy man. His riches were so vast that words fail to tell the extent of them. But he had a neighbor who was as poor as the rich man was rich. The neighbor had nothing. His clothes were ragged and dirty. He was suffering from malnutrition. He had no home, not even a hovel to call his own, but was forced to spend his days and nights clutching his rags miserably about him, suffering from exposure.

The rich man noticed the plight of the poor neighbor, and set about to remedy the situation. He said to the poor man, "You are in a terrible state. You need a home to live in and nourishing food. You need to be properly clothed. If you will come to me, I will give you all you need, and more besides."

But instead of coming to the rich man, the poor man backed off and would not come near. "I can't come to your house in these clothes. I would bring disgrace to you if folks saw me at your table in such poverty."

"That's true," the rich man agreed. "But here is a change of raiment that I will give you, if you will come to me and accept it. And then you will be suitably clothed to come to my house."

When Christ offers to us His robe of righteousness to cover the filthy rags of our sin, we must accept it in order to benefit from it. The rich man could have provided enough clothes for a whole city, but if the poor man refused to put them on, they would not benefit him.

There *are* conditions to salvation—there are conditions to entering the heavenly home. We must be suitably attired—clad in the garments of Christ's righteousness—in order to enter there. We must have come to repentance. We must have new hearts. We must have faith. We must be obedient. But for all the requirements that God makes, He also provides gifts to meet the requirements, if we will only accept. God never sends us a bill without enclosing enough money to pay it. We must repent before we can be forgiven. But if we come to Him, He will provide the gift of repentance, and when we accept it, we are justified. This doctrine is just one more truth that reveals Jesus—He is not willing that *any* should perish, but that all should come to repentance.

NOW IS THE TIME TO DECIDE

Therefore choose life, that both thou and thy seed may live. Deut. 30:19.

There's an old evangelistic phrase that you may have heard, "Getting people across the line." This term has been used many times in reference to getting people to make decisions regarding some point of doctrine, usually the Sabbath. But it is a principle in decision making, when it comes to spiritual things, that all decisions should be based on commitment to Jesus. If that commitment has not already been made, then it is futile to pull for decision on any other point. If a person has not already made a decision for Christ and been converted, then he or she is not ready to make a lasting decision on doctrinal issues.

God has very simple methods for decision making. John 10:1-5 describes His method. The first thing He does is make Himself known to His sheep. He realizes that when the sheep know Him and have learned to recognize His voice and decided to follow Him, the decisions along the path of following Him day by day will naturally come. Our first method in seeking to bring others to decision should be to lead them to know God and His voice themselves.

The primary force in all spiritual decision making is the Holy Spirit. It is His work to confront each individual with decision at the time that He knows they are the most approachable, and in a manner that they will be most likely to respond to.

The Bible is clear that we ought to make decisions and that we ought to make them every day. 2 Corinthians 6:2 says that *now* is the accepted time. Joshua urged the people of Israel to choose. "Choose you *this day* whom ye will serve" (Joshua 24:15). Notice that he wanted them to choose *whom* to serve, not what to do. The decision to serve Jesus and allow Him control in our lives is a daily decision.

If the Holy Spirit has been speaking to you to make a decision in your life, don't procrastinate. The longer you put it off, the harder the decision will be. *Steps to Christ*, page 32, says that thousands have erred, to their own destruction, in putting off decision. Probably every person has some decision that has been on his mind, a conviction from the Holy Spirit. Why not decide now? If you have a decision you need to make, make it today.

"FOLLOW ME"

And the sheep follow him: for they know his voice. John 10:4.

A tour group traveling in the Middle East was told by the tour guide to watch for the sheepherders. "A shepherd never drives his sheep, but rather leads them," he said. So they began watching for an opportunity to see this in action. But the first group of sheep they saw were being *driven,* urged on with sticks and stones and shouts. They checked the matter out to discover what had happened to the sheepherding business, and learned that they had happened upon a group of sheep being taken by the butcher!

Jesus said, "If any man will come after me, let him deny himself, and take up his cross, and *follow* me" (Matt. 16:24). He said that the sheep hear the voice of the shepherd that they know, and *follow* him (John 10:4). He said, "If any man serve me, let him follow me" (John 12:26). He told the rich young ruler to sell all he had, and *follow* (Matt. 19:21). And He invited the disciples to *follow* Him to become fishers of men (Matt. 4:19).

When we follow someone we trust, it is the opposite of being coaxed or pushed or coerced. Jesus invites us to follow. And in Revelation 14:4 we find a group of people who have become so involved with the One who is both Shepherd and Lamb that they follow Him wherever He goes.

Luke 9:57-62 tells of a group who had trouble with the idea of following Jesus. They made excuses. They had other things they wanted to do instead. And Jesus indicated to them that they could not have divided hearts. Those who follow Him must be totally committed. But the key is that they were asked to *follow* Him. First Peter 2:21 says that "hereunto were ye called: because Christ also suffered for us, leaving us an example, that ye should *follow* his steps."

Only the Holy Spirit knows the timetable for each soul. We don't. We must allow Him to do His work. He is the one who must bring each of us to decision. And the basis of all decision is to decide to follow Christ. Decision is meaningful only in that setting. When we have chosen to follow Christ and have learned to know His voice, then He can lead us to whatever else He desires for us in terms of decisions. The Holy Spirit leads each one individually in deciding to follow Christ and in continuing to follow Him day by day.

WISDOM FROM THE WISEST MAN

Remember now thy Creator in the days of thy youth, while the evil days come not, nor the years draw nigh, when thou shalt say, I have no pleasure in them. Eccl. 12:1.

King Solomon was known as the wisest man who ever lived. He came to the throne before he was 18. He hauled in gold from Ophir, and silver from the mines in Spain. He imported precious stones and spices from Arabia, and ivory from India. Ten thousand people ate at his table every day. His fleets brought in resources from foreign shores amounting to $10 million annually. The queen of Sheba came to see his kingdom for herself, and when she left she said that the half had not been told. Solomon spoke 3,000 proverbs—and he had to be old enough to die before he knew enough to live!

Near the end of his life he said, "Let us hear the conclusion of the whole matter." Are you interested in what the wisest man who ever lived had to say as to the conclusion of the whole business? He had learned from God and from the school of hard knocks. Here is his conclusion: "Fear God, and keep his commandments: for this is the whole duty of man. For God shall bring every work into judgment, with every secret thing, whether it be good, or whether it be evil" (Eccl. 12:13, 14).

Notice the sequence. *Fear God,* and keep His commandments. Of course, this is talking about something more than just being *afraid* of God. Respect God. Hold Him in awe for who He is, our Creator. This is what Solomon was talking about. God had been very patient with Solomon. He should have been dumped from the throne as far as our standards are concerned. Have you ever studied some of his debauchery during the time that he rebelled? He tried to pack in all the so-called pleasures of this life, but they turned sour. He discovered that he could not keep the commandments without putting God first.

The problem that we all have with the Ten Commandments is that there is no power there. Have you found that out? Jesus' wisdom is revealed there, and the great lawmakers of all times have been unable to improve on the Ten Commandments. But there is no power in the law itself. The law reveals to us our need of a Saviour. It points us to Christ. It is in Christ that we find pardon and the power to fulfill all the demands of the law.

THE LAW REVEALED IN A LIFE

Think not that I am come to destroy the law, or the prophets: I am not come to destroy, but to fulfil. Matt. 5:17.

The law is a transcript of God's character. The same things that are said about God are said about His law. God is truth (John 14:6). His law is truth (Ps. 119:142). God is righteous (Ps. 145:17). His law is righteous (Ps. 119:172). God is perfect (Matt. 5:48). His law is perfect (Ps. 19:7). God is holy (Isa. 6:3). His law is holy (Rom. 12:7). God is unchangeable (Mal. 3:6). The law is unchangeable (Matt. 5:18). God is spiritual (John 4:24). His commandments are spiritual (Rom. 4:17). God is forever (Ps. 9:7; 90:2). His law is forever (Ps. 111:7, 8; 119:44).

This means that it always has been and always will be wrong to kill and steal and lie and covet and take God's name in vain and all the rest of it. There is no time when the commandments will be changed, by situational ethics or anything else. Why? Because the Ten Commandments are what God is, and what Jesus is.

A woman goes to the dry-goods store for material to make a dress. She rummages through the bolts of cloth until she finds one that appeals to her. She pauses, fingers the cloth, holds it up to the light. The proprietor comes by and says, "Do you like that cloth?" "Well," she says, "I think so. I was just trying to visualize how it would look made up into a dress." The shopkeeper takes her to the front window and points out a dress made from the same cloth. And the woman says, "In the bolt it was beautiful. But made into a dress it is even more beautiful! I'll take it!"

We look at the Ten Commandments and realize the wisdom there revealed. We admit that not a single improvement could be made—except for one. To see the Ten Commandments made up into a life. Whereas these principles were beautiful on tables of stone, they are much more beautiful made up into a life—the life of Jesus. Jesus reveals the Ten Commandments. He came to this earth, and through depending moment by moment upon His Father's power, kept every one of the Ten Commandments perfectly. He offers to us today the same power that He had. Through dependence upon Him we may reveal to the world the beauty of character that will bring glory to Him. The Ten Commandments may be made up into our lives as well.

JESUS REVEALED BY A ROCK

And in the days of these kings shall the God of heaven set up a kingdom, which shall never be destroyed. Dan. 2:44.

Nebuchadnezzar was the ruler of the whole world. He must have been capable and brilliant to accomplish such a feat. He could walk on the veranda of his palace, look at his hanging gardens, and compliment himself on the great empire that he had built. He had "I" trouble, just as Lucifer had. He did not give God the glory or the credit or the praise, but said rather, "Is not this great Babylon, that *I* have built?" He was a self-made man, and self-made men always love to worship their maker.

Earlier the God of heaven had tried to get through to this heathen king and let him know that there was Someone bigger than he. Nebuchadnezzar had a dream. However, he forgot it, and thus Daniel became involved in the picture. God revealed the dream to Daniel, and Nebuchadnezzar recognized his dream. Daniel also gave him the interpretation of his dream. Nebuchadnezzar was told that he was the head of gold. However, that wasn't the end of the dream. Nebuchadnezzar didn't like the part about the chest and arms of silver, and the other kingdoms to follow. So he decided to build an image like the one in his dream, but *all* of gold. And you remember the rest of the story. The God of heaven once again revealed Himself to Nebuchadnezzar.

But I'm more interested in the *rock* of Daniel 2 than in anything else. We have sometimes spent a lot of time studying the four kingdoms, and the ten kingdoms, and have not spent as much time on the real hero of the story, the rock, cut out without hands.

Which would you choose if you were offered a choice between gold and a rock? At first glance it would seem that the gold would be the better choice. But God sees things differently than we do. The rock that is cut out of the mountain, *without hands,* is chosen to represent Jesus. And all the gold and silver and brass and clay are lost sight of. They are broken in pieces and become like the chaff of the summer threshing floors, and the wind carries them away. The kingdoms of this world pass away into nothing, and all that man values in place of God is ultimately seen to be worthless. But "in the days of these kings shall the God of heaven set up a kingdom, which shall never be destroyed . . . and it shall stand for ever."

FALLING ON THE ROCK

For they drank of that spiritual Rock that followed them: and that Rock was Christ. 1 Cor. 10:4.

If you study the symbol of the rock or the stone throughout Scripture, you will discover that it is a symbol of Jesus Christ. In the days of Israel's exodus from Egypt to Canaan, you have Moses striking a rock in the wilderness. The rock was a representation of Christ. Our text today says it in so many words: "and that Rock was Christ."

Jesus used the analogy of a rock, and in Matthew 7:24, 25 spoke of the necessity of building upon a rock instead of upon the sand. Paul said that other foundation can no man lay, than that which is laid, Jesus Christ. Jesus is the cornerstone in Scripture.

Isaiah 8:13-15 says that the Lord will be a "stone of stumbling," and a "rock of offence." Psalm 118:22 refers to the Rock. Jesus quoted from the Old Testament in Matthew 21:42-44, saying, "Did you never read in the scriptures, The stone which the builders rejected, the same is become the head of the corner: this is the Lord's doing, and it is marvellous in our eyes? . . . Whosoever shall fall on this stone shall be broken: but on whomsoever it shall fall, it will grind him to powder."

Each of us is offered a choice today. Do you choose to fall on the Rock or do you choose to let the Rock fall on you? If I don't know what it means to fall on the Rock, the day will come when I will pray to the rocks and mountains to fall on me, and hide me from God's face. There are only two choices—to fall on the Rock or to have the Rock fall on you. But *falling on the Rock* is an intangible phrase. What does it mean? Romans 9:33 explains what falling on the Rock signifies. "Behold, I lay in Sion a stumblingstone and rock of offence: and whosoever *believeth on him* shall not be ashamed." So what's the issue? In Romans, the issue of whether I fall on the Rock or the Rock falls on me is the issue of faith and works. It's that simple. If I try to live a good life through my own efforts, and do not know what it means to believe on *Him* for salvation in all of its aspects, then the Rock will fall on me. It is only by falling on the Rock and being broken, by coming to the end of our own resources and becoming involved in fellowship and communion with Jesus, that we are secure.

JESUS REVEALED IN HUMILITY

Let this mind be in you, which was also in Christ Jesus: who, being in the form of God, thought it not robbery to be equal with God: but made himself of no reputation, and took upon him the form of a servant. Phil. 2:5-7.

A Seventh-day Adventist evangelist was confronted with the question of why his church was so particular about the Sabbath when others were not. He said, "We believe in observing the Sabbath in honor of Creation, because that's what the Bible says. And we want to follow what the Bible says."

The person who was confronting him replied, "No one really follows all that the Bible says. It can't be done. If you really believed and followed everything the Bible says, then you would wash one another's feet!"

And the Adventist evangelist said, "We do!"

It's true that there are very few in the Christian churches of today who believe in celebrating all the parts of the Lord's Supper. Some take only the wafer or the bread, some take the bread and the cup, but very few follow the foot-washing ordinance as well.

John 13 is the only place in the four Gospels that describes the ordinance of foot washing. Let's read it, beginning with the first verse: "Now before the feast of the passover, when Jesus knew that his hour was come that he should depart out of this world unto the Father, having loved his own which were in the world, he loved them unto the end. And supper being ended, the devil having put into the heart of Judas Iscariot, Simon's son, to betray him; Jesus knowing that the Father had given all things into his hands, and that he was come from God, and went to God; he riseth from supper, and laid aside his garments; and took a towel, and girded himself. After that he poureth water into a bason, and began to wash the disciples' feet, and to wipe them with the towel wherewith he was girded."

What a picture! The Creator of the universe stooping to wash the tired, dusty feet of the creatures that He had made. It was a sandbox illustration of His incarnation, when He laid aside His kingly robes in heaven and came down to be born as one of us, that He might be able to minister to our needs. Jesus is revealed in the Communion service in a special way. He is revealed as the One who was not ashamed to call us brethren, to meet us where we are, and to cleanse us from the defilement of sin.

IT IS HARD TO BE WASHED

If I wash thee not, thou hast no part with me. John 13:8.

I f I then, your Lord and Master, have washed your feet; ye also ought to wash one another's feet. For I have given you an example, that ye should do as I have done to you. . . . If ye know these things, happy are ye if ye do them" (John 13:14-17). Here are given three reasons why we should wash one another's feet. First, because Jesus commanded it. He told us that we should. Second, because He set the example for us. And third, because we will be happy if we do it.

Are you really happy to wash someone else's feet? Are you happy to have someone else wash your feet? There are some who find real meaning in this service and have learned to see Jesus revealed in the Communion ordinances. If they take part in the service one week at their home church, and visit another church the following week where there is another Communion service scheduled, they are overjoyed. But there are others who partake in one church, and if they find another church having the Communion service the following week, they say, "Forget it. We already did our duty for this quarter!" There are some who find the service so distasteful that they stay home on Communion Sabbath, and don't even become involved once a quarter.

A student said to me during one Week of Prayer Communion service, "I usually wash my feet myself!" And we began to talk about the significance of that. To let someone else do for you what you usually do for yourself carries a message. It can be humbling to let God do for us what we are accustomed to doing for ourselves or what we *want* to do for ourselves.

Do you find it harder to wash someone else's feet or to get your own feet washed? Usually the response is that it is harder to get your own feet washed. It's embarrassing. There is something deep inside that goes along with the idea expressed by the student. We don't want to admit that we need something done *for* us—that we can't do everything ourselves. Peter found it humiliating to have his feet washed, and objected to the necessity until Jesus showed him that it was only by his humbling himself to accept of Jesus' cleansing that he could have a part with Him. It is as we allow our pride to be humbled today, and accept of Jesus' ministry in our behalf, that we find cleansing.

CLEANSED FOR COMMUNION

Jesus saith to him, He that is washed needeth not save to wash his feet, but is clean every whit. John 13:10.

Then cometh he to Simon Peter: and Peter saith unto him, Lord, dost thou wash my feet? Jesus answered and said unto him, What I do thou knowest not now; but thou shalt know hereafter. Peter saith unto him, Thou shalt never wash my feet. Jesus answered him, If I wash thee not, thou hast no part with me" (John 13:6-8). Peter found it hard to get his feet washed. Why? Why do you suppose Peter found it hard? Did he think that Jesus, as the Son of God, was above this menial sort of task? Was he feeling guilty already for not having volunteered himself? It was the custom that a servant would wash the feet—and if a servant was not available, then someone would volunteer to do the job. But you don't expect volunteers for this from a group of disciples who have been bickering and arguing about who is going to be the greatest.

Then Jesus said, "If I wash thee not, thou hast no part with me. Simon Peter saith unto him, Lord, not my feet only, but also my hands and my head. Jesus saith to him, He that is washed needeth not save to wash his feet, but is clean every whit" (verses 8-10). Peter had already been washed by Jesus' cleansing power. Baptism, where the head and hands, as well as the feet, are washed, is a symbol of the cleansing of the whole person. The Communion is a symbol of the cleansing needed because of our falling and failing as we grow. When we accept Jesus as our personal Saviour, because of His righteousness, we stand before God as though we had never sinned. And His justifying grace is available to us day by day according to our need.

Because of the example Jesus set in this service, we know that if we are to have a part with Him we will be involved in the Communion service in all its aspects. If He does not wash us, we have no part with Him.

Those in the early church followed this practice for a time, but then many found it to be inconvenient, and the practice was largely abandoned. However, the symbol is incomplete without the foot-washing service being included. It is only as we are washed by His blood, cleansed anew, that we are fitted to partake of the bread and the wine that are the symbols of communion with Him.

CELEBRATING DELIVERANCE

Forasmuch then as the children are partakers of flesh and blood, he also himself likewise took part of the same; that through death he might destroy him that had the power of death, that is, the devil; and deliver them who through fear of death were all their lifetime subject to bondage. Heb. 2:14, 15.

The key word for the Communion service is deliverance. Deliverance from Egypt, deliverance from the guilt of sin, from the power of sin, and from a world of sin. The Communion service goes clear back to Egypt—not simply to Jesus and the disciples in the upper room. The reason that they were in the upper room in the first place was in order to celebrate the Passover. They were remembering the time when the blood was put on the doorposts and the angel passed over.

You remember that night; the Israelites were going to leave at midnight. The firstborn was awake, unable to sleep, anxious that the blood be on the doorpost. And the blood on the doorpost pointed forward to the blood of Jesus. There was power in the blood, clear back in the days of Egypt. For those who placed the blood on the doorpost, there was a wonderful deliverance. And for those who refused, there was tragedy. So Jesus and His disciples met in the upper room to celebrate that deliverance.

The day after the Communion service in the upper room, Jesus fulfilled all that had been a symbol from the days of Egypt until the Last Supper. The fulfillment was far greater than the symbol. Calvary was far greater than putting blood on the doorpost in the days of Egypt, as much as the reality is greater than the symbol that prefigures it. But as we look at this deliverance, and at the symbols of the Lord's Supper today, we find that it still speaks to us of deliverance. When we accept what Jesus has done for us, not only are we forgiven but we stand before God as though we had never even sinned. God offers more than forgiveness. And this good news is designed to bring peace to every heart.

There is power in the blood of Christ and in the deliverance that He brings, not only to forgive us but to change our lives as well. The deliverance that is symbolized by the Communion service is available to each of us today as we accept of both His forgiveness *and* His power.

THEY SHALL BE MINE

And they shall be mine, saith the Lord of hosts, in that day when I make up my jewels; and I will spare them, as a man spareth his own son that serveth him. Mal. 3:17.

One of the charges that Satan has hurled against God down through the ages is that God is selfish. Satan wanted what God had, and when it was not given to him, he accused God of being self-centered and stingy. At first glance, it might appear that Satan has a point. Look at Haggai 2:8. God says that the silver and the gold are His. Look at Psalm 50:10-12. God says, "For every beast of the forest is mine, and the cattle upon a thousand hills. I know all the fowls of the mountains: and the wild beasts of the field are mine. If I were hungry, I would not tell thee: for the world is mine, and the fulness thereof." Sounds rather possessive, doesn't it? But the charge of Satan was answered at the cross. Calvary proved that God is not selfish but willing to spend and be spent. There *is* self-sacrifice with God.

But the reason that God says He owns it all is because He does! He is the One who created it all, including us. We are only creatures. The earth is His. But there is one thing that is not His. *We* are not all His. He has given us freedom of choice, and the only way that He can say that we are His is if we choose to be His. There is a promise concerning this found in our text today. "And *they shall be mine,* saith the Lord of hosts, in that day when I make up my jewels." There comes a day when the ones that God wants more than anything else—who are of more value to Him than animals or gold or the thousand hills—become His. He has all the rest of it. But there is a group of people who are going to be His, as well. Are you one of them today? Have you made that choice?

When we consider the subject of stewardship, we are not talking merely about dollars and cents. The most precious gift that we can bring to the Lord is not our money, but ourselves. Without the gift of a loving heart, the gift of simply money is worthless. God already has all the silver and the gold—it is His to begin with. And while the heart that loves cannot but bring gifts as well, the first and primary gift that we must bring to Him is the gift of ourselves. True stewardship begins in choosing to belong to the Lord ourselves, in loving and serving Him.

HOW MUCH DO YOU HAVE LEFT?

For all they did cast in of their abundance; but she of her want did cast in all that she had, even all her living. Mark 12:44.

Some people consider tithing an Old Testament teaching. They think that when Jesus told the Pharisees that they tithed mint, and small things like that, and neglected the bigger things, He was downgrading the idea of tithing. But Jesus made it clear that while we ought to do the one thing, we should not leave the other undone either.

One day a widow woman came to the Temple and put into the offering container only two mites. From that experience Jesus drew some important lessons concerning giving. One of them was this—that heaven places value upon the gift in an entirely different way than we do. Jesus said that this woman put in more than all the rest. How can that be? Because God measures our giving not by how much we give, but rather by how much we have left after we have given. So if someone puts in $10,000, and has $10,000 left, he has given far less than one who puts in 2 cents and has nothing left.

Of course, it is possible to give all the cash you have and still own a house in the city and a house in the country, and a boat in the harbor, and three new cars! Our possessions are to be considered also when we figure out how much we have left. 1 Corinthians 4:7 says, "What hast thou that thou didst not receive? now if thou didst *receive* it, why dost thou glory, as if thou hadst not received it?" Whatever our wealth, be it money *or* possessions, it is God that gave the power to get it (Deut. 8:18), and thus He has a claim upon all that we have been given.

The first portion of our money that is the Lord's in a special sense is the tithe. But we have not finished when we have returned our tithes to the Lord. He has invited us to bring our freewill offerings as well. Malachi 3:8 says that God has been robbed in tithes *and* offerings. And even beyond that, God has a claim on *all* that we possess. "Some think that only a portion of their means is the Lord's. When they have set apart a portion for religious and charitable purposes, they regard the remainder as their own, to be used as they see fit. But in this they mistake. All we possess is the Lord's, and we are accountable to Him for the use we make of it."—*Christ's Object Lessons*, p. 351.

OPEN HEAVEN'S WINDOWS

Bring ye all the tithes into the storehouse, that there may be meat in mine house, and prove me now herewith, saith the Lord of hosts, if I will not open you the windows of heaven, and pour you out a blessing, that there shall not be room enough to receive it. Mal. 3:10.

One time there was a man who decided that the way he would pay tithe would be to tithe his talents instead of his money. He was very stingy with his money. He probably still had the first nickel he had ever made. But he could play the violin. So the way he paid his tithe was to play his violin for Sabbath school!

There have been others who have set aside their tithe in actual money, but have decided to use it as they see fit, instead of turning it in to the church. Some have decided that the church school fund needs the money more than the church—or that some mission project has the greater need. But God has given clear instructions as to what the tithe consists of, and as to what our responsibility is in giving it.

Our text for today says, "Bring ye all the tithes *into the storehouse,* that there may be meat in mine house." What is the storehouse? Let's allow the Bible to interpret itself, and turn to Nehemiah 13:12. "Then brought all Judah the tithe of the corn and the new wine and the oil unto the treasuries." If you have a margin in your Bible, you will see a marginal reading by the word "treasuries," which refers you back to Malachi 3. The storehouse and the treasuries are the same. Nehemiah 10:38 says, "And the priest the son of Aaron shall be with the Levites, when the Levites take tithes: and the Levites shall bring up the tithe of the tithes unto the house of our God, to the chambers, into the treasure house." Notice that the tithe is to be brought to the storehouse, to the treasury, to the house of our God. It is not our responsibility, unless we have been placed in charge of the funds of the Lord's house, to try to decide whether the funds are being used appropriately.

God's blessing, His promise to open the windows of heaven and give more than there is room to receive, is given to those who bring their tithes *into the storehouse.* When we bring our tithes to Him, He is enabled to pour out His blessings upon us as He has promised.

YOU CAN'T OUTGIVE GOD

Give, and it shall be given unto you; good measure, pressed down, and shaken together, and running over, shall men give into your bosom. For with the same measure that ye mete withal it shall be measured to you again. Luke 6:38.

Have you ever tried to outgive God? There are people who have set out deliberately to do that very thing, and have found that it is impossible. Does the idea sound exciting to you or scary? Malachi 3 insists that the person giving does not even need a right motive. It gives a carte blanche promise that those who return to God what is His, in tithes and offerings, are going to receive a blessing. And while it is obvious that the one who gives from the motive of love for God is going to receive the greater blessing, the promise is for anyone who is willing to give.

Malachi 3:10 is the only place we know where God has said, "Test Me. Try Me out." Have you read about the businessmen who have tried Him out? People have gone into partnership with God, in terms of money, and have discovered that His promise is sure. Some do it for business purposes, others from love for Him. But when you discover that God's promise is sure, even for your lesser motives, it does something to change your motives, doesn't it?

The statistics show that probably only 50 to 60 percent of Seventh-day Adventists are faithful tithepayers. But those who are not faithful stewards are showing at least a lack of faith, and possibly ignorance and even stupidity! Will you forgive me for that last one? But it is being smart to realize that nine dollars with God's blessing goes much further than ten dollars without His blessing. It's a simple principle. If you have tried it you know it's true, and there is no debate. In fact, eight dollars with God's blessing goes much further than ten dollars without it! The question in Malachi is not regarding simply tithes but tithes *and offerings.* Some forget that when they have returned their tithe they have simply been honest— they have not yet been generous! It is when we return our tithes to Him because it is His money, and bring our offerings *as well,* that we find His promise is still good for today. It is impossible to be more giving, more generous, more unselfish, than God is. You can't outgive God. The more we give to Him, the more He blesses.

THE STRONG MAN

When a strong man armed keepeth his palace, his goods are in peace: but when a stronger than he shall come upon him, and overcome him, he taketh from him all his armour wherein he trusted, and divideth his spoils. Luke 11:21, 22.

Have you ever wondered what these verses meant? There's a similar verse in Mark 3:27: "No man can enter into a strong man's house, and spoil his goods, except he will first bind the strong man; and then he will spoil his house." The mind is the "strong man" of every individual. The enemy who comes trying to destroy us has to first bind the strong man. The big battle in this conflict between good and evil is the battle for your mind.

The subject of health has always been of great interest to Seventh-day Adventists because there is a definite connection between health and our minds. At the very beginning, when sin first entered, Satan first of all had to bind the strong man. And he succeeded in that. But when Jesus came on His mission of salvation, He bound Satan and Jesus has been the victor ever since. However, when it comes to the battle for each individual, Christ and Satan are in constant conflict, and it isn't just at the beginning but at every stage of the Christian life. It is the battle for our minds.

Jesus made it clear that it is the mind that counts. It is not the outward actions that are of primary importance. "Man looketh on the outward appearance, but the Lord looketh on the heart" (1 Sam. 16:7). God has always looked at the heart. And when we speak of the heart, we are referring to the mind, even though there are other meanings the word *heart* may have in Scripture. The heart, or mind, is the strong man of each person.

Before we come into personal relationship with the Lord Jesus, we have what is called in Romans 8:7 the carnal mind. But God has made provision through the gospel to renew our minds (Rom. 12:2). *Testimonies*, volume 3, page 162, says that if men do not keep their bodies holy, they are unfit to be spiritual worshipers. Seventh-day Adventists believe in the harmonious development of the physical, mental, and spiritual powers, and have long emphasized this. There is a close connection between the body and the mind. It is through the mind that we commune with God and thus become one with Him.

293

WHO'S IN CONTROL?

Beloved, I wish above all things that thou mayest prosper and be in health, even as thy soul prospereth. 3 John 2.

What is it you usually think of when you think of health? Many think of Seventh-day Adventists as the people who don't eat meat. But diet is not the major issue in health. Jesus promised His followers that He and His Father would come and dwell with them. He said that He would manifest Himself to us. How does He do this? Well, we could say, By the things of nature; but He does that for everybody, including the skeptic and infidel and agnostic. People who curse God have much of the natural manifestations of God. So His manifestation must be by means of a more direct communication.

"The brain nerves that connect with the whole system are the medium through which heaven communicates with man and affects the inmost life. Whatever hinders the circulation of the electric current in the nervous system, thus weakening the vital powers and lessening mental susceptibility, makes it more difficult to arouse the moral nature."—*Education*, p. 209. There are three parts of the brain—and the first that is affected by stimulants is the higher center, where spiritual communication takes place.

The body and mind are closely related. "The body is the only medium through which the mind and soul are developed for the upbuilding of character."—*The Ministry of Healing*, p. 130. So the mind is the only medium of communication with God. And the body is that through which the mind and soul are developed. Whatever affects the body affects the mind. It is through the mind that God manifests Himself to us, so when the body and mind are affected, our communion with Him is affected.

So what does insufficient sleep do in terms of affecting communion with God? What does lack of exercise do to our communion with God? What does overeating do in terms of communion with God? What do drugs and alcohol and other harmful substances do in terms of communion with God? Are these fair questions? Satan is able to come in and control us when he manages to control our minds. But the clearer our minds become, and the more healthy our bodies, the easier it is for us to let God control us according to His will.

PREVENTIVE MEDICINE

Then shall thy light break forth as the morning, and thine health shall spring forth speedily: and thy righteousness shall go before thee; and the glory of the Lord shall be thy rereward. Isa. 58:8.

Daniel and his three companions refused to be defiled with the delicacies from the king's table. They knew that what they ate and how they lived had a definite effect on spiritual life. Seventh-day Adventists have believed that for a long time. We believe that our bodies are the temples of God (1 Cor. 3:16, 17) and that God wants us to use our bodies and our spirits to glorify Him (1 Cor. 6:19, 20).

When it comes to health and healing, we have the eight simple, natural remedies. They are not only remedies but also preventatives. "There are many ways of practicing the healing art; but there is only one way that Heaven approves. God's remedies are the simple agencies of nature. . . . Pure air, sunlight, abstemiousness [temperance], rest, exercise, proper diet, the use of water, trust in divine power—these are the true remedies."—*Counsels on Diet and Foods*, p. 301. These are both the means to recovery and the means to prevent becoming sick.

Have you ever taken a few minutes to check how you are doing in these eight areas? Usually, if there are health problems, there are difficulties in one of these eight areas, if not in several of them. You might want to try checking yourself sometime. And there is a spiritual counterpart for these remedies as well. Jesus is the "*Sun* of righteousness." We are invited to drink of the *water* of life. Jesus has given us the Sabbath for *rest*, and has invited us to come to Him for rest every day. Prayer is the *breath* of the soul. *Exercise* is the Christian witness. The proper *diet* is to eat the bread of life. These are the ingredients for a healthy spiritual life, as well as for a healthy physical life.

Four of these eight remedies, in the spiritual realm, are the cause, and four are the result. Pure air, prayer; proper diet, God's Word; water, the Holy Spirit and the water of life; and exercise, witness; all have to do with the relationship with God, and are the cause of a healthy Christian experience. And the result of these are the other four: temperance, rest, the sunlight of God's presence shed abroad, and trust in divine power.

JESUS REVEALED BY YOUR DRESS | OCT 16

Whose adorning let it not be that outward adorning. . . . But let it be the hidden man of the heart, in that which is not corruptible, even the ornament of a meek and quiet spirit, which is in the sight of God of great price. 1 Peter 3:3, 4.

Is there anything wrong with washing your face? Is there anything wrong with combing your hair? How about wearing a watchband? Is it OK to wear a necktie? Should Christians wear clothes that are in style? Should they try to look nice? Are scarves or pins acceptable? What about lace, ribbons, or buttons? Is it wrong to dye your hair or wear a wig? Is it wrong to wear makeup? If a wristwatch is all right, then what about a pendant watch? Is there any difference between wearing a colored scarf and a small silver necklace? What about a wedding ring? Is all jewelry to be forbidden?

While there are differing standards in different parts of the country, different schools, different cultures, there *are* principles that are given in Scripture that apply everywhere. In Revelation 12 God uses a woman to represent His true church. Notice how she is dressed: "And there appeared a great wonder in heaven; a woman clothed with the sun, and the moon under her feet, and upon her head a crown of twelve stars" (verse 1).

Revelation 17:4 describes the false church, also represented by a woman—this time a harlot. Notice what she was wearing: "And the woman was arrayed in purple and scarlet colour, and decked with gold and precious stones and pearls, having a golden cup in her hand full of abominations and filthiness of her fornication." Of course, these verses are symbolic. There might be people who don't believe in wearing anything at all who would find comfort in Revelation 12:1! But God has had something to say about nakedness in other places in Scripture. So obviously that isn't the point. The principle is the contrast between natural, simple attire, and extravagance.

What is the reason for these restrictions? Because the adorning of the outside is simply a symptom of an inward lack. God wants us to have the inward adorning of a meek and quiet spirit, not the outward adorning that draws attention to ourselves. The application of these principles will have to be made in the framework of our own personal communion with Him.

296

THE ROOT OF THE MATTER

And now also the axe is laid unto the root of the trees. Luke 3:9.

Mr. Jones had a tree in his front yard that he wanted removed. One summer afternoon he made a decision. The tree really had to go, and it was time for action. He borrowed an extension ladder from a neighbor down the road, and went to work. He began pulling off the leaves, handful by handful. It was a hard job, and took several days. But at last he was done. He returned the ladder, confident that his problem was solved.

All went well for a few months. Mr. Jones had almost forgotten about the tree until one day the following spring when he noticed that new leaves had sprouted out all over it. It had happened so slowly that he couldn't even pinpoint when it occurred. But there it was. The tree wasn't dead at all, but alive and flourishing.

Mr. Jones borrowed the ladder again, and again went over the tree carefully, branch by branch, removing all the leaves. But the next spring they grew again, and the next, and the next. Finally his neighbor stopped him as he was setting up the ladder for yet another try and said, "Look—I don't mind your using my ladder. But why don't you just wait till autumn, like the rest of us, and *rake* up the leaves? Wouldn't that be easier?"

"But you don't understand," Mr. Jones replied. "I'm not just trying to get rid of the leaves. I'm trying to kill the tree!"

His neighbor went away shaking his head, but returned a few minutes later carrying an axe. "If you want to kill the tree, here's what you need," he advised. "If you chop the tree down, it will be sure to die."

Have *you* ever spent your time picking leaves, trying to kill a tree? You may think you never have. But how often we as Christians try to die to self by working on the fruit, instead of the root. "We may pick the leaves from a tree as often as we please, but this will not cause the tree to die; the next season the leaves will come out again as thick as before. But strike the ax at the root of the tree, and not only will the leaves fall off of themselves, but the tree will die. Those who accept the truth, in the love of it, will die to the world, and will become meek and lowly in heart like their divine Lord. Just as soon as the heart is right, the dress, the conversation, the life, will be in harmony with the Word of God."—*My Life Today*, p. 265.

BLACK, WHITE, OR GRAY?

Love not the world, neither the things that are in the world. 1 John 2:15.

Have you ever heard that Seventh-day Adventists don't dance, don't go to shows, don't go to worldly places of amusement? Or are the church standards regarding worldly pleasures and love of the world outdated? Are they simply relics of a legalism that we have outgrown? There are other churches that used to believe as we do, but they have "adjusted to modern times." Where do you make the division? And how do you know where the line should be drawn between what is simply custom and what is right and wrong?

1 John 2 says, "Love not the world, neither the things that are in the world. If any man love the world, the love of the Father is not in him." That's a rather general statement. "For all that is in the world, the lust of the flesh, the lust of the eyes, and the pride of life, is not of the Father, but is of the world." That's a little more specific. "The world passeth away, and the lust thereof: but he that doeth the will of God abideth forever."

This doctrine of the church, perhaps more than any other, illustrates the fact that there are some things that appear to be neither black nor white, but are gray. You can't find chapter and verse discussing them specifically, and the devil has done his best to introduce a lot of gray areas, because he likes to work with gray. He can get people from white to black through the shades of gray. It's much harder to take people from white straight to black. That's why the deceiver enjoys the gray areas.

If you study the case histories of people who have gone from white to black, no one ever really makes the transition in one big jump. They always go in little, tiny steps. Sometimes the only thing wrong with step number one might be that it leads to step number two. There might not be anything that you can put your finger on that is inherently wrong in a particular thing, except where it leads. That's where the gray area comes in. How do you know where to cut it? How do you know where to draw the line? This is where Jesus has to be revealed in the gray. If Jesus doesn't reveal Himself to us in the gray area, we're sunk. But He has promised to be with us, and to reveal Himself to us, even in the gray. "And thine ears shall hear a word behind thee, saying, This is the way, walk ye in it, when ye turn to the right hand, and when ye turn to the left" (Isa. 30:21).

THE DOWNWARD PATH

There is a way that seemeth right unto a man, but the end thereof are the ways of death. Prov. 16:25.

The downward way at times *appears* to be right. But the Bible principle of how to deal with gray areas is to ask where they lead. Jesus admitted to His disciples that He wasn't taking them out of the world (John 17). But He did pray to His Father that they be kept from the evil.

Many of the worldly pleasures that have come in recent years don't show up in Scripture as such. There is not always specific chapter and verse to guide us. That's why we have to underscore the fact that the Bible, for the Christian, is going to have to be used in at least two ways—for information *and* for communication. Which is the *primary* purpose of the two? Which is more important? Maybe we shouldn't even try to separate them. We tend to separate them because we have often been given the impression that all you have to do is memorize 500 Bible doctrine texts, and you are secure. But information alone will not be sufficient.

The primary purpose of God's Word is to lead us to know God, and to come into fellowship and communion with Jesus. But, of course, communication is based on information. You have to have both. If communication wasn't based solidly on information, you would be wide open to error. Your communication with God has to be based on the information He has given through His Word. It cannot be based simply upon your own experience. It cannot be based upon feelings. So let's hang on to communication based solidly on information. But the information given is not always specific, and it in itself is not enough.

So how do you draw the line between the things you watch on TV? How do you decide whether you should even own a TV? Where do you draw the line between playing Frisbee on the front lawn with the kids, and major league competition? There are some who think bowling is a sin, and others who think it's a healthy exercise. The important question is, "What has God told *you* about it?" The only way you can expect to get clear signals from Heaven on a gray area in your own life is through your personal relationship with the Lord Jesus. It is only through personal communication with Him that you are able to keep an open channel to hear what God wants to tell you regarding His specific will for you.

299

NO ONE LIVES TO HIMSELF

But take heed lest by any means this liberty of yours becomes a stumblingblock to them that are weak. 1 Cor. 8:9.

The number one prerequisite for knowing God's will specifically for you in any area is to have an ongoing, vital, personal relationship with Him day by day. The person who suddenly decides he wants to know God's will in a particular area, who has had no time for relationship with God before that point, will find it very difficult to get the signals straight. But once a person does have a vital relationship with God, he will find that there are guidelines given in Scripture to aid in determining what is right or wrong in the gray areas, where specific details for every situation have not been given.

Some things that are all right to do if you are alone on a desert island would not be all right to do if you are living in a community. Let's notice it in Scripture. Romans 14:7, "For none of us liveth to himself, and no man dieth to himself." Verse 10, "Why dost thou judge thy brother? or why dost thou set at nought thy brother?" Verses 12-16, "Every one of us shall give account of himself to God. Let us not therefore judge one another any more: but judge this rather, that no man put a stumblingblock or an occasion to fall in his brother's way. I know, and am persuaded by the Lord Jesus, that there is nothing unclean of itself: but to him that esteemeth any thing to be unclean, to him it is unclean. But if thy brother be grieved with thy meat, now walkest thou not charitably. Destroy not him with thy meat, for whom Christ died. Let not then your good be evil spoken of."

In those days they had the practice of dedicating foods to idols. This food was then sold in the marketplace. Some of the Christian brothers were having problems when one of the other church members ate of the meat that was offered to idols. It had nothing to do with flesh, necessarily, but rather with *food* offered to idols. But Paul says, If someone is going to stumble over it, don't cause them to stumble. The issue of *influence* is a big one by which to determine the Lord's will in a gray or uncertain area. If our actions will hinder the spiritual growth of any of those around us, then we must take this possibility into account when we make our decisions in areas where God's will has not been specifically revealed.

KNOWING GOD'S WILL

For I came down from heaven, not to do mine own will, but the will of him that sent me. John 6:38.

Nine tenths of the difficulty of knowing God's will for our lives is met when we come to the point where we are willing to listen objectively to God's direction. How can this be done? Humanly, it is impossible. Only God can accomplish it for us. It is going to have to be done by His grace and His power.

And isn't this demonstrated in the life of Jesus? You'll have to admit that it must have been within God's will for Jesus to have a drink of the water at the well of Samaria. But when He had a chance to talk to someone about deeper wells and longer-lasting waters, the disciples were surprised at how quickly He forgot His own needs.

In John 4:34 Jesus said, "My meat is to do the will of him that sent me." He pointed this out as His mission, His purpose in life, again and again. And finally, at the close of His ministry, in the Garden alone, struggling and sweating drops of blood, He said, "Father, if thou be willing, remove this cup from me." He had a preference in the matter, but He immediately surrendered His wishes and His will to His Father. "Nevertheless not my will, but thine, be done" (Luke 22:42). He was willing for His own wishes to be submitted to God.

There is a quotation that some of us carry around, longing for the reality in terms of growth and experience for it to be accomplished in our own lives: "Christ in His life on earth made no plans for Himself. He accepted God's plans for Him, and day by day the Father unfolded His plans. So should we depend upon God, that our lives may be the simple outworking of His will. As we commit our ways to Him, He will direct our steps."—*The Ministry of Healing*, p. 479. That was the example that Christ left for us.

Wouldn't you like to live so close to the Lord that He would be able to flash His plans to you individually for the day? Wouldn't you at least like to be open to His plans, so that if He interrupts plans you have made for yourself you do not resist Him? As we grow more and more into the likeness of Jesus, we will be more sensitive to what His plans are, so that the plans we follow will be the plans He has made, instead of simply our own.

EIGHT STEPS FOR GUIDANCE | **OCT 22**

I will instruct thee and teach thee in the way which thou shalt go: I will guide thee with mine eye. Ps. 32:8.

If we would know God's will for us in any particular question, we must, first of all, by God's grace, come to the place of having no will of our own in the matter. This can be accomplished only through God's power, and through the personal relationship with Him. Second, don't go by feelings. You may *have* feelings on the subject, and, in fact, the Holy Spirit often will give impressions and convictions that will be very close to the area of feelings. But the important thing is not to make your decision based on feelings alone. (Don't make your decision based on any single aspect, but put all of the information you have together, and make the decision based on all areas.)

Third, seek God's will as revealed in His Word. There will be times when His Word does not reveal, for instance, whether you should move to Florida or Michigan. But there are principles that apply to many situations. And this brings us again to the fact that the primary purpose of God's Word is for communication as well as for information.

Fourth, take into account providential circumstances. Be sensitive to the open and closed doors. Note the direction He has been leading you in the past, and try to see whether the present decision somehow fits into the picture.

Fifth, take the decision to the Lord in prayer. Seek His guidance on your knees, through communication with Him. Take time to listen to the still small voice. Spread out your case before the Lord, and give Him your consent for Him to work out His plans for you.

Sixth, counsel with Christian friends. Godly parents, teachers, ministers, can often give important insights because of their experience and their life with the Lord. Here again, don't *depend* upon others to make your decisions for you, but listen to what they have to say, and add it to the total picture before deciding.

Seventh, *make a decision!* Don't sit on the fence forever. Decide. And then tell God in prayer what your decision is and move ahead on that decision. And, eighth, invite Him to stop you if you have somehow gotten your signals mixed up. As we allow the Lord to guide us, we will be led by Him. He has promised to fulfill the purposes He has for our lives.

JESUS REVEALED BY DOCTRINES

My doctrine is not mine, but his that sent me. If any man will do his will, he shall know of the doctrine. John 7:16, 17.

Jesus is the Man of the Bible. He is the theme of the entire book, the central character of each story. He was the Word who spoke all things into existence. He was revealed through symbols and types. And He is revealed by the doctrines of the Bible as well. Sometimes we have separated the doctrines from the theme of salvation by faith in Christ. Some have had trouble discovering the importance of the doctrines in light of the truth that our acceptance with God is based only on coming to Jesus for the salvation that He has freely provided. But we have only scratched the surface of the exciting and rewarding study of how the doctrines of the church reveal Jesus in a special light.

Jesus came to live and die for us, that He might offer us salvation. He promised to come again for us, taking us to the heavenly country He has prepared for those who love Him. His love for us is revealed in the complete provision He has made to save us from the world of sin.

He has made every effort to make sure that we understand the issues in sin, so that we can choose life instead of death. Even His dealings with Satan and the angels who fell show us how fair and how patient He is and how determined He is that no one will fail of understanding the truth.

He has shown Himself to be interested in our physical lives. He is revealed as a practical God, who knows from personal experience the needs of humanity. He has instructed us in the best way to live while here on earth, and has made provision to wake us up if we fall asleep before His return.

He has revealed His power for cleansing our hearts, and given us the Sabbath to be a special sign of His power to make us holy. He is revealed in the sanctuary as the Lamb of God. He gave us a sandbox illustration of the methods of communication with Him, and opened the way to the Holy of Holies to give us the assurance that the law can still be kept through His power.

It is as we study the doctrines in the light of Jesus, and what they teach us about Him, and our relationship with Him, that we find meaning in the distinctive teachings of our church, and become prepared to share these truths with the waiting world around us.

SANCTIFIED FOR JESUS' SAKE | OCT 24

A new heart also will I give you, and a new spirit will I put within you: and I will take away the stony heart out of your flesh, and I will give you an heart of flesh. Eze. 36:26.

God's people had been unfaithful to Him. They had profaned His name, and because of that the heathen got a wrong image of God. God wanted to set the record straight. He came with a message through Ezekiel: "Say to the house of Israel, I'm going to do something, but it isn't for your sake. It's for My holy name's sake. The heathen are going to know that I am the Lord when I shall be sanctified *in you* before their eyes" (Eze. 36:22, 23). This sanctification is the work of the Holy Spirit in cleansing us from unrighteousness. It is not primarily for our sake, but *for God's sake.*

Now look at verses 25 and 26 of the same passage: "Then will I sprinkle clean water upon you, and ye shall be clean: from all your filthiness, and from all your idols, will I cleanse you. A new heart also will I give you, and a new spirit will I put within you."

Notice the sequence given here. First, God gives the reason why He is going to cleanse His people. Second, He says He is going to sprinkle them from all of their uncleanness and filthiness. And third, He's going to give them a new heart. Sometimes we say that the new heart is referring to the experience of conversion. This message was given to people who were already God's people. It is possible, therefore, to be among God's people and to even have been born again, and in a sense still need a new heart. The heart that is given to us at the new birth is not necessarily a cleansed heart. This is demonstrated in the lives of godly people in Scripture. It is indicated in *Steps to Christ,* page 18, where it says that we will be given a new heart, *leading to* a new life. It doesn't all happen overnight.

Suggested here is an ongoing process that is the work of God through the power of the Holy Spirit. It is not something we do for ourselves. The only part we can really play in the process is to be open to God's leading, and allow His Spirit to do His work. The way we can be open is to choose to respond to the Holy Spirit's promptings, and deliberately come into His presence day by day for relationship and fellowship with Him. It is this response on our part that enables Him to work in our lives.

GOD'S BIGGER BUSINESS

He restoreth my soul: he leadeth me in the paths of righteousness for his name's sake. Ps. 23:3.

In the last day, that great day of the feast, Jesus stood and cried, saying, If any man thirst, let him come unto me, and drink. He that believeth on me, as the scripture hath said, out of his belly shall flow rivers of living water. (But this spake he of the spirit, which they that believe on him should receive)" (John 7:37-39). So the rivers of living water are connected with the Holy Spirit. Jesus, who was filled with the Spirit from His birth, is also included in the symbol. He said, "Come unto *me*, and drink." But the Holy Spirit under the symbol of water has to do with cleansing.

One of the aspects of the Holy Spirit's work is to cleanse the heart of the Christian. What does it mean to have a cleansed heart? There might be two descriptions. The behaviorist would define a cleansed heart in terms of actions, of victory over sinful deeds. But the relationist would define a cleansed heart more in terms of relationship with the Lord Jesus. To have an uncleansed heart means to be in known separation from God. The cleansed heart will not be found going along day by day in separation from God. Relationship is by far the bigger of the two issues.

All our struggles with sin and temptation and falling and failing are because we are living a life independent of the Lord Jesus and trying to meet the enemy in our own power. It cannot be done. And it is only as we realize this, and place ourselves day by day under God's control, that His Spirit can lead us to the point of depending upon His power all the time.

The work of the Holy Spirit in us is not what saves us eternally. Our acceptance of the cross and the blood of Jesus secures our eternal salvation. That is finished. Now God wants us to go on to bigger business—namely, bringing glory to Him in our lives before the universe. It is a self-centered view to think that the biggest business in the world is to get ourselves to heaven. We may cooperate with the Holy Spirit to bring glory and honor to Jesus now. That's the most important business.

THE GREATEST BATTLE

Knowing this, that our old man is crucified with him, that the body of sin might be destroyed, that henceforth we should not serve sin. Rom. 6:6.

The crisis of surrender, of cleansing, of filling by the Holy Spirit, is a subject that is sometimes debated by people because the impression has been given that conversion and surrender usually happen at the same time. But even though this may be God's ideal for us, it is still true that the initial conversion experience and absolute, or constant, surrender are often far apart. This is not to say that conversion is not a form of surrender. But the human heart, though converted, apparently has a way of not staying in the surrendered stance, but rather of swinging back and forth between total dependence upon God and dependence upon self. This painful swing leads to a crisis—the crisis of absolute surrender.

All conversions are not alike, as we know. One person has a tremendous upheaval; for another person, conversion is almost imperceptible. For those who have grown up in the church, it is comfortable to cling to the idea that conversion can be almost unnoticed, that we might never know the date or time or occasion that it happened. But notice this description of conversion: "Christ is constantly working upon the heart. Little by little, perhaps unconsciously to the receiver, impressions are made that tend to draw the soul to Christ. These may be received through meditation upon Him, through reading the Scriptures, or through hearing the word from the living preacher." Sounds pretty good so far, doesn't it? Sounds as though we'd probably not even notice anything happening. But look at the next sentence: "*Suddenly,* as the Spirit comes with more direct appeal, the soul gladly surrenders itself to Jesus." Did you catch the transition? Suddenly! As the Spirit comes with more direct appeal! "By many this is called sudden conversion; but it is the result of long wooing by the Spirit of God."—*The Desire of Ages,* p. 172. (Italics supplied.)

But even if it were possible for conversion to be imperceptible in your experience, absolute surrender will not get by you in the same way. Absolute surrender will be a crisis in your life that you will be aware of. *Steps to Christ,* page 43, says that the warfare against self is the greatest battle ever fought. Such a battle will not go by unnoticed.

LIFE'S GREAT CRISIS

Whosoever shall fall upon that stone shall be broken; but on whomsoever it shall fall, it will grind him to powder. Luke 20:18.

What kind of crisis is the surrender of the will? On the basis of the experiences of Bible characters, we are going to take the position that absolute surrender will be a big crisis for those who have failed in the little crises.

This principle is true of life in general. If a child fails to learn his multiplication tables, there is going to be a big crisis when he reaches college calculus. If a parachutist has never made any practice jumps, there is going to be a big crisis when he is 10,000 feet up in the air and the pilot says, "Jump!" Scuba diving can be a big crisis for someone who is afraid to get into the bathtub.

For the young person who finds ways to use a pay phone without putting in the money, or who helps himself to a candy bar from the local grocery store, the day may come when he is called into court to face a charge of grand larceny. No innocent baby goes from the cradle to becoming a criminal in one big jump. One reason that Abraham finally found himself in the big crisis with Isaac on the mountaintop was because he had failed in a series of smaller ones. The reason why Peter, after denying Jesus, found himself grinding his face in the dirt in Gethsemane, wishing he could die, was because he had failed in smaller tests before that time. We are told in *The Desire of Ages,* page 382, that if Peter had learned his lesson in some of the smaller tests, he would not have failed when the big test came upon him.

"Day by day God instructs His children. By the circumstances of the daily life He is preparing them to act their part upon the wider stage to which His providence has appointed them. It is the issue of the daily test that determines their victory or defeat in life's great crisis."—*Ibid.*

There are a series of little events, all based upon one issue: Am I going to trust God or myself? If I continue to fall and to fail the little tests, I can plan on a big wrestling with the angel some night by the brook Jabbok. If you are curious as to how you will fare in the big crisis, check to see how you are doing on the little ones day by day, and you will have your answer.

BEWARE OF SATAN'S SHORTCUTS

And I saw three unclean spirits like frogs come out of the mouth of the dragon, and out of the mouth of the beast, and out of the mouth of the false prophet. For they are the spirits of devils, working miracles. Rev. 16:13, 14.

Would you rather die or be healed by the devil? Most of us think that that would be an easy decision to make. But there are people who have been hit with some long-lasting illness or fatal disease who have had to think twice about that kind of decision. Would you rather die or run even a 10 percent risk of being healed by the devil? Is it possible that it might not be God's will to heal you, but it might be the devil's will?

Let's look at it in a different way. Would you rather burn at the stake or give up your faith? Isn't that the same issue? Most of us say that if we'd lived back in those days and they had asked us to give up our faith, we would have stepped forward, with the martyr's blood thrilling through our veins, and said, "You can burn me." But it might be a different story when the green wood is kindled for a slow fire.

Perhaps we could frame it one other way. Would you rather continue to struggle with failure and defeat in your life until God is able to lead your stubborn heart to surrender completely to Him, or would you rather have victory instantaneously given to you by the devil, without the surrender? Does the devil ever give victory? Perhaps you will want to ponder that question.

There are three major forces in the religious world that students of the book of Revelation will remember. These three forces in the last days just before Jesus comes are identified as Catholicism, Protestantism gone bad, and spiritualism. It's very interesting to note that in recent books world leaders in religious circles have gone on record as saying that they see three distinct forces in the religious world today, Catholicism, Protestantism, and neopentecostalism—the charismatic movement. This third one is growing by leaps and bounds. It is jumping all denominational barriers, including our own. And I believe that it has underground forces at work in almost every part of the country. We may see much more of it before we're finished.

For this reason it is meaningful to study the Holy Spirit, and the issues in the modern manifestations of the true and the false, as we near the end.

SEARCH FOR THE SPECTACULAR

And he doeth great wonders, so that he maketh fire come down from heaven on the earth in the sight of men, and deceiveth them that dwell on the earth by the means of those miracles which he had the power to do. Rev. 13:13, 14.

The devil is known as a roaring lion. He has been saving some of his most effective tricks for last. He is determined to get not just the drunk in the gutter but the saint on the pew, as well. One method he is going to use is the spectacular.

Most of us are impressed by the sensational. We don't need to deny that. We can try to be as stoical as possible, but deep down inside we are impressed by out-of-the-ordinary, unusual things. If someone were to go floating up from their pew to the ceiling during church, we'd be impressed. It would be sensational. We might be impressed for different reasons, but we'd still be impressed!

We're impressed with fabulous offers, giveaways, and shortcuts. When I was an academy student, I heard, from what I thought were authentic sources, that Henry Ford was going to give away a free Ford for a certain penny. Supposedly there were only a few of them made. Well, my father was holding evangelistic meetings downtown. Guess who was in the back room going through the offering! I found one of those pennies! I replaced it with one of my own, one that wasn't worth a new Ford, and hurriedly sent it in. Finally I got a letter back from Henry Ford's office. That's *all* I got back from Henry Ford's office! It conveyed his regrets.

The disciples in the days of Jesus were impressed by the spectacular. You can read about it in Luke 10:17. Seventy disciples came back. They had been empowered for service by the Lord Himself. And as they returned, they expressed the item of highest interest to them: "Lord, even the devils are subject unto us through thy name." They had seen some sensational things take place. But if you'll pardon my paraphrase, Jesus, in effect, said "Big Deal!" He told them that the devil had fallen like lightning from heaven a long time ago. And He tried to draw their minds back to the real issues of salvation. In the face of the spectacular today, we, too, need to be reminded that the greatest news is still the news of salvation in Jesus.

THE SENSATIONAL IS NOT ENOUGH

If they hear not Moses and the prophets, neither will they be persuaded, though one rose from the dead. Luke 16:31.

It is the dead that are raised, the blind whose eyes are opened, and the spectacular things that draw our attention. But how long has it been since you came home rejoicing because someone's name had been added to the book of life?

Heaven looks at things so differently from the way we do. The miracles at which we wonder seem simple to God. But when someone comes to Jesus, all heaven rejoices. We put the faith healers on the television screen, and report them in the newspaper. But you don't see special features about someone who has just accepted Jesus and had his name written in heaven.

In Luke 16 is the story of the rich man and Lazarus. There have been all kinds of attempts to explain that story. We understand that the story was a parable that Jesus used to illustrate a point. One of His lessons was the deceitfulness of riches. He didn't happen to be talking on the state of the dead at that time. But the other point was more subtle, one that Jesus used as a method of reaching the Jewish nation, depicting their plight. They were like beggars sitting at the gates of a rich man's palace. But in the middle of the story, He had the rich man in the fires of torment. The rich man said, "Please send someone back to tell my five brothers so they won't end up as I have." And the answer comes, "They will not believe, though one rose from the dead."

We think that someone rising from the dead would convince anyone. But it didn't back then, and it won't today. The Jewish leaders were *not* convinced, even when One rose from the dead. And Jesus was not the only one who rose from the dead. Lazarus' story must have hit the press of the Jerusalem *Times* too. But none of it caused them to believe.

To Elijah in the cave, Jesus made it clear that it wasn't the spectacular that counted. It wasn't the earthquakes and the fires and the winds. It was the still small voice. In Acts 8 you have Simon the sorcerer, who was impressed only by the spectacular, and wanted to buy the power to do the same. He was told to repent. We must not depend on the spectacular today, to prove or to convince of truth. We must not join the search for the sensational, for the sensational is never a sufficient basis for our faith.

A WARNING FOR THE ELECT

For there shall arise false Christs, and false prophets, and shall shew great signs and wonders; insomuch that, if it were possible, they shall deceive the very elect. Matt. 24:24.

Some people rise and fall with appeals to the emotions through the sensational and spectacular. This will always be a clever ploy in the hands of the enemy. I'd like to remind you that miracles and sensational happenings are no proof of the power of God.

Revelation 13 makes clear that there is an apostate power that does great wonders, even making fire come down from heaven on earth in the sight of men, and deceiving them that dwell on the earth by means of those miracles that he has power to do in the sight of the beast. This power says to them that dwell on the earth that they should make an image to the beast that had the wound by the sword and did live. This power has the ability to work miracles—not just feats that look like miracles, but miracles. And those three unclean, froglike spirits, the spirits of devils, do work miracles and go forth to the kings of the earth and the whole world, to gather them to the battle of the great day of God.

In Luke 3 we read of a woman who was bound by Satan for many years. Jesus released her on the Sabbath. The people in the crowd griped and complained. Jesus said, "Isn't it sensible to release this woman who had been bound by Satan?" If Satan has the power to bind people, then it would be reasonable to expect that in certain cases he would have the ability to release the bonds.

We know that Job got boils, and we know from whence his boils came. And if the devil can produce the stimulus that will make boils, he ought to be able to stop the stimulus, and let the natural miracle-working power of the human body bring healing. We know about Pharaoh and the magicians in the courts with Moses and Aaron. We know about their rods turning into snakes. We have some evidence, based on the premise that the devil cannot create, that the magicians' rods did not really turn into snakes, but only appeared to. But if he cannot create, he certainly can counterfeit closely! All of which leads us to this conclusion: Our basis for faith must be in Jesus and in the faith relationship with Him, not in the spectacular.

DON'T TRADE JESUS FOR VICTORY

But thanks be to God, which giveth us the victory through our Lord Jesus Christ.
1 Cor. 15:57.

The person who is preoccupied with his performance, who is looking for victory, looking for a changed life, above all else, is wide open for the charismatic movement of today. Charismatics offer a changed life quickly and easily. You don't have to sweat it out with an angel by the brook Jabbok. You can go and get someone to place his hands on your head, have nice "vibes" go through you, and get victory *now*. In the Seventh-day Adventist Church, with our concern over right living, there could be a wide cross section open for that. Why? Because for many, while they have learned that a changed life is important, they have not learned that relationship and communion and dependence on Jesus is the only way that a real change in the life can happen.

If I were the devil, I think I would be happy to ease off on my temptations for someone to commit a certain sin for a while, if in so doing I could get that person under my control. That would be a good trade, wouldn't it? And the person who sees Christianity as primarily a matter of behavior could be very easily led into such a trap.

But for the person who is locked in on the relationship of faith with Christ, for the person who realizes that the entire basis of the Christian life is fellowship and communion and dependence upon Jesus, for that person spiritual life is not dependent upon sudden, spectacular changes.

It is true that the Holy Spirit *does* work to change our lives. The Holy Spirit *does* bring victories. The Holy Spirit *does* accomplish many wonderful things, and the visible work of the Spirit will continue to increase until the end of time. But our basis for judging whether a work is of God or from another power must always be based solidly on Scripture, interpreted in the context of an ongoing, vital relationship with God. A changed life doesn't prove anything. What counts is who changed it, and for what reason, and what motive. What *we* see as changed lives is always only external. We don't know hearts. And we must never become more interested in victory over our sins than in Jesus. When we focus our attention on Him the changed life that we need will be the inevitable result.

TRUTH MIXED WITH ERROR

Now the Spirit speaketh expressly, that in the latter times some shall depart from the faith, giving heed to seducing spirits, and doctrines of devils. 1 Tim. 4:1.

Do you believe that you should judge the Bible by your experience or that you should judge your experience by the Bible? When something has happened to you, when you have experienced something, it is very difficult not to believe in it. It's hard not to accept something you have experienced as real. And yet our own experience by itself is not a safe guide, in spite of how real and valid and convincing it may seem to us.

When Saul sought out the witch of Endor to learn what would happen at the battle that he was about to engage in, he experienced something real. Not only that, but the prediction that he was given in that setting, by the spirit posing as Samuel, proved to be correct. But that did not mean that it was from God.

Satan "will present his temptations to men in a manner to pervert the senses of all who are not shielded by divine power."—*The Great Controversy*, p. 554. In the end of time, we are told that miracles will be performed, that the sick will be healed. Satan is a real being, and the works that he does are real also. It is true that there are many hoaxes performed by magicians and others who can make it appear as if things are happening that actually are not. But even if you could prove the absence of hoax, and the presence of the supernatural, that does not prove the supernatural to be of God.

It is when truth is mixed with error that it is the most dangerous. If there is a brown jar that contains poison, with a skull and crossbones on the label, clearly marking it poison, will it be as dangerous as poison in a green bottle marked "7-Up"? Satan knows better than to come openly with his devices. He knows that the best lies are those that are only partly untrue. He knows that the best way to reach people with his power is to come disguised in such a way as to appear as an angel of light. It is then that we are more ready to accept his devices.

It is only in dependence upon Christ, in acquaintance and friendship with Him through an ongoing relationship based on His Word, that we can be secure against the devices of Satan.

WHAT IS TRUTH?

Because thou hast kept the word of my patience, I also will keep thee from the hour of temptation, which shall come upon all the world, to try them that dwell upon the earth. Rev. 3:10.

You cannot judge truth on the basis of the presence of undeniable power, or by miracles, or healings. You cannot judge truth on the basis of warmth and fellowship and love, or even changed lives. So on what can you judge truth? How can anyone come up with conclusive proof?

Well, it is certain that we *can* know truth. We have been promised, "Those who are earnestly seeking a knowledge of the truth and are striving to purify their souls through obedience, thus doing what they can to prepare for the conflict, will find, in the God of truth, a sure defense. 'Because thou hast kept the word of my patience, I also will keep thee,' . . . is the Saviour's promise. He would sooner send every angel out of heaven to protect His people than leave one soul that trusts in Him to be overcome by Satan."—*The Great Controversy*, p. 560. We have big forces on our side that we can count on.

The first way to test the truth of supernatural manifestations is by the Word of God. Even people who apparently love one another and Jesus and the Bible, but who do not keep the commandments of God, cannot necessarily be depended upon to be from God. "If they speak not according to this word, it is because there is no light in them" (Isa. 8:20). If a group is experiencing wonderful manifestations, but at the same time is teaching that you don't have to obey all of God's law, there's a big clue right there. Although it may be true that there are sincere *individuals* that God is leading to Himself in every group, this fact does not prove that we should abandon the truths that have been revealed to us as a church and go to join them. They may be on their way up, but if we join them, we may pass them on *our* way *down*.

An equally important safeguard against deception is to have the righteousness of Christ in the life, to be in vital relationship with Him. Even a head knowledge of Scripture will prove insufficient to take us through the times ahead. But as we continue the fellowship with Christ, solidly based on His Word, we will be secure against all the wiles of the enemy.

HOW TO SPOT THE PHONY

Let no man deceive you by any means. 2 Thess. 2:3.

A hillbilly came out of the mountains with an $18 counterfeit bill. He had intended to print $20 on it, but made a mistake in his printing. But it looked so good he decided to try cashing it anyway. He arrived at the store in the valley and gave the bill to the proprietor. The proprietor accepted the bill and asked, "Would you prefer three sixes or two nines?"

There's no sense in making a counterfeit unless there is a real. Those people who are adept at making counterfeit money are the ones who know the real. As we consider the modern manifestations of the Holy Spirit, we know that for every genuine revival, there will be an attempt at a counterfeit on the part of Satan.

All of us are terribly impressed by the spectacular, and we might as well admit it. The enemy is going to try to deceive, if possible, the very elect. The Bible reports miracles, and gives evidence that the devil himself can at times perform them. So even though we might be impressed by the spectacular, we can never judge truth by it. Truth must be judged by the Bible, in the context of our personal relationship with God.

In Revelation 17 the true church is represented by a pure woman, and the false (or counterfeit) church, by a harlot. God has always had a tender regard for His church, and He manifests His power and gives His gifts to the church. The true church of the last days will be the one that can expect the genuine manifestations of the Spirit's working. The counterfeit workings of a supernatural type will be expected in the counterfeit church. Some people will at this point sit back smugly and say, "That's right, and we're the true ones." Are you sure? The false church is spoken of in Revelation as Babylon. Babylon is a classic example of man trying to save himself. And if you are still trying to save yourself in some way, you can be partaking of the spirit of Babylon whether you are in one of the churches called Babylon or not. If you have not yet reached the end of your own resources and learned the necessity of coming to Jesus day by day for salvation and for relationship with Him, you are a part of Babylon. Until you know Him for yourself, you will not be safe from deception, no matter how many *facts* you know about the last days. It takes both.

315

INFORMATION IS NOT ENOUGH

I am the way, the truth, and the life. John 14:6.

Many Seventh-day Adventists feel quite secure from some of the counterfeits that are being publicized today. We *know* better than to believe that people come back to life again and claim to have been taken right to heaven when they died. We *know* better than to believe the stories told by beings on UFOs, that they used to live on this earth hundreds of years ago. We know all about these kinds of things, and we think we will never be deceived.

But there is something more—and the something more has to do with the fact that God's Word has at least two purposes. It is true that God's Word is for teaching truth. Jesus said it: "Thy word is truth" (John 17:17). But the other purpose of Scripture is that we come to Him so that we might have life. The two purposes could be summed up by (1) the Bible for information, and (2) the Bible for communication. It's possible to be acutely aware of the teachings of the Bible and have texts memorized concerning information, and still be deceived because we haven't discovered personal communication with Jesus through the Bible. The primary purpose of the Bible is for fellowship and communion with the Lord Jesus Christ, and to experience a relationship with Him that is *based* upon information.

One of the greatest concepts of how we can be sure that we are not among those that are deceived was stated by Ellen G. White in the *Review and Herald*, December 24, 1889: "There is a work for this time to be done in fitting a people to stand in the day of trouble, and all must act their part in this work. They must be [1] clothed with the righteousness of Christ [notice the sequence of importance], and [2] be so fortified by the truth, that the delusions of Satan shall not be accepted by them as genuine manifestations of the power of God."

Every topic you begin with should end at the same point—do you know a relationship with Jesus for yourself today? Do you know how to spend quiet time with Him day by day with His Word and in prayer? There will come a time when people who know all the *facts* of the Bible will be deceived nonetheless, because they don't know Jesus. It's going to take more than information. To stand in these last days, we must have a vital relationship with the Lord Jesus that is solidly based on the truth of the Bible.

THE MARKS OF GOD'S CHURCH

Here is the patience of the saints: here are they that keep the commandments of God, and the faith of Jesus. Rev. 14:12.

Which church is it that has the two distinguishing marks spoken of in our scripture for today? It isn't a church that simply talks about the commandments of God, and believes in them. It's a church that *keeps* them. This church doesn't simply think that the faith of Jesus is a good thing, and important—it *has* the faith of Jesus. It doesn't rely on the fact that the forefathers and pioneers in the church kept all the commandments of God and had faith in Jesus. Whenever you look at the remnant, through whom you can expect the mighty working of God's power, you're looking at a group that has *both*. You cannot expect the mighty outpouring of God's Spirit and a revival of primitive godliness among people who place great emphasis on the commandments but who don't know Jesus, anymore than you can expect it among people who put a lot of emphasis on knowing Jesus but who don't pay much attention to the commandments. Both are equally important.

Some years ago God gave a direct message to our church, describing why it is that some people go off looking for special experiences in a holiness or pentecostal meeting. It was written in the book *Evangelism*, pages 598, 599: "We as a people have fallen into . . . error. We acknowledge the claims of God's law, and teach the people the duty of rendering obedience." (Notice the word *duty.*) But "we fail to have that trust, that faith, which keeps the soul abiding in Christ. . . . Through a lack of faith, many who seek to obey the commandments of God have little peace and joy. . . . They are not anchored in Christ. Many feel a lack in their experience; they desire something which they have not; and thus some are led to attend holiness meetings, and are charmed with the sentiments of those who break the law of God."

As God leads *individuals* to the place of both keeping His commandments *and* having the faith of Jesus, His purpose is that His *church* will finally have both as well. If you resist either necessity, you will lose out in the end. But for those who seek the faith relationship with Jesus day by day, and by beholding His matchless charms are molded into His image and led to obedience, there is safety from the storm that is breaking around us.

317

SINCERITY IS NOT ENOUGH

For it had been better for them not to have known the way of righteousness, than, after they have known it, to turn from the holy commandment delivered unto them. 2 Peter 2:21.

Have you ever heard stories of mothers on the other side of the world who threw their babies to the crocodiles as part of their worship of heathen gods? I don't know whether there are still mothers who do this, but if and when they did, you'll have to admit that it would have taken a mighty sincere mother to throw her baby to the crocodiles—either mighty sincere or mighty something else! It is possible for a poor heathen mother, coming out of the darkness of heathenism, to be in the process of being led by God into greater light and truth, and a clearer understanding of what God is like. We don't have to sit in judgment upon a mother who would sacrifice her child. We don't have to decide her eternal destiny individually. We can look at the episode and weep, and can allow for God to bring her out of that. But should we, with what we know, and what we understand, and with the information that we have available, go and join her? Should we throw *our* babies to the crocodiles, too, just because we are convinced that she was sincere?

We don't have to judge anyone's eternal destiny, or even speculate on his sincerity, concerning certain charismatic movements in the world today. Even though much of the charismatic movement we see currently could be simply a veiled manifestation of spiritualism, we don't have to judge the individuals. But those who leave the plain teachings of the Bible and join with charismatic groups will be deceived. If we find a vacuum in our lives, it can be filled by going to our closets with God's Word and seeking a personal relationship with Him.

Our correct understanding of Bible information gives us no reason for complacency. As members of the "remnant church," we sometimes think that we are invulnerable. But the truth is that the Holy Spirit will be poured out through those who keep the commandments of God and who also have a faith in Jesus that is real, not just theoretical. God's Spirit will not be poured out in its fullness until the majority of His people are cooperating with Him. And if I refuse to be a part of that group, then I will be left out in the end.

THE SPIRIT OF TRUTH

Howbeit when he, the Spirit of truth, is come, he will guide you into all truth. John 16:13.

The first work of the Holy Spirit is found in John 16:7-9. "Nevertheless I tell you the truth; It is expedient for you that I go away: for if I go not away, the Comforter will not come unto you; but if I depart, I will send him unto you. And when he is come, he will reprove the world of sin [He will convict or convince the world of sin], and of righteousness, and of judgment: of sin, because they believe not on me." Please underscore the Bible definition of sin given here. Sin is something more than doing wrong things—transgressions. The real issue is to not believe and trust in the Lord Jesus Christ. And the Holy Spirit has this reminder as His first work.

His first work involves the entire world. No one is left out. The poor heathen in some far-flung country is convinced of sin even before the missionary comes. The Holy Spirit has been there first. It is His work to convince the world of sin. Not one person is passed by. While you and I are sleeping, the Holy Spirit is somewhere doing His work of conviction.

If all there is to salvation is to be convicted of sin, everyone would be saved. But there is something further in the work of the Holy Spirit, and that is His second work, found in John 3:3-5. "Jesus answered and said unto him, Verily, verily, I say unto thee, Except a man be born again, he cannot see the kingdom of God. Nicodemus saith unto him, How can a man be born when he is old? . . . Jesus answered, . . . Except a man be born of water and of the Spirit, he cannot enter into the kingdom of God." To be born again is to be born of the Spirit. The second phase of the Holy Spirit's work is His regenerating work, which takes place only in the hearts and lives of the people who respond to it. In order for everyone to be saved, all would have to respond to the Holy Spirit's second work. Here's where the big difference lies.

The Bible makes it clear that God wants everyone to be saved but that only those who respond to His invitation can receive the new birth that is possible for each one. As we choose today to accept anew the work of the Holy Spirit in our lives, He will do His converting work. As we respond to Him, we will be brought into harmony with God.

319

THE SWORD OF THE SPIRIT

And he shall go before him in the spirit and power of Elias, . . . to make ready a people prepared for the Lord. Luke 1:17.

John the Baptist had been given a particular message of preparation. He had been sent as the forerunner of Jesus, to prepare, as much as possible, the people of his day to accept Jesus when He came. If you have ever studied John's mission and message, you have perhaps wondered at the sort of person that he was. No one would consider John the Baptist to be a diplomat! He came with the spirit and power of Elijah—who had met people at the top of Mount Carmel and demanded, "How long halt ye between two opinions? if the Lord be God, then follow him" (1 Kings 18:21). John the Baptist was not soft-spoken. He didn't mince words. He uttered scathing rebukes. He called the people a generation of vipers.

Have you ever pondered the message of John the Baptist, and wondered why he used such a hard-hitting approach? Our evangelists usually try to come on a little more tactfully. But not John the Baptist. He was used by the Holy Spirit as a sword to cut deeply for the purpose of preparing the way for Jesus to enter. "God does not send messages to flatter the sinner. He delivers no message of peace to lull the unsanctified into fatal security."—*The Desire of Ages*, p. 104.

There are times when the Holy Spirit cuts deeply today. The Holy Spirit doesn't spare our feelings or try to make us feel comfortable, but cuts deeply into our souls with the burning message of conviction. He works to make us painfully aware of our shortcomings, our hypocrisy, of our lack of trust in God. He points out our sin, our selfishness, and our lack of concern for the things that really count. His first purpose is to convince us of our deep need of the salvation that God has to offer, that we might be motivated to come for that salvation. It is only those who are sick, and who *know* that they are sick, who are willing to seek the help of a physician. And it is only those who are sinners, who *know* their condition as sinners, who are willing to come to God for the salvation that He has provided.

Today, when we feel the sword of the Spirit cutting deeply into our complacency, we can be thankful that He is alive and well, still doing His work of bringing us to Jesus to find healing and rest.

COME, HOLY SPIRIT

For our gospel came not unto you in word only, but also in power, and in the Holy Ghost, and in much assurance. 1 Thess. 1:5.

There's a big difference between simply speaking words and having the Holy Spirit make those words effective by His power. "Only when the truth is accompanied to the heart by the Spirit will it quicken the conscience or transform the life. One might be able to present the letter of the Word of God, he might be familiar with all its commands and promises, but unless the Holy Spirit sets home the truth, no souls will fall on the Rock and be broken."—*The Desire of Ages*, p. 672.

The first work of the Holy Spirit is His convicting work. Our greatest need is to realize our need of salvation. How many people who have been born and reared in religious circles, and are third- and fourth-generation church members, have had this lack as one of their problems. Some people say, How can you recognize your need if you have never been out in the world? How can you realize your need if you have never known anything else but going through the regular routine of religion and formal worship? The Holy Spirit is responsible for bringing each person to realize his need, and although He can make use of the troubles and sorrows of sin to point it out, He can also work in the heart by uplifting Jesus and showing us how far we fall short of His standard, even when everything is going well.

Sometimes we try to help other people realize their need by pointing out to them their need. But if we are working apart from the inspiration of the Holy Spirit, who alone knows the proper timetable for each one, we end up with zero. On the other hand, we can talk about the Holy Spirit, and how it is His work to bring conviction, and then sit back and wait for Him to work. But the Holy Spirit wants to use us, to control us, to work through us, in order to reach other people. Jesus told His disciples that He wanted to send the Comforter to *them*. The Holy Spirit is sent to *us*, to live in us, and by cooperating with Him we can be used of God to reach other hearts. God intends to work through us. It is not His purpose for us to work without the Holy Spirit, nor for the Holy Spirit to work apart from us. We are to cooperate with Him.

Now is the judgment of this world: now shall the prince of this world be cast out.
John 12:31.

The Holy Spirit convinces the world of judgment—"Of judgment, because the prince of this world is judged" (John 16:11). What does this tell us about the function of the Holy Spirit? Well, obviously, if the prince of this world is judged, and he is the chief sinner, then all his followers are going to be judged, too. The minute that Hitler, during World War II, found the whole world caving in on him, all his followers were in trouble as well. The minute that Goliath went down under the slingshot of David, all of Goliath's supporters knew they were finished, and they began to run. So the Holy Spirit convinces us that at the cross, when Jesus said, "It is finished," the devil knew that he was finished, and everyone who has been born in a world of sin, and who has rejected Jesus' righteousness, knows that he has nothing but a fearful looking for of judgment.

On the other hand, the war is over. The war has been won. And if you are on the winner's side, then the fact of judgment, that the prince of this world is already judged, doesn't bring condemnation or fear, only hope, gratitude, and peace. It depends on whose side you are on. Each of us today has the privilege of choosing anew to be on the winning side.

When Goliath's head was cut off, those on David's side uttered a shout of victory. So when we are told that if we believe on Christ we are not even going to come into judgment (John 5:24), we can rejoice. The convicting work of the Holy Spirit can bring hope and comfort. When He is come, He will reprove the world of sin, of righteousness, and of judgment.

Allow the Holy Spirit today to convince you that if you are living a life apart from Jesus, regardless of how good or how bad that life is, you are living a life of sin. Don't choose to live without fellowship with Jesus. Take courage that as we come into continuing acceptance of Christ, His righteousness at the Father's right hand is enough. He is able to bring His people faultless before His throne with Him. Judgment is nothing to fear; it is cause for rejoicing, for the war has been won. It was won at the cross, and salvation is assured. This is the truth that the Holy Spirit is seeking to bring to our understanding.

THE RENEWING BY THE HOLY SPIRIT

For we ourselves also were sometimes foolish, disobedient, deceived, serving divers lusts and pleasures, living in malice and envy, hateful, and hating one another. But after that the kindness and love of God our Saviour toward man appeared. Titus 3:3, 4.

You can keep your new translations on this passage! I like the way it reads in the King James Version. Aren't you glad that the kindness and love of God appeared? "Not by works of righteousness which we have done, but according to his mercy he saved us, by the washing of regeneration, and renewing of the Holy Ghost: which he shed on us abundantly through Jesus Christ our Saviour; that being justified by his grace, we should be made heirs according to the hope of eternal life" (Titus 3:5-7). Here you have the beautiful picture of salvation from sin coming to every believing heart. It describes the regenerating work of the Spirit, the renewing of the Holy Ghost, and the work of the Holy Spirit to transform lives.

Is this accomplished by a single acceptance of Jesus? Is justification everything, or is sanctification also part of salvation? *My Life Today,* page 313, answers, "When souls are converted their salvation is not yet accomplished. They then have the race to run; the arduous struggle is before them to do, what? 'To fight the good *fight of faith.'* . . . There is no release in this warfare; the battle is lifelong." Even though the work of the Holy Spirit in regeneration is a tremendous work, there is more. The work of the Holy Spirit in the ongoing Christian life has just as much to do with salvation as does the work of Jesus on the cross. It's all salvation. One is salvation from our past sins, one is salvation from our present sinning. And we have the promise that finally we will be saved from a world of sin. All is by Christ, and all comes by faith. There is no difference.

What happens at conversion? At the new birth we receive a supernatural change of attitude toward God, and a new capacity for knowing Him (*The Desire of Ages*, p. 189). We are given the equipment to get started with—it is not the end of the Christian life, but rather the beginning. As we begin to fight the fight of faith, to seek Jesus day by day, after the Holy Spirit has done His converting work in our life, we will be led daily in a continuing walk with Christ.

HOPELESSLY RELIGIOUS

That which is born of the flesh is flesh; and that which is born of the Spirit is spirit.
John 3:6.

When we are born into this world of sin, we are born with the absence of any joy in holiness or joy in communion with God. That's the dilemma of being born a sinner. But at the same time, the human being is born hopelessly religious. We *insist* on worshiping something. Our problem is that we often don't recognize that this vacuum within is a God-shaped vacuum. So until people discover the truth of the gospel, they will direct their worship to things, other people, or themselves. No one is born again until the Holy Spirit is able to lead him to the place of being fed up with worshiping anything else but God.

I was told as a preacher that one of my responsibilities was to help people become converted. If this is true, how can this be accomplished? Is there anything we can do to help someone else to the point of conversion? Well, it is for sure that when it comes to our first birth, we have no choice or direction in the event. It happens to us, but we didn't choose it. But when it comes to being born again, we do have a choice. God gives us life and strength and health for the purpose of providing us the opportunity to come to Him for life. God offers us more than life here, with its threescore years and ten. He offers eternity—the choice of the second birth.

One of the first things we can do in seeking to bring others to choose conversion is to uplift Jesus. It is as Jesus is lifted up, and the Holy Spirit is enabled to speak to the heart by the awareness of His love, that hearts are softened and attracted and broken.

The Holy Spirit has a timetable for each one of us—Nicodemus waited and pondered for three years. If Nicodemus had come to some of us, as he came to Jesus that night, we would have had him in the baptismal pool by the following Sabbath. But Jesus was willing to wait for the Spirit's schedule, and when Jesus was lifted up, Nicodemus responded and became a faithful follower of the Lord. It is the Holy Spirit's work to bring people to the place of being willing to worship something besides things, other people, and self. And then, as Jesus is uplifted, hearts are won and sinners are converted.

THE SPIRIT WORKS AS HE WILL

The wind bloweth where it listeth, and thou hearest the sound thereof, but canst not tell whence it cometh, and whither it goeth: so is every one that is born of the Spirit. John 3:8.

A man who was a great scholar came to Jesus one night. He was a teacher, an intellectual, a thinker. He came to Jesus and said, "I notice that You're a great teacher. And I'm not so bad myself. Why don't we have a discussion?" But Jesus said, "What you need is to be born again."

Nicodemus had been worshiping something other than God. But he was drawn to Jesus. He came to have a discussion with Jesus. He didn't fully realize his need, and when Jesus said, "Except a man be born again, he cannot see the kingdom of God" (John 3:3), Nicodemus didn't understand. He proved that the unconverted man doesn't comprehend spiritual things, for he said, "How can a man be born when he is old?" It is only through the regenerating work of the Holy Spirit that we can even understand about salvation by faith in Jesus, which is what the "kingdom of God" refers to (*Christ's Object Lessons,* p. 62).

Jesus gave to Nicodemus that night His clearest presentation on the new birth. But was Nicodemus born again that night? The evidence we have is that he walked away through the darkness, pondering, thinking, wondering. For three years Jesus let the seed He had sown do its work. The new birth comes at the proper time for each person, and not even Jesus rushed the timetable. The timetable is not a clock or some number of years. It has to do with conditions. With some people the conditions necessary are fulfilled very quickly. For others, it may take a lifetime before they get fed up with life apart from God. For Nicodemus it took three years. But at least by the time of the Crucifixion Nicodemus was able to accept the work of the Holy Spirit in regeneration. One of his first acts, along with Joseph of Arimathea, was to provide a decent burial for Jesus. This rich man became poor, and was ridiculed by his former friends, because of his loyalty to Jesus. But once Nicodemus had surrendered to the regenerating work of the Holy Spirit, he was willing to become poor, because of love for the One who became poor in our stead so that we, through His poverty, might become rich.

THE CLEANSING OF THE SPIRIT |

And I will pray the Father, and he shall give you another Comforter, that he may abide with you for ever; even the Spirit of truth . . . for he dwelleth with you, and shall be in you. John 14:16, 17.

A new heart is not necessarily a cleansed heart. A new mind is not necessarily a cleansed mind. This is why the continuing work of the Holy Spirit is a necessity. The Holy Spirit can convict us of sin and lead us to conversion, to being born again, but that is only the beginning. His work does not stop there. In *Steps to Christ,* page 18, we are told that when we receive a new heart, this *leads to* a new life. Conversion is only the beginning—it is not the whole picture.

The regenerating work of the Holy Spirit simply prepares us for His further work, which is the cleansing of the Christian. What does it mean to be cleansed by the Holy Spirit? Jesus said that He would pray the Father and we would be sent another Comforter to abide with us. It would be the Spirit of truth, who would dwell with us and would be *in* us. The New Testament teaching is that there is an indwelling presence of God, which gives transforming, overcoming power. We are told that a new heart will be given to us. If we confess our sins, God will forgive and *cleanse us* from all unrighteousness (1 John 1:9). What does this mean? Is it simply cleansing the records of heaven? No, it is cleansing *us.* And it is through the Holy Spirit that this happens.

Notice Ephesians 3:16-19: "He would grant you, according to the riches of his glory, to be strengthened with might by his Spirit *in the inner man;* that Christ may *dwell in your hearts* by faith; that ye, being rooted and grounded in love, may be able to comprehend with all saints what is the breadth, and length, and depth, and height; and to know the love of Christ."

"Sin could be resisted and overcome only through the mighty agency of the Third Person of the Godhead. . . . It is the Spirit that makes effectual what has been wrought out by the world's Redeemer. It is by the Spirit that the heart is made pure. Through the Spirit the believer becomes a partaker of the divine nature. Christ has given His Spirit as a divine power to overcome all hereditary and cultivated tendencies to evil."—*The Desire of Ages,* p. 671. It is through the Holy Spirit's cleansing that we can overcome.

KEEP YOUR EYES ON JESUS

But if the Spirit of him that raised up Jesus from the dead dwell in you, he that raised up Christ from the dead shall also quicken your mortal bodies by his Spirit that dwelleth in you. Rom. 8:11.

The work of God *for* us is accomplished by Jesus and through the power of the Holy Spirit. And the work of God *in* us is accomplished by Jesus and through the power of the Holy Spirit. It is Jesus and the Holy Spirit working together in both. There is no need to distinguish between them. It is by the Spirit that the heart is made pure. The work of the Holy Spirit, following conversion and regeneration, is to cleanse the Christian. This is one of the unique missions of the people who are symbolized by the three angels—to emphasize something in addition to justification, that is, the transforming, victorious power of the Holy Spirit.

The subject of the cleansing work of the Spirit was not clearly taught by Luther and other Protestant leaders. One of the unique contributions by the remnant church to the world is to emphasize both the work of justification *and* cleansing, which are both of God and the Holy Spirit.

One of the problems is that many people who become Christians experience only the first works of the Holy Spirit, in convicting of sin and converting the sinner. But they have done nothing to cooperate with the Holy Spirit in the work of cleansing. They go to church and sit on the pew week after week, and yet know nothing of a daily experience with Jesus, which is the factor that enables the Holy Spirit to do His cleansing and sanctifying work. *The Desire of Ages,* page 302, says, "If the eye is kept fixed on Christ, the work of the Spirit ceases not until the soul is conformed to His image." It is through constant communication and fellowship with God that we cooperate with the Spirit for His cleansing work in our lives.

The Holy Spirit is the breath of spiritual life in the soul. The impartation of the Spirit is the impartation of the life of Christ. It imbues the receiver with the attributes of Christ (*ibid.,* p. 805). It is by choosing the continuing relationship with Jesus that we allow the Holy Spirit to accomplish for us the cleansing that He has in mind.

But ye shall receive power, after that the Holy Ghost is come upon you: and ye shall be witnesses unto me both in Jerusalem, and in all Judaea, and in Samaria, and unto the uttermost part of the earth. Acts 1:8.

The work of the Holy Spirit is to bring power for witnessing, power for service. The promise of power, after the Holy Ghost was come, was fulfilled after the waiting time in Jerusalem following Christ's ascension. Jesus told His disciples to wait until something happened. Of course, if they weren't able to know what it was, or able to tell when it happened, they could hardly have known when to stop waiting. They might still be tarrying there in Jerusalem! So the very fact that Jesus said, "Tarry until . . ." indicated that they could expect something obvious to happen.

Is there something that we have not experienced in its fullness today? "The descent of the Holy Spirit upon the church is looked forward to as in the future; but it is the privilege of the church to have it now. Seek for it, pray for it, believe for it. We must have it, and Heaven is waiting to bestow it."—*Evangelism*, p. 701. Have you ever heard of the latter rain? Do you pray for the latter rain or do you pray for the Holy Spirit? Is there a difference? Yes, there is. The latter rain is the *last* outpouring of the Spirit. When you pray for the latter rain, you are praying for the last one. Only God knows when the last one can be relevant, because only God knows when the world is going to end. When you pray for the latter rain, in a sense you are praying for the end of the world, and maybe that wouldn't be a bad idea. But God gives a simple invitation to the church to pray for the Holy Spirit, which has no timetable on it as suggested by the word *latter*. It is something that has been present and potential and possible ever since the day of Pentecost, and even before.

If we are invited to pray for the Holy Spirit, and the invitation is to the church, then it would have to be something in addition to the converting work of the Spirit that we are asking for. When we seek power for witnessing, we are seeking something in addition, even to power for overcoming and victory. When the Holy Spirit is given in His fullest sense, He is given to make us witnesses for Christ, to share His love with others.

GROWTH IN SURRENDER

But grow in grace, and in the knowledge of our Lord and Saviour Jesus Christ. 2 Peter 3:18.

The first phase of the Holy Spirit's work in this world is to convict the sinner. The second phase is to convert the sinner. The third work is to cleanse the Christian, and the fourth work is to commission for service.

It is during the cleansing work of the Holy Spirit that the fruits of the Spirit are developed and manifest in the life. It is not the *gifts* of the Spirit that change our lives—their purpose is to make us useful in God's service. Our lives must be cleansed *before* we are totally empowered for service.

When a person is converted he has come to the place of giving up on himself and depending totally on Christ. If he were to stay in this stance the rest of his days and depend totally on Christ all the time and never on himself, he would not fall or fail. So long as we rely upon God's power we do not fall; the devil has no power over us. But growing Christians are cruelly aware that they *do* fall and fail. This is because we do not stay in total dependence upon God's power. We depend upon Him part of the time and part of the time we go back to our old habit of depending upon self.

At the beginning of the Christian life, when a person is born again, he experiences a sample of what God has in mind for him. As he grows he learns to depend upon God's power more and more constantly. We are perfect in birth, when we are born again; and as we grow, we can be perfect in growth. When we have learned to depend upon God's power all the time and never upon our own power, we will be perfect in maturity.

The cleansing work of the Holy Spirit begins at the time of conversion, and brings growth in the constancy of surrender. Surrender is an all-or-nothing thing at any given point. We can never depend partly on God and partly on ourselves. The only way partial or incomplete surrender happens is as we depend upon God part of the time and on self part of the time. The growth in the Christian life is progressing toward a more constant dependence upon His power. This is not our work, because "no man can empty himself of self. We can only consent for Christ to accomplish the work."—*Christ's Object Lessons*, p. 159. Christ does this work through the power of the Holy Spirit as we continue our daily fellowship with Him.

THE GIFTS ARE FOR SERVICE

Now concerning spiritual gifts, brethren, I would not have you ignorant. 1 Cor. 12:1.

It is the work of the Spirit to empower for service. Here is where the supernatural manifestations of the Holy Spirit are seen. It is under this work of the Spirit that the gifts of the Spirit are given. Here is where we see such things as prophecy and tongues and healings and miracles. The supernatural manifestations are always given for service.

No one gets the gifts of the Spirit, and empowering for service, without having first received the fruits of the Spirit through the cleansing work of the Holy Spirit. In the genuine working of the Holy Spirit, the fruits of the Spirit come before the gifts. This tells us that we cannot expect a drunk coming out of the gutter and wandering into a gospel meeting somewhere to suddenly get the gifts of the Spirit, just because someone places hands on his head. You can't expect that.

There was a man in Phoenix who was having a terrible time. He beat his wife, and yelled at his kids, and broke the furniture, and got drunk. One night, as a completely discouraged man, a backslider, he was considering suicide. He passed a tent, but went back in to the meeting. Someone put his hands on him, and he "got the Holy Spirit." He began "talking in tongues" right there. What would you make of that?

Not only did he talk in tongues but following this experience he quit beating his wife, and breaking furniture, and all the rest of it. It appeared that victory came to him through the gifts of the Holy Spirit.

If you will study the subject of the gifts of the Holy Spirit, you will discover that they are never given to change a person's life. They are not to make us holy, they are not to make us happy. They are to make us *useful*. Any other use and purpose for the gifts of the Holy Spirit is a deception. It is the *fruit* of the Spirit that brings transformation of life. And not until that has happened are the gifts of the Spirit given. You can never find the miraculous manifestations of the Spirit given anywhere in the Bible for the purpose of transformation or cleansing. They are always for service and witness. If you have this sequence clearly in mind, you have tools with which to face the spectacular manifestations of today without being deceived.

330

THE HOLY SPIRIT IS A PERSON

It is expedient for you that I go away: for if I go not away, the Comforter will not come unto you; but if I depart, I will send him unto you. John 16:7.

Have you ever felt like an "it"? I've heard people say that. "I don't feel like a person, I feel like an it." A thing. And yet, how much of the time we call the Holy Spirit an It. Regardless of our theology, whether we believe that the Holy Spirit is a person or not, we keep calling Him an It! Maybe it's all right in a sense, but we ought to realize more often, even in our designation of Him, that the Holy Spirit is a person. And we ought to think of the Holy Spirit as a person all the time experientially. The Holy Spirit *is* a person.

There are some who think of the Holy Spirit as simply the spirit of God or of Christ and not really the third person of the Godhead. He is considered to be primarily an influence, and not a real person, not a separate entity. But the Bible teaches that the Holy Spirit is a separate personality. Luke 3:21, 22 is one text on the subject; it tells of the Holy Spirit descending on Jesus in a bodily shape. Matthew 28:19 lists the Holy Spirit as a separate person. John 14:16 records Jesus' request that the Father give another Comforter besides Himself. John 16:7 says that the Spirit could not come until Jesus went away. And Acts 2:33 calls the Holy Ghost the "promise" that we receive of the Father.

John 14:26 tells that the Spirit's work is to bring to our remembrance the teachings of Jesus. John 15:26 says that the Holy Spirit testifies of Jesus. Romans 8:9 describes the Spirit's indwelling. Acts 16:7 tells of the Spirit's guidance. John 16:13 says that the Spirit guides us to truth. And John 16:14 says that the Spirit glorifies Jesus.

If you will study these references and others like them, you will discover that there are indicated three distinct persons of the Godhead. You will see that the Holy Spirit is a separate person, that He is one with the Father and with Jesus, and that He is given a special work on this earth of bringing us to God and working in our lives. We can be thankful today for the Person who is the Holy Spirit, who loves us and seeks to bring us to salvation.

For as many as are led by the Spirit of God, they are the sons of God. Rom. 8:14.

Which is more important—to try to get more of the power of the Holy Spirit or to try to let the Holy Spirit get more of us? In heathen religions, getting power is apparently the goal. A witch doctor is the one who has obtained most of the power of the heathen gods, and in that way he has more power over the other people in his village. But God does not operate in that way. The secret of the greatest power with God is to allow Him to have the greatest power with us. The more fully we are under His absolute sway, the more constantly we depend upon Him, the more He is able to work in our lives.

This is the unique Christian approach to religion. Christianity is not for the purpose of getting power over others, as the heathen do. To allow the Holy Spirit to gain control of us and have power over us is to come to the point of subordination and surrender. This brings humility. If you can think of the Holy Spirit, with all His might and all His love and all His mercy, as one of the great members of the Godhead, condescending to come and dwell in us, that in itself is a humbling thought and might keep us from the dangers of becoming drunk with power.

Satan always uses the power that he has to force those under his control to do his biddings. There is no freedom in being controlled by the power of the devil. His primary purpose is to keep all people under his control and in bondage forever. One of the hallmarks of false religions is their lack of freedom of conscience. At Satan's directions, the most cruel persecutions have come as a result of trying to force the minds of others to conform. But the Holy Spirit's control is never of this variety. The Holy Spirit, as an integral part of the Godhead, shares the respect that all of the Godhead have for man's power of choice. Man is free at any time to choose to leave the Spirit's control, and it is only as man continues to choose that control that the power of the Holy Spirit is manifested in his life.

God is not interested in a forced loyalty or obedience. God knows that love cannot ever be forced, but is only awakened by love. It is as we respond to the love of the Holy Spirit, as He seeks to draw us, that we know the peace and freedom that come from being controlled by God.

332

YOUR FRIEND, THE HOLY SPIRIT

But when the Comforter is come, whom I will send unto you from the Father, even the Spirit of truth, which proceedeth from the Father, he shall testify of me. John 15:26.

When we say that the Holy Spirit is a person, we are not speaking of a physical body such as we know. We are speaking of knowledge, feelings, and emotions, and will—the power of choice. It is not necessary to personality to have hands and feet. There are people who have personality who have no hands and feet. But the elements of knowledge, emotion, and power of choice are essential to personality.

In 1 Corinthians 2:11 it speaks of the Spirit: "For what man knoweth the things of a man, save the spirit of man which is in him? even so the things of God knoweth no man, but the Spirit of God." The Spirit of God *knows*. Here you have evidence that the Spirit of God possesses knowledge, one of the ingredients of personality. In 1 Corinthians 12:11 we have evidence that the Holy Spirit has the power of choice and therefore is an intelligent being, something more than simply an influence. He divides the spiritual gifts to different people "severally as he wills." As *He* wills! It takes an intelligent being to have the power of choice.

One of the reasons that we can be sure that the Holy Spirit is a person is because only a person can be treated with rebellion. You can vex and grieve only a person who has personality and a mind. The Holy Spirit is a person, for it is possible to wound Him, grieve Him, and refuse His love (Eph. 4:30).

In Romans 15:30 we read, "I beseech you, brethren, for the Lord Jesus Christ's sake, and for the love of the Spirit, that ye strive together with me in your prayers to God for me." Whenever you think of the Holy Spirit, do you usually think of Someone who is a loving person? Or do you think of a Being lurking somewhere in the shadows, not too close, checking up on you? Do you think of the Holy Spirit as one who is easily hurt, sensitive? Do you think of Him as impatient, easily grieved? Or do you have the picture of a loving person when you think of the Holy Spirit? He is one who stays with you and does not easily give up. God is love. The Holy Spirit is love. He stays by your side, seeking to bring comfort. He is your Friend.

WHOSOEVER WILL, MAY COME

And grieve not the holy Spirit of God, whereby ye are sealed unto the day of redemption. Eph. 4:30.

Have you ever had the idea that the Holy Spirit is easily hurt? At first glance, this text could give that impression. But it is a mistaken impression. The Holy Spirit is *not* easily hurt—in fact, I don't believe that the Holy Spirit ever gives up. I don't believe the Holy Spirit leaves us. It is possible for us to leave the Holy Spirit, and it is possible for the Holy Spirit to accept our leaving Him, because of the respect He has for our power of choice. But the Holy Spirit simply does not come to some point where He says, "I'm giving up now—it's no use." Not at all. One of the greatest attributes of the Holy Spirit was demonstrated by the children of Israel. Think of their lives of rebellion and apostasy, of their ups and downs. Yet for hundreds of years, God through the Holy Spirit kept working with them, never giving up.

Has the Holy Spirit given up on the individual within the nation of Israel, even today? No—He still hasn't. We have evidence that right up to the close of time, the Holy Spirit does not give up, in spite of everything. One of the greatest traits of the Holy Spirit is the way He stays with a person, not being pushy—but being persistent. Some of you have had evidence of this in your own life.

When a person comes along who is absolutely certain that he has committed the unpardonable sin, it is not so. The fact that one is still concerned and seeking after God is an evidence that God is still seeking after him by the power of the Holy Spirit. The unpardonable sin is a very difficult sin to commit.

The invitation by Jesus that whoever comes to Him He will in no wise cast out has no date on it. Anyone, no matter how far he has gone, if he will come to Jesus and respond to the drawing love of the Holy Spirit today, will be freely accepted and forgiven. God does not give up on man easily. The only way it happens is when man finally gives up on God, and refuses to be drawn to change that decision. But the love and patience of God, and of Jesus, and of the Holy Spirit, continue to this very day. If you come to Him today, you will be accepted.

COMFORTED BY THE HOLY SPIRIT

Likewise the Spirit also helpeth our infirmities: for we know not what we should pray for as we ought: but the Spirit itself maketh intercession for us with groanings which cannot be uttered. Rom. 8:26.

The Holy Spirit prays for us. The third mighty person of the Godhead is involved in intercession on our behalf. He is on our side. He's for us. He's our Friend. Jesus also is our Intercessor. Hebrews 7:25: "Wherefore he is able also to save them to the uttermost that come unto God by him, seeing he ever liveth to make intercession for them." With Jesus and the Holy Spirit both praying for you and interceding for you, how can you miss? There must be a great deal of stubbornness in the human heart that would cause anyone to be lost with this kind of force on our side.

God has not made it easy for anyone to be lost. He wants each one of us to come to Him and have life eternal. He has made every provision for every need that we have. And the only reason a person is lost someday is because he is just plain stubborn, and holds out in his stubbornness. It is his own resistance. Let's not forget that the only thing necessary for salvation is for us *not* to resist the mighty forces of heaven. If we do not resist, we will be drawn to Christ. I don't want to resist Him today, do you?

God invites us to become His sons and daughters, to accept Him as our Father. Jesus and the Holy Spirit are united with Him in seeking to draw us to the place of accepting that relationship with Him. They are united in the work of presenting every enticement to convince us of their love.

The Holy Spirit is called a Comforter. Have you ever needed comfort? Did you ever fall down when you were small and scrape your knee, and Mother was there to bring comfort? Have you ever known sorrow as you grew older, and had parent or brother or sister or friend to comfort you and bring help, to be there with you? The Holy Spirit is by our side today to bring comfort, to bring help, to bring us to Jesus. In the daily life, in the battles with the enemy, in times of discouragement, He is always there to bring comfort. When you've ended up bruised and bleeding, and afraid that God couldn't forgive you, the Holy Spirit is there. He is by your side today.

THE HOLY SPIRIT IS OUR GUIDE | NOV 25

He shall glorify me: for he shall receive of mine, and shall shew it unto you. John 16:14.

The Holy Spirit is given to lead us to Jesus. His work is to glorify Christ. When we become preoccupied with the Holy Spirit and are more interested in the manifestations of the Spirit than we are in Jesus, we have gone beyond what even the Spirit Himself would be comfortable with. That is because the Spirit bears witness to, and testifies of, Jesus. Whenever you hear someone talking primarily about the Holy Spirit and His supernatural works, and very little about Jesus, you can immediately suspect, on the basis of God's Word, that it's the wrong spirit working through him. If it is the wrong spirit, such as an evil spirit in spiritualism, you can be sure that that spirit does not like to hear Jesus uplifted. It is the false manifestation of the Spirit that calls attention primarily to the Spirit instead of to Jesus Christ. The Holy Spirit "shall not speak of himself" (John 16:13; we can look at this text in two ways).

The Holy Spirit also guides us into truth. "When he, the Spirit of truth, is come, he will guide you into all truth" (verse 13). We don't have to depend upon our own feeble human understanding in any situation. The Holy Spirit is willing and ready to bring us divine guidance, to direct our thoughts, to indite our prayers, to show us more of Jesus and His will for us. "It is not in man that walketh to direct his steps" (Jer. 10:23). We don't have the wisdom to choose rightly, apart from the direction of the Spirit. But the Holy Spirit leads us to understand the will of God for us, as we depend on Him for guidance.

The Holy Spirit wants to be our guide, not only in living the Christian life but in witnessing as well. He can give us the sensitivity that Jesus had of when to speak and what to say to each person within His sphere of influence. We do not have to rely upon our own power but can trust the Holy Spirit to bring us His power to know how to "speak a word in season to him that is weary" (Isa. 50:4).

The most outstanding thing about the way Jesus witnesses was that He depended upon power from above Him in knowing how to reach out to others. He did not depend upon His inherent wisdom as God, but gave us an example of being led and guided by the Spirit to reach hearts.

GOD JUSTIFIES PUBLICANS

And he spake this parable unto certain which trusted in themselves that they were righteous, and despised others. Luke 18:9.

Two men went up into the temple to pray; the one a Pharisee, and the other a publican. The Pharisee stood and prayed thus *with himself,* God, I thank thee, that I am not as other men are, extortioners, unjust, adulterers, or even as this publican. I fast twice in the week [the Pharisee was probably slim and trim], I give tithes of all that I possess [the church that he attended was probably financially secure]. And the publican, standing afar off, would not lift up so much as his eyes unto heaven, but smote upon his breast, saying, God be merciful to me a sinner. I tell you, this man went down to his house justified rather than the other: for every one that exalteth himself shall be abased; and he that humbleth himself shall be exalted" (Luke 18:10-14).

We notice first of all that this parable was spoken for certain persons who trusted in themselves. The initial thrust of this parable is for the Pharisee. Notice that both men went to the Temple to worship, but only one worshiped God, because you can't worship God and self at the same time. They both went there to pray, but only one prayed to God. The Pharisee prayed to himself.

The Pharisee reminds us by contrast of what Jesus said in Matthew 9:13, "I am not come to call the righteous, but *sinners* to repentance." And He said in Matthew 5:20 that unless your righteousness exceeds the righteousness of the Pharisees, there's no hope. The problem with the Pharisee is that he had the idea he could save himself. Anyone who thinks he can save himself is becoming his own God. The hardest hitting warnings in all of Scripture are against that. Trying to take the place of God is called *blasphemy* by Jesus (John 10:33). And blasphemy doesn't get very good marks.

It is possible to be a Pharisee today. It is possible today to be guilty of the sin of blasphemy. There is nothing in our tithepaying, or our fasting, or any of our good works, to commend us to God. Each one of us must recognize anew each day that we are sinners, in need of God's mercy. As we bow in humility with the publican, we too will receive of God's justifying grace, and have peace with God.

SALVATION IS A GIFT

But when thou makest a feast, call the poor, the maimed, the lame, the blind: and thou shalt be blessed; for they cannot recompense thee: for thou shalt be recompensed at the resurrection of the just. Luke 14:13, 14.

We are reminded in the story of the Pharisee and the publican that salvation is a gift. It isn't something that we can secure by our fasting or by our tithing, or by any good work that we might do that we think would make us righteous. Salvation is a gift.

Jesus came one day to the Temple with His disciples. He saw the money-changers, and the buyers and the sellers, and He drove them out, saying, "Make not My Father's house a house of merchandise." There's something deeper here than just the doves and the pigeons and the lambs. God's house is not a marketplace. Salvation is not to be bought and sold. It is a gift, freely given to all who will accept. Jesus indicated in our text for today that the ones who can't pay are invited to the gospel feast. He calls the poor, the maimed, the lame, and the blind—those who cannot repay Him for His kindness—to come to His table. And He invites us to relate to other people in the same way that He deals with us.

The publican prayed, "God be merciful to me a sinner." Do you have to be bad in order to make this kind of confession? Do you have to be scooped out of the gutter? Do you have to be a criminal? Paul wasn't. He was a Pharisee of the Pharisees. He lived a blameless life, so far as outward actions were concerned. But one day he had seen so much of the love and righteousness of Jesus that he was willing to say, I am the chief of sinners.

But it's more than just a matter of saying the right words. It is only through the power of the Holy Spirit that conviction can be brought so that we *mean* the words we say. The Holy Spirit brings conviction as we look to Jesus and learn of Him and His love for us. If I want to be sure to stand in the publican's shoes today and experience true repentance, what do I do? I go and study about Jesus, and what He has already done for me; and it will break my heart. I will realize that I am one of those who cannot repay Him, and yet was invited to His table. When this happens, we accept the sacrifice provided for us, and we, too, will be justified.

ACCEPTANCE FULL AND FREE

Anyone who gives heed to what I say and puts his trust in him who sent me has hold of eternal life, and does not come up for judgment, but has already passed from death to life. John 5:24, NEB.

The key word in the theme of justification *by faith* is the word *acceptance.* When you study what Jesus had to say about justification, and as you see how He treated people, you can't miss this conclusion. We are always accepted just as we are. We don't change ourselves in order to come to Him. Jesus loves to accept us just as we are. This is true not only for the beginning of the Christian life but for every day as well.

Luke 15:2 says, "This man receiveth sinners." In John 6:37 Jesus said, "Him that cometh to me I will in no wise cast out. John 3:17, "God sent not his Son into the world to condemn the world; but that the world through him might be saved." Jesus said to the woman dragged to Him, "Neither do I condemn thee" (John 8:11). Jesus said, "I came not to judge the world, but to save the world" (John 12:47). And in our text for today, Jesus said that those who trust in Him don't come up for judgment.

Isn't it good news, my friend, to know that we don't have to face the judgment? This acceptance is full and free, and it is based on what Jesus has already done for us. It's good for every day. It causes the poor publican who can't even get into the back row or lift his eyes up to heaven to be able to go to his house on the other side of town, holding his head high. He realizes that he is worth everything to God. He is accepted, he is forgiven, he is justified.

Jesus said that forgiveness is unending for anyone who comes, and who keeps coming, to Him. Will this lead to license? No, because the more you are forgiven, the more you love. And the more you love, the more you obey. God's forgiveness, when rightly understood, does not lead us to play loose with God's grace, but leads to love. And love leads to obedience. It's just that simple.

Once again I'd like to remind you of the friendly arms that still open to receive us when we come. Jesus said in Luke 23:34: "Father, forgive them; for they know not what they do." That forgiveness, that acceptance, is available to you today, as you come to Him.

PEACE WITH GOD

These things I have spoken unto you, that in me ye might have peace. In the world ye shall have tribulation: but be of good cheer; I have overcome the world. John 16:33.

God's kind of forgiveness is far more than the simple forgiveness that we know. When you forgive me, you can still have memories of my horse running through your petunias! But when God forgives me, I stand before Him as though I had never even sinned! *Steps to Christ,* page 62, shares the promise "He died for us, and now He offers to take our sins and give us His righteousness. If you give yourself to Him, and accept Him as your Saviour, then sinful as your life may have been, for His sake you are accounted righteous. Christ's character stands in place of your character, and you are accepted before God just as if you had not sinned."

Jesus said to His disciples in the upper room, before Peter denied Him and before they all forsook Him and fled, "Now ye are clean" (John 15:3). Ye *are* clean. Did that mean that they would never fall again? No, but at that moment they stood before God as though they had never sinned. They were clean through what Jesus had done and was doing for them. We can have this peace with God today. Jesus said, "In me ye might have peace" (John 16:33). "If the Son therefore shall make you free, ye shall be free indeed" (John 8:36). Peace with God? No question about it.

This seems to many of us a truth almost too good to be accepted. But it's still the truth, whether we accept it or not. Is there someone who says, "It sounds good, but it's not for me; I've gone too far"? Then notice these encouraging words: "Put away the suspicion that God's promises are not meant for you. They are for every repentant transgressor. Strength and grace have been provided through Christ to be brought by ministering angels to every believing soul. None are so sinful that they cannot find strength, purity, and righteousness in Jesus, who died for them. He is waiting to strip them of their garments stained and polluted with sin, and to put upon them the white robes of righteousness; He bids them live and not die."—*Ibid.,* pp. 52, 53. This peace and acceptance and forgiveness by Jesus is yours today, if you accept it.

WE PREACH CHRIST CRUCIFIED

And being found in fashion as a man, he humbled himself, and became obedient unto death, even the death of the cross. Phil. 2:8.

Have you ever felt that you were becoming calloused to the cross? Have you ever felt that you have heard so much about it, and seen so many pictures, that it no longer moves you? 1 Corinthians 1, beginning with verse 18, says, "For the preaching of the cross is to them that perish foolishness; but unto us which are saved it is the power of God. For it is written, I will destroy the wisdom of the wise, and bring to nothing the understanding of the prudent. Where is the wise? where is the scribe? where is the disputer of this world? hath not God made foolish the wisdom of this world? For after that in the wisdom of God the world by wisdom knew not God, it pleased God by the foolishness of preaching to save them that believe. For the Jews require a sign, and the Greeks seek after wisdom: but we preach Christ crucified, unto the Jews a stumblingblock, and unto the Greeks foolishness; but unto them which are called, both Jews and Greeks, Christ the power of God, and the wisdom of God."

One of the apparent handicaps of the early church was that they had to present a God that had been crucified. This was unheard of in the history of gods. And when the Christians came along and preached Christ crucified, it seemed to do away with their whole message.

In the days of the early church, people knew what crucifixion meant. Some people today have reacted against spending time dwelling on the cross; they feel that we should not focus so much on all the blood and gore. But we need to recognize that there was blood, and there was pain, and there was hurt. It would be a tragedy if we forgot the reality of the cross. Perhaps we should be reminded of the stark facts of crucifixion, and what was involved in the death that Jesus died for us, since in our culture today it is no longer a familiar sight.

Jesus, with His divine nature, suffered every pain and every insult, to as much greater a degree as His nature is greater than ours. When we come to understand a little more of the extent of His sacrifice for us, we understand better how much He loves us, that He would be willing to give His life for our salvation.

341

EVEN THE DEATH OF THE CROSS

He humbled himself, and became obedient unto death, even the death of the cross. Phil. 2:8.

Today's text is the same as yesterday's, but we are not finished with it yet. In the days of Christ, crucifixion was used by the Romans as a deterrent from crime. Criminals were crucified in a most public place, where many people would see them. There was no cloth draped gracefully around their bodies, as the artist pictures.

There is evidence that, in some cases at least, the spike was driven through both heels, just in front of the Achilles' tendon. It was driven into the cross with such force that in some cases archeologists have discovered buried in the casket, with the body, large hunks of wood that came loose when the bodies were torn from the cross.

After the soldiers had nailed the victims securely sideways through the heels, they twisted them around, and nailed their arms tightly through the wrists. You will discover that if you try standing against the wall in that twisted position for just a little while, your muscles begin retching. And as though that weren't enough, some sadist would then drive a spike through the private parts of the individual as well.

Then they would drop the cross into the hole prepared, and the teeming throng of people would walk by and stare. Can you picture Jesus hanging there? Jesus, the One who had created the people who crucified Him?

But something else is even heavier. We are told that so great was the anguish that Jesus went through because of the burden and weight of the sins of the world, that the physical pain was hardly felt. The sense of separation from His Father's presence was more than He could bear, and it broke His heart.

As we look upon the cross of Christ, and get a glimpse of the price paid for our salvation, we "begin to comprehend something of the righteousness of Christ, and exclaim, 'What is sin, that it should require such a sacrifice for the redemption of its victim?' . . . A knowledge of the plan of salvation will lead him [the sinner] to the foot of the cross in repentance for his sins, which have caused the sufferings of God's dear Son."—*Steps to Christ*, p. 27.

342

CHRIST DIED FOR OUR SINS

For I delivered unto you first of all that which I also received, how that Christ died for our sins according to the scriptures. 1 Cor. 15:3.

It is good news today that Christ died for our sins according to the Scriptures. When we grapple with the subject of the atonement, we are into something that is over our heads. We are thinking about a topic that is bigger than we are. It is one that we will be trying to understand throughout eternity.

The cross was real, and it was bad, and it hurt, from all human perspective. Yet the pain of the cross was hardly felt by Jesus, because of the greater issues involved. What was it that broke Jesus' heart, and why did He die? "'But he [Jesus] endured the suffering that should have been ours, the pain that we should have borne. All the while we thought that his suffering was punishment sent by God. But because of our sins he was wounded, beaten because of the evil we did. We are healed by the punishment he suffered, made whole by the blows he received'" (Isa. 53:4, 5, TEV).

The concept that Christ died for *our* sins, that He was our substitute, is a concept found all through Scripture, in spite of the fact that there are those who would minimize that truth. Christ died for *our* transgressions, and was wounded for *our* sins. As substitute and surety for sinful man, Christ suffered under divine justice. It was because of the burden of His being our substitute that His physical pain was hardly felt (*The Desire of Ages,* p. 753).

In the attempt to present a loving God who is not angry and has to be appeased by blood, some say that the cross was not necessary but incidental, that Jesus merely came to show how much God loved us, that God is good and kind, and not that concerned with justice.

We need to remember that God is a God of justice, and since Jesus is God, He also is a God of justice. Any government will stand only as long as it has laws. No government is stronger than its laws, and no law is stronger than the enforcement of its penalty. God is the originator of justice. It is because the law could not be set aside, and penalty had to be enforced, that Jesus came to die for us. He showed the other side of God's character—His mercy and love that would pay the penalty for us, so that we might live.

JESUS, OUR SUBSTITUTE

What then? shall we sin, because we are not under the law, but under grace? God forbid. Rom. 6:15.

One day when I was a pastor in Oregon I was detained at an appointment, which put me behind schedule for a funeral service. I was going through a back road, spraying gravel and dust all over, trying to get to the place of the funeral on time, when a second cloud of dust arose behind me. It turned out to be the cloud of a law-enforcement officer who was trying to catch me. When he finally stopped me he was angry. He said, "Who are you, anyway? I thought I was following a stolen car!"

I told him who I was and where I was going. He suddenly calmed down and said, "I don't know what to do with you. If I give you a citation, it will come out in the newspaper tomorrow, and your parishioners will know all about it. Besides, I don't think a citation is the answer, anyway."

And I said, "No, I don't either!"

After he had shifted from foot to foot for a little while, he said, "I'm going to let you go. Go on. You're on your own."

I thought as I started down the road that this was the greatest motivation I'd ever had to obey the law. But the reason I was motivated to obey the law was because of the other times when I didn't get that kind of treatment. I knew what justice was, and that's why mercy meant something to me.

The illustration is very feeble. If we were going to make it more like the atonement, the officer would not simply have permitted me to go free. God Himself doesn't do that. God has never been able to forgive sin. He forgives *sinners.* The reason we know He cannot forgive sin is because Jesus died. So the officer, to fit the analogy rightly, should have pulled out his wallet and handed me the money for the fine. Or he would have gone to court *for* me. That's what Jesus has done for us—He has paid the penalty in our behalf.

It is because God is a God of love that He is a God of justice. But because of His love, He is also a God of mercy. Satan didn't understand that. When he caused human beings to sin, he exulted. He thought that this would prove that God's law could not be kept, and that if a loophole were found for humanity, he would be able to get back into heaven again himself. But Jesus came as our Substitute, to make a way of escape for us. Thus God's justice and mercy could both be revealed.

344

GOD SUFFERED TOO

God was in Christ, reconciling the world unto himself. 2 Cor. 5:19.

Both Jesus and the Father were involved in the atonement together. God suffered when Jesus suffered. God was there at the cross, even though Jesus was unable to sense His presence. That's why Paul says that "God was in Christ, reconciling the world unto himself." God could not change His law, but He sacrificed Himself in Christ.

Have you ever wondered why, if God loved the world so much, He didn't come Himself? Why did He send His Son? If you are a parent, you probably don't need to ask that question. The father suffers more when he sees his son suffer. Haven't you ever been by the bedside of a loved one, someone who was suffering pain, and wished before God that you could trade places with the patient? It is much harder to watch. God died too, in a sense. Away with the pagan idea that God was angry and that Jesus was appeasing Him. They both suffered together.

Jesus took our place. His death was not incidental. It wasn't just another martyrdom. Jesus suffered the horror of the second death in your place and in my place. This is what broke His heart and made the physical pain hardly felt. I am thankful that He was wounded for our transgressions, bruised for our iniquity, aren't you? I'm thankful that He is a God of justice, because it means that we can have security forever. And I'm thankful that He is a God of love, and that His justice did not destroy His mercy.

The sacrifice of Jesus is full and complete. There is pardon for every person who will respond to His invitation and come to Him for rest. It is not enough to come once, but we must come again today, and every day, and fall at His feet in repentance and humility, accepting anew of His death in our place. As we do this, and continue to do this, we are assured of life eternal, because He paid the penalty for the wages of sin *for* us. He died so we don't have to die. Because He lives, we can live forever, if we will only accept His merits on our behalf. No work of man can add to the fullness of the salvation provided. As we see His loving acceptance, our hearts will respond in love to Him, and He will work in us to accomplish all that He has in mind for us—our complete recovery from the penalty, the power, and the presence of sin.

JUSTIFICATION BY FAITH

Therefore being justified by faith, we have peace with God through our Lord Jesus Christ. Rom. 5:1.

Because of Jesus' death on the cross, He can offer life and forgiveness to each one of us. But I would like to remind you that justification is no good unless it is accepted. Although Jesus' sacrifice was complete and sufficient, so that the sins of the whole world could have been erased, the whole world will not be saved. The atonement of Christ does no good to anyone unless they accept it personally. And the atonement must be accepted daily, through the ongoing relationship with Christ. It is more than a matter of a one-time nodding of the head toward Heaven. We must come to Jesus every day and accept anew of His death in our behalf.

When you give someone a gift, in order for that person to profit from that gift he or she must receive it. A gift is no good unless it *is* received. As beautiful as the doctrine and truth of justification is, as wonderful as what God has done for us may be, and as much as the sacrifice of the cross stands out in all of history, these things do not benefit anybody until they are received.

But there is far more than just the matter of our own salvation involved in our relationship with Him. God created man for fellowship with Him in the first place. Because of Adam's sin, the race has been separated from God. The death of Christ brings us back to oneness with Him, where it all started. The broken relationship is restored at justification.

Justification is mankind being put right with God through what Jesus has done. It is a provision in heaven for the redemption of the whole human race. It has as its foundation the spotless righteousness of Jesus. But justification will not benefit any sinner until it is accepted by that sinner. The Bible does not teach that justification is by grace alone. It is always by grace through faith. Faith is essential on the part of the sinner. Faith, or trust, immediately involves two parties, one trusting the other. When we trust in Jesus for salvation, there comes into existence a saving relationship. This is more than a legal declaration in heaven. This is the beginning of a friendship and fellowship with God. It is only through this relationship with God that the Christian life can begin or continue. "This is life eternal, that they might know thee" (John 17:3).

COMING . . . AND STAYING

Afterward came also the other virgins, saying, Lord, Lord, open to us. But he answered and said, Verily I say unto you, I know you not. Matt. 25:11, 12.

There is a big difference between "only believe" and the genuine faith relationship with God. The nominal Christian world has for years held onto "only believe" as its brand of faith. But intellectual assent has never been sufficient for salvation. The person who has a vital relationship with God, from which genuine faith springs, is the only one who can really accept of Christ's sacrifice on a continuing basis.

Insofar as our reception of eternal life is concerned, the relationship of knowing God, of loving Him, of trusting in Him, is the entire basis of the Christian life. Eternal life is based upon Jesus and what He has done, but there is a part we have to play. We must accept and receive it, or we never benefit from it personally.

When we first accept of His grace, at justification, the relationship with Christ begins. As we continue to accept of His grace on a daily basis, the relationship continues. It's like a marriage. Which is more important, getting married, or staying married? In the end you'll have to admit that this is a nonsensical question! You can't stay married if you have never gotten married in the first place, and getting married is worth nothing unless you stay married. They are both important; they are both necessary. Coming to Jesus is important. Staying with Jesus is important. Both are equally vital.

Jesus told about a wedding party in Matthew 25. When it got down to the nitty-gritty, and the five foolish virgins were asking admission to the wedding, the Lord answered them, I know you not. It's said again in Matthew 7:23, "Then will I profess unto them, I never knew you: depart from me, ye that work iniquity." The ones to whom these words were addressed had done a lot of working. They had said, Lord, Lord. They knew how to mouth the name of Jesus. They had cast out devils and been involved in many wonderful works. But they didn't know Him. Do you know Him today? Have you accepted again today of His sacrifice? Have you spent time in communion with Him?

JESUS KEEPS WALKING WITH US

And they went to another village. Luke 9:56.

Relationship with God is not based on your behavior. Relationship is based on your communion with Him. Anyone who thinks that their relationship is based on their behavior will give up their relationship sooner or later. Anyone who gives up their relationship because of their behavior is a legalist.

There is a difference between getting discouraged over your behavior and being disappointed in your behavior. I am disappointed in my behavior many times, but I am not discouraged with the relationship! Why? Because Jesus had a nice way about Him of going right ahead with disciples who fell and sinned again and again. Read it in Luke 9:55, 56. They wanted to call fire down and burn up the miserable Samaritans. Jesus rebuked them, and He may rebuke you and me, too. But He kept walking with them. They went on to another village—together.

If it weren't for this realization of God's continuing walk with us, many of us would have given up long ago. "The one thing essential for us in order that we may receive and impart the forgiving love of God is to know the love that He has to us. Satan is working by every deception he can command, in order that we may not discern that love. He will lead us to think that our mistakes and transgressions have been so grievous that the Lord will not have respect unto our prayers and will not bless and save us. In ourselves we can see nothing to recommend us to God, and Satan tells us that it is of no use; we cannot remedy our defects of character. When we try to come to God, the enemy will whisper, It is of no use for you to pray; did not you do that evil thing? Have you not sinned against God and violated your own conscience? But we may tell the enemy that 'the blood of Jesus Christ his Son cleanseth us from all sin.' When we feel that we have sinned and cannot pray, it is then the time to pray. Ashamed we may be and deeply humbled, but we must pray and believe."—*Thoughts From the Mount of Blessing,* p. 115.

Take courage today, for Jesus continues to walk with you as you continue to seek fellowship with Him day by day. When we remain in fellowship and communion with Him, He is enabled to do His work of grace in our lives. Sooner or later, His power will be seen greater than our failures, and He will complete the work that He has started.

THE GOD WHO IS MAN

And the Word was made flesh, and dwelt among us, (and we beheld his glory, the glory as of the only begotten of the Father,) full of grace and truth. John 1:14.

When we talk about Jesus and who He was, it becomes very fascinating to discover what He said about the subject Himself, as recorded in the four Gospels and the Spirit of Prophecy commentaries on the four Gospels. Among those who like to talk theology, the subject of the nature of Christ is one of the most divisive and difficult of all. Sometimes we have wasted endless hours on it, and whole churches have been split over it. So it is intriguing to find what Jesus had to say about it Himself.

Almost all evangelical, fundamental, Bible-believing Christians believe that Jesus was God. We probably don't have to spend much time trying to prove that point. But let's notice a few of the major texts concerning it. "The Word was with God, and the Word was God" (John 1:1). God Himself spoke at the baptism of Jesus, saying, "This is my beloved Son" (Matt. 3:17). Even the devil knew who Jesus was, because he came to Jesus in the wilderness of temptation and tried to tempt Jesus to turn stones into bread. If he didn't know that Jesus was God, he wouldn't have wasted his time on such a temptation. None of us has ever been tempted with that one! And on more than one occasion, the devil or some of his cohorts said, "We know who You are, the Holy One of God." We are told that Jesus knew that He came from God, and that He was God (John 13:3).

So Jesus was God. He continued to be God when He became man. And He continues to be God, at the right hand of the Father today.

But Jesus was also man. He was human. "The Word was made flesh, and dwelt among us" (John 1:14). As a man, He exhibited certain traits that human beings are known for. He got tired (John 4:6). He went to sleep in the bottom of a boat (Mark 4:38). He got hungry and thirsty (John 4:7, 8). He was thirsty on the cross (John 19:28). He found out, as a man, what it is like to experience the needs that we experience.

Because He was man, He is touched with the feelings of our infirmities and understands our weakness. Because He was God, He is able to save unto the uttermost all who come to God by Him.

NO ADVANTAGE OVER US

Wherefore in all things it behoved him to be made like unto his brethren, that he might be a merciful and faithful high priest in things pertaining to God, to make reconciliation for the sins of the people. Heb. 2:17.

Jesus was born God. He was also born a man. Sometimes we debate about how much of a man He was, how human He was. Was He just like us, or not? In *The Desire of Ages,* page 117, we discover three ways in which Jesus was like us. He became a man, after 4,000 years of degenerating human nature. The race had been diminishing in terms of physical strength. Jesus was shorter than Adam. He got tired, when perhaps Adam wouldn't have. The race had also been degenerating in mental power. Inherently, Jesus wasn't as smart as Adam. Apart from God, Adam would have been smarter than Jesus. It sounds almost sacrilegious to say it, but it's the truth. Jesus accepted the weakness of humanity in terms of mental power.

The third way in which Jesus was weaker than Adam was in moral strength. He didn't have the willpower and backbone to control His actions, apart from God, that Adam would have had. He wasn't inherently worth as much as Adam in grit and determination and willpower. Jesus accepted all these weaknesses that were passed on by the great law of heredity (*The Desire of Ages,* p. 49). But it made no difference so far as what we see produced in the life of Jesus, because He wasn't depending upon willpower. He wasn't depending upon His weak human nature. He was depending instead upon God's power. And that's the difference.

The law of heredity doesn't mean that sin is passed through the genes and chromosomes. In other words, just because a man is a drunkard doesn't mean that his son will have a weakness for drink. But a man who is a drunkard can pass on physical, mental, and moral weakness, and because of that, his son can be more susceptible to the problem of sin, no matter what form it takes.

Satan will never be able to charge God with giving Jesus an advantage in overcoming sin, because Jesus accepted not only human nature as Adam was created but the weakness and decay that resulted from sin. He lived life as we must live it, by depending upon the power of God to sustain Him. He had no advantage over us.

350

JESUS, THE SECOND ADAM

And he that sent me is with me: the Father hath not left me alone; for I do always those things that please him. John 8:29.

Although Jesus took human nature when He was born into this world, He was never a sinner, He never sinned. Sometimes we debate whether Jesus was like Adam before the Fall or after the Fall. That question will keep you going till midnight! But in a sense, it is the wrong question, because in some ways Jesus was like Adam before the Fall, and in some ways He was like Adam after the Fall. And that's why the question becomes so complicated. Jesus was like Adam after the Fall in terms of physical, mental, and moral strength (*The Desire of Ages,* p. 117). But Jesus was like Adam before the Fall in that He was sinless.

Jesus had all the liabilities of Adam. This means that He was able to be tempted. It means He was able to give in to temptation. It means He could have fallen and failed and sinned. Jesus had all these liabilities. But there was no sin in Him. "No trace of sin marred the image of God with Him [Jesus]. Yet He was not exempt from temptation."—*Ibid.,* p. 71.

This means that He had a spiritual nature, or a spiritual side to His nature, that carried with it no propensities to sin. The spiritual nature of Jesus had no tendencies toward sin. The spiritual aspect of Jesus' nature had no desire for sin. Can you say that about yourself? Can you say that about anyone else who was ever born into this world? No, our spiritual natures are fallen.

Then did Jesus have an advantage over us? Yes, He had an advantage over us! Luke 1:35 says He was born "that holy thing." We weren't. Jesus was never tempted to continue in sin. That's one of our biggest temptations. There are people who have struggled for years with the momentum of sin that has built up—it's a heavy temptation. Jesus never had that. Jesus hated sin. From a child, He hated sin. You cannot say that about us. These were advantages.

But in *The Desire of Ages,* page 119, you will find it stated that Jesus had no advantage over us! How can you explain that? Because Jesus never used the advantage of being born God. He lived life as we must live it, by dependence upon His Father and relationship with Him.

JESUS WAS NOT FORSAKEN

The words that I speak unto you I speak not of myself: but the Father that dwelleth in me, he doeth the works. John 14:10.

Satan represents God's law of love as a law of selfishness. He declares that it is impossible for us to obey its precepts. . . . Jesus was to unveil this deception. As one of us He was to give an example of obedience. For this He took upon Himself our nature, and passed through our experiences. . . . He endured every trial to which we are subject. And He exercised in His own behalf no power that is not freely offered to us. As man, He met temptation, and overcame in the strength given Him from God. . . . His life testifies that it is possible for us also to obey the law of God."—*The Desire of Ages,* p. 24.

How did Jesus live His life of obedience to God? Through dependence upon a power from above Him, rather than depending upon the power within Him. His weakened human strength would have been insufficient. He lived through dependence upon another power, in the same way that you and I can live. Jesus said, in John 5:30, "I can of mine own self do nothing."

Jesus' life was a life that was lived as a result of the faith relationship with His Father. He became a mighty demonstration of the fact that this is available to every one of us. Not even His miracles were performed by His divine power. They were performed by faith and prayer (*ibid.,* p. 536), by the power of God through the ministry of angels (*ibid.,* p. 143).

In coming to the close of His life and finding Him struggling in the Garden and sweating drops of blood, some of us have concluded that from then on, He had to go it alone. That although throughout His life He had been living in dependence upon His Father, from Gethsemane to the cross He had to do it alone. But Luke 22:43 says that an angel came from heaven to the Garden and strengthened Him. On the cross, when Jesus said, "My God, My God, why have You forsaken Me?" we have said, From then on, He was on His own. But God and the angels were there at the cross (*ibid.,* p. 754). Jesus didn't *feel* as though His Father was there. He *felt* forsaken. But God was there, in Christ, reconciling the world unto Himself.

JESUS, OUR EXAMPLE

For even hereunto were ye called: because Christ also suffered for us, leaving us an example, that ye should follow his steps. 1 Peter 2:21.

All through His life, including His perfect sinless behavior, including His miracles, including Gethsemane and the cross, Jesus lived through a power from above Him. It was always through the faith relationship of prayer and communion with God that Jesus experienced this power.

Not even by a thought did He yield to temptation. So it may be with us (*The Desire of Ages*, p. 123). His sinless life was given as our example (*ibid.*, p. 49). By His own obedience to the law, Christ proved that through His grace, the law could be perfectly obeyed by every son and daughter of Adam (*Thoughts From the Mount of Blessing*, p. 49). Jesus' life in you will produce the same as in Him (*ibid.*, p. 78). We are to overcome as Christ overcame (*The Desire of Ages*, p. 389). "The Saviour was deeply anxious for His disciples to understand for what purpose His divinity was united to humanity. . . . God was manifested in Him that He might be manifested in them. Jesus revealed no qualities, and exercised no powers, that man may not have through faith in Him. His perfect humanity is that which all His followers may possess, if they will be in subjection to God as He was."—*Ibid.*, p. 664.

Don't let anyone tell you that we cannot perfectly obey the law of God. There's too much evidence that this is not true. And it all comes from Jesus and the life that He lived, and the teachings that He gave concerning His own life and how He lived it.

Jesus becomes an example to us, if we consider the issue of sin in terms of relationship rather than simply behavior. The real issue is relationship with God and dependence on Him, versus choosing to try to control ourselves. Jesus was our example in living His entire life through dependence upon God.

When I study this subject, I feel as though I'm on holy ground. It is humbling to realize that Jesus came and lived like I have to live. Does this make me feel as though I'm far behind? It surely does. Does it discourage me? No, because Jesus has given too much evidence already that He loves us and will continue to help us understand how He lived His life, so that we too can overcome. We can take courage from that today.

A WAY OF ESCAPE

For we have not an high priest which cannot be touched with the feeling of our infirmities; but was in all points tempted like as we are, yet without sin. Heb. 4:15.

Even though Jesus took on Himself our infirmities, or weaknesses, He lived without sinning, doing always those things that pleased His Father. Not only did He not sin, but He was sinless. He loved righteousness and hated iniquity. He was tempted more than anyone who ever lived, but He overcame in the same way that we can overcome. It is often asked, "Didn't Jesus have an advantage over us?" Of course He did. He was born God. But He never used this advantage, because He laid down the power of divinity within Him and lived His life as a man through the power of His Father from above Him. He gave us an example of victory from above rather than from within.

Obviously then, man's beginning is different from that of Jesus. This leads some to insist that there would have to be a doctrine to explain how Jesus could be born sinless, of human parentage. But there are some things that we cannot and do not need to explain. "The incarnation of Christ has ever been, and will ever remain, a mystery. That which is revealed, is for us and for our children, but let every human being be warned from the ground of making Christ altogether human, such an one as ourselves; for it cannot be."—*The SDA Bible Commentary*, Ellen G. White Comments, on John 1:1-3, 14, p. 1129.

Another mystery that we often waste endless hours in discussing is how Jesus could be in every way tempted as we are. "It is a mystery that is left unexplained to mortals that Christ could be tempted in all points like as we are."—*Ibid.*, pp. 1128, 1129.

The two mysteries concerning the nature of Christ are (1) how He could be born sinless of human parentage, and (2) how He could be in all points tempted as we are.

On the other hand there are two things of major importance that we should remember concerning the nature of Christ. Number one, He had no advantage over us in meeting sin and the devil, and number two, He overcame sin and the devil in precisely the same way we can overcome. By His death, Jesus provided a way of escape for us, that we might not die; and by His life He gave us an example of how to live.

FOUNDATION AND WALLS

For which of you, intending to build a tower, sitteth not down first, and counteth the cost, whether he have sufficient to finish it? Luke 14:28.

Satan's original charge was that the law of God could not be obeyed. When man broke the law of God, Satan rejoiced and added another charge, that man could not be forgiven. He had no idea that God would pay the penalty Himself. But Jesus' life and death proved that sinners could be forgiven and that the law of God could be perfectly obeyed, not only by Jesus but by those who live the life of faith as He did.

This twofold message of forgiveness and obedience is the heart of the remnant mission during the time of the three angels, and the final work of Christ in heaven. Jesus as our High Priest provides forgiveness for sinners and power to obey. These two truths are equally necessary. It is extremely important that the remnant church understand this twofold work of Christ in heaven, otherwise it will be impossible for them to fulfill their mission. Justification by faith, God's work for us, and the righteousness of Christ, which includes God's work in us, are the themes to be presented to a perishing world.

It will come as a surprise to some to discover that when you study the life and teachings of Jesus, you will find that Jesus had far more to say about the work of God *in* us than He did about the work of God *for* us. The analogy of the foundation and the walls of a structure could be a good example. Justification by faith is the foundation of salvation, and sanctification by faith represents the walls to be built on that foundation. Although the walls cannot be secure if the foundation is not solid, the foundation alone is not sufficient.

In Luke 14:29 Jesus told of a man who began a structure by building a foundation, but was unable to complete the job. For years the nominal Christian world has been in that position. They have had only a foundation, and have never gone forward to complete the building. On the other hand, perhaps our problem as Seventh-day Adventists has been that we have spent much futile effort trying to build walls when we have tended to take our foundation for granted. But it takes both walls *and* foundation to make a building that will stand.

BUILDING ON THE FOUNDATION

And for their sakes I sanctify myself, that they also might be sanctified through the truth. John 17:19.

The mission of the remnant people was to build on the foundation of the Reformation. That's why we have so much information concerning sanctification. The world is still waiting to hear the twofold message of justification by faith, and sanctification by faith as well.

Some feel that the good news of sanctification is that Jesus is our substitute in living the Christian life. This is not the case. Please notice a difference here, for it is very important. Those who believe that Jesus continues to be our substitute in living, as well as in dying, believe that we can't obey—so He has obeyed *for* us. His sanctification is in our place. If this is true, then we will be sinning and falling and failing right up to glorification; but, they say, Jesus' life will substitute for our lives, and our lack of obedience will be covered by His obedience.

Sanctification by faith, on the other hand, accepts Jesus as our example. It finds Him to be our pattern in sanctification, that we might be sanctified in the same way in which He was sanctified. In sanctification by faith, we are invited to live as Jesus did, through dependence upon a power from above, and the same obedience that He experienced we can experience as well, through the faith relationship with God.

"Christ declared He sanctified Himself, that we also might be sanctified. He took upon Himself our nature, and became a faultless pattern for men. He made no mistakes that we also might become victors, and enter into His kingdom as overcomers. . . . We are to be brought into a sacred nearness with the world's Redeemer. We are to be one with Christ as He is one with the Father. What a wonderful change the people of God experience in coming into unity with the Son of God! We are to have our tastes, inclinations, ambitions, passions all subdued, and brought into harmony with the mind and Spirit of Christ. This is the very work that the Lord is willing to do for those who believe in Him. The Spirit of Christ is to have a controlling influence over the life of His followers. . . . The grace of Christ is to work a wonderful transformation in the life and character of its receiver."—*My Life Today*, p. 252.

OUR GREAT DEFENDER

Jesus answered, My kingdom is not of this world: if my kingdom were of this world, then would my servants fight. John 18:36.

What is the method of sanctification? It is by faith alone. In John 15:5 Jesus said, "Without me ye can do nothing." He's talking about producing the fruits of the Spirit and the fruits of obedience in the Christian life. If without Him we can do nothing, then it's all going to have to be done by faith in Him.

In our text for today Jesus said, "If my kingdom were of this world, then would my servants fight." Whether fighting sin and the devil, or whether fighting men who are under the control of Satan, as were the Jewish leaders, Jesus does not ask us to try to defend ourselves. Our part is to remain in relationship with Him, depending on Him for deliverance.

Some people asked Jesus what they should do that they might work the works of God. Jesus said, "This is the work of God, that ye believe on him whom he hath sent" (John 6:29). Jesus says, He that eateth Me shall live by Me. What does that mean? Verse 63, "The words that I speak unto you, they are spirit, and they are life." In Mark 14:38 He said, "Watch ye and pray, lest ye enter into temptation." Here He gives us another clue as to how to depend on Him.

The methods of sanctification are through His Word, through prayer, through watchfulness concerning relationship with Him, through dependence upon Him. In John 1:29 we read that it was said of Jesus, "Behold the Lamb of God, which taketh away the sin of the world." This verse can be seen in several ways. First, "Behold the Lamb of God, which taketh away the sin of the world" can refer to Jesus' death as the Lamb of God for the sins of the world. Second, it can refer to relationship, "*Behold* the Lamb of God." It is by beholding that we are changed. And third, it can refer to sanctification, "Behold the Lamb of God, which *taketh away* the sin of the world." In Luke 10:42 Jesus told Martha that there is only one thing needful, and that is to sit at His feet. This is accomplished through His Word and through prayer. It is through this relationship that we accept His justifying grace, and it is through this relationship that we are enabled to behold Him, which results in our lives being changed into His image.

357

YOU CAN'T EARN A GIFT

Whosoever will save his life shall lose it: and whosoever will lose his life for my sake shall find it. Matt. 16:25.

In our text for today Jesus is saying, in essence, that you cannot accept a gift and also earn it. This is one of the big, mountainous questions that face us today. Can we ever earn or merit God's grace, whether it's in the realm of justification or sanctification? The answer to both is No. We can never earn or merit or work for God's grace. It is a gift. It is always a gift.

If we try to save ourselves, we are going to end up forsaking Jesus. This is shown in Matthew 26:51-56. It's the story of Peter and the other disciples. They were sure that they would die for Jesus. They loved Jesus. They had worked and traveled with Jesus for more than three years. But they thought they could take care of themselves. Instead of spending time in the Garden watching and praying, they simply buckled their swords a little tighter and went to sleep. They thought they were prepared for any emergency. But notice the commentary in *The Desire of Ages* on the sequence of events that night. It's found on page 697: "The disciples were terrified as they saw Jesus permit Himself to be taken and bound. They were offended that He should suffer this humiliation to Himself and them. They could not understand His conduct, and they blamed Him for submitting to the mob. In their indignation and fear, Peter proposed that they save themselves. Following this suggestion, 'they all forsook him, and fled.'"

Whether I'm trying to save myself in justification, trying to earn or merit my forgiveness, or trying to save myself by overcoming and obedience and victory in sanctification, in the end I'm going to forsake Jesus. If we try to weave ourselves into the picture, in whatever area of salvation, whether justification, sanctification, or glorification, then we are trying to save ourselves, and ultimately we'll follow the example of the disciples, who forsook Him. It is blasphemy for a man to try to be God or to try to save himself, no matter in what aspect of salvation. We can be saved only through Jesus, through accepting His merits and through continuing the faith relationship with Him.

DON'T WORK ON THE FRUIT

"If you love me you will obey my commands." John 14:15, NEB.

How many of us have wasted time and effort trying to obey, when Jesus said, "If you love me you will . . ." Genuine obedience and growth and victory are natural and spontaneous in the Christian life. One premise almost everyone agrees on is that justification is the root and sanctification is the fruit. But if this is true, and we do not work on our own justification, but rather accept it as God's free gift, how much more should we accept as God's gift the *fruit* of justification? In *The Desire of Ages,* page 677, we read how Jesus told His disciples that they were not to labor to bear fruit but rather to put their labor toward abiding in Him. To believe that sanctification is the fruit of justification, and at the same time to believe that you are supposed to work hard on your obedience and victory, presents a great incongruity. You don't labor on fruit. It is the result of something else, and you never put forth effort on the result. You put your effort toward the cause of the result.

Jesus made many statements regarding fruit that are significant to this subject. One is found in Matthew 7:16-18: "Do men gather grapes of thorns, or figs of thistles? Even so every good tree bringeth forth good fruit; but a corrupt tree bringeth forth evil fruit. A good tree cannot bring forth evil fruit, neither can a corrupt tree bring forth good fruit." Notice that bearing good fruit is natural for a good tree.

In Matthew 23:26 Jesus said, in effect, If you will wash the inside of the cup, the outside *will* be clean. How many of us have wasted our time and years and effort trying to clean up the outside instead of going to the cause of the problem? If we put our attention on the cause and clean the inside, the outside will be clean. These are simple examples from the teaching of Jesus that genuine obedience is natural and spontaneous in the Christian life.

Then where is cooperation? It seems quite obvious. If obedience is the fruit of faith (*Steps to Christ*, p. 61), then our efforts and our cooperation would be toward becoming good trees, instead of toward producing good fruit. The only way we can become good trees is by coming to Christ day by day, allowing Him to do His work of grace in our lives. As we do this, the fruit will develop naturally and spontaneously.

LORD, SAVE US!

And he saith unto them, Why are ye fearful, O ye of little faith? Matt. 8:26.

The essence of Jesus' teaching was self-surrender (*The Desire of Ages*, p. 523). Until he has given up on himself, no one understands how obedience and victory can be spontaneous. Perhaps that's one of the reasons why we can have so much trouble with the question of whether obedience is natural or deliberate. The person who insists on deliberate obedience, on forcing himself to obey, is the one who hasn't surrendered himself yet. But the one who has given up on himself and realizes that he can't do it is the one who begins to experience natural and spontaneous obedience. And if self-surrender was the substance of Christ's teachings, then this places obedience by faith rather high on the priority list.

When the disciples were sinking out on the sea, they didn't say, "God, help us." They said, "Lord, *save us!*" A person who looks toward Heaven and says, "God, I need some *help*" may be admitting something about his lack of surrender. If I say to you, "I wish you'd come over and help me mow my lawn," and you, being in a friendly sort of mood, say, "Yes, I'll come over," what do you expect? Do you expect me to say, "There's the lawn, here's the mower, and I'll be out back in the hammock"? What do we mean by the word *help*? We mean we'll do it together. You'll do part, I'll do part. In fact, the word *help* usually indicates that the person to be helped does *most* of the work, and the one "helping" just adds a little extra.

When a person is going down in the water for the last time, he doesn't say, "God, help me." He says, "God, *save me!*" What does that mean? It means, "God, You're going to have to do it *all.*" Peter, when he was sinking, said, "Lord, save me."

In Matthew 13:45, 46 Jesus talked about the pearl of great price. He said that you have to sell everything you have in order to get the pearl. In Luke 14:33 He said that we can't be His disciples unless we have given up on everything—it will cost everything we have. And all through the Gospels Jesus speaks of the cross—*our* cross—which is death for us. *We* must die, we must give up on ourselves, before we can understand what sanctification and obedience and victory are all about.

BRINGING GLORY TO GOD

Let your light so shine before men, that they may see your good works, and glorify your Father which is in heaven. Matt. 5:16.

For the person who has given up on himself, there is then the privilege of accepting Christ's righteousness. There are two aspects to the righteousness of Christ—first, Christ's righteousness *for* us, and second, the righteousness of Christ *in* us. There are people who have given up and accepted Christ's righteousness for them who have not given up and accepted Christ's righteousness in them. It is possible to give up on one but not the other, and in that case you have the most subtle form of holding on to the old problem of salvation by works. Even though I believe the cross and the finished work of Christ is enough to save me, if I haven't given up on trying to change my life, trying to manufacture genuine obedience on my own steam, trying to force myself to victory, then I am still a victim of salvation by works on that level. Accepting of His righteousness on both fronts is a tremendous privilege that we cannot dodge or miss in the great theme of salvation by faith in Christ alone.

The object of the Christian life is the reproduction of the character of Christ in His followers. The object of the Christian life is fruit-bearing, for God's glory. (See *Christ's Object Lessons*, p. 67.) Is the object of the Christian life to reproduce His character so that we can be saved? No. It is so there can be honor and glory brought to God. In Matthew 5:16 Jesus made it clear that the fruits of righteousness are for glorifying God. John 15:8: "Herein is my Father glorified, that ye bear much fruit." John 17:10, Christ is glorified in us. Our works, our sanctification, our obedience, our victories, are not for saving us in heaven, they are for bringing glory to God. But if a person is interested only in getting to heaven, and not interested in bringing glory to God, then we might seriously question whether salvation in heaven can be expected by that person.

In *Christ's Object Lessons*, page 384, we are told that sanctification is Christ in the life. What is the purpose of having Christ in the life? It is to bring honor and glory to God, as others see Christ in us. There is still bigger business than the certainty of our own salvation, and that bigger business is bringing glory to God, as we share His love with others.

NO CONDEMNATION

And when they had nothing to pay, he frankly forgave them both. Tell me therefore, which of them will love him most? Simon answered and said, I suppose that he, to whom he forgave most. And he said unto him, Thou hast rightly judged. Luke 7:42, 43.

What is the purpose of studying the Bible, of praying, and of the relationship of a daily devotional life with God? It is for the purpose of studying God's great grace, His forgiveness, His love, and what He did for us at the cross. It is by studying and contemplating His mighty love, and His acceptance of us, that sanctification takes place. Because the more you're forgiven, the more you love; and the more you love, the more you will obey (John 14:15). It is meaningful to discover that sanctification comes by justification.

In John 8:11, when the woman was dragged to Jesus, Jesus said to her, I don't condemn you. There is no one today who is condemned by Jesus. Jesus did not come to condemn the world but to save the world. It's only when we understand this that we can go and sin no more. One is the result of the other. We don't go and sin no more by trying hard not to sin. That's a dead-end street. The only way we can ever hope to go and sin no more is by discovering and continually being reminded day by day, that God doesn't condemn us. It is good news again today that there is no condemnation for those who are in Christ Jesus.

In order to understand sanctification correctly, we must be clear on the subject of justification. If we don't have it clear in our minds that we are accepted before God when we accept what Jesus did for us at the cross, then we will become confused. We will think that our obedience is the basis for our acceptance, and we will get discouraged when we find we're not doing that well in overcoming. But we can stand uncondemned today in God's presence as we accept what Jesus has done for us. We will always need the covering of His blood.

Although obedience is not a condition of acceptance with God, it is a condition for salvation. When we come, and continue to come, to Him, He is enabled to work in us to fulfill the conditions necessary for salvation, and He has promised that He is able to finish the work that He has started in our lives (Phil. 1:6).

WHAT ABOUT PERFECTION?

Be ye therefore perfect, even as your Father which is in heaven is perfect. Matt. 5:48.

There is a vast difference between the legitimate study of the subject of perfection and becoming involved in perfection*ism*. A person who is into perfectionism is one who becomes preoccupied with perfection. He thinks of little else. He focuses *his* attention primarily on the subject of perfection, and everybody else's as well. The perfectionist is the one who insists that the sinful nature gets eradicated before Jesus comes, that not only can we overcome but we can become sinless in ourselves. I would like to disclaim any kind of identity with perfection*ism*—but the doctrine of perfection is a good Bible doctrine, a good Bible teaching, which Jesus Himself taught.

In our text for today it says, "Be ye therefore perfect, even as your Father which is in heaven is perfect." There are those who would like to say that the word *perfect* in the Bible means nothing more than *mature*. And it's true that the original word includes the idea of maturity. But the word *mature* is a *stronger* word than *perfect*. It carries with it the idea of ultimate perfection. Jesus allowed for growth in the Christian life. This is clear in Mark 4:28: "First the blade, then the ear, after that the full corn in the ear." A blade can be a perfect blade, and an ear can be a perfect ear. But the full corn in the ear is not only perfect but mature as well. So we are told that at every stage of development we may be perfect (*Christ's Object Lessons*, p. 65). You can have a perfect baby, one that gurgles and coos. You can have a perfect 1-year-old, who chatters and jabbers. But if a person is still gurgling and cooing and jabbering at age 20, we get nervous!

I'm thankful for the concept of perfection given by Jesus, aren't you? It may be very likely that some of us are still in the stages of growth! But we can still be perfect for the stage that we're in.

Let's not make excuses while we are growing in Christ. Let's not make excuses for sinning, or assume that because we have not achieved perfect maturity that it is not possible—that we will continue to fall and fail indefinitely. Perfection—perfect maturity—is God's goal for each of us.

SAINTS DON'T CLAIM PERFECTION | **DEC 23**

Christ Jesus came into the world to save sinners; of whom I am chief. 1 Tim. 1:15.

The purpose for perfection, whatever perfection God has in mind for His children, is to bring honor and glory to Him. Those who obey God bring rewards for His suffering (*Thoughts From the Mount of Blessing*, p. 89). Those who obey God, and who by His grace understand perfection of character, bring honor to Christ (*Christ's Object Lessons*, p. 102). Those who obey God bring honor to Christ, because the honor of God is involved in the perfection of the character of His people (*The Desire of Ages*, p. 671). "Let your light so shine before men, that they may see your good works, and glorify your Father" (Matt. 5:16).

Perfection is not the basis of our salvation. Jesus' death on the cross, accepted on our behalf, is the basis of our salvation. But obedience and Christian perfection bring glory to Him. However, perfection is never apart from God; therefore, *we* don't bring honor to Him, He brings honor to Himself through us. If it's Christ dwelling within, then *He's* doing it. Are we going to exonerate God by our holy lives? No—God wants to exonerate Himself by whatever we allow Him to do in our lives.

But we must always remember that the religion of Christ includes more than forgiveness. It includes setting us free from the power of sin here and now. This doesn't mean we will no longer *be* sinners. Even the apostle Paul admitted that he was the chief of sinners. He wasn't saying that he was sinning all the time. We will join him in that acknowledgment.

Anyone who claims to be perfect or sinless is simply advertising the fact that he's not. *We* can never claim perfection, because the closer we come to Jesus, the more faulty we will appear in our own eyes. The apostle Paul proved it. "The nearer we come to Jesus and the more clearly we discern the purity of His character, the more clearly we shall discern the exceeding sinfulness of sin and the less we shall feel like exalting ourselves. Those whom heaven recognizes as holy ones are the last to parade their own goodness."—*Christ's Object Lessons*, p. 160. But although we cannot claim to be perfect, yet as we keep our eyes fixed upon Christ, we can be perfect at every stage of growth.

GOD ON TRIAL

Fear God, and give glory to him; for the hour of his judgment is come: and worship him that made heaven, and earth, and the sea, and the fountains of waters. Rev. 14:7.

God has been accused before the universe. God is on trial. God is up for judgment. It is the hour of *His* judgment that is come. While it is true that there is a pre-Advent judgment of *people*, which involves an examination of the heavenly records and a revelation concerning the names written in God's book, there is something more. In addition to this, the hour of *God's* judgment has come; and there is a close relationship between the judgment of God and the judgment of His people.

In this heavenly court scene, where God is on trial, there is a prosecuting attorney. Revelation 12 talks about him. He is the dragon, that old serpent called the devil, and he has many accusations. One of his great accusations is that God is *not* love. Since the beginning of time he has worked to convince people that God is not love. Another of his charges is that God cannot forgive the sinner. While it is true that God cannot forgive sin, God *can* forgive *sinners* because of the cross.

The devil knew of God's justice, that His whole government was just. He knew that if God went against His own character of justice, His government would fall. What he did not understand was the love of God, which had conceived of a plan, before the foundation of the earth, making provision to forgive sinners and still maintain justice.

Satan thought he had God in a corner. Either sinners wouldn't be forgiven, and man would perish; or else sinners would be forgiven, God's government would go down, and Satan and his angels would gain control of the universe. But a cross on a lonely hill forever settled this issue. When Jesus cried, "It is finished," the devil knew that his doom was sealed. He knew that *he* was finished, and that all that remained for him was to get as many as possible to suffer and perish with him.

The cross of Christ settled forever the accusations against God's mercy versus His justice. God was proved to be a God of love, and when men are led to behold the cross, they will see that God has been judged, and that He has been vindicated.

THE ACCUSER CAST DOWN

And I heard a loud voice saying in heaven, Now is come salvation, and strength, and the kingdom of our God, and the power of his Christ: for the accuser of our brethren is cast down, which accused them before our God day and night. Rev. 12:10.

Satan's charge that God could not be just and at the same time forgive sinners was answered at the cross. Another charge that the enemy leveled against God was that even if sinners could be forgiven, God's law could not be kept. He accused God of making a law that was impossible to obey. In *Christ's Object Lessons*, page 314, this charge is specifically stated: "Satan . . . claimed that it was impossible for man to obey God's commandments." Let's not forget who it is who makes this claim. This is Satan's claim, this is *his* charge. And anyone else who claims that it is impossible for man to obey God's commandments is simply echoing Satan's original charge. It is true that in our own strength we are not able to obey. "But Christ came in the form of humanity, and by His perfect obedience He proved that humanity and divinity combined can obey every one of God's precepts. . . . When a soul receives Christ, he receives power to live the life of Christ."—*Ibid.*

Since Calvary, Satan's charge that mankind cannot obey God's commandments has become a major issue in the judgment of God. This issue wasn't completely answered by Jesus' life; it is a charge that has to be answered by God's people as well. And right here is a problem area in the popular Christian world. It has always been much the same. If people hear about the finished work of Christ and how our salvation is certain because of the cross, they will say "Amen" and "Praise the Lord." But when they hear about God's power to overcome sins, about victory and obedience, they get strangely quiet.

Many people are frightened about the possibility of overcoming. For some reason there seems to be a fear that grips people concerning victory and obedience. It is becoming an unpopular topic even within our church, and this trend ought to say something to us. It ought to say something to people who have a special mission, a mission that goes *beyond* that of Luther or the Reformers. We have a unique contribution to make to the religious world, and obedience through faith is a significant part of it. We still have a part to play in honoring God's name before the world.

THE HONOR OF GOD

That the righteousness of the law might be fulfilled in us, who walk not after the flesh, but after the Spirit. Rom. 8:4.

Why should the possibility of overcoming and victory frighten us? Why should we be nervous about the idea that God wants to prove that He is right, through His people? The word *vindication* has been used in this connection. Some question whether or not anything *we* can do will vindicate God. But the real issue here is, "Is God right or is He not right? Is God true or is He false? Is He able to do what He says or not?" This is the devil's challenge.

One main reason why people are edgy and frightened about the idea of overcoming is that they still have the idea that their eternal destiny is based on their behavior. This, then, leads them to a great lack of assurance. But if we really believe that our eternal destiny is settled as we continue to accept Christ's sacrifice at the cross, then we don't have to get nervous at all about the possibility of overcoming. We can rejoice at the thought! It is only the legalist, who is still trying in some way to save himself, who gets nervous when he hears about what God intends to do through His people in terms of overcoming and victory.

We are told that "the very image of God is to be reproduced in humanity. The honor of God, the honor of Christ, is involved in the perfection of the character of His people."—*The Desire of Ages*, p. 671. This is part of the issue in the great judgment of God.

"The law requires righteousness—a righteous life, a perfect character; and this man has not to give. He cannot meet the claims of God's holy law. But Christ, coming to earth as man, lived a holy life, and developed a perect character. These He offers as a free gift to all who will receive them. His life stands for the life of men. Thus they have remission of sins that are past, through the forbearance of God." Now notice what immediately follows: "*More than this,* Christ imbues men with the attributes of God. He builds up the human character after the similitude of the divine character, a goodly fabric of spiritual strength and beauty. Thus the very righteousness of the law is fulfilled in the believer in Christ. God can 'be just, and the justifier of him which believeth in Jesus.' Rom. 3:26."—*Ibid.*, p. 762. (Italics supplied.)

PERFECT OBEDIENCE POSSIBLE

Bringing into captivity every thought to the obedience of Christ. 2 Cor. 10:5.

There ought to be a solution somewhere to the dilemma concerning obedience, and victory, and perfection, and the other questions being discussed in the church today. Even the theologians don't agree on Paul. Theologians and church historians don't agree on Luther. Greek scholars disagree on the Greek. And the people who use the Spirit of Prophecy statements at random, one here and one there, come up with opposite conclusions. But since "no other light ever has shone or ever will shine so clearly upon fallen man as that which emanated from the teaching and example of Jesus" (*The Desire of Ages*, p. 220), let us turn to the teachings of Jesus to find out whether He had anything to say about these issues. If you study carefully the four Gospels, along with the inspired commentary on the life of Christ, *in context,* you will find simple answers to some of the current questions. Here are a few excerpts taken from Scripture and the inspired commentary on the point of victory and overcoming:

Not even by a thought did Jesus yield to temptation—so it may be with us. Jesus had no advantage over us in overcoming. There are no command- ments which cannot be obeyed by all. We can obey as Jesus did. Jesus' mission was to bring us back to obedience. The law can be perfectly obeyed by every child of Adam, through grace. You must be perfect. Perfect righteousness we can attain; God will accomplish this for us. Jesus' life in you will produce the same as in Him. Satan is the one who tells us we cannot remedy our defects. Those who have no relationship with Christ do not believe in power to over- come. The object of the Christian life is the reproduction of Christ's character. The character of Christ is to be perfectly reproduced in His people.

There are far too many of these statements to be ignored. You cannot dodge these premises and still face the truth that has long been truth in our church. While it is true that Jesus was God, and divine as well as human; and that we are only human, we can still do as Jesus did through His power. We will never *be* as Jesus *was.* But this has nothing to do with the fact that power is available, through the Holy Spirit, to *live* as He *lived.*

VINDICATING GOD

"And I will vindicate the holiness of my great name, which has been profaned among the nations, and which you have profaned among them; and the nations will know that I am the Lord, says the Lord God, when through you I vindicate my holiness before their eyes." Eze. 36:23, RSV.

God is wanting to vindicate Himself through us before the world. *We* will never vindicate God, but the evidence is that God will vindicate Himself through us. How is this going to happen? There's only one way. In the sanctuary, where Jesus ministers today, we find the method. There is the altar of burnt offering, reminding us of the sacrifice of Jesus on the cross that makes it possible for us even to enter the sanctuary. Inside, there is the table of shewbread, which represents Jesus, the Bread of Life, the Word of God. There's the altar of incense, which has to do with the righteousness of Christ and the prayers of the saints. On the other side are the golden candlesticks, with oil and light: the Holy Spirit and Christian witness. The methodology of relationship with Christ—Bible study, prayer, Christian witness, and righteousness of Christ and the Holy Spirit—is found in the sanctuary. And in the Most Holy Place are found the Ten Commandments, which through the presence and power of Jesus can still be kept.

"Perfection*ism*" is not a safe topic. But *perfection* is a Bible teaching. We cannot reach a goal that we are not aware of. Perhaps that's one reason why we are told about it. We don't have to spend a lot of time dwelling on what we *must* be, but we can spend some useful, thankful hours dwelling on what we *can* be. There's a big difference between saying, "You have to reach this goal by the time probation closes," and saying, "God is going to lead His people to victory." There's a big difference between saying, "I must," and saying, "He can."

When we do away with basing assurance on our level of perfection, let's not do away with perfection itself. At the very end, obedience or disobedience is the primary question to be decided (*The Desire of Ages*, p. 763). Our assurance is based on our continuing acceptance of what Jesus did at the cross, and when that is settled, we can accept perfection and obedience and victory with joy. Jesus is our High Priest, and He brings not only forgiveness from sin but power as well, for those who are tempted.

PERFECTION IS GOD'S WORK

Being confident of this very thing, that he which hath begun a good work in you will perform it until the day of Jesus Christ. Phil. 1:6.

We are never going to become perfect by dwelling on being perfect. It is by dwelling on Jesus, on His love, on His sacrifice for us, on His spotless character, and then becoming involved in sharing His love with others, that we are changed into His image. The one who is the most involved in trying to help someone else know Jesus is the one who will be motivated to dwell most on Jesus himself. Let's get rid of all that we depend on instead of God, whether it's in justification, sanctification, or glorification. Let's make Jesus our dependence.

Don't let the idea of perfection discourage you. In the first place, Jesus Himself allows for growth, and in the second place, even if you *are* perfect, *you* will be the last to know it, because your attention will be so completely focused on Jesus that you will not be looking at yourself. Checking yourself to see how perfect you have become is a dead-end street. It is in looking to Jesus that you are safe.

While we are growing into the experience of total dependence upon God's power all of the time, remember this statement: "If in our ignorance we made missteps [Did Abraham? Yes. Did David? Yes. Did Elijah? Yes. Did the disciples? Yes.], the Saviour does not forsake us. We need never feel that we are alone. Angels are our companions. The Comforter that Christ promised to send in His name abides with us. In the way that leads to the city of God, there are no difficulties which those who trust in Him may not overcome. There are no dangers which they may not escape. There is not a sorrow, not a grievance, not a human weakness, for which He has not provided a remedy."—*The Ministry of Healing*, p. 249.

I am thankful today that although I am desperately in need of the grace of the Lord Jesus, and in my ignorance have made many missteps, yet He has not left me—and He has not left you. Are you thankful for that?

Let's not try to drag God's standard down to our level of performance. Neither let us ever get discouraged because of our performance, but keep our eyes always on Jesus, continuing to choose His control, and the work that He has begun in our lives He will complete.

HE IS ABLE

But seek ye first the kingdom of God, and his righteousness; and all these things shall be added unto you. Matt. 6:33.

There was a father who wished his son would stop chewing his finger-nails. He talked to him about it, but the son responded that his father's smoking bothered *him*. So they made a deal that the father would give up his smoking if the son would give up chewing his fingernails. Now the father is chewing his fingernails, and the son has taken up smoking!

What sort of resolutions do *you* make at the beginning of a new year? I'd like to suggest that almost all resolutions have to do with some problem in behavior. They are connected with something that should have been done that wasn't, or something that shouldn't have been done that was.

Our scripture today reminds us that the God we serve is big enough to take care of all the necessities of our lives, when we seek Him first. He can take care of not only our physical necessities but all the rest of our needs as well—including the sorts of things we usually make resolutions about.

Have you ever discovered that your promises were like ropes of sand? *Steps to Christ,* page 47, talks about it. Have you ever discovered for yourself the truth that "our hearts are evil, and we cannot change them" (*ibid.,* p. 18)?

All our efforts toward fixing up the external, behavioral areas of our lives are of no avail, because they simply focus our attention on ourselves and draw our minds away from Jesus, who is the only source of power. He has said that all power is given unto Him in heaven and in earth. He is able to take care of that problem in your life you have been struggling with all year—the one you made the resolution about last year, and failed after the first three days. He's big enough to take care of every problem we face today.

I would like to invite you today to make a resolution not to make any more resolutions except one. It's the only resolution worth making. It has to do with the heart, not with externals only. And there is only one resolution that affects the heart, the motives, and purposes. It has to do with choosing the relationship with Jesus day by day, of seeking to know Him, of spending time with Him who is the answer to all life's questions.

JESUS, YOUR BEST FRIEND

And this is life eternal, that they might know thee the only true God, and Jesus Christ, whom thou hast sent. John 17:3.

Do you know what it's like to be lonely? So alone that none but your own thoughts are ever your companion? Do you know what it's like as a child to want to play with other children, and meet only ridicule? Do you know what it's like to wish for a retreat in the quiet of your own home, but even there find mocking and sarcasm? Do you know how it hurts to have no one to talk to, no one to share with, even if he only listens? Have you ever felt the pain of rejection or the bitter disappointment of broken trust?

Have you ever been invited by someone to get acquainted, and then had him come after dark so no one would see you together? Have you ever had people follow you everywhere so that they might distort something you say, and justify putting you to death? Have you ever returned to your hometown acquaintance, seeking to give friendship, only to have rocks thrown at you?

Have you ever given of yourself until there was nothing left to give? Have you struggled against all the forces of evil, struggled until you actually sweat blood? Have you ever been rudely jostled by calloused men, while you were restrained by love from retaliating?

Have you ever felt the sharp pain of thorns pressed deep into your scalp and temples? Have you ever had someone spit upon your bruised and bleeding face? Do you know how it feels to struggle through your own blood drops while dragging heavy timbers? Do you think you could stagger on, willingly, dying for those who hate, despise, and reject you?

Have you ever felt the tearing, grinding crunch of nails being pounded through your hands and feet? Have you ever felt with every nerve of your body the jolt of a cross dropping into its deep, ugly hole? Have you ever hung from wounds gaping ever wider, while crowds taunted you and threw rocks at your lacerated body?

Have you ever hurt? Have you ever suffered? Have you ever died, alone, for those who refused to let you be their friend? While on this earth, Jesus did. And all the time, He longed for companionship and communion.

He still does. Won't you be His friend?

SCRIPTURE INDEX

DANIEL

2:44 . . . . Oct 3
9:7 . . . . Mar 26

HOSEA

11:8 . . . . Aug 10

AMOS

8:12 . . . . May 19

NAHUM

1:7 . . . . Apr 2

MALACHI

3:10 . . . . Oct 11
3:17 . . . . Oct 9

MATTHEW

4:19 . . . . Aug 11
5:6 . . . . Mar 24
5:15 . . . . Aug 4
5:16 . . . . Dec 20
5:17 . . . . Oct 2
5:22 . . . . Jul 27
5:28 . . . . Jul 26
5:29 . . . . Jun 14
5:48 . . . . Dec 22
6:24 . . . . Jun 18
6:33 . . . . Dec 30
7:13 . . . . Mar 4
7:14 . . . . Mar 14
7:16, 17 . . . . . Apr 1
8:2 . . . . Jan 16
8:26 . . . . Dec 19
9:12, 13 . . . . . Feb 5
10:31 . . . . . . Aug 23
10:34 . . . . . . Mar 1
10:39 . . . . . . Feb 27
11:28 . . . . . . Jan 20
11:29 . . . . . . Mar 18

13:24, 25 . . . . Sep 25
15:22 . . . . . . Apr 27
16:24, 25 . . . . Aug 3
16:25 . . . . . . Dec 17
18:21 . . . . . . May 30
19:16 . . . . . . Jan 14
20:28 . . . . . . Aug 6
21:44 . . . . . . Feb 25
23:25 . . . . . . Jul 15
23:26 . . . . . . Jul 7
24:24 . . . . . . Oct 31
24:27 . . . . . . Aug 21
25:11, 12 . . . . Dec 6
26:13 . . . . . . Jan 25
26:39 . . . . . . Feb 28
26:41 . . . . . . Jul 17

MARK

1:24 . . . . Aug 26
1:35 . . . . Apr 11
2:27, 28 . . . . . Sep 3
4:26-28 . . . . . Jun 17
7:7 . . . . Sep 7
8:35 . . . . Apr 30
11:22 . . . . . . May 15
12:44 . . . . . . Oct 10

LUKE

1:17 . . . . Nov 9
2:44 . . . . Apr 13
3:9 . . . . Oct 17
4:16 . . . . Aug 16
6:38 . . . . Oct 12
6:45 . . . . Jun 27
7:26 . . . . Sep 23
7:42, 43 . . . . . Dec 21
7:47 . . . . May 31
9:23 . . . . Mar 20
9:24 . . . . Aug 2
9:56 . . . . Dec 7

9:62 . . . . Apr 18
10:42 . . . . . . Jan 23
11:5, 6 . . . . . Apr 29
11:21, 22 . . . . Oct 13
12:15 . . . . . . Mar 21
13:8, 9 . . . . . Jan 9
14:13, 14 . . . . Nov 27
14:28 . . . . . . Dec 14
15:18 . . . . . . Jan 19
16:31 . . . . . . Oct 30
17:26 . . . . . . Sep 26
18:8 . . . . May 13
18:9 . . . . Nov 26
18:13 . . . . . . Feb 9
                 Apr 23
19:5 . . . . Feb 17
19:9 . . . . Feb 19
19:10 . . . . . . Jan 12
20:18 . . . . . . Oct 27
21:25, 26 . . . . Aug 20
22:31, 32 . . . . May 17
23:34 . . . . . . Jan 5
24:32 . . . . . . May 14

JOHN

1:9 . . . . Feb 1
1:14 . . . . Dec 8
3:3 . . . . Feb 16
3:5 . . . . Apr 19
3:6 . . . . Nov 13
3:7 . . . . Apr 20
3:8 . . . . Nov 14
3:11 . . . . Aug 1
3:14 . . . . Aug 14
3:16 . . . . Jan 2
3:17 . . . . Jul 5
5:24 . . . . Nov 28
5:39, 40 . . . . . Feb 4
6:29 . . . . May 12
6:35 . . . . Apr 3

PHILIPPIANS

1:6 . . . . Dec 29
2:5-7 . . . . Oct 5
2:8 . . . . Nov 30
             Dec 1
2:10, 11 . . . . . . Feb 29
2:13 . . . . Jul 6
3:7, 8 . . . . Feb 8
3:10 . . . . Mar 28
3:14 . . . . Apr 21
3:20, 21 . . . . Aug 18

COLOSSIANS

1:9 . . . . Mar 9
2:6 . . . . Jun 3

1 THESSALONIANS

1:5 . . . . Nov 10

2 THESSALONIANS

2:3 . . . . Nov 4

1 TIMOTHY

1:15 . . . . Dec 23
4:1 . . . . Nov 2
6:12 . . . . Feb 15
            Mar 19

2 TIMOTHY

2:15 . . . . Feb 3

TITUS

2:11 . . . . Mar 5
3:3, 4 . . . . Nov 12
3:5 . . . . May 11

HEBREWS

2:3 . . . . Apr 14
2:14, 15 . . . . . . Oct 8
2:17 . . . . Dec 9
4:15 . . . . Dec 13
10:23, 24 . . . . Aug 13
10:35 . . . . May 20
10:37 . . . . Aug 22
10:38 . . . . Jun 2
11:1 . . . . May 6
11:6 . . . . Jan 13
11:8 . . . . Jan 10
11:16 . . . . . . May 21
11:32 . . . . Jun 24
11:33, 34 . . . . . Jun 15

JAMES

1:2, 3 . . . . . . May 18
1:4 . . . . Jul 30
1:5 . . . . Jul 4
1:14 . . . . Jul 25
2:19 . . . . Mar 15
3:11, 12 . . . . . Jul 16
4:10 . . . . Apr 22
5:16 . . . . May 28

1 PETER

1:2 . . . . Jun 30
1:18, 19 . . . . Mar 29
2:21 . . . . Dec 12
3:3, 4 . . . . Oct 16
5:7 . . . . Jan 26
5:8 . . . . Jul 20

2 PETER

2:21 . . . . Nov 7
3:9 . . . . Jan 6
3:18 . . . . Nov 18

1 JOHN

1:3 . . . . Apr 16
1:8 . . . . Jun 5
1:9 . . . . May 27
2:1 . . . . Jun 23
2:4 . . . . Jun 28
2:15 . . . . Oct 18
3:2 . . . . Aug 17
3:4 . . . . Jul 24
3:5 . . . . Jul 18
3:6 . . . . Jul 10
5:4 . . . . Jul 21

3 JOHN

2 . . . . Oct 14

REVELATION

2:10 . . . . Sep 15
3:5 . . . . Sep 28
3:10 . . . . Nov 3
3:21 . . . . Jul 19
7:3 . . . . Sep 10
12:10 . . . . Dec 25
12:17 . . . . Sep 24
13:13, 14 . . . . . Oct 29
14:7 . . . . Dec 24
14:9, 10 . . . . . . Sep 13
14:12 . . . . Nov 6
15:2 . . . . Sep 12
            Sep 14
15:3 . . . . May 4
15:4 . . . . Aug 24
16:13, 14 . . . . . Oct 28
20:6 . . . . Aug 25
22:17 . . . . May 22